D1452713

Czechoslovakia: The Short Goodbye

CZECHOSLOVAKIA: THE SHORT GOODBYE

Abby Innes

Yale University Press
New Haven and London

Designed by Adam Freudenheim
Set in Stempel Garamond by Best-set Typesetter Ltd., Hong Kong
Printed in Great Britain

Library of Congress Cataloging-in-Publication Data

Innes, Abby.
    Czechoslovakia—the short goodbye / Abby Innes.
      p. cm.
    Includes bibliographical references and index.
    ISBN 0-300-09063-3 (hb : alk. paper)
    1. Czechoslovakia—Politics and government—1989–1992. 2. Czech Republic—Politics and government—1993–3. Slovakia—Politics and government—1993– I. Title.
DB2238.7 .I55 2001
943.705—dc21

2001039024

A catalogue record for this book is available from the British Library
10 9 8 7 6 5 4 3 2 1

CONTENTS

Acknowledgements   vi

Prologue   ix

1   The state under siege   1

2   The return of history?   43

3   The political divide   75

4   Renegotiating the state   115

5   A Lenin for the bourgeoisie   147

6   The short goodbye   176

7   The new state builders: 1993–2000   220

Appendix: 1990 and 1992 election results   273
Czech and Slovak political parties   276
Notes   279
Bibliography   314
Index   327

ACKNOWLEDGEMENTS

There are many people who, through their scholarship, support and generous help, have been invaluable to the completion of this book. In a previous life this text was my Ph.D. thesis, and for his excellent supervision and boundless support I am beholden to Brendan O'Leary at the London School of Economics – a more inspiring teacher is not to be found. For the humane and extremely useful viva I am indebted to Walker Connor and Dominic Lieven – I hope they can see the improvements they suggested in this text – I tried! For believing that this new script was worth publishing, and for their great assistance in putting together what follows, I am hugely grateful to the ever-reassuring Adam Freudenheim and Robert Baldock at Yale – though, if you read the sections on neo-liberalism you will understand why Robert, suddenly looking concerned, asked 'You do think the end of Communism was a *good* thing, don't you?' (the answer *was* 'Yes!').

For making my every stay in the former Czechoslovakia a delight over many years, and for their endless supply of friendship, sober knowledge, far-from-sober discussion and practical help I am indebted to Christoph Barmann, Sharon Fisher, Victor Gomez, Jan Hanzl, Michal Pleticha, Chris Pomery, Petra Klvačová and to Quentin and Marketa Reed, Jonathan Stein and Anja Tippner – all of whom are quoted extensively one way or another in this book – Quentin, Jonathan and Sharon in several cases directly from their own excellent texts. For the same reasons most particular thanks must go to Michaela Kaplanková and David Řehák. They heard everything written here in countless guises and yet never questioned my right to criticise the country they love, rather, they persisted in providing me with some of the very best times of my life – for this they are owed a thousand thanks – and this book is dedicated to them. From the United States I would like to thank Shari Cohen, Anna Gryzmala-Busse, Veljko Vujacic and Jason Wittenberg most especially for their friendship and for their spirited fights through the manuscript. I would also like to thank Grzegorz Ekiert for being a constant source of great advice and support and Valerie Bunce and Carol Skalnik Leff for their most timely encouragement. The detailed comments of two other, anonymous readers for the book were fantastic and very gratefully received.

For their insights on many of the key issues in the text I am indebted to Aleš Čapek, Ján Čarnogurský, Ivan Gabal, Fedor Gál, Jan Klacek, Daniel Lipšič, Katarina Mathernová, Jan Mládek, Jiří Pehe, Michal Vašečka, Thomáš Vrba, and last but certainly not least Václav Žák – a very patient man. When living in Prague I was also helped enormously by the staff at the Czech Centre for Economic Research and Graduate Economic Studies. I am indebted to the Massachusetts Institute of Technology for providing me with the privilege of 'Visiting Scholar' status for two years, and to University of California Press for allowing the reproduction of parts of an article published in *East European Politics and Societies*, Volume 11, Number 3, 1997. Last but not least, I am most grateful to the British Economic and Social Research Council for the funding of the doctorate.

On the home front I would like to thank Pippa Humpries, Jenny Lister, Poppy Miller, Lisa Molander, Jo Malt and honorary Norwich girl, Sonja Lambert – they know quite how crazy I would have gone without them. Through the years it has taken me to write this text my family, Jean and Michael Innes, Simon, Jo, Hannah and family-James provided every imaginable form of assistance and comfort (the Nancy Mitford novels in Prague were strange but perfect), and I thank them from the bottom of my heart. Finally, I want to thank Denis Gromb – for everything! Any errors in the following pages are, without a doubt, my own.

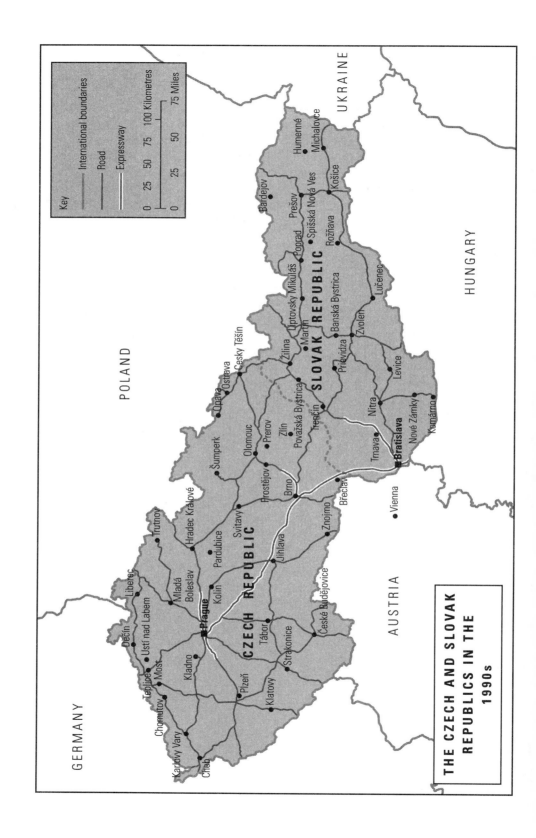

THE CZECH AND SLOVAK
REPUBLICS IN THE
1990s

PROLOGUE

There is a profound belief, particularly among policy-makers in the West, that post-Communist Europe is converging with Western Europe; that liberal democracy is the only game in town and that it is merely a matter of time before post-Communist legacies and troubles everywhere are resolved into civil and familiar forms. The abject failures of Communism as a system seem to encourage us, whether we are on the Western political right or left, to wish it away, and we interpret the 1989 revolutions in Central Europe as proof of a profound liberal consensus. As a result, the divergent developmental paths of the Communist period – the openness and relative prosperity of Yugoslavia, the stagnant, neo-Stalinist orthodoxy of Czechoslovakia, the constant democratising pressures among the Poles – seem to be forgotten, and we prefer to hark back to the interwar period when forming our expectations of the region. We look for signs of liberal democratic vitality in Central Europe, and we find them. We go to the Balkans looking for ethnic strife, and it stares us in the face, confirming our lowest expectations and worst fears.

The fate of Czechoslovakia, one of the most orthodox Communist states of the late 1980s but in the interwar period the most advanced state of the region, both in levels of economic development and in democratic strength, provides a critical test case for the impact of Communism, for the magnitude of its legacy. To the outside world, at least, the transition from Communism seemed set fair in Czechoslovakia. The peaceful – and famously 'velvet' – anti-Communist revolution of 1989 was swiftly followed by the election of the dissident playwright Václav Havel as president. A country capable of selecting such a thoughtful intellectual as head of state was not seen as likely to go astray. This impression was confirmed on 1 January 1993 when the Czechs and Slovaks proceeded to divide their country into two independent republics in perfect peace. No shot was fired and no borders were disputed. The end of the Czechoslovak state was so peaceful and so rapid that it was seen as a model: an exemplar for the frictionless parting of nations.

Czechoslovakia was the last of Eastern Europe's three Communist-era federations to collapse, following Yugoslavia in 1990–1 and the Soviet Union in December 1991. This succession of state failures was only a little less rapid than the toppling of Soviet Communism itself, and these three cases are frequently taken together as demonstrating, beyond doubt, the 'return of history' to post-Communist Europe: potentially, a return to ethnic conflict, a return to divisions between advanced territories and backwaters, between sophisticated urban electorates and 'backward rural masses', even a return to liberal political elites fighting militant nationalists, utopians and populists. Czechoslovakia supposedly cut across these divides; the idea that the Czechs are European and the Slovaks are 'Eastern' is a well-worn stereotype of the region.

The notion that history 'returned' presupposes that the Communist system acted merely as a lid upon culture and identity, that it failed to transform the deeper character of these societies in any profound way. In Czechoslovakia's case, the Slovak separatism of the interwar period was deemed to have re-emerged as a fatally divisive force, like the proverbial genie, uncorked from the bottle. What Yugoslavia had threatened in terms of a region-wide resurgence of ethnic hostility Czechoslovakia supposedly confirmed. In the light of what became a genocidal war in Yugoslavia, however, the absence of violence between Czechs and Slovaks rendered their divorce a virtuous and hopeful (even miraculous) event in Western eyes, confirming re-emerging regional and national stereotypes as markers for policy. The 'velvet divorce' entrenched stereotypes not only of Czech liberal political virtue as against Slovak nationalist vice but also of the relatively 'civilised' nature of Central European politics compared with those of the Balkans. There exists, as a result, a fully refreshed stereotype of a (still only relatively) rational 'Central' Europe distinct from an incurably 'Asiatic' East, which, obsessed with historical grievances and, typically, bitter ethnic conflicts, is pushed beyond the European pale. Even though careful scholars have not seen developments in this region in such simplistic terms, many policy-makers in the West viewed the separating Czechs and Slovaks as marching purposefully into two different worlds.

Examining the history of Czechoslovakia and the forces that threatened its security throughout the twentieth century, this book argues that attributing the final divorce to an irreconcilable nationalist conflict is in fact deeply misleading. The explanation developed here is that the separation was neither an expression of deep nationalist enmities between Czechs and Slovaks – their often fractious history notwithstanding – nor was it merely a symptom of the transition, of the multiple stresses afflicting the state. Rather it was a process manufactured by a ruthlessly pragmatic Czech right, abetted, when push finally came to shove, by a populist and opportunist Slovak leadership. On closer inspection, both political forces, Czech technocrats and Slovak populists, bear many of the hallmarks of a distinctly Communist political culture.

The break-up of Czechoslovakia illustrates, perhaps better than any other post-1989 event in the region, how strongly the Cold War legacy influences our reading of present-day Eastern Europe: 'we won' – and Communism can be forgotten. Western observers were so relieved by the peacefulness of the Czechoslovak separation that they hardly inquired into the abuses of state power that went into procuring it – and, as this book will show, there were many. What this book seeks to illustrate is that even the most advanced country of this region did not go unshaken by the Communist experience; Communism's impact was transformative after all.

The significance of the Czechoslovak divorce is not limited to the fate of the other Soviet-style federations but speaks to issues that affect the entire post-Soviet bloc. The impression that a Slovak nationalist explosion was forestalled by a Czech liberal political elite has perpetuated deeply rooted Western assumptions about the strength of ethnonationalism, not only in this particular case but across the region. The impression that it was Czech free-marketeers who saved Europe from more ethnic turmoil has, moreover, reinforced the liberal image of the post-Communist economic reform project as such, regardless of the fact that governments of practically every shade in Eastern Europe have pursued marketising reform for the simple reason that, where elections are essentially free, the economy must show *some* prospects of growth if any government is to be re-elected.

If we recognise that no government in Central Europe has managed to ignore the massive marketising and liberalising pressures of transition (and, more recently, accession to the European Union), then we can begin to ask more appropriate questions about how political parties are meant to compete meaningfully in elections when so much of public policy cannot be avoided – stalled or corrupted, maybe, but not avoided. We might also note that the plausibility of the claim that marketisation is an imperative to which everything else must succumb has proved a powerful tool for elites justifying behaviour that in less pressured circumstances would be viewed with outrage. Right-wing governments in this region have proved quite as capable of corruption and instrumental uses of the state as those originating from the post-Communist left.

The story of the break-up of the Czechoslovak federation and of the early years of the new independent states is an instructive one, revealing that Czech and Slovak post-Communist politicians remained not only practically free from public constraint but also distinctly authoritarian in their attitudes toward the state and its purpose – not to mention spectacularly deceitful to their electorates. The assumption that politicians, once elected, have a right to rule as they wish, to mould the state to their own ends and to mythologise their actions as they go, has clearly been carried through from the Communist era into the politics of the new independent states of Czechia and Slovakia. There is, moreover, an obvious reason for this. The difficulties of managing the transition to a democracy are phenomenal, and while dismantling the Communist state, the opportunities and electoral strategies most appealing to a vote-seeking politician in the short term have rarely been those most conducive to building democracy in the long run.

1

THE STATE UNDER SIEGE

Assessing the resilience of a state on the basis of its history is not easy at the best of times. Czechoslovakia has, moreover, been so steeped in misfortune that the question of how it stayed together so long is at least as arresting as that of why it fell apart. In its seventy-four years of existence Czechoslovakia emerged from World War I in chaos, weathered multiple ethnic grievances and economic depression, was broken apart in turn by Slovak separatism and by Nazism and was then put back together only to be subjected to forty years of Soviet Communism. After an anti-Communist revolution and three years of social, economic and political disintegration and reform, euphemistically referred to by political scientists as 'transition', the country finally collapsed.

Ascribing Czechoslovakia's downfall to 'the return of history', is therefore, just plain confusing: it implies that a particular aspect of the state's history must have proved fatal, whereas in fact the historical record is one of radically shifting contexts and quite amazing contingency. With a past like this, separation might have resulted not so much from mutual hostility as from the tired indifference of two peoples who, having endured war, fascism and Communism, viewed the bloody national conflict in Yugoslavia with dismay and concluded that they had no wish to follow that path.

This first chapter concentrates explicitly on national provocations before 1989. In considering the issues generally seen as in conflict within Czech and Slovak memory, the purpose is to assess the condition of Czech – Slovak relations over time, and to alert the reader to the fuller implications of post-1989 political rhetoric. This chapter also seeks to identify the extent to which, by 1989, there were any over-riding economic, political and military reasons for a common Czech and Slovak state.

CZECHOSLOVAKIA 1918–38: A MARRIAGE OF CONVENIENCE

The Czechoslovak Republic was founded in October 1918 as a union of regions from opposite sides of the Austro-Hungarian tracks. The industrially advanced Czech lands (Bohemia, Silesia and Moravia) came from the Austrian side of the old Habsburg Empire, the still predominantly agrarian Slovakia from the Hungarian[1].

Before 1918 Czechs and Slovaks had been divided not only legally, administratively and traditionally but in many other ways. Before the Great War the Czech economy was among the most industrialised and urbanised of the Habsburg Empire: Czechoslovakia contributed some 60 per cent of overall taxation revenue, was the industrial powerhouse of the region and employed almost half the Austro-Hungarian Empire's labour-force and boasted a per-capita income not far below that of Germany[2]. Slovakia, on the other hand, although the most developed area of Hungary, had remained predominantly agrarian and unmodernised under Hungarian tutelage: in 1914 Slovak industrial development was in its infancy.

These very different economies sustained very dissimilar societies in terms of class structure, social mores and traditions, and the contrast was accentuated by religious differences. Slovakia was predominantly and profoundly Catholic, the Czech lands were also more Catholic than Protestant but philosophically anti-clerical, a confirmation of their relative modernity, with its attendant secularisation. When it came to political culture the Czechs were far more conscious of themselves as a mature political nation deserving a state of their own. In this respect the experience of these territories under the deadening hand of imperial rule had proved extremely important. Slovakia under Hungarian rule had suffered greater national repression and isolation than the Czechs had under Austria.

During the nineteenth century Hungary had attempted the systematic assimilation of the Slovak minority and all but crushed Slovakia's attempts at national assertion. The start of the twentieth century brought a further deterioration in the condition of Hungary's national minorities as the Hungarians sought to eliminate self-determinist impulses root and branch. Hungarian was the exclusive language of instruction in all schools after 1907, a potentially fatal blow to Slovak national identity. Before 1918 the Slovak region was never at any stage permitted administrative or economic recognition distinct from other Hungarian regions. It also lacked a major urban centre on which a nationalist-minded intelligentsia might converge.

In comparison with the other minorities within Hungary, the Slovak voice was scarcely audible. The Hungarians had been forced through painful experience to acknowledge Serb and Romanian national movements, but they could never be persuaded that Slovak nationalism was anything more than an aberration which, as Macartney points out, 'they also believed to be curable'[3]. Slovakia's miniature political and intellectual elite (predominantly and disproportionately Protestant[4]) was well aware of its lack of a historic claim to statehood. By 1918 it saw little choice but to appeal directly to the newly vaunted but hardly attainable 'right of self-determination'.

The Czechs, in contrast, possessed by 1918 a strong national tradition as well as a large educated class[5]. Perhaps most importantly, they could also claim ancient statehood in the form of the Kingdom of Bohemia and the Margravate of Moravia, and they had a history of national independence until the outset of the Thirty Years' War (1618–48). The Czechs joined the Habsburg monarchy in 1526[6] along with the Hungarians and considered themselves by rights their equal. Angered by the creation of the Dual Monarchy of Austria-Hungary in 1867, the Czechs grew increasingly disillusioned by and hostile to rule from Vienna.

While the Slovaks in the late nineteenth century found themselves under growing threats of total assimilation, the Czechs, the third strongest ethnic group in Austria-Hungary, experienced a cultural and economic renaissance on a sufficient scale to challenge the traditional dominance of Germans in the area. The economic strength of Bohemia and Moravia brought with it not only a developing middle class but also new and independent Czech institutions – their own bank in 1868, a national theatre in 1881 and university in 1882. Bohemia's capital, Prague, had long been a cosmopolitan and much admired European city and throughout the latter half of the nineteenth century it acted as the locus of an ascendant Czech nationalism. An almost entirely German city until the middle of the nineteenth century, Prague was only 6 per cent German by 1910[7]. In strong contrast to Slovakia, therefore, the Czech National Revival proceeded apace from 1848 to the outbreak of World War I, and through its many cultural and political associations had popularised the Czech aspiration to independence. Slovakia, dominated by the Hungarians for over 1000 years, was in an altogether weaker position in its claims for national recognition, let alone statehood.

What brought two such apparently disparate nations together in 1918? The traditional explanation, presented in the state-building rhetoric of the new Czechoslovakia, was based on the understanding that, as neighbouring Slavs, the Czechs and Slovaks shared deep common roots of culture and language. These supposed commonalities, however, were a constant source of debate. Even the state's founder,

Thomáš Garrigue Masaryk (of Slovak/Moravian origin but born in Slovak Moravia and hence viewed by Slovaks from Slovakia as a Czech!), believed that 'Slovaks and Czechs formed a single nation, separated only by differences in language, history and culture'[8]. If one understands 'nation' to refer to a group of people who believe they are ancestrally related[9], Masaryk's verdict implied very little kinship indeed. Language, history and culture are, in most circumstances, critical markers of national difference, and with such divisions paralleled by deep social and economic disparities, Czechs and Slovaks would require an overarching common interest if they were to avoid conflict. In 1918, however, such a common interest did, apparently, exist.

A more convincing explanation for Czechoslovakia's existence came from the calculations of the Czech and Slovak political elite and the state-makers of the Paris Peace Conference in 1918, and their understanding of Germans and Hungarians. Czechoslovakia was, to a critical degree, a product of its massive minorities[10]. During the First World War the previously limited business and culture-oriented contacts between Czechs and Slovaks broadened as the two political leaderships joined in mutual support of their respective national claims. Masaryk, the principal initiator of this collaboration, calculated early in the war that neither region was likely to achieve independent statehood alone[11], nor, if independence was achieved, could they sustain it in the face of those German and Hungarian minorities who would find themselves demoted from overlords to underdogs. It was undoubtedly with such thoughts in mind that Masaryk, as early as 1907, made pointed references to the two million Slovaks in upper Hungary as 'belonging to our nationality', and as 'co-nationals'[12].

There were also international pressures for the creation of a unified Czechoslovak state, and, concomitantly, for a unified 'Czechoslovak people' to act as the bulwark against the strength of other minorities. Without the proclamation of a 'Czechoslovak people' Czechoslovakia would have been a state lacking an absolute national majority, and the question might then reasonably have been asked why it should include three million Germans. Without the German territories, however, the Czechoslovak economy would have been considerably weakened[13]. A strong Czechoslovakia constrained Germany, an obvious gain in the eyes of the Great War victors, and the ethnic German territories stood within the natural and historical military border of the Czech lands, as was made all too clear in 1938.

If Czechoslovakia, however, was not to be dependent for life upon the persistent untrustworthiness of its neighbours, it needed to develop a state identity that was not simply about defensible frontiers and economic viability but was also positively attractive to its constituent members. As soon as Czechoslovakia was born, however, the profound inherited differences between Czechs and Slovaks manifested themselves – as friction.

NATIONAL STEREOTYPES AND THEIR SOURCES

The Pittsburgh Agreement, 1918

One of the most embittering experiences for Slovaks was that as soon as the new state was formed, the language of 'fraternity' prevailing before 1918 translated into a Czech assumption of the role of the older brother. Czechs wore their historic nationhood and economic success as a badge of maturity and deemed their own goals the most appropriate for Slovak development. On the reverse view many Czechs, including those more sympathetic to Slovak particularism, were dismayed at the seemingly endless demands of Slovaks for both improved conditions and greater equality. The Czechs' resentment of Slovak ingratitude and their surprise at the coherence of Slovak nationality – about which they had known little before 1918 – provided fertile ground for unflattering stereotypes on both sides.

To many in Slovakia's political and cultural elite, especially its young Catholic contingent, grievances over the term 'Czechoslovak' arose almost immediately, provoked by the very founding documents of state. On 30 October 1918 a Slovak document – the Martin Declaration – endorsed Czech-Slovak unity but was obscure as to the status of the Slovak nation within a Czechoslovak state[14]. The Martin Declaration, however, came two days after a proclamation of statehood by the Prague National Committee, to which a pro-Czech Slovak representative, Vavro Srobar, was the sole Slovak signatory. The 28th of October duly became the Czechoslovak Republic's official anniversary date. This first declaration, with its minimal Slovak participation, was assumed by Czechs from the outset as legitimating not only a unitary, Prague-centralised state but also membership in a 'Czechoslovak nation' and use of a 'Czechoslovak' language[15]: terms to be found throughout the 1920 constitution. In his opening address to the National Assembly on 14 November 1918, Prime Minister Karel Kramář explicitly defined Czechoslovakia as a 'Czech state' and welcomed the Slovaks as 'lost sons' who had now 'returned to the nation's fold, where they belong'[16]. When another document, the Pittsburgh Agreement of 30 May 1918, became known in Slovakia in 1919[17], it provided a focus for those who wished to reassert Slovakia's national rights.

Signed by the future state President, T. G. Masaryk, and by Czech and Slovak émigré groups in the United States, the Pittsburgh Agreement, like the Cleveland Accord of 1915[18], stipulated a separate administration, parliament, and even courts for Slovakia[19]. According to Masaryk, however, the Agreement was 'concluded to appease a small Slovak faction which was dreaming of God knows what sort of independence for Slovakia . . . I signed the Convention unhesitatingly as a local understanding between American Czechs and Slovaks upon the policy they were prepared to advocate'[20]. Legally, Masaryk was in the right; the concluding clause of the agreement stated that its US signatories were in no way competent to bind the nation to the Agreement's contents, since only the state itself, following independence, could decide its fate[21]. Though Masaryk had conceded that 'a demand for autonomy is as justifiable as a demand for centralism, and the problem is to find the right relationship between the two'[22], practical developments in the new Czechoslovakia had already been firmly on the centralist side.

The disparagement of the Pittsburgh Agreement had a decisive impact on party political developments in the new state, resonating, in particular, within the Slovak People's Party (HSPP), hitherto pre-occupied by Catholic rights and education. Father Andrej Hlinka, its leader, had promoted and endorsed the principle of Czech-Slovak unity on several occasions before 1918, but he had remained suspicious of Czech anti-clericalism[23] and had argued passionately for Slovakia's distinctiveness after the war. The Agreement tipped the HSPP toward a defensive position of Slovak autonomism, and, as we shall see, this position grew ever more assertive as Slovak grievances mounted through the 1920s and 1930s.

The initial shift toward Slovak autonomism in the HSPP was expressed in the Žilina Memorandum in 1922. The Memorandum accused Prague, and Masaryk in particular, of a breach of faith in failing to implement either the Cleveland or Pittsburgh 'Treaties' – a status these documents had never had, although nationalist histories have long granted it. Thereafter Hlinka campaigned to present Pittsburgh as the ideal and unfairly forsworn guidelines for the reform of the state and for the full recognition of the Slovak nation[24]. The failure of Prague to acknowledge even the spirit of these two Agreements marked them down in Slovak eyes as the first of several instances of broken Czech promises of constitutional equality.

It is important to note that, despite its solid Catholic pedigree and attempts at agitation, Hlinka's Slovak People's Party (known as L'udáks or Populists) did not fare as well in the first, 1920 election as subsequent nationalist and L'udák histories have implied. The

1920 election, coinciding with a postwar recession, indicated that 'Czechoslovakia' at this stage remained a feasible project: it revealed a political consensus across the territory that had every appearance of transcending national differences. Both the Czech and Slovak electorates favoured the left, and 1920 represented the high point in interwar social democratic support. The social democratic left was loyalist as far as the state was concerned. More preoccupied with social than 'narrow' national questions, they supported multi-national states in principle whilst opposing 'nationalist particularism', accepting that the prioritisation of Slovakia's national grievances could only mean the incitement of additional national tensions. In the early 1920s, moreover, the evidence suggests that Slovaks were more engaged by urgent socio-economic issues than by aspirations to threaten the recently achieved order and the relative freedoms of the Czechoslovak unitary state.

Bureaucracy: the glass ceiling

The First Republic lost a tremendous opportunity for cohesion by thwarting social mobility for the growing Slovak middle classes and persisting with Czech administrative dominance. No sooner had the Czechs arrived in Slovakia in 1918, it seemed, than they began to replace the Hungarians as administrators and choose Slovak Protestants to assist them, though Protestants represented a small minority in Slovakia, some 18.7 per cent of the population in 1910[25]. Slovakia's governance had immediately fallen to the so-called Slovak 'Hlasists'[26], close and predominantly Protestant followers of Masaryk. Though it was only a hastily constituted Slovak National Council that had empowered Vavro Šrobár, a leading Hlasist and a Catholic, to represent Slovak interests in Prague, he became the sole Slovak representative on the so-called Czechoslovak National Council[27]. In the Slovak nationalist canon, Šrobár's subsequent advocacy of Prague centralism and Prague's apparent Protestant chauvinist administration marked him thereafter as a traitor to the national cause.

Returning as Minister for Slovakia in December 1918 Šrobár abolished the limited organs of Slovak administrative autonomy that had grown out of the grassroots of Slovak society, using his powers in ways that could only increase hostility to Prague among Slovaks already antagonised by the 'one-nation' principles of Czechoslovakism. Endowed with wide powers of decree and also with units of the Czechoslovak legionnaires, Srobar dissolved the Slovak National Council (SNC) immediately on coming to office and the local councils, formed under SNC auspices, soon after, in January 1919. Following the first parliamentary elections, Slovakia's special caucus was also dissolved in April 1920[28], and Šrobár's own administration lasted only until May[29]. Thereafter, Slovak deputies seemed destined to speak from within Czech-dominated, state-wide parties, albeit representing Slovak wings of those parties.

Slovak nationalist historians have naturally emphasised how the Hlasists appointed Czech Protestants to public positions in Slovakia, some of whom undoubtedly viewed themselves as 'bringing enlightenment to a backward country'[30]. Though this was not another case of 'iron centralism', as Slovak nationalists have subsequently claimed, the security-conscious Hlasists were sufficiently dogmatic in their purging of Hungarianised Slovaks – who, because of the past assimilationist role of the Church, were predominantly Catholic – as to appear anti-Catholic as a matter of policy[31]. In branding as 'Magyarone' those Catholics who had worked for the Budapest government before the war, however, Prague applied a double standard, since in the Czech lands experienced Czechs who had worked for the Viennese government were actually encouraged to offer their services to the new administration[32].

From the Slovak point of view the Czechoslovak regime thus appeared philosophically and legislatively anti-clerical. Czech politicians seemed bent on separating Church and state, and were quick to nationalise primary and secondary education, previously the preserve of religious authorities. Agrarian reform also threatened the Church estates, and even anti-Hungarian priests in Slovakia found that they were denied the flourishing parishes for which they had hoped. The journalist Ferdinand Peroutka concluded that 'in probably the most complete way, they [the Protestants] excluded Catholic representatives from public service and the enjoyment of glory'[33]. As a consequence, the profoundly conservative, parochial, and socially influential clergy in Slovakia concluded early on that it was they who would have to find a convincing explanation for national inequalities, if Slovakia was not to be radicalised by secular ideas of class and emancipation. When the reality of Slovakia's persistent relative economic backwardness also sank in, support for the Slovak People's Party grew as the division between those who opposed and those who supported Prague rule began to cut more clearly down religious lines.

Undoubtedly it was this religious cleavage that supported the development of a Slovak (political) party belying notions of a single Czechoslovak identity. In another age such a development might have proved sustainable. In 1930s Czechoslovakia, however, Slovak Catholic discontent was an Achilles heel. The Hlinka Slovak People's Party had, by the 1930s, created a strong alliance of co-religionists, frustrated clergy, Catholic laymen, and also 'Magyarone' Slovaks behind the cause of autonomy. Untried as it was, autonomy seemed the idea holding the greatest hope of relief from Czech dominance.

The Hlinka Slovak People's Party (HSPP)

According to the historian Robert Seton-Watson, Father Andrej Hlinka was a priest 'of the twelfth rather than the twentieth century'[34]. In Czech eyes, Hlinka was too overtly tolerant of the now officially despised 'Magyarone' Slovaks; indeed, he was suspected as prone to Hungarian manipulation. In Catholic Slovakia, by contrast, Hlinka was considered a patriot who had suffered for his efforts against Hungarian repression and had earned Czech animosity only by drawing attention to the iniquities of Czech power. Prague's mistrust and a tendency of the Czechoslovak parliament toward character assassination increasingly marked Hlinka out as Slovakia's *ami du peuple* – a powerful position in an era of increasingly radicalised politics across Europe.

By linking a wide range of Slovak grievances to perceptions of Czech religious bias, Hlinka's clerically based party was able to frame a Slovak national agenda literally as an article of religious faith. The party's main political rivals in Slovakia increasingly forfeited support through their relative abstraction from Slovak realities but also because of their continued unwillingness to touch upon national issues in a state with so fragile an ethnic balance. After the social democracy movement divided into warring Communist and Social Democratic Parties between 1920 and 1921 both groups seemed incapable of noting Slovak difficulties without first appraising them through the prism of international Socialist strategy, a practice diminishing their initial support to a smaller, if consistent, core. The Slovak section of the Agrarians (unified in 1922) might have laid claim to significant support had not their leader, Milan Hodža, established himself as one of Hlinka's main adversaries at the same time as appearing deeply attached to his position and influence in Prague. In 1920, Hodža had gone so far as to prophesy that Czech and Slovak cultures would converge and their languages merge – a recitation of the Czechoslovakist creed. The Czechoslovak People's Party, led by Jan Šrámek, might also have laid claim to Slovak Catholic sympathies had it not fallen out with the Hlinka Party in the early 1920s over religious education. As coalition king-makers between 1921 and 1938, however, Šrámek's populists held so great a stake in the Czechoslovak establishment as to lose the disenchanted Slovak vote almost entirely to Hlinka's L'udáks[35].

Party Strength in the First Republic: Election results by region (% of votes cast)

	1920	1925	1929	1935
BOHEMIA				
Agrarians	12.4	13.2	13.6	12.7
Social Democrats	22.4	10.4	13.8	12.9
National Socialists	11.2	11.7	13.9	11.6
Czechoslovak Populists	5.6	8.0	6.6	6.0
National Democrats	8.8	5.8	5.2	7.6
Small Tradesmen	2.4	5.2	4.6	6.4
Communists	–	12.6	10.3	9.0
German Parties	32.5	27.0	26.1	28.7
MORAVIA				
Agrarians	12.9	11.5	12.3	14.2
Social Democrats	22.0	9.6	14.8	13.3
National Socialists	6.2	7.0	9.7	9.8
Czechoslovak Populists	18.9	21.3	17.7	15.6
National Democrats	6.2	2.5	3.1	3.9
Small Tradesmen	2.9	4.6	4.3	6.1
Communists	–	11.1	8.9	8.6
German parties	21.3	22.7	21.8	22.2
SLOVAKIA				
Agrarians	18.0	17.4	19.5	17.6
Social Democrats	38.1	4.2	9.5	11.4
National Socialists	2.2	2.6	3.0	3.2
Czechoslovak Populists	17.5	1.3	2.6	2.3
Hlinka Slovak Populists	–	34.3	28.3	30.1
Communists	–	13.9	10.7	13.0
German-Magyar Christian Socialists	18.5	6.9	15.9	14.2

Source: Carol S. Leff, *National Conflict in Czechoslovakia: The Making and Remaking of a State, 1918–1987* (Princeton, 1988), p. 52.

Most of the interwar Czechoslovak cabinets were constituted by Socialist-Agrarian coalitions including all but the National Democrats and the Communist Party[36]. Agrarian-Clerical coalitions governed only between 1925/7 and 1929, and these included not only the National Democrats and eventually the Hlinka Slovak People's Party but also representatives of four out of the seven German groups. This eventual co-option of German parties and the Slovak populists was bought at the cost of 'abandoning extreme centralism, of toning down anti-clerical tendencies and of stiffening tariffs in the interests of the Agrarians'[37]. The price seemed eminently worth paying to bring the hitherto uncooperative principal minority – the Germans – and the obstructionist HSPP into the state's mainstream. Neither, however, stayed long.

Having emerged as the strongest party in Slovakia, the HSPP demanded greater decentralisation from Prague. In 1927, the county system was abolished and the administration reorganised along provincial lines, creating a 'Slovenská Krajina', which transformed Slovakia from an object to a source of power[38]. Though the HSPP thereafter participated in government (after a full two years of negotiations), the frail accord lasted only until the trial for treason of Hlinka's adviser, Dr Vojtech Tuka, in 1929. The so-called Tuka affair[39] had a fateful impact on the political environment as a whole. It rocked HSPP support, which had wavered following its move into the government coalition, and caused a final breach between the HSPP and all mainstream political groups, bar Šrámek's Populists, despite the brief rapprochement after 1926. Tuka's imprisonment put an end to Hlinka's attempt at constructive engagement with the Czechoslovak political establishment, and the affair pushed the HSPP into a more extremism-prone opposition than they had ever previously entertained[40]. The Depression then improved L'udák electoral fortunes, relatively well attuned to Slovak social and economic grievances as the Hlinka party had become[41].

Electoral fortunes in Slovakia during the First Republic

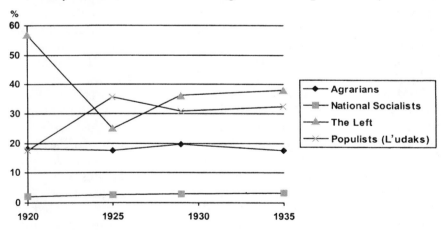

The Left = Social Democrats + Communists + German-Magyar Christian Socialists
Populists = Czechoslovak Populists + Hlinka Slovak Populists (L'udáks)

The betrayal of Czechoslovakia

It was a mark of the coalition dynamics in the First Republic and the failure to integrate Slovakia's more outspoken political forces that it was not until the mid-1930s that regional economic disparities were debated in any direct and politically sensitive way[42]. The assumption throughout the 1920s and early 1930s had been that Slovakia would catch up economically with the Czech lands, despite the tendency of Czech industry to treat Slovakia as a colony, left to provide agricultural products, labour and raw materials. Czechoslovakia's initial *laissez-faire* politics had in practice done little positively to advance Slovakia's relatively underdeveloped economy. The state's concern, when it came, was far too late: by the mid-1930s, continuing economic inequality had helped create a convergence of Slovak grievances that looked set to pitch the entire state into crisis.

On 5 November 1935 President Masaryk appointed the Agrarian Milan Hodža as Prime Minister – the only Slovak premier in the history of the First Republic. After the shocking success of the covertly pro-Nazi Sudeten German Party in the 1935 election it was hoped that a Slovak Prime Minister might at least reinforce the core state relationship, leaving Hodža little choice but to open discussions with the Slovak autonomists. He was, however, in a clear bind; for Czechs, his credibility partly depended upon his presumed powers in Slovakia, but if he accepted HSPP demands for economic and administrative concessions and implementation of the Pittsburgh Agreement he would lose his place in Prague. As an established Pragocentric politician, moreover, Hodža had poor prospects in an autonomous Slovakia. The negotiations, begun at the end of January 1936, ended in complete failure in late March[43]. Thereafter the HSPP assumed its full potential as a major threat to the Czechoslovak state[44].

Hodza's coalition negotiations revealed that by 1935 the Hlinka Slovak People's Party had succumbed to the radicalisation sweeping Europe. The HSPP's moderates were increasingly pushed aside by a faction intent on closing ranks with the Sudeten German Party, the Czech Fascists and others of the extreme right. Since the mid-1930s Hlinka had acted as arbiter between moderates who were more faithful to the Republic, led by the ideologist Jozef Tiso, and neo-fascist and separatist radicals, which notably included the younger party leaders. In 1937, L'udák agitation increased and culminated in anti-Czech demonstrations and accusations that the government had Bolshevised the Republic[45], citing the May 1935 Soviet-Czechoslovak Treaty of Mutual Assistance as evidence. Anti-Czech, anti-Communist and anti-Semitic propaganda became the favoured weaponry of the day[46]. Hlinka's death on 16 August 1938 opened the HSPP fully to the factional contest, and the moderates seemed as good as defeated. The HSPP presented its programme for autonomy – the 'Whitsun Programme' – to parliament on 17 August. Their platform was framed exactly to the demand for 'national self-determination' to be invoked by Hitler's Germany in the Saarland, Austria, and eventually in the Sudetenland: Czechoslovak territory. In the context of the time, therefore, the HSPP aligned itself with the spread of Nazism and the *de facto* destruction of the Czechoslovak state. By September, conditions were moving dramatically in the Populists' favour.

As the extreme right had begun to hold sway, Milan Hodža had attempted a last and desperate acceleration of governmental reforms as a basis for negotiations with Germany, including a new statute of national autonomy, but the time for such efforts had passed. Unwilling to step beyond appeasement of the growing Nazi threat, France and Britain, despite the former's treaty obligations, had made it clear to the Czechoslovak government back on 19 August that it should comply with Hitler's demands for the Sudeten territories. With Czechoslovakia's fate sealed, Slovak Ľudák behaviour became transparently pragmatic: when the Polish and Hungarians raised territorial claims on Czechoslovakia in early September, the Ľudáks retained the demand for autonomy but decried the prospect of any forceful solution to Czechoslovak statehood. As Hitler's 1 October deadline for handing over the Sudetenland drew closer, Ľudák leaders proposed a Polish-Slovak union to forestall the Hungarian occupation of Slovakia in the event of Czechoslovakia's destruction[47].

The Munich Conference of Germany, Italy, France and Britain on 29 September signed away Czechoslovakia to the German sphere of influence, forcing Prague to cede to Germany the Sudetenland – Czechoslovakia's frontier territories with Germany and her military fortress line – leaving Czechoslovakia unprotected and in Hitler's grasp. On 6 October, Slovakia's centrist parties capitulated to the Slovak autonomists and embraced the Whitsun Programme as their own, informing the new Syrový Government in Prague[48] that all Slovak parties now supported Slovak autonomy. The Czechs conceded without debate, besieged by the loss of the Sudetenland and assailed by Hungarian and Polish territorial demands[49]. A nominally 'federalist' Second Czecho-Slovak Republic was established on the same day.

Slovakia's sudden autonomy meant a fundamental shift in regime under a now extremist-ridden HSPP, led since Hlinka's death by Dr Jozef Tiso. Slovak elections were held from which the

Communists and Social Democrats were excluded, and all other parties were merged with the L'udáks. Independent associations such as trade unions were swiftly brought under HSPP authority. Tiso meanwhile sought to hold off the independence so desired by the L'udák radicals so as to try to consolidate a measure of economic self-sufficiency[50]. The Czechs' response, military intervention, the suspension of Tiso's government and the introduction of martial law in Slovakia, only hastened the fatal blow from Germany. Tiso was presented with a German ultimatum: Slovakia could assert full independence or suffer Hungary being given a free hand in her former territory. Slovakia duly declared itself independent on 14 March 1939 – becoming, in effect, a Nazi puppet state. On the 15th, the Slovaks requested Hitler's 'protection', and Germany annexed what remained of the Czech lands, establishing the Reich's 'Protectorate of Bohemia and Moravia'[51].

Slovakia's autonomy, won in 1938 and completed in March 1939, stunned Czechs as a betrayal of Czechoslovakia and of the democratic principles that had flown about the masthead of the new state in 1918. This was a feeling shared by many Slovaks. Though the true level of public support for the HSPP is ultimately hard to judge, there is little evidence that there was a Slovak majority who preferred the resolution of national differences by the dismemberment of the state, let alone the crushing of Czechoslovakia by German forces dictating the installation of Nazism. The early enthusiasm of the Catholic majority in Slovakia should not be interpreted simplistically. As others have explored in great depth, support for the new regime can be attributed either to the perception that Slovakia had finally seized its fate into its own hands or to a genuine hostility to all aspects of the First Republic. There is evidence to support both interpretations[52], but not to resolve the issue.

FIRST REPUBLIC – DOOMED TO FAIL?

In the long term the apparent betrayal of the First Republic produced powerful national stereotypes. Masaryk's frequently overbearing presidential influence had been directed toward fostering progressive and 'state-building' parties whose priority would be 'state', rather than religious, ethnic or even party, interests. The priorities of the Slovak L'udáks had always represented an attack on the Masarykian philosophy as such. Tiso's brand of clerico-fascism provided Czechoslovak history with evidence of Slovak disloyalty and difference, but also of a latent, 'demonic' Slovak nationalism. Subsequently, Czechs have rarely failed to allude to the 'liberal' state's betrayal at moments of

Czech–Slovak tension, and for many years afterwards they clearly expected Slovak acts of atonement and contrition.

For many Slovaks the events of 1938–9 only exacerbated Slovakia's already overlooked frustrations with the inequalities of Czech rule. The failure to grant Slovaks significant autonomy throughout the First Republic had marked Masaryk's establishment notion of 'Czechoslovakia', with an irreducible defect for Slovak pride. Many Slovaks had increasingly felt that Slovakia had been co-opted into a notion of 'Czechoslovak' identity only to safeguard the stability of a Czech-dominated state. This interpretation grew once the rewards accruing to Slovakia for its Czechoslovak status were seen to be inadequate, albeit for different reasons in different quarters. The logic of the state's built-in flaw and the reasoning to which Czechs had recourse between 1918 and 1938 were nevertheless powerful; granting Slovak aspirations to administrative autonomy could trigger irredentist claims by both Germans and Hungarians[53].

To complicate matters further the 'Slovak question' in the First Republic had been 'triangular', i.e. not simply between Czechs and Slovaks as homogeneous opponents but between Czechs, Slovak autonomists and Slovak integrationists[54]. This triangular relationship would persist, with some variations, after the Second World War and until the state's demise in 1992. The integrationist first generation of 'Czechoslovakists' within Slovakia (among them the bulk of Slovakia's young Protestant intellectuals) had clearly believed that Slovakia could only benefit from the modernising and Westernising influence of the Czech territories and should adopt a suitably loyalist attitude. From the beginning, however, the Czechoslovak project was a hostage to the fortunes of its Slovak population, predominantly Catholic and agrarian as that population for the moment remained: with hindsight, an unlikely seedbed for the visions of progressive, Westernising, and secular intellectuals.

Demographic developments, moreover, worked against assimilation into a homogeneous Czechoslovak identity. The Slovak population had grown rapidly after 1918 through the combined effects of an increase in the Slovak birthrate, a decline in emigration and the re-Slovakisation of the previously Magyarised population. The 1921 census revealed the sweeping away of the apparent Hungarian majority in many Slovak cities. Combined with a continuing process of urbanisation, concentrated in Bratislava and Košice[55], and a comprehensive improvement in the entire education structure within Slovakia, conditions had turned to favour those who wished to distinguish the Slovak national identity as sustainable and as distinct from the Czech.

Had the fate of Czechoslovakia been sealed from the start by the mis-equation of its minorities?[56] It is a seductive explanation. The combined imperatives facing Czechoslovakia in 1918 suggest a state besieged. To begin with, Slovak goodwill appeared considerable. The evidence is that the coexistence with and the assistance of the Czechs was initially welcomed by most Slovaks as the realisation of an ethnically 'natural', economically beneficial, non-assimilationist and relatively non-centralising Slavic state. In these early years Bratislava became the headquarters of new and resuscitated parties, newspapers, home to a national university and other diverse cultural and educational institutions, able to function with relative freedom[57] and to bear the marks of a 'capital' city. Above all, in terms of its own cultural security, Slovakia won formal demarcation as a distinct territory – for which many Slovaks were undoubtedly grateful. On the down side, the weakness of the 'Slovak element' in Czech collective awareness turned out to be critical.

The term 'Czechoslovak' had become a rich source of contention almost immediately after the state's formation: 'the emergence of the new state in October 1918 was not accompanied by a clear delineation of what the term Czechoslovak meant. Some persons thought it descriptive, others saw it as prescriptive. Some thought it was related to politics, while others cast it solely into the ideological sphere. There was disagreement whether its significance was primarily internal or external. By 1938, the Czechoslovak concept was beginning to give way to recognition of distinct Czech and Slovak nations . . .'[58] As the journalist Ferdinand Peroutka put it at the time, how could Slovaks not be antagonised when 'there did not exist a Czechoslovak nation. How else could one refer to it other than as a demand?'[59] The development of national stereotypes and grievances was critical in the demise of the First Republic, but it remained equally the case that the First Republic had been denied any attempt at the constitutional arrangements to which multi-ethnic states may typically, and often successfully, resort. The Czechs discovered the strength of Slovak national identity in the direst geopolitical circumstances imaginable, and there was no hope of remedy when, in Churchill's memorable phrase, 'the whole equilibrium of Europe [had] been deranged'[60].

THE SECOND WORLD WAR

Slovakia's experience of the Second World War was very different to that of the Czech lands, where open occupation resulted in greater repression, resistance and use of terror. Germany relied on the HSPP to arrange the particulars of Slovakia's alliance, including the maintenance of 'order' and the subordination of the economy to German war needs. Economists of all political hues have agreed that the Slovak economy prospered under German tutelage – with certain undoubtedly popular spin-offs. Jewish property was given to 'Christian' Slovaks rather than to the Germans[61], and Slovakia remained unengaged in the war until 1941. The Slovak-born historian Stanislav Kirschbaum has gone so far as to argue that 'the Slovak Republic not only took the Slovak people far down the road of modernisation but it served the Slovaks well especially in the social and cultural field, and played an extremely important role in the development of the national consciousness of the people'. For the sake of his argument the Slovak people are portrayed as having been fully behind Tiso, relieved at 'liberation' from Czech domination[62]. Such positive interpretations of a clerico-fascist dictatorship, and such single-minded belief in the goodness of the Slovak national idea *per se*, subsequently persuaded more than a few people, but particularly Czechs, of the inability of nationally minded Slovaks to recognise, let alone mind, fascism when they see it[63].

The Tiso regime claimed in the early war years to represent the lesser of possible evils, and Tiso proved adept at keeping Germany at arm's length from general domestic affairs. To this end, however, the Ľudáks perjured the Christian values to which they supposedly aspired. Between 25 March and 20 September 1942 – arguably the year of the regime's greatest confidence – over 57,000 Jews were deported: two-thirds of Slovakia's Jewish population. One factor distinguishing Tiso's regime from those abiding by Nazi racial theory was that it had excluded baptised Jews from its anti-Jewish legislation, decreeing instead that converted Jews and their parents, with other, more pragmatically selected groups, such as young men in forced labour battalions, should be held in exempted categories, according to the medieval Catholic logic at work. Under the euphemism of 'evacuation', Slovakia's non-baptised Jews were delivered first into Nazi hands. Subsequent deportations were suspended for a while owing to pressure from the Lutheran clergy, and also from some of the Catholic clergy once the Vatican had instructed them as to the true meaning of the term 'resettlement'. In late 1943 and early 1944 Tiso himself refused further deportations, although agreeing to establish further concentration and labour camps within Slovakia[64]. Most of Slovakia's remaining 30,000 Jews were nevertheless deported in 1944, following the German occupation. Active resistance began to grow in the last year of the war and, crucially, the Slovak army proved disloyal to the Tiso regime; it had little stomach for a fight with the Russians, historically seen as Slavic brethren[65], and when circumstances improved the army switched sides.

THE SLOVAK NATIONAL UPRISING, 1944 – SLOVAK REDEMPTION OR NATIONALIST CONSPIRACY?

With the downturn of Hitler's fortunes tactical considerations arose of how an anti-fascist insurrection might be secured, and with whose assistance[66]. Slovakia's underground resistance had begun to increase, swelling the ranks of army officers, Czechoslovak loyalists and Communists who had formed its core[67]. During the period of Soviet-Nazi collusion, that is, until the Nazi invasion of the USSR in 1941, the Soviets had positively encouraged Slovak Communists to anticipate postwar independence or, more specifically, a Soviet Slovakia. They had therefore effectively nurtured both the tactical and the heartfelt nationalist sentiments already developing within the Slovak Communist movement. After the Nazi invasion of the USSR, however, the Soviets needed the trust of the Allies, and they duly shifted in support of the 'bourgeois' and decidedly Czechoslovakist government in exile in London, even as they continued to send ambiguous messages to the divided audiences in Czechoslovakia itself. With this deeper isolation from Czech and Soviet influences, Slovak Communists had necessarily opened their eyes to the maturing sense of national self-assertion within Slovakia, and their own nationalist sentiments had evolved unhindered.

The Agrarians, the bulk of Slovakia's underground democratic opposition or 'Civic-bloc', supported Czechoslovakia's restoration, and together with the Communists, whom they presumed they could restrain, they clandestinely re-formed the Slovak National Council on 20 November 1943. The programme that emerged from the Council, the so-called 'Christmas Agreement', called for a restoration of Czechoslovakia but as a federation on the principle of 'equal with equal'. In the conditions of the time it was evident that a proposal for anything less would be unacceptable, a naïve platform and an unsustainable denial of the mistakes of the First Republic. Aided by pro-Czechoslovak officers, the Slovak National Council prepared an anti-Ľudák coup, its declared purpose, Czechoslovakia's basic restoration, to be followed by the reconstruction of constitutional relations.

Soviet partisans were parachuted into Slovakia in the summer of 1944, and when German troops entered Slovakia on 29 August, the signal was given for the Slovak National Uprising[68]. Its bloody suppression, due to Soviet non-cooperation, to the withholding of promised assistance, and, more bitterly still, to the Soviet veto of proffered British support[69], was, for prospective Czech–Slovak relations, less important than the fact of the Uprising itself.

For Czechs the contribution of the Uprising to the developing national stereotype of Slovakia remained unusually constructive – a redeeming act – even though, during the Communist years, the Party variously claimed it as a Czech and even Russian-inspired event[70]. The Uprising 'saved Slovak nationalism', acting as a purgative of the idea that Slovak nationalism was irredeemably collaborationist or 'Ustashist'[71]; it thus re-endowed Slovaks with some powers to make claims upon the future[72]. After the war, however, the Uprising's main protagonists fell victim to Communist historical revisionism and Party in-fighting, and the consequences of the Uprising are still much debated by Slovaks[73]. For the significant number of moderate nationalists in the Slovak Communist movement the defeat of the Uprising could only mean their more profound defeat strategically, within the now re-emergent pan-Czechoslovak Communist movement.

BOLSHEVIK CZECHOSLOVAKISM 1945–8

Essentially the same reasons existed for the re-creation of a common Czechoslovak state in 1945 as had existed for its creation in 1918. Despite the immediate mass expulsions of Germans and Hungarians at the close of the Second World War – today we would call it ethnic cleansing – a significant Hungarian minority remained in Slovakia and provided the majority of Slovaks with a compelling reason for restoring a stronger state[74]. For the Czechs, the threat of a revanchist Germany loomed large. The brutal expulsion of ethnic Germans from the Czech lands, ending in the main by November 1946, could not wipe away Germany's historical connection to the area, and Czechs were unlikely to anticipate a democratic and contrite Germany rising from the ashes of the Third Reich. As in 1918, the Allied peace-makers were keen sponsors of a renewed Czechoslovak state. The Allied Powers acted on the assumption that the legal continuity of the interwar states should be restored wherever they had been violated by Nazism or its consequences.

The impulse behind the restoration of Czechoslovakia, however, was not simply pragmatic. Despite the previous eight years, it seems that it was still widely felt across Czechoslovakia that the interwar state had by no means been a disaster; on the contrary, it could be remembered as the most advanced state of the region, both politically and economically. Optimists could argue that Czechoslovakia was a thwarted plant – nipped in the bud by economic depression and German military force. In Slovakia, a consensus also apparently existed that in a new Czechoslovakia the mistakes of the previous Republic might be rectified and a new partnership created. The fact of the independent Slovak state had meant a coming of age for Slovak national consciousness, and even for those who had fought against the clerico-fascist regime; Czechoslovakist, Protestant Slovaks pledged allegiance to a new Czechoslovak state 'without the old centralist mistakes'[75].

In March 1945 the Slovak National Council – still powerful at home – passed a resolution echoing the Christmas Agreement. *The Standpoint and Requirements of the Slovak Nation* proposed that Czechoslovakia be formed as a loose federation, with only foreign trade, defence and foreign affairs to be under central authority; temporarily, Slovakia was even to administer customs and currency as a separate territory[76]. Also in March 1945 the Slovak National Council went to Moscow to meet with the Czechoslovak Communists in exile and the (London) Czechoslovak Government. Here they discovered that the Slovak voice would be heard only at the discretion of these 'Czechoslovak' forces. The future of Czechoslovakia was to be decided at round-table talks between the two exiled parties (Moscow and London), with the SNC delegates being brought in only on issues pertaining exclusively to Slovakia[77].

While the Slovak National Council's role in the Uprising and Slovakia's aspiration to equality were recognised in Moscow, the SNC's federal model remained patently unacceptable – not to the Soviets – but to the 'Muscovite' Czechoslovak Communists, who stood at the forefront of Czech efforts to reduce Slovak powers, regardless of their earlier promises to their Slovak comrades. Guided by the Soviet model of regional cultural autonomy and rigid political centralisation, Czech Communists clearly viewed themselves as the leading nationality in their republic. Like the Russians in the USSR, the Czechs designated themselves the nationality of greatest maturity in dialectical terms, best placed to direct the new state toward the socialist future[78]. However much this was understood by Slovaks as a transparent reworking of the 'older Czech brother' as the 'older Czech comrade', the Czechoslovak Communist Party was the only power that Slovak Communists were unable, following the discipline and context of the time, to resist. The last stages of the war had clearly pushed events in the Muscovites' favour. Through the winter of 1944 and 1945 the Soviet army overran large parts of Czechoslovakia, and the Muscovite Communists could subsequently employ some strategic subtlety in their dealings with the non-Communist political parties gathered in Moscow. The latter accepted the Communists' proposal for a 'National Front of the Czechs and Slovaks', the Communists camouflaging their intentions by offering the equitable distribution of three posts to each of the six parties represented at the Moscow conference[79].

The Moscow negotiations produced a programme for the Third Czechoslovak Republic. Announced on 5 April 1945 in Košice, the new Czechoslovak Government promised guarantees of Slovakia's. autonomous status. The exact divisions of competence remained to be resolved, however, and this ambiguity turned out to be a false hope for the Slovak National Council. Against the Council – still constituted by the Slovak democrats and the Communists – were ranged not only Czechoslovak Communist Party discipline but also financial considerations; Slovakia remained the weaker power economically and depended entirely upon a Czech sense of enlightened self-interest for any chance of an equalising constitutional settlement. By the end of May 1945 it was clear that the Slovak Communists were really outflanked; they had no robust ideological justification for their claims and, perhaps more importantly still, they lacked the support of those now Prague-aligned Slovak Communists who had not participated in the Uprising[80]. Fatally for Slovak interests, a joint-session decree resolved that the Communist Party of Slovakia would become merely a part of a united Communist Party of Czechoslovakia and would be subject to a common leadership[81]. This common leadership's first instruction to Slovak Communists was to drop their federalising proposals. They conceded, convinced that unanimity was crucial in the favourable postwar environment for Communism.

Follow-up negotiations to the Košice Programme brought about successive 'Prague Agreements', the first on 2 June 1945, the second on 11 April 1946. These agreements began the steady erosion of Slovak autonomy. An interim confederative arrangement enshrined in the first gave way to an extension of presidential powers to cover Slovakia in the second, though Slovak members of parliament maintained some rights of confederative veto[82]. Following the humiliation of the senior Slovak Communists of the Uprising, Karol Šmidke, Gustáv Husák and Ladislav Novomeský[83], the wartime common front of the Democratic Party and Slovak Communists finally collapsed, leaving the way open to a Czech, and this time Communist-led, reassertion of centralised power.

The 1946 election revealed to Czech Communists the reality that support for Communism in Slovakia was relatively weak. For Slovak Communists the results meant the fatal weakening of their still cherished autonomist platform. On 26 May 1946, the Communists triumphed in the Czech lands with 40.17 per cent of the vote, but were defeated in Slovakia, even with 30.37 per cent. The Slovak victors, with a massive 62 per cent, were the Democratic Party, but a Democratic Party which had made a deal with moderate L'udáks and so inherited the Catholic vote. The Slovak Communists thus found themselves in the awkward position of wanting to defend the jurisdiction of a Slovak National Council set to be dominated by the 'bourgeois' Democratic Party. This case was simply unsustainable – contesting the policy of recentralisation for the sake of a Democratic Party with new clerico-fascist overtones amounted to an unthinkable breach of Communist discipline and doctrine. Shortly afterwards the Communist Party invited its partners in the Czech National Front (Social Democratic, National Socialist and Czechoslovak People's Parties) to cooperate in restricting Slovak national powers and curtailing clerical influence.

The result of these events was the Third Prague Agreement of 28 June 1946, which further restricted Slovak authorities, most notably those of the Slovak National Council, whose legislation would henceforth require central ratification. To reinforce the point that the SNC was no longer deemed a 'progressive social force' the agreement was signed, not on behalf of the Slovak National Council but by the 'Slovak National Front'. When the agreement was ratified by the Slovak National Council on 16 July 1946, Lettrich, chairman of the Council and leader of the Democratic Party, proposed the motion on the understanding that 'the Slovaks were making a big sacrifice in the interest of the Republic and expressed the hope that their gesture would find a ready response on the part of the Czechs'[84]. The Slovak understanding of 'Czechoslovakism' nevertheless looked set to be reconfirmed, this time by Czech Communists who decried the 'bourgeois' First Republic.

Following the Communist *coup d'état* of 25 February 1948, the all-important Constitutional Committee fell to the disposal of the Party. Grounds for the coup had been prepared by Tiso's trial and execution as a war criminal and the uncovering of a (fabricated) L'udák conspiracy at the centre of Slovakia's Democratic Party. The new Communist Prime Minister and soon to be President Klement Gottwald entrenched as far as possible the idea that Prague should maintain strict and central powers. The newly purged Constitutive Assembly abolished the Slovak right to a veto in Slovak affairs on 16 April 1948, and on 9 May it approved a new constitution. This removed those vestiges of autonomy left by the Third Prague Agreement while nevertheless declaring the Czechoslovak Republic to be a state of 'two Slav nations possessing equal rights'[85].

The statement about 'nations' and state was at least now relatively accurate following the massive ethnic cleansing of Hungarians and Germans. *De jure*, however, Slovakia's formal constitutional status was restored to that of part of a unified, Czech-dominated Czechoslovak state. *De facto*, moreover, Slovakia's constitutional status had become an irrelevance, since legality was now the property not of parliament but of the Presidium of the Central Committee of the Czechoslovak Communist Party and, eventually, of its political secretariat. With the expulsion of the Germans, Czech administrative dominance was clearer than ever before and Czech national identity unchallenged within the Czech lands for the first time since 1918[86]. The democratic division of powers was at an end; of greater significance for Slovakia than constitutional changes was the formal unification of the Slovak Communist Party and the Czechoslovak Communist Party into one in September 1948.

The assimilation of the Slovak Communist Party into the Czechoslovak Party was almost a caricature of prewar democratic developments, and it was viewed by some as an act of Czech revenge[87]. Communist practice could still be filtered through national perceptions. Those principles supposedly derived from scientific law, such as the belief that material equality dissolved national sensibility, were often interpreted as old-fashioned national manoeuvring. The preferential investment in Slovakia, which began in the 1950s and was accelerated after 1968, was often perceived stereotypically by Czechs as merely an intensification of Slovakia's prewar tendency to exploit Czech idealism. On the Slovak side, the Communist doctrine of democratic centralism and the leading role of the Party could be seen as a minimal facade for continuing centralised rule from Prague. Both impressions arguably had a basis in fact.

Czechoslovakia at this point was in an extraordinary position – broken apart by war and now hammered back together by Communism and politically transformed; the huge tensions and divisions of the interwar and wartime period were now supposed to be swept aside by an entirely new order of society. Socialism, or rather, by 1949, Stalinism, purported to bring about harmony and reconciliation on all fronts. This, however, was an enforced harmony, and, as already suggested, it did not mean the resolution of the national question, but the aggravation and obscuring of it. Given the *realpolitik* reasons for Czechoslovakia's creation in 1918, the expulsion of the vast majority of Sudeten Germans from Czechoslovak territory appeared, ironically, to destroy one of the platforms upon which Czechoslovak solidarity had depended. In practical terms, however, the fact of

Slovakia's siding with Germany in the late 1930s had already destroyed the internal cohesion that the German threat was supposed to create. A possible solution to Slovakia's deeper grievances might have been federalisation – the cherished hope of the Slovak resistance movement. With federation denied, however, it asked a great deal of socialism that it should transcend (and not simply repress) Czech and Slovak differences. Was it conceivable that Czechs and Slovaks would be reconciled under a secularising, homogenising and modernising ideology that, in many respects, stood as a utopistic caricature of the Czech liberal vision of the 1920s?

THE 1950S: SHOW TRIALS

The Prague leadership responded to Soviet pressure for ever greater obedience to Moscow with the full Stalinisation of the Party and its tactics. The result in terms of Czech–Slovak relations was that the forces behind Slovak nationalism, in its clerico-fascist, but also in its more benign pro-federal forms, were systematically attacked. When attempts to uncover the true scale of the ensuing political trials were inaugurated under Alexander Dubček's liberalising offices in 1968, reports concluded that some 83,000 citizens had fallen victim, even before those persecuted through collectivisation were taken into account. The Catholic Church found itself under pressure at every level: clergy, laymen, believers, and even officials connected to charitable church institutions. Of greater importance for the position of Slovaks within the Communist polity, however, were the trials at the senior Party level.

In accordance with the Stalinist strategy of the time – random and targeted terror – President Klement Gottwald purged the Party of those prominent Slovaks who had ever proposed improvements in Slovakia's political status, and those whom the Party could usefully suspect of such a thing. Relatively unsurprising was the crushing of the Democratic Party – its membership of over 300,000 was reduced to a few hundred officials. More shocking was the swathe cut through Communist veterans of the Slovak National Uprising and the wartime partisan struggle. In Slovakia, all but three of the political commissars and commanders of the partisan movement were arrested and the army *en bloc* found itself 'beheaded' of its experienced officer corps. Some 273 top Party officials were tried between 1952 and 1954. The two main characteristics of the trials were that those Party-faithful who had helped establish the existing system and had been the Party's backbone through the war were now in the dock, and secondly, that these trials were a direct reflection of Soviet international interests and Stalinist paranoia[88]. The trials of the early 1950s[89] were directed at three distinct groups in senior Party positions: those who had spent time abroad ('cosmopolitans', 'Titoists'), Jews ('Zionists') and Slovak 'nationalists' ('bourgeois nationalists').

Top-level purges had begun in earnest when the Central Committee expelled thirteen members and two candidates of this senior Party organ in February 1951. Amongst the expellees were the Slovak war veterans Gustáv Husák, Ladislav Novomeský and Karol Šmidke – already in disfavour and reprimanded for 'bourgeois nationalism' at the Ninth Congress of the Slovak Party in 1950[90]. During trials designated for 'nationalists', Husák was jailed under a life sentence[91], and Novomeský sentenced to ten years for the 'betrayal', paradoxically, of the Slovak National Uprising. The prosecutor's paranoid identification of these Communists with the bourgeois, fascist nationalism of the Hlinka Slovak People's Party meant that the memory of Slovakia's wartime betrayal was once again recycled and Czech recriminations for Czechoslovakia's betrayal implicitly renewed. It was typical of the perverse psychology of the terror that the trials attempted to associate these 'bourgeois nationalists' not only with fascism but also with Zionism. Eleven out of the thirteen senior Communists executed in the trials were Jews, and efforts were clearly made to mobilise latent Slovak anti-Semitism to further discredit popular Slovak leaders before they came to trial[92].

The cold-bloodedly tactical nature of the purges, aimed first and foremost at appeasing Moscow, was undeniably terrible for Slovakia, silencing many of its most respected leaders and coming as it did a mere five years after the constitutional promises following the end of the war. Any political expression of Slovak national grievance or aspirations, even as Slovakia underwent forced heavy industrialisation and collectivisation, was rendered taboo not just through the 1950s, but for the foreseeable future. Stalinism ensured that Slovaks experienced only the repression of the burning issues of their political culture – national recognition and equality of political representation. Czech national chauvinism was arguably no longer necessary when assertions of national identity were systematically suppressed. Though Slovaks would eventually rise to the very top of the Communist ladder, their experiences as a nation in the 1950s are essential in explaining how antagonistic were the common Czech insinuations, after 1968 and again after 1989, that Czechoslovak Communism had been a system somehow more of Slovakia's making, more sympathetic to the Slovaks' putative 'primitive political culture'.

1968 – BRATISLAVA SPRING?

By 1963 it was clear that the Czechoslovak economy was beginning to stagnate. In such circumstances Slovakia looked set to lose the preferential investment that had revolutionised its economy in the 1950s, a prospect which could only draw together the two taboo issues of nationality and systemic change. The Soviet leader Nikita Khrushchev went public with his denunciation of Stalinism at the Twenty-second Congress of the Soviet Communist Party in October 1961, and even Czechoslovakia's most habituated Stalinists could not withstand the pressure from Moscow to acknowledge past excesses. Thousands of victims of Stalinist injustices were discreetly released, but the state recoiled from the prospect of public redress. Many of those in the regime of Antonín Novotný were all too evidently implicated in the brutality they were now expected to unmask and criticise, including Novotný himself[93].

First Secretary Novotný cremated the embalmed remains of his Stalinist predecessor, Klement Gottwald, and accepted that a massive statue of Stalin overlooking Prague should be removed. Tokenism, however, was his limit. When an up-and-coming Slovak apparatchik, Alexander Dubček, pressed for political rehabilitations and articulated the problems of Slovak underdevelopment, it seemed highly likely that Party hard-liners would teach him the lessons conventionally reserved for 'nationalists'[94]. Remarkably, Dubček not only survived, testimony to the growing weakness of the Novotný regime, but found himself on a commission investigating the political crimes of the 1950s.

When the shocking results of the Kolder Commission were presented to the Central Committee in April 1963, Dubček again lobbied for comprehensive rehabilitations, including the clearing of all accused of 'bourgeois nationalism'[95]. The report was made public in August 1963, and it added to the stir caused by Khrushchev's attempted reforms of the 'model' Soviet system. In Slovakia Dubček had in April sharply criticised the Slovak First Secretary, Karol Bacílek, for his part in the repression and had been chosen as Bacílek's replacement. Though Novotny tried to overwhelm Dubček with conformists, the Slovak party, having assimilated its success in defying Novotný, rallied to his defence, and henceforth his rise in Slovakia undoubtedly carved out not only national, but also reformist, territory inside the still repressively centralised state.

The reaction of the Slovak press was increasing openness. The Slovak writers' congress in April 1963 brought forth bitter accounts of earlier repression and recriminations against their still high-ranking instigators[96]. In spring 1963, the weekly magazine of the Union of

Slovak Writers, *Kultúrny život* (Cultural Life), began to address formerly taboo subjects. With a circulation of over 100,000, *Kultúrny život* was one of the few publications with a state-wide circulation and readership. The Slovak Party paper *Pravda* (Truth) also began to criticise Party policy[97] – an unheard-of apostasy[98]. A war of attrition ensued between Dubček, with the growing body of Czech and Slovak reformers at his side, and the old guard. From 1963 onwards Dubček's activity could not but reawaken Slovak hankerings after meaningful powers of national representation[99], significant institutional changes, even federalism[100]. To separate this desire for federalisation from a desire for liberalisation would be unwarranted, however. For many of those proposing it, federalisation represented a democratising project – a guarantee that Slovakia as a community would no longer find itself systematically at one remove from decision-making. Although Slovaks would later be accused by Czechs of having pursued their national interest at the expense of democratisation, the reality was that in the early 1960s the impulse for reform was very much emanating from Slovakia. Moreover, as the reform movement flourished across the country, Slovak institutions and public opinion continued to participate and endorse every aspect of the democratising project.

When a showdown within the Party finally took place in 1967 the Slovak question emerged as only one point in the catalogue of failures for which the regime was finally called to account[101]. Czechs fearful that Dubček would come to the fore of the Party as a Slovak nationalist seemed reassured of his even-handedness within a few months of his gaining the Party leadership, when Czech opinion polls rated him highly[102]. The Central Committee elected Dubček First Secretary on 3 January 1968, leaving Novotný the Presidency only until 22 March.

'FEDERALISATION' – A COMPROMISE

Since 1948 the idea of federalisation had lingered in the shadow form of institutional asymmetry, i.e. in the survival of moribund Slovak organs without Czech equivalents and a Slovak branch of the Communist Party subordinate to the Czechoslovak Party[103]. This asymmetry had encouraged the already strong tendency of Czechs to identify Czechoslovak institutions as correspondingly Czech, a fact that was now decried in 1968 in the reforming Action Programme that emerged under Dubček's leadership[104]. When the issue of how to reform the state re-emerged the debate centred not on the question of whether to federalise it, but how. The asymmetrical model was evidently no longer acceptable to most of the Slovak elite. The aspirations of Slovakia's wartime resistance movement had clearly taken root as a profound Slovak consensus[105]. On 15 May 1968, a committee was established to prepare a draft law on federalisation. The Slovak National Council unilaterally prepared a draft proposing two semi-independent states: the Czech Republic and the Slovak Republic, in which the federation was reduced to an 'umbrella construction' with powers mainly over defence and foreign policy. The Czechs presented two different drafts. One suggested a strong federation; the other also proposed, remarkably and for the first time, a looser bond between the two republics[106], though in a version still viewed by the Slovaks as unacceptably asymmetrical.

In June 1968 the National Assembly approved the 'Constitutional Law on the Preparation of the Federation', founding at last a Czech National Council as an equivalent institution to the Slovak National Council. Slovak rights of veto were also reintroduced for matters covering Slovak national interests – the principle previously cancelled by the Prague Agreements. The Slovak victory was by no means secure, however. The members of the new Czech National Council were not to be elected but 'presented' by the National Front, a reflection of the continuing Czech perception that the Czech National Council could only be a redundant body so long as the state National Assembly continued to exist[107].

Czech Communists had accepted the principle of federalisation, but its impetus had been Slovak. Czechs evidently realised that the Party needed re-legitimising, and that the solution for Slovakia was obviously constitutional. However, as would shortly become clear, the federation was put in place to satisfy Slovak aspirations and not out of any independent Czech desire to decentralise power. The entire project was put in doubt, moreover, when, on 21 August 1968, five armies of the Warsaw Pact occupied Czechoslovakia in order to destroy the reform movement, and Dubček was taken, separated from his colleagues and blindfolded, to Moscow.

Dubček's Action Programme had proposed a reconstitution of the emasculated Slovak National Council as a working legislature and the establishment of a Slovak Council of Ministers as an executive – both to be animated by an enhancement of Slovak competences[108]. Even if the Soviets were appalled by Czechoslovakia's experimental socialism they were not blind to the problem of legitimacy and thus, having followed the lesson of the 'Slovak' time bomb, they duly applied their own experience of exploiting constitutional guarantees. It was agreed, with Soviet encouragement, that federalising constitutional changes would be formally promulgated as of 28 October 1968.

As it transpired, Constitutional Act 143/1968 recognised the inalienable right of the Czech and Slovak nations to self-determination, even to the point of secession. But also explicitly, and crucially for post-1989 discussions, it declared the essential 'sovereignty' of the republics: the Czech Socialist Republic and the Slovak Socialist Republic. The relationship of republic to federation was to be based formally on cooperation rather than subordination. The federal government and its organs could perform activities on the territory of the republics only if given explicit legal authorisation[109]. A federal bicameral parliament was to be the supreme legislative body and this would become tricameral when considering constitutional legislation, which would have to pass by a three-fifths majority in both the Chamber of the People and the now nationally separated Chambers of the Nations. The constitution thus provided a guarantee against '*majorizácia*' – the power of the Czech majority to outvote the Slovak minority on issues involving national interests.

Though many among Dubček's supporters had realised that there was no surer way to reinforce the state than by fulfilling Slovak aspirations as quickly as possible[110], clearly not all Czechs understood enlightened self-interest in the same way. In the commentary of the time it was not unusual to find the birth of the Czech republic interpreted as 'an exigency to which the Slovaks have led us . . . Czech public opinion understands the federalisation of Czechoslovakia in no way as their victory, but as historical necessity'[111].

The federal package that emerged was nevertheless even theoretically inconsistent. Though parity between the two republics was a central characteristic of parliamentary structures, including committees, the principle was not applied to bureaucratic, ministerial or government appointments, where majority rule continued[112]. Thus the principle of national parity applied most strongly in those institutions weakest in a Communist system – the national legislature and constitutional court – and was weakest of all in the federal bureaucracy, where decision-making and implementation had a critical impact on policy[113]. As post-invasion 'normalisation' took hold, moreover, the reshaped Communist Federal Assembly became as toothless as those that had gone before. Though the new Federation law was based on divided sovereignty 'from below', the pyramidal nature of the Communist system once again dictated that real power came from above – not from government, but from Party structures, according to the principle of democratic centralism. The executive power-sharing virtues of the constitution provided little protection in practice, and its confederative elements were likewise a facade (foreign policy, defence, currency, federal material reserves and federal legislation were the only policies supposedly under the exclusive purview of federal organs)[114].

The 1968 amendments to the 1960 constitution, while rapidly over-ruled in practice, were also formally weakened by amendments in 1970 which further diluted the original division of competences. Where the 1968 law had referred to the 'integration of two socialist economies', decentralising various economic competences, the 1970 revision pro-claimed the Czechoslovak economy to be unified. Further changes consolidated the coordination of security and social control from Prague, and dual citizenship, briefly symbolising the primacy of Czech and Slovak nationality, was also abolished[115]. Even before 1970, a fatal blow had fallen with the Soviet-enforced prevention of the federalisation of the Communist Party. Proposed in Dubček's Action Programme, Party federalisation had been seen as an essential condi-tion for the real differentiation of policy. Through the 1970s and 1980s Czechoslovakia was re-established as a pillar of Soviet orthodoxy, surpassed in its conservatism only by East Germany[116].

BETWEEN SCYLLA AND CHARYBDIS

Though public support for reform had become marginally deeper and better defined in the Czech lands than in Slovakia – an unsurprising consequence of the former's longer history of self-government – 1968 was neither intrinsically nor solely a Czech phenomenon. The abiding Czech historical perception that it was, that democratic rather than structural reform impulses were essentially Czech, came from an important continuity in Czech political expectations. As one historian has noted, 'the Czech population considered the Czechoslovak Republic to be their state and, in general, had no objections to the cen-tralised system. Czech demands were for democratisation'[117]. These same preconceptions have tended to blur the extent to which Slovaks had perceived federalisation not just as a good in itself[118], a narrowly nationalistic demand, but as a peculiarly Slovak prerequisite for those same democratic goods supposedly desired only by the Czechs.

Slovakia's theoretical right of veto for constitutional legislation was a major point of tension in 1968, as it would be again after 1989. For Slovaks, federalisation was not only consistent with democratisation, but the veto provided a structural guarantee that Slovak interests could not be simply overridden by the natural Czech majority in a working parliament. Unfortunately for Czech–Slovak relations, the Czechs persisted in understanding democracy as a system in which the indi-vidual, and not the nation, was the exclusive source of authority. In the Czech conception of democracy, therefore, majority rule was the only valid basis of decision-making: a patently disingenuous idea in a distinctly bi-national state. Moreover, the Slovaks could cite economic reformist arguments on their side; the Czech preference for centralised rule by the 1960s ran against the economic reform arguments of the day, which generally recommended that the centre relinquish its complete and initiative-inhibiting control.

The Czech insistence that the reform impulses of 1968 were essentially Czech is also simply a-historical, not least in terms of leadership. Alexander Dubček, a Slovak who had fought as a partisan during the National Uprising, and was as strongly aware as anyone of Slovakia's impoverished past, was also a socialist of almost Fabian instincts, with profound beliefs in the necessity of democratic freedoms. As he insisted subsequently, 'I was not so naive as not to see that it would only take time before the changes we made yielded to a full multi-party democracy. I knew that, and Brezhnev knew that, of course. So why won't the critics see it?'[119] The Soviet crackdown and the ensuing twenty years of Communist 'normalisation' clearly had a strong editing effect on public sentiment. The particular conformism of the Slovak Party *apparat* following 1968 appears to have eradicated from Czech memory all recollection of the highly contrasting state of affairs in Slovakia in the early 1960s.

More than any other period under Communist rule, the aftermath of the so-called Prague Spring brought existing national stereotypes back to the political surface and reinforced them for another generation. To a striking degree the events of 1968, far from engendering new prejudices, only reworked the old, recycling, rather than reinterpreting the past[120]. The despair felt by pro-reform Czechs and Slovaks alike at the destruction of 'socialism with a human face', moreover, lent a distinct bitterness to the charges that emerged in the aftermath. Two of the most enduring views to emerge from the '68 experiment and its demise would greatly inform evaluations of the 'other side' during disputes in the 1990s.

THE CZECH VIEW

Though there was an attempt among Czech politicians of the right after 1989 to play down the popularity as such of the '68 reform movement, demoting it to a factional battle between Party cliques, a second mainstream Czech view maintains that the liberalising impulses of 1968 were intrinsically Czech. According to this view, Czechs alone had called for cultural and political emancipation, and Prague had formed the centre of radical activity[121]. Slovak reformers, this view insists, worried only about Slovakia's status. As Petr Pithart, Prime Minister of the Czech Republic between 1990 and 1992, put it, 'The reform movement which culminated in 1968 bore the distinct seal of the Czech genius loci. Slovakia left its mark in its emphasis on a greater degree of national self-determination, which could only mean a weakening of the democrats' position'[122]. According to this reading, Slovakia remained more watchful and typically conservative, if not indifferent to rolling back the Communist state. Slovakia's real endeavours were opportunist and, worse still, selfishly nationalistic. According to an old, and now repeated, Czech saw, nationalism always brought out the worst in the Slovak tendency toward primitive politics, vehemence and self-dramatisation, something the liberal and rational Czechs had always found hard to understand. Slovakia sought only federalisation out of the revolutionary flux in 1968, and engaged in a Faustian bargain with the Soviet occupiers to secure it – just as after Munich in 1938 they were shaming not just their nation but also the state in benefiting from its humiliation. With federalisation secured, Slovaks exploited their 'fifth column' status to extract massive Czech subsidies for Slovak industry, and encouraged Soviet patronage and protection. Gustáv Husák, the author of the greyest days of Communist 'normalisation', this argument ran, was reasserting through Party favouritism the Slovak nationalism for which he had been imprisoned after the Second World War.

THE SLOVAK VIEW

Not surprisingly the Slovaks' version of events differs radically. From their perspective, the events of 1968 amounted only to the fuller realisation of the Slovak reformist movement and Dubček's influence. These had already taken hold in Slovakia in the early 1960s, when Slovak economists insisted that the economy required liberalisation and a parallel, political opening. These facts were lost in an international glamorisation of 1968 which focused entirely on Prague, more beautiful and sophisticated as that city was. While the Czech Antonín Novotný still clamped down on the Czechs, Slovakia had enjoyed so much freedom in its publishing that censored Czechs had sought refuge in Bratislava publishing houses – another fact forgotten in the 1970s and 1980s, when the dissident movement was, for complex reasons, disproportionately Czech.

Dubček – Novotný's undoing, the undisputed instigator of state-wide Party reform and the democratising April Action Programme –

this exasperated view points out, was a Slovak. Not a Czechoslovakist Slovak or an opportunist Slovak, but a reasonable Slovak. The
continued pursuit of federalisation was an attempt to wrest at least
some good, and a good already long promised and repeatedly denied,
from Czechoslovakia's shattered sovereignty – relatively acceptable to
the Soviets as the idea was. Finally, and crucially, though the Czechs
never stopped complaining about it, federalisation under Communism
turned out to be a sham, a constitutional facade for continuing centralised power. Czechs remained in the driving seat and deep down
still begrudged all Slovak attempts to build even economic equality,
Slovakia's only real compensation for being in the state in the first
place. Federalisation of the Party had never been permitted and
Slovaks had found themselves politically unarmed. After 1968 they
could no longer even demand 'federalisation' since formally it existed,
and the national issue had once again become taboo.

THE VERDICT ON THE FEDERATION AT THE END OF THE 1980S

The last twenty years of Czechoslovak Communism could be characterised as a phenomenal balancing act. The prevailing post-invasion
policy was one of 'no surprises'[123]. The leadership of Soviet normalisation in Czechoslovakia, while not entirely senile and decrepit by
Soviet standards, was nevertheless unchanging, and it engaged with
the national question only minimally and only in the language of
economic achievements, namely, the claim that Czech and Slovak
economic conditions were finally equalised. It is hard to give the
flavour of normalisation in Czechoslovakia and of the sense of profound stagnation in every aspect of social and political life, but if you
can imagine living in a melancholic, low-budget, black-and-white,
twenty-year-long version of the film *Groundhog Day*, you will have
some idea of the atmosphere of the time. What diagnosis, then, could
reasonably be offered for the future of the Czechoslovak state on the
threshold of 1989, when the dominant characteristic of the state was
that its national question had been deeply repressed for the previous
twenty, indeed forty, years?

Of course, no definitive judgement is possible, but what is most
striking about the condition of national relations at the end of the
1980s is precisely their uncertainty – their extreme contingency.
Formally, the Czechoslovak state was a federation with a powerful
right of veto for Slovakia in constitutional affairs; in practice, the constitution was quite meaningless as real power continued to emanate
from the centralised and unified, Czech-dominated Czechoslovak

33

Communist Party. Bi-national relations were nevertheless maintained via long-developed political ties, factional balances within the Party, personal connections, understandings and obligations, all in a system in which the explicit discourse of national interest was not permitted. Although Czechs and Slovaks had accumulated a fund of potentially corrosive political events, the Communist historical record, the only record available to the vast majority of Czechs and Slovaks under the age of fifty, portrayed national relations as perpetually harmonious and fraternal. From the late 1940s onwards, the clerico-fascist Slovak state was portrayed in Communist history as a German imposition, opposed by the vast majority of Slovaks, who were, needless to add, profoundly Communist in their aspirations and mentality, just like the Czechs! Since Communist renderings of history had nevertheless been completely internally inconsistent, modifying interpretations of events to suit the vagaries of Soviet foreign policy, the condition of Czechs and Slovaks alike was one of not knowing what history to trust. As the dissident playwright Václav Havel so eloquently put it, the main endeavour of Communist rule over the years had become one of 'organised forgetting', the only context in which Communist achievements might shine.

Economically, the picture in the late 1980s was likewise contingent. The Communist Party had claimed for over a decade that economic equality between the two republics stood as one of the lasting achievements of socialism. Moreover, economic data were aggregated across the state as a whole, making it extremely difficult to prove or disprove any claims about separate national economic performance or about the degree of economic dependence of one republic upon the other. Emergency reforms proposed in 1988, however, indicated an economic crisis precisely because they were based explicitly on the conclusion that the 'equal' Slovak economy was fundamentally less able to absorb investment compared to the Czech. In 1988 even the Panglossian Czechoslovak Communist Party understood crisis management as necessitating a reorientation of investment to the more profitable Czech lands. What impact this admission might have on national relations given the end of Communism, however, was anybody's guess[124].

In geopolitical terms, membership of the Soviet-dominated military alliance, the Warsaw Pact, had ensured that the existence or non-existence of Sudeten Germans within a Czechoslovak state hardly mattered; Czechoslovakia's geopolitical position was fixed as a front-line state of Communist orthodoxy, ranged against the capitalist West. Again, what sense of common geopolitical interest in a Czechoslovak state would exist in a new military world order could not be anticipated. The total collapse of the Warsaw Pact through

1989–1990 and the withdrawal of Soviet troops from Czechoslovak soil by June 1991 would place Czechoslovakia, like every other state of the Soviet bloc, in a security vacuum, a fact that, intuitively at least, would seem to render secession exceptionally risky, and make the maintenance of as large as state as possible unusually attractive.

The picture of Czech–Slovak relations is hardly clarified by public opinion polls, for obvious reasons a somewhat neglected tool under Communism. In one of the few surveys on this topic, conducted by Radio Free Europe and based on 1,200 interviews among Czech and Slovak visitors temporarily in Western countries between 1974 and 1975, 72 per cent of Czechs and 81 per cent of Slovaks thought the federal government treated both republics 'equally'. 17 per cent of Czechs as against 2 per cent of Slovaks felt the government favoured Slovakia, whereas only 12 per cent of Slovaks felt the government favoured the Czech lands, as against 1 per cent of Czechs. With such a small and unusual sample, however, the RFE survey is essentially a shot in the dark. In a domestic poll taken in April–May 1989 the majority of both the Czech and Slovak respondents were found to believe that relations between Czechs and Slovaks were either friendly or 'rather friendly' (63 per cent), a lower count than the 79 per cent of respondents in 1983 who had evaluated their relations positively. Czechs, moreover, were again less positive than Slovaks about national relations (66 per cent versus 76 per cent)[125].

To try to relate vaguely worded and isolated polls of the 1970s to the vaguely worded polls of 1990 is, I would argue, a treacherous exercise. Moreover, to credit the expressed opinions of the 1970s and 80s with predictive properties is to ignore the potential of the anti-Communist revolution of 1989 to rekindle either optimism for the future of a common state *or* optimism regarding the opportunities for small, newly independent nations within a fully liberated Europe. It would be equally unwise to ignore the potential for a new, non-Communist political leadership to reframe the national question in an attractive and manageable light. The picture, again, is one of extreme contingency.

Though the legitimacy of the existing Czechoslovak state was profoundly in doubt by 1989, the year of Communism's collapse, the circumstances outlined above ensure that the exact nature of that illegitimacy will remain unclear. It was in the nature of the regime, and of dissent, that only dissident circles were able to evince nationalist and oppositionist attitudes, and such dissident circles were a tiny minority of the population: a very particular cross-section of the religious, artistic and intellectual elite of the two republics. When these same dissidents came to power through the anti-Communist revolution of November 1989, however, their perceptions of national tension became deeply significant.

The two national dissident elites appear to have acted as a repository of some of the most comprehensive national stereotypes, uninhibited and unaltered as such national stereotypes had been by any open ethnic conflict or overt weakness in the 'normalised' Communist state. As we shall see in later chapters, the role of these dissident figures from the 1970s and 1980s in the Czechoslovak debate in 1990 to 1992 would be formative, though not decisive. Their respective national views, already established by 1968, had been greatly reinforced by the apparently diverging development of anti-Communist protest between the two republics under normalisation.

When the dissident Charter 77 movement was founded in a desperate effort to hold the Communist regime to its commitments to the Helsinki Final Act of 1975, those that risked everything to sign it were disproportionately Czech. Among the first 243 signatures collected when the Charter was created, only one was that of a dissident living permanently in Slovakia – Miroslav Kusý[126]. As František Kriegel complained to *Die Welt* in 1977: 'The Slovak minority exercises power over the Czech majority, although the federation meant to establish parity. But today, Slovaks hold all the key positions, and considerable financial resources are flowing to Bratislava. They [the Slovaks] have thus accomplished much more than they had been aiming at, and therefore, they will also not identify with our cause[127] [Charter 77]'[128].

Alexander Dubček, ever the federalist, described the Charter as 'a courageous initiative in the tradition of Czech political and cultural defiance going back to Austria-Hungary'[129]. The overbearing 'Czechness' of its organisation, however, was later cited by others as actually accounting for Slovak non-participation. The Slovak writer Vladimír Mináč went so far as to call the Chartist movement 'Czechoslovakising'[130]. Indeed, no Slovak input into the Charter had been sought before its publication[131] – as with Ludvík Vaculík's trenchant critique, 'Two Thousand Words', issued in 1968[132] – an important reflection of the deep and persistent Pragocentrism of Czech dissent.

Commentators have noted a systematic discrepancy between the Czech and Slovak republics in the level of anti-Communist activism[133], pointing out that of the individual instances of regime retaliation against dissidents in the late 1970s only 4–5 per cent occurred in Slovakia, and over half of these targeted just two Slovak individuals. Others have pointed out, however, that the Slovak proportion of dissident activity increased steadily into the 1980s[134], and indeed, Czech assessments of Slovak protest routinely ignore the real and unprotected locus of Slovak dissent – their persistent religious affiliation. Despite the regime's attempts to co-opt the Catholic Church throughout the 1970s, mass pilgrimages and religious demonstrations were proof of a profound and sizeable Slovak opposition to the culture of Communism – if not active 'pro-democracy' dissent – and yet this appears to have done little to halt the Czech intellectuals' recourse to stereotypes. If the Communist regime of the 1970s pursued a carrot-and-stick policy toward religious believers it was always clear, at least to Slovaks, that any independent religious initiatives and associations would face the same abuse experienced by the Chartists in Prague. In a signature campaign in 1988 calling for religious freedom some 300,000 of the 500,000 names collected were Slovaks. By way of reaction, the regime brutally repressed the subsequent candlelight gathering in Bratislava of 2000 believers led by František Mikloško[135]. That Slovak religious protest was persistently disregarded as 'dissent' by the Czechs is thus noteworthy, particularly since Czech dissidents were content to view religious protest in Poland as both anti-Communist *and* pro-democratic.

Clearly, among many in the Czech intellectual elite there was a mistrust of this separate Slovak religiosity which bordered on the chauvinistic. Religious affiliation was not readily accepted as indicative of the liberal yearnings supposedly prevalent among Czechs. It was instead considered a sign of an essentially unreconstructed and pre-democratic political culture – by implication, the culture of the clerico-fascist Slovak state of the Second World War. For the Czech dissidents to hold such a view, however, was to be wilfully blind to their own isolation. As the Polish dissident Adam Michnik commented in 1982, 'The underground in post-1968 Czechoslovakia . . . includes . . . small groups of déclassé oppositionists whose spiritual atmosphere resembles the first Christian communities hiding in the catacombs more than they resemble an illegal political opposition movement'[136]. In practice, Slovakia's isolation from Czech dissident activity was actively enforced by the Communist regime[137]. Moreover, by focusing on Slovakia's lack of secular anti-state organisation as positive evidence of apathy, and by maintaining so low an opinion of Slovak political culture, many in the Czech dissident elite unintentionally reinforced the regime's own efforts[138].

While Radio Free Europe felt able to conclude that 'traditional rivalry between Czechs and Slovaks' was 'at an encouragingly low ebb in 1974 – early 1975'[139], a resurrection of the kind of alliance of the national reformist-dissident elites witnessed in the 1960s appeared ever more elusive in the 1980s[140]. The Slovak dissident elite was particularly isolated, having lost not only the sympathy of the Czechs but the strength of their own numbers in 1968, deliberately divided as they had been by nominal federalisation and the softer purges inflicted on the Slovak wing of the Communist Party[141].

In November 1989, the entire character of the state was thrown into question by the anti-Communist revolution sweeping at last across Central and Eastern Europe. The Czechoslovak state's attempt to simply hold the nationalities question at arm's length now collapsed along with the rest of the *status quo*. The so-called 'Velvet Revolution' in Czechoslovakia not only aimed at destroying the previous rules of the political game, but more successfully broke the bi-national political ties sustained by the factional balances and personal networks maintained within the Czechoslovak Communist Party. The already ambiguous political relationship between the two republics was now reduced to its most unstable institutional basis: a dubiously confederative constitution and parliament, a legal framework which, in the absence of the all-regulating Party, was untried in practice, extremely decentralising in some of its provisions and respected neither by the federal centre nor by the republican periphery. Even the term Czechoslovakism carried ambiguous connotations in Slovakia. When said in derogatory tones 'Czechoslovakist' was a shorthand expression for 'someone who believes, or is clearly assimilated, in a composite national identity, though historically this identity is merely a guise for Slovak assimilation into Czech culture'.

Without consensually established and binding connections it seemed unlikely that the market and democracy would diminish national friction, at least in the short term. On the Slovak side it seemed more probable that Slovaks would see democratisation as the opportunity for achieving in practice the deep federalisation that until now had existed only in the unexamined texts of the constitution. On the Czech side it appeared that a dissident-dominated government, more than others, would treat such overtures with suspicion. A domestic consensus regarding Czechoslovakia's history and function scarcely existed, raising the further complication that the state after 1989 might suffer as much from unstable and ideologically driven interpretations of its history as it would from historical events themselves[142].

HOW TO INTERPRET THE BREAK-UP?

Within three years of the 1989 revolution the Czechoslovak state had ceased to exist. The circumstances in which the state collapsed, moreover, suggest many possible explanations. Nationalism, the ambiguous nature of the state, social, economic and political uncertainty and radical change, political entrepreneurialism and state-building, institutional failure, economic inequality, latent grievances and populism were all present to some degree in post-1989 Czechoslovakia. In what ways would each of these issues play out over the critical three years between 1989 and 1992? Did some political figures, societal grievances or institutional failures prove more important than others?

The political puzzle of the separation unfolds in the following way: Czechoslovakia's peaceful anti-Communist revolution produces a broadly 'liberal' federal government of Czechs and Slovaks; they commit themselves to a renewal of federalism. Two years later diverse political parties, including the offspring of the Czech and Slovak revolutionary civic movements, submit themselves to an election; every party (excepting a small Slovak National Party) declares itself in favour of a common state. Barely two weeks later the victors, the Czech leader Václav Klaus and the Slovak leader Vladimír Mečiar – both professedly pro-federal before the election – announce that Czechoslovakia is to be broken apart. Within seven months they dissolve the Czechoslovak state and launch the independent Republics of Czechia and Slovakia. Though the majority of the electorate is against the split, there is no referendum. While the President, Václav Havel, is internationally respected as the tribune of the 1989 revolution, he is powerless to stop the divorce.

How is such a radical turn of events to be explained? How have Czechs and Slovaks explained it to themselves? In what follows I investigate how Czechoslovakia was partitioned against the popular will and how politics have operated in the newly independent states. The book explores competing explanations for the divorce in chapters that isolate, in turn, the critical dimensions of the break-up; party political developments, the constitutional talks and economic performance. The final chapter charts the political evolution of the independent republics since the separation.

APPROACHES TO THE BREAK-UP

Apart from the essential question 'why?' the end of Czechoslovakia in December 1992 poses two additional and, in the circumstances of state separation, highly unusual questions – 'why did it fall apart so quickly?' – i.e. without any serious attempt at an alternative configuration – and 'why did it fall without violence?' Given the many alternative sources of friction it is worth establishing some benchmarks, some reasonable standards of proof and evidence to help us judge between possible alternative causes.

Even without heightened nationalist feeling the theoretical literature on federations did not bode well for a bi-national, democratised Czechoslovakia, it being difficult to create a consensus in conditions that would naturally encourage an adversarial approach. Democratic federal systems typically operate on the basis of the bargaining between shifting coalitions of groups. Compromises can be secured only when, and because, no single group or coalition of groups is in a continually dominant position. As a result, so political theory anticipates, the danger of an irreconcilable confrontation in a two-unit federation is so great that sooner or later it must end in civil war, secession, or both[143]. Further conditions of successful federations 'would be the requirement that no single member state should be in such a dominant position that it can dictate the policies of the federal government' and 'the development of a party system which will provide those political linkages across the boundaries of the member states, without which the process of bargaining and compromise essential to federal politics cannot take place'[144].

The assertion that the oppositional characteristics of a bi-communal federation doom it to collapse should not, however, be accepted uncritically in the Czechoslovak case. Such an argument – dependent as it is on the idea that institutions themselves create structures of incentives – glosses over many of the distinct problems of the Communist inheritance and the post-Communist transition, and to ignore these is to adopt a distinctly fatalistic attitude to the separation. To keep our options open, therefore, the theoretical arguments set out below entertain the possibility that the Czechoslovak state after 1989 was neither democratic nor federal, but in 'transition'.

The alternative explanations are, of course, not plucked from thin air but have been framed around the major known facts of the Czechoslovak divorce. Another consideration has been that these exploratory theories should allow us to consider many types of explanation and a wide range of possible causes. I have tried to cover the critical dimensions of Czech and Slovak political life, constitutional, party political and bureaucratic developments – what we might call 'institutional developments' – together with political ideas, national identities, social divisions, public opinion, economic issues and last, but not least, the geopolitical context. These theories are not intended to be mutually exclusive, but, rather, exploratory ideas. They are as follows:

1) The inevitability argument – nationalism

This contends that ethnonationalism was at the root of the separation and that the anti-Communist revolution of 1989 did not so much engender conflict as reveal and unleash it. This argument is investigated in the next chapter.

2) The inequality argument – relative deprivation

Observing that economic relations between the Czech lands and Slovakia had always been fraught, and that after 1989 economic reform proved especially controversial, this argument suggests that it was Slovakia's persistent relative deprivation in particular that motivated secessionist impulses (in both republics), which in turn led to separation. This argument is explored in Chapters 2 and 5.

3) The institutional argument – 1. Separate party systems

This view proposes that, once separate party systems emerged in a democratic setting, political interests and party competition, and thus electoral incentives, were structured in such a way as to make consensus building between parties from the two separate party systems impossible. Divergence was, therefore, institution-led. This thesis is examined in Chapter 3.

4) The party competition argument – party autonomy

This argument contends that the process of party formation and the post-election fragmentation of the Czech and Slovak anti-Communist civic movements into competing factions permitted the development of highly oligarchic and autonomous political parties. The resulting vagueness of party programmes and campaigns, particularly on the alternative models of state design, left the way open for unaccountable elite action. This thesis is also examined in Chapter 3.

5) The institutional argument – 2. Path-dependency

This view proposes that once pre-Communist, Communist and post-Communist institutions (in particular, Communist constitutional rules and parliamentary structures) were animated in a democratic setting, political interests were structured in such a way as to make consensus building impossible. Divergence was, therefore, institution-led, i.e. constitution-led. This thesis is examined in Chapter 4.

6) *The democratisation argument – state-restructuring*

This argument contends that there were fundamental differences and incompatible notions of what kind of democratic state should be built and, consequently, of how the state should be restructured. Diverging perceptions of democratising, and of concomitant state-restructuring needs among Czech, Slovak and federal governing elites led to growing conflict and the breakdown of common institutions. This thesis is examined in Chapter 5.

7) *The realist argument – leadership choices*

Following the party autonomy argument, this 'realist' account contends that in the absence of democratic and representative institutions the fullest rein was given to elite decision-making, and the separation was duly concocted by leaders with demonstrably rational private power interests in republican independence. This thesis is examined in Chapter 6.

2

THE RETURN OF HISTORY?

It was not uncommon, after 1989, to hear that Communism in Eastern Europe would be replaced by nationalism, the assumption being that Communism had functioned as a form of societal deep-freeze, locking in the cultures of the interwar period. Those who expected the collapse of the Cold War *status quo* to reopen old wounds of ethnicity in European politics found it easy to believe that Czechoslovakia could succumb to a nationalist conflict once cut loose. The notion that Eastern European national grievances are peculiarly resilient, moreover, has intellectual underpinnings which predate the Cold War.

In modern times, there have been fewer states which correspond to ethnic cultures in Central and Eastern Europe than in Western Europe. Instead, different states in Eastern Europe, *purporting* to be ethnically homogeneous 'nation-states', have tended to compete for populations and territory, and nationhood criteria have often been asserted for the brutal extension and assumption of political power[1]. The resulting tangled web of actual and potential national conflicts in Eastern Europe has prompted several scholars to condemn the impulse to nationhood in this region *in toto*, as altogether different from, and far more dangerous than, that in the 'West'. One of the first scholars to account for this tendency, Hans Kohn, argued – as far back as 1944 – that by having to rely on ethnicity as the only available justification for territorial claims, Eastern European nationalism was from its inception[2] biased towards authoritarian and 'irrational' forms; potent ethnic myths and legends were more frequently invoked in the attempt to prove that a certain national group was originally 'sovereign' over a given territory. The tendency of Eastern nationalism towards ethnic 'mysticism' – because it could not be rooted in any liberal traditions or within existing states – Kohn argued, set these nationalisms apart from the Enlightenment and supposedly more rational nationalism of Western Europe, which had emerged as ideologies of liberalisation in territories already well-defined by history and law[3]. Kohn's line of theory, with its emphasis on powerful myths of heritage and ethnic survival, would lead us to expect Eastern European nationalism to be exceedingly resilient, able to survive – in however abstract a form – an experience even as repressive as Communism.

Whether or not one believes that nationalism was 'bound to return' after 1989, one thing at least is clear, and that is that the end of Communism made overt nationalism possible. During the Cold War even weak states could survive purely on their condition as pillars of the East–West *status quo*. In the post-Cold War era, in contrast, nationalist and secessionist claims were peculiarly tempting because eastern bloc states could no longer appeal to the Soviet Union to stop them[4].

If the return of nationalism is to blame for the break-up of Czechoslovakia then we should be able to look back at the period between 1990 and 1992 and discover the evidence. We would expect to find political movements with a separatist nationalist programme and to see that these movements succeeded electorally – they would have been popular and had a mass following. One would also have expected to see strong nationalist and separatist sentiment in public opinion polls and among those politicians who had ultimately decided Czechoslovakia's fate[5]. If nationalist parties had actually proved weak and unpopular, however, and levels of public nationalist sentiment had been low – if few politicians had used the nationalist card, and, more specifically, if those politicians clearly responsible for the decisions breaking up the federation had avoided overt nationalism and carried no personal nationalist preoccupations of their own – then the argument that the collapse of Czechoslovakia was inevitable, that it was broken apart by a re-emergent nationalism, should be accepted as incorrect or, at best, as an inadequate account of the story as it could be observed.

While an 'inevitability argument' about the return of nationalism is worth exploring, it is self-evidently controversial as an explanation for the end of Czechoslovakia, and not simply because it is the official explanation of the Czechs, the strongest side in the dispute. Even if we were to reject the inevitability argument as simplistic, however – if we were to point out that Communist socialisation must have had at least *some* mollifying impact on national grievances – it is still possible to imagine conflicts arising *after* 1989 that were quite capable of provoking fresh nationalist arguments or reinvigorating the more muted conflicts of the 1970s and 1980s.

Perhaps the most frequently heard thesis in this respect – and, for us, an alternative explanation for the break-up – is that renewed economic tensions between Czechs and Slovaks may have acted as fertile ground for the regeneration of a nationalist idea. The historical fact of unequal economic development between Slovakia and the Czech lands, tensions over preferential investment in the republics throughout the 1970s and 1980s, and the unique scale of the economic reforms proposed in 1990 together suggest tremendous scope for nationalist mobilisation based on economic competition and economic grievances – or 'relative deprivation', as this category of nationalist conflict is often called.

The relative deprivation theory of nationalism was conceived by Ernest Gellner and championed by Tom Nairn in his writings on Scottish nationalism. In this interpretation, intellectuals or politicians in relatively poor regions mobilise the masses because, without economic strength, 'the people is all they have got'[6]; the ornaments of national culture and nationalist rhetoric are just a facade for the practical defence of economic interests. Interestingly enough for our case, Nairn also admits of a cross-category, where the more developed regions also defend their economic interests against what they perceive to be the 'backwardness around them'[7].

Over the years these theories have been criticised for many reasons as inadequate explanations for the emergence of nationalism as such[8], but they still suggest a solid basis for the *resurrection* of secessionist impulses in the Czechoslovak case. One could envisage, for instance, a scenario of conflict between two essentially economically motivated nationalisms: the Czechs perceiving themselves to be shedding the expensive, 'backward' Slovaks in a bid for accelerated entry into Western European institutions, the Slovaks perceiving themselves to be escaping the exploitative Czechs.

If at minimum 'economic factors are very apt to serve as catalytic agent, exacerbator, or choice of battleground' in a nationalist conflict[9], then Nairn's ideas may at least cast some light upon the mobilising tactics of Czech and Slovak nationalists after 1989. It may be that an emphasis upon sharp economic differences and national discrimination provided the best available strategy for the entrepreneurs in Czechoslovakia's new political elite.

If this more pragmatic explanation for a nationalist revival is to be taken seriously then we should find strong economic grievances – in Slovakia's case, against Czech economic manipulation; in the Czech case, against something along the lines of Slovakia's debilitating economic archaism – and we should then find these grievances translated into separatist nationalist political movements able to mobilise mass support. If, however, this second nationalist thesis is also misplaced, then we would find that economic grievances were not translated into separatist nationalist sentiment and that nationalist or separatist parties were perceived as performing badly on economic issues. Although the question of nationalist strength is treated in the following chapter, the further political implications of economic inequalities in Czechoslovakia are examined in Chapter 5.

ATTRIBUTING BLAME

With hindsight, the collapse of Czechoslovakia looks inevitable. The existence of entrenched and unflattering national stereotypes, the historically deep conflicts over political power and economic resources, and the speed with which the terms of the Czechoslovak divorce were eventually settled – in scarcely seven months at the end of 1992 – all suggest a case of *fait accompli* and imply that the 1989 revolution in Czechoslovakia did not so much provoke a national conflict as uncover one. Such an interpretation of the break-up, moreover, has an important political sponsor. Both during and after the divorce, at home and abroad, the Czech political right has explained the separation of Czechoslovakia as a revealed nationalist conflict, and they have laid the blame for the divorce squarely at the door of the Slovaks.

The main architect of right-wing thought in the Czech Republic following the 1989 revolution was Václav Klaus, the Federal Finance Minister and chief author of Czechoslovakia's economic reforms from 1990 to 1992. Following the pivotal elections of June 1992 Klaus had become Prime Minister of the Czech Republic and by 1 January 1993 he had secured its independence. In December 1993, accepting the Konrad Adenauer Foundation Prize in Prague, Klaus reflected that 'the existing Czecho-Slovak state arrangement [had] ceased to meet the needs of Slovak national emancipation. The partition of the common Czechoslovak state must', he argued, 'be seen as a peaceful agreement on matters that elsewhere threaten to become, and in some places have become, grave national conflicts'[10]. Back in November 1992, arguing against a constitutionally required referendum on the future of the state, Klaus had insisted that such a referendum would change nothing. 'This state', he claimed, 'would be uncontrollable, ungovernable, chaotic, and it would draw us into the depths and entice us into a situation close to what we see in the Balkans'[11]. Similarly, in October 1992, at a rally during the separation talks themselves, Klaus's party colleague Milan Uhde observed that the Czech state was not being established at the choice of its inhabitants but that 'The Slovak nation did not feel free with us and we decided to respect that feeling'. Klaus then concluded, to applause, that 'Good relations with Slovakia are more important than haggling about a couple of billions'[12].

Implicit in these pronouncements is the idea that the 1989 revolution had released in Slovakia a long-suppressed but still vital will to self-determination. The Czechs, for their part, had simply admitted the depths of Slovak national desires and – with some sadness – let them go. In this reading of the separation the Czechs emerge as an enlightened folk, ready to sacrifice their illusions of ethnic fraternity to spare Europe from any further ethnic grief. The picture of a liberal and liberalising Czech nation frustrated by 'more primitive' Slovak political forces has, of course, a direct resonance with the dismemberment of Czechoslovakia in 1938.

The purpose of this chapter is to discover how accurate a portrayal of the divorce this is. If one accepts the conclusions of the previous chapter, that Czech and Slovak relations under Communism had actually become profoundly ambiguous and contingent, then a critical investigation of why the country broke up should start from an agnostic position. The obvious questions to begin with are whether nationalism did emerge in any significant way in Czechoslovakia after 1989, whether a separatist nationalism emerged on the Slovak side or the Czech, or both, and finally, whether or not such nationalism was actually a determining factor in the break-up of the state.

In order to assess the role of nationalism in the break-up of Czechoslovakia we need a straightforward definition of 'what nationalism looks like in practice'[13] – a reference point by which to judge the arguments and events of the early 1990s. Given that we are looking at the break-up of a state it is the basic political power of nationalism that we need to capture, and to this end John Breuilly has restricted the term nationalism to nationalistic political action[14]. 'Nationalist' actions and arguments are characterised by three basic assertions, that:

- There exists a nation with an explicit and peculiar character.
- The interests and values of this nation usually take priority over all other interests and values.
- The nation must be as independent as possible. This usually requires at least the attainment of political sovereignty[15].

A nationalist movement, therefore, is one which aims to take state power on the basis of a nationalist programme[16], or which generally aspires to advance the interests and values of the nation above all else (including in negative ways, such as by taking actions against those groups or individuals interpreted as 'not of the nation'). For the purposes of identifying the salience of nationalism in the Czechoslovak separation it is not actually necessary to resolve the deeper questions of what caused this nationalism in the first place. The political power of this ideology in practice between 1990 and 1992 is what counts for us. The question is whether separatist nationalism had really arrived as a force with significant decision-making powers in either the Czech or Slovak Republics by 1992.

Such a practical interpretation of nationalism as observable political action has its critics. Breuilly has often been accused of using a definition so minimal and so practical that it fails to capture nationalism's more subtle manifestations: the nationalism that is not articulated but which, 'one way or another', still manages to mould political action towards nationalist ends. This objection is frequently made by those who emphasise the resilience and complexity of national consciousness; however, in the post-Communist context in particular such objections should be treated cautiously. An insistence that nationalism may have been weak in explicit terms but extremely strong in implicit forms can come perilously close to an insistence that 'love for *x*' – a religion, an attitude, a certain symbol – is always and ineluctably *really* an expression of 'love for the nation', even if a given community no longer recognises or acknowledges such connections itself. A good deal of the evidence from the Czech and Slovak Republics in the 1990s, moreover, would suggest that politicians had great difficulty in rediscovering what 'resonated' in Czech or Slovak national terms, leading them to resort instead to extremely emotive evocations of external enemies and 'innate' domestic heroism – cabalistic themes as redolent of the 'combat tasks' of Communism as they were of the 1930s and questions of national identity. Such urgent rhetorics, moreover, consistently failed to impress a majority of either Czechs or Slovaks.

Nationalist sentiment might be high but powerless, in which case a collapse of the state would remain unexplained. Alternatively, politicians may use nationalist rhetoric either to justify a policy, to gain support, or to explain events after the fact, but we should not assume that the electorate interprets these actions uncritically – or that a break-up justified officially in terms of nationalism was actually legitimated by popular nationalist feeling. In what follows I look at the electoral strength of nationalism and the militancy of the nationalist ideas expressed in party politics[17].

As it transpires, nationalist parties as set within Breuilly's definitional limits were by no means decisive in the Czech or Slovak Republics after 1989. Militant Slovak nationalists – those who aspired to full Slovak independence – saw their popularity decline between 1989 and 1992, having proved particularly inept at mobilising economic grievances, even though these were the most important grievances registered in Slovak opinion polls during this period. Those parties that took up the issues of social and economic reform more successfully mobilised only 'soft' nationalist sentiments, i.e. national disagreements that fell far short of secessionism. In Slovakia such nationalism as there was between 1990 and 1992 proved Janus-faced, insofar as there was considerable mobilisation against the domestic Hungarian minority and a far less successful attempt at mobilisation against the Czechs.

NATIONALISM IN THE SLOVAK PARTY POLITICAL SCENE

Two anti-Communist civic movements emerged out of the spontaneous demonstrations and improvised tactics of the 1989 revolution in Czechoslovakia: the Czech Civic Forum (CF), with Václav Havel as its chief spokesman, and the Slovak sister organisation, the Public Against Violence (PAV). Together these movements articulated and sustained the revolutionary mass protests during the ten days it took to shake the Communist regime from power.

The Slovak Public Against Violence was politically all-embracing when it started; it included former dissidents, artists, ecologists, and – before the formation of the Catholic Christian Democratic Movement in February 1990 – Catholic dissidents, with the lawyer Ján Čarnogurský[18] pre-eminent amongst them. To strengthen its ranks the PAV also took on board reform Communists, notably, part of a Slovak movement of Communists purged after 1968 calling themselves 'Revival' (*Obroda*). The Slovak hero of the Prague Spring, Alexander Dubček, also re-emerged during this time as a hugely popular and respected figure for the PAV; he reassured the dissidents that the reform Communists would participate in the pro-democracy movement in good faith – a significant guarantee, given that the people of *Obroda* were unknown to the Slovak public at large[19].

On 26 November 1989, in the midst of the revolution, the Public Against Violence issued a statement of its democratic aspirations – 'A Chance for Slovakia'. In addition to calls for the basic liberal freedoms of elections, the press and association, this included a bid for the creation of a genuine parliament in Slovakia as part of a rebalancing of Czech–Slovak relations. Both the Czech and Slovak civic movements soon afterwards declared their shared objective – Czechoslovakia's transformation into a democratic federation[20] – and the new political order thus proclaimed itself unequivocally for the common state.

With the collapse of Communism in Czechoslovakia the formal, previously 'paper-tiger' parliamentary structures of the federation came into their own, and the country looked forward to multi- rather than one-party rule. The Czech and Slovak National Councils, in addition to the Federal Assembly, were reanimated as working institutions under the non-partisan Government of National Understanding[21]. The activation of the Slovak National Council meant the re-creation of a domestic political platform: a real, republic-level legislature for Slovakia, albeit still subordinate to the federal legislature. If Slovak nationalists were to emerge as a political force to be reckoned with, then this would be their forum. The elections in June 1990, however, confirmed a victory for the avowedly pro-federal Slovak Public Against Violence and Czech Civic Forum. Party political developments in both republics between 1990 and 1992, moreover, would go on to indicate only a decline in support for radical secessionist nationalist, forces.

The fate of nationalist parties in Slovakia between 1990 and 1992 suggests that Czech claims of a Slovak nationalist renaissance are straightforwardly untrue. Nationalism, let alone separatism, was not the main preoccupation of either the secular or the religious Slovak dissidents who had emerged in the 1980s. To voice such nationalist concerns would, of course, have been a particularly dangerous form of dissent. After 1989 it became apparent that the religious dissident elite in Slovakia had retained some sense of Slovak national identity and aspiration, rooted in familial political heritage and Catholic tradition. This historically-founded scheme, however, would fail to resonate among the wider population to anything like the degree its political leaders expected.

When the Catholic dissident leadership put together a new political party in Slovakia in February 1990 – the Christian Democratic Movement (CDM) – its very origins in the Catholic nationalist past proved a burden as it faced the electorate. In effect, the CDM leadership discovered quite how much Communism had destroyed the association of Catholicism with politics, and how small the social base for politicised Catholicism had become. Not only did the Slovak voters prove forward-looking and interested in practical rather than nostalgic politics, they were also particularly wary of anything that smacked of a return to 'black', i.e. fascist, clericalism. By April 1992 some 40 per cent of Slovaks believed the CDM would not hesitate to lie or use undemocratic tactics in order to gain power; and, amazingly, despite the CDM'S dissident leaders, 35 per cent of Slovaks actually believed that they would try to introduce a new totalitarianism should they succeed[22]. These were remarkable public judgements indeed, and they indicate a good deal of success for the forty years of anti-Catholic Communist propaganda.

Immediately following the CDM's formation tensions arose over the thorny issues of where to place the wartime Slovak L'udák state in the new party canon. The younger Christian Democratic leadership, forged out of religious dissent through the 1980s, aimed to direct the party's older factions away from any reversion to militant separatism and towards a more moderate nation-building nationalism typical of Western European Christian Democracy. In the process, however, the diverse voices of the CDM managed to signal quite contradictory messages to the electorate[23] and they steered what appeared to be a deeply confused course in terms of their policy toward the common state. Out of his deep religious convictions Čarnogurský supported *eventual* independence for Slovakia, arguing that the country's destiny was to become a Catholic oasis within a region of Godless consumerism 'some time in the future' – by no means a call for 'independence now'. Čarnogurský's line seemed equivocating if not millennialist (not to mention electorally blind on the consumption issue), and the CDM's support at the polls suffered accordingly.

Given Czech claims about the revelation of deep Slovak nationalist feeling after 1989 it is striking that truly radical, i.e. separatist, nationalists in Slovakia raised their heads above the parapet only a full six months after the formal defeat of Communism. The founding congress of the new Slovak National Party (SNP) was not held until May 1990, making it the latecomer on the Slovak electoral scene. Its leadership, moreover, seems to have adopted nationalism in a spirit of speculative political investment rather than missionary zeal. The Slovak National Party was conceived in December 1989 and founded by political entrepreneurs, not, in contrast to the Christian Democratic Movement, by idealists. These relatively young political adventurers – the Party's leaders were all strangers to dissident circles and under the age of fifty – guessed that they would win good electoral prospects from taking on the trappings of the First Republic's Slovak National Party. As one of the leaders, Vladimír Miškovsky, admitted, he had surveyed the political scene looking for a place to fit himself in. His goal had been political power and not visionary achievement: 'once you find a position, you go with it', he concluded[24].

As with other political formations of under-fifties, with no connections to dissident circles, the hallmark of the SNP's politics was a seemingly bottomless pragmatism. A Slovak National Party had existed in the interwar period, indeed was the oldest Slovak political party historically, but this new SNP formation had no familial or traceable connections to the original organisation. Indeed, the idea of taking the name of the oldest party came from the historian Anton Hrnko, former leader of the Communist Party unit in the history institute at the Academy of Sciences[25].

Slovakia's most determined and ideologically driven nationalists after 1989 were imports: lobbyists from historically militant Slovak emigrant organisations[26]. These returning nationalist émigrés were evangelical in their nationalism[27], and their pro-independence rhetoric and dogmatism probably did more harm than good to the nationalist cause; certainly the vast majority of the Slovak population appeared to find them histrionic rather than inspiring. These émigrés duly found it hard to gain a foothold in their most obvious candidate party – the Christian Democratic Movement. From the beginning of 1990 the CDM had nurtured relations with Western European Christian Democrats (who on the whole were none to keen to reminisce about the Second World War) whilst discreetly trying to figure out quite how much of the clerico-fascist past they could prudently employ at home in order to capture the L'udák pensioner vote. An open association with returning elderly Catholic separatists, so directly evocative of the fascist past, was precisely what the younger leadership of the CDM had wished to avoid, and Ján Čarnogurský decisively rejected the émigrés' calls for immediate Slovak independence.

The returning émigré nationalists found more favour with the Slovak National Party, who were opportunistically hunting for ideas just as the émigrés were hunting for a party. However, even though the SNP were willing to countenance a pro-independence platform when other political parties still considered it taboo, they too remained wary of the émigrés' clerical links. With the Christian Democratic Movement as their obvious electoral rivals the SNP sought to establish themselves as non-Catholic nationalists in order to distinguish themselves electorally; but given the lack of a secular nationalist tradition in Slovakia this led them into distinctly paradoxical readings of Slovak history. For example, the SNP attempted to foster approval for the Slovak wartime state – as Slovakia's one moment of political independence – even as they edited out and deplored its Catholic associations. The SNP also criticised the CDM for its connections with the clerico-fascist Slovak state even as they tried to appropriate that state's dubious heritage for themselves – and as the SNP's cynicism revealed itself, so the relationship with the nationalist émigrés went sour[28].

Public opinion polls at the end of May 1990 gave the Slovak National Party a mere 3.8 per cent of popular support[29]. Within a few weeks, however, the SNP won 13.9 per cent of the Slovak National Council vote in Czechoslovakia's first free elections. This result made the SNP the rival third largest Slovak party in the Council along with the Communist Party and the fourth largest party in the Czechoslovak Federal Assembly. The sudden success for the SNP came as a surprise in both republics. The vote followed a tortuous and, for both Czechs and Slovaks, disturbing dispute over the renaming of the

Czechoslovak state, and it was decisively through this dispute that the SNP had emerged into the public eye.

In January 1990 Czechoslovakia's dissident-turned-President, Václav Havel, had suggested that the state should be called the 'Czechoslovak Socialist Republic', deleting the word 'Socialist'. To the growing incredulity of practically everyone involved, the ensuing row lasted almost four months. The controversy over how to rename the state was the first post-revolutionary signal that Czechs and Slovaks conceived of the common state in different ways, and would seek to reform it with potentially conflicting priorities in mind. The Federal Government of National Understanding had agreed that inter-governmental negotiations for the reform of the state should begin after the first elections in June 1990. The naming debate duly turned into an opportunity for political parties on both sides to adopt positions before the elections and before the serious process of constitutional talks began. In this context a vote for the still vaguely defined but professedly 'pro-Slovak' Slovak National Party in June 1990 may be interpreted as expressing an extremely wide variety of Slovak aspirations. It is also essential to note that at this stage – in the run-up to the first election – the National Party's electoral platform was not yet openly secessionist. In the June 1990 election itself the SNP offered aspirations only to 'enhanced autonomy' for Slovakia, changing its line to secessionism only after the elections were over. Once 'outed' as separatists, the aim of drawing Slovaks behind the militant nationalist cause would prove straightforwardly over-ambitious, and when smaller, rival nationalist parties emerged and refused to coalesce with the Slovak National Party, public support for nationalism only dissipated further[30].

As political opportunists first and foremost the SNP concluded that playing on and provoking public grievances was the safest electoral bet, and their eventual call for independence, like their increasingly racist abuse of Slovakia's Roma minority, should be understood in this light – as tactics for drawing a crowd. SNP tactics, moreover, were repeatedly ill-judged. The Party horrified many in both republics by participating, along with members of the Christian Democratic Movement, in celebrations of the First Republic populist Andrej Hlinka at Ružomberok on 26 August 1990. The rally offered a memorandum calling for Slovak sovereignty and independence ('sovereignty' implying an ambiguous degree of Slovak 'authority' but 'independence' being an unequivocal demand for international legal personality); pro-Tiso calls were heard and Christian Democratic Movement leader Ján Čarnogurský was jeered as a moderate[31]. The CDM distanced itself from the memorandum, and far from stimulating a wave of nostalgia the move to endorse L'udák heritage only put the Slovak National Party further beyond the pale for a sizeable Slovak majority.

The Slovak National Party's fight for a new language law in autumn 1990 represented the high point of nationalist militant action and provocation within pre-1993 Slovakia. The Slovak National Party thereafter endeavoured to join with the recently politicised and increasingly nationalist cultural organisation *Matica Slovenská* ('Mother Slovakia') in organising rallies and demonstrations. SNP rhetoric was nothing if not single-minded; their programme remained ill-developed in economic and social policy and, having finally declared themselves for independence, they shifted wholesale to campaigning on negative, symbolic and racist issues. Through 1991 to 1992 the SNP focused on renaming towns, streets and squares, attacking the use of the Hungarian language and establishing Slovak as the exclusive official language. They also spearheaded repeated attempts to declare Slovak sovereignty in the Slovak National Council and to identify enemies of the people among Slovakia's traditional scapegoats – Jews[32], Roma, Hungarians and federalists[33].

Public opinion polls consistently showed that the vast majority of Slovaks shared very different preoccupations. Civic problems such as unemployment and inequality regularly topped the league table of public concerns, followed by anxiety over social breakdown as expressed through crime, drug abuse and family break-up[34]. Concerns about the environment and health-care surpassed those about Slovak sovereignty, and the efforts of the Slovak National Party produced only steadily declining support[35].

The significance of the Slovak National Party lay in its capacity to shock. Elected into parliament in 1990 as newcomers with an open promise to champion Slovak interests, they had abused their parliamentary platform to introduce ever more incendiary legislation, most notably the anti-Hungarian 'Language Law', finally defeated in October 1990[36], and their repeated attempts to declare Slovak sovereignty, which never succeeded but which sent the Czech press – not surprisingly – into regular paroxysms of indignation. By the time of the second election, in June 1992, the Slovak electorate knew a great deal more about the Slovak National Party than it had done in 1990 and its vote was duly cut in half – to 7.9 per cent of the vote in the Slovak National Council. By 1992, however, the Slovak National Party had impacted in one significant respect upon Czech–Slovak relations. Most importantly, as we shall see, they did much to disinter the spectre of Slovak nationalism in the eyes of Czech journalists.

The profound failure of secessionist nationalists in Slovakia was very much confirmed by a still clearer verdict in the same election for a new and militant nationalist party calling itself the Slovak Christian Democratic Movement (SCDM). This nationalist and leftist party, led by Ján Klepáč, emerged as a faction within the more moderate Christian Democratic Movement and openly harked back to the wartime Slovak state. The SCDM plagued Čarnogurský's moderate brand of religious nationalism until breaking away just before June 1992. As a more militantly nationalist Catholic party, however, it proved even less inspiring to the public imagination than the SNP and failed to enter parliament after this critical second election.

All importantly, whereas in Britain the Scottish National Party has managed to cultivate the perception that its emphasis on 'Scotland first' directly assists the Scottish economy[37], neither the Slovak National Party, the Slovak Christian Democratic Movement nor the Christian Democratic Movement achieved such a connection with the Slovak economy. The result was a majority feeling in Slovakia that separatism and indeed more moderate nationalism as such were blunt political instruments with which to tackle Slovakia's economic woes. Up until mid-1992 the ratio of Slovaks who supported the common state stayed basically stable at 8:2, and had hit the ratio 7:3 only at its very lowest point[38].

In assessing the strength of nationalism as a political force in pre-divorce Slovakia the pivotal question is how to classify the victorious party by the time of the June 1992 election, the Movement for a Democratic Slovakia (MDS), led by the lawyer Vladimír Mečiar. In the immediate aftermath of the revolution the reform Communists of the Public Against Violence had proposed Mečiar as Interior Minister for the Government of National Understanding. Having demonstrated a clear political acumen and gained popularity in this position Mečiar was duly appointed Slovak Prime Minister for the PAV after the 1990 elections, until ousted by the party in April 1991 for his erratic behaviour. Having formed the Movement for a Democratic Slovakia as his new political platform Mečiar's star rose inexorably in opposition; was this, as is so often assumed and claimed, because the MDS was a nationalist, even secessionist party?

Critically, Mečiar championed the cause of Slovak autonomy within Czechoslovakia, specifically, equality for Slovakia within a Czech and Slovak federation. As PAV Prime Minister, however, he had condemned extreme nationalists and secessionists whilst bargaining hard for equality during constitutional negotiations (see Chapter 4). More problematically, Mečiar's definition of 'equality' was highly changeable, so much so as to make a categorisation of his new party as straightforwardly 'nationalist' inadequate. After splitting off from, and thereby destroying, the mass anti-Communist movement, Public

Against Violence, in April 1991, the Movement for a Democratic Slovakia had streaked ahead of its competitors with a populist programme of quite startling ideological elasticity.

The distinction between the clear separatist politics of the Slovak National Party and the populist[39]/ambiguously autonomist politics of the breakaway Movement for a Democratic Slovakia under Mečiar is all-important. In autumn 1991 the MDS announced an 'Initiative for a Sovereign Slovakia', and the ensuing rally attracted some 30,000 demonstrators. It also included speeches from the Slovak National Party[40]. The use of the national issue by the Movement for a Democratic Slovakia, however, was facile and tactical; it stood as an addition to a populist agenda that had also included highly vocal commitments to the federal idea and support for the 'Czechoslovakist' President Havel – a former pillar of the allegedly 'Czechoslovakising' Charter 77 movement. Mečiar's political skill lay in his ability to position himself as the champion of all Slovaks. With Slovak public opinion divided fairly evenly over models for a common state[41] this meant Mečiar's optimal electoral position was to avoid any definite position on the state arrangement whatsoever, whilst maintaining credibility as the man who could secure the best deal by 'caring most' about a fair solution. Mečiar's charismatic leadership and his abilities as an entrepreneur of public grievances combined to produce an astute and flexible populism.

The 'Initiative for a Sovereign Slovakia' was notable as the Movement for a Democratic Slovakia's opening shot in the 1992 electoral campaign. It secured public support early by promising not independence but a full post-election referendum on the constitutional future. In other words, Mečiar, alone among Slovak politicians, entered the 1992 election campaign promising an open public choice on the future structure of the Czechoslovak state[42]. Neither should the title itself – an 'Initiative for a Sovereign Slovakia' – be interpreted as conveying an essentially separatist message. Use of the term 'sovereign' by this stage could not be read simply as meaning complete independence, a bid for international legal personality. By 1992 the term had become utterly confused in the public realm, employed as frequently by Mečiar to imply basic cultural freedoms within a common state as it was by the Slovak National Party to mean independence. However, while sovereignty carried this highly ambiguous meaning in Slovak public debate, it is not difficult to see why many Czechs read it as a clear call for secession.

The presence of the Slovak National Party at the Movement's election rally, and Mečiar's mimicry there of certain SNP grievances, particularly against President Havel, who between 1990 and 1992 had persistently annoyed Slovaks with comments about Slovak political immaturity, illustrated not programmatic separatist nationalism on Mečiar's part but more simply a pure populist strategy of mobilising any available grievances, whatever their strength. By shifting between nationalist, non-nationalist, and anti-nationalist rhetoric Mečiar could present himself both as a force for moderation and as a champion of the people. With the Slovak National Party, the Movement for a Democratic Slovakia and the Party of the Democratic Left (PDL) (the former Communists) together in opposition in Slovakia after April 1991, it remained necessary for the MDS to distinguish itself from nationalist and leftist rivals while poaching their strongest electoral

Electoral performance of nationalist parties in the Slovak National Council 1990 and 1992 (% votes)
Non-nationalist parties are in italics

Parties: in order of separatist militancy	June 1990	June 1992
Slovak National Party	14	8
Slovak Christian Democratic Movement	–	below 3% threshold
Christian Democratic Movement	19	9
Movement for a Democratic Slovakia	–	37
*Public Against Violence**	29	*below 3% threshold*
*Coexistence and HCDM***	9	7
*Party of the Democratic Left****	13	*15*
Democratic Party	4	*below 3% threshold*
Green Party	4	*below 3% threshold*

* When Public Against Violence split in April 1991 it broke into two factions, Vladimir Mečiar's Movement for a Democratic Slovakia and the rump PAV, which became the liberal Civic Democratic Union. The PAV/CDU failed to enter the Slovak National Council in June 1992.
** Hungarian Christian Democratic Movement.
*** The Party of the Democratic Left broke away as a fully independent party in December 1991 from the briefly federal Communist Party of Czechoslovakia.

issues. As it turned out, these did not include separatism. It should be noted that in April 1992 – two months before the general election – some 59 per cent of Mečiar supporters polled expressed their preference for a continuation of a common state even against the offer of a confederation, a model supported by 22 per cent of MDS voters. Only 19 per cent of Mečiar supporters favoured Slovak state 'sovereignty'[43]. Mečiar's MDS, then, entered the 1992 election not as a separatist party in any sense, but as the 'people's party' – as the only party that would let 'the people' decide.

NATIONALISM IN THE CZECH PARTY POLITICAL SCENE

The Czech political picture was hardly more threatening in terms of thriving secessionists. Between 1990 and 1992 only one openly separatist nationalist party emerged in mainstream Czech politics, the intellectual and conservative Civic Democratic Alliance. The CDA was one of the first small parties to establish itself (December 1989) and it stood allied to the Civic Forum, the Czech anti-Communist movement. As the Civic Forum split decisively into party factions early in 1991, the CDA gained electoral rivals; firstly, the neo-liberal Civic Democratic Party (CDP), led by the Federal Finance Minister, Václav Klaus, and secondly, the centrist-liberal and dissident-dominated Civic Movement (CM), led by Federal Foreign Minister Jiří Dienstbier. Of these three 'Civic' enterprises, only the Alliance would go on to develop an openly nationalist electoral strategy.

By 1992 the Civic Democratic Alliance had developed an electoral programme openly expressing impatience with the continuing constitutional disagreements with Slovakia. Although opinion polls were not so detailed as to tell us precisely which CDA ideas were popular or unpopular, it is striking that the agenda of the Alliance was in most respects completely in accord with the dominant mood of the Czech electorate. They were competent and credible on two major issues of apparent Czech public consensus: market reform and anti-Communism, as they possessed both liberal economists and dissidents in their leadership. As a faction within government since 1990 these leaders (particularly the economists Vladimír Dlouhý and Tomáš Ježek) would also become popular and were able to boast experience in policy-making. Throughout the constitutional talks with Slovakia, however, between 1990 and 1992, the CDA was particularly and publicly unyielding. Of all their policies, their electoral recommendation that Czechs should follow their economic self-interest in becoming independent was the most obviously discordant with public opinion[44], and it was apparently their militancy on this issue that proved electoral suicide. In the June 1992 election the Alliance failed even to cross the 5-per-cent threshold for entry into the Federal Assembly.

Beyond the mainstream there was (and remains) a party of the extreme racist right within the Czech lands, the Association for the Republic/Republican Party of Czechoslovakia, led by Miroslav Sládek. Sládek's political sophistication resembles that of Russia's Vladimir Zhirinovsky more than that of France's Jean Marie Le Pen or Austria's Jörg Haider. The political leaders at the federal level, and Václav Havel in particular, were the main source of Sládek's purple prose until 1993. True to their basic populism and Communist Party roots, the Republican Party tended to equate Czech and Slovak as 'the nation', and the Republicans were not so much separatist as obstructionist in mainstream politics *tout court*. As a former propagandist for the Communist Party, Dr Sládek proved extremely skilful, in an exhibitionist kind of way, at keeping his party in the public eye. The Republican Party was effectively neo-fascist, and adopted the 'policies' of political disruption, racism and xenophobia which it stuck to throughout the 1990s with a depressing consistency.

By June 1992 the Republicans, formed in Bohemia in 1990, had garnered some 6 per cent of the Czech National Council vote, mainly from the north-western reaches of the country where long-unsolved economic and social problems combined with environmental devastation to alienate younger voters in particular from the political mainstream. The Republicans' electoral dependence upon racist mobilisation is confirmed by a clear correlation between Republican voters and concentrations of the ever-persecuted Roma minority[45]. Mercifully, Sládek was kept on the fringes of Czechoslovakia's national problems, restrained by the mainstream Czech right's admirable refusal to collaborate.

In the Czech lands the most successful political party by 1992 was the Civic Democratic Party, with the Civic Movement its main urban liberal rival. Václav Klaus's CDP avoided explicit nationalist rhetoric and identification from 1990 to 1992, claiming consistently that nationalist preoccupations were parochial and narrow-minded and only delayed the progress of economic reform. Klaus always portrayed his party as transcending narrow nationalistic concerns and representing the democratic interests of the entire Czechoslovak state. Klaus, however, followed in a long tradition of Czechs who equated Czech and Czechoslovakia 'national' interest as one and the same, regardless of the dire impact this tendency had long had on Slovak perceptions of Czech arrogance. Klaus's main liberal competitors, the Civic Movement, in contrast, positively championed the causes of re-legitimating the federation and Slovak equality. In the Czech Republic, as in the Slovak Republic, therefore, the single openly secessionist parties that existed had been pushed to the electoral margins.

A puzzle remains then as to why Czech and Slovak politicians failed quite so completely in producing a common policy on the reform of the Czechoslovak state between 1990 and 1992. Whatever the forms of injustice exercised by the Czech Republic upon the Slovaks, or by the Slovaks upon the Czechs, one thing is already apparent; a consistent and militant nationalist rationale, let alone a secessionist or separatist rationale, was the dominant feature of neither Czech nor Slovak

Electoral performance of nationalist parties in the Czech National Council 1990 and 1992 (% votes)
Non-nationalist parties are in italics

Parties: in order of separatist militancy	June 1990	June 1992
Civic Democratic Alliance	–	6
*Civic Forum**	*50*	–
Civic Democratic Party and Christian Democratic Party	–	*30*
Movement for Self-governing Democracy/ Society for Moravia and Silesia	*10*	*19*
*Christian and Democratic Union***	*8*	–
Christian Democratic Union/ Czechoslovak People's Party	–	*6*
Republican Party of Czechoslovakia	–	*6*
*Communist Party of Czechoslovakia****/ Left Bloc*	*13*	*14*
Czechoslovak Social Democracy	–	*7*
Liberal Social Union	–	*7*

* The Civic Forum was divided into the Civic Movement, the Civic Democratic Alliance and the Civic Democratic Party by the June 1992 elections; the Civic Movement and the Civic Democratic Alliance failed to enter the federal parliament, but the latter entered the Czech National Council.

** The Christian and Democratic Union had divided into the Christian Democratic Party and the Christian Democratic Union by June 1992.

*** The Communist Party was the dominant force in the 'Left Bloc' left-wing electoral coalition, which ran in June 1992.

party politics. As the election results in June 1992 would show, separatism amongst voters was rarer still. An investigation of the 1992 election reveals more systematically the remarkable lack of nationalist ideology extant at the moment that turned out to be the very crisis point of the state.

1992 JUNE ELECTIONS – HOBSON'S CHOICE

Party attitudes would prove decisive for the future of Czechoslovakia in June 1992 and yet neither the Czech or Slovak political parties nor their constituencies were openly, let alone militantly, nationalistic[46]. In June 1992 the call for separation could be heard only from the fringes of Slovak politics in the shape of the Slovak National Party and, in a more defensive version, from the Civic Democratic Alliance in the Czech lands. Separation, nevertheless, occurred seven months later.

The final victory in June 1992 of Klaus's right-wing Civic Democratic Party–Christian Democratic Party coalition in the Czech Republic and of Mečiar's Movement for a Democratic Slovakia in Slovakia meant, in theory, the election of two fresh sides ready to agree a new constitutional arrangement. Instead these two leaders instigated a divorce. The subsequent argument of the Czech right, that the 1992 election had constituted a referendum on the future of Czechoslovakia, is simply inaccurate. The claim that the election represented the people's clear decision obscures the fact that both election victors had claimed throughout their campaigns to have only the best interests of the common state at heart. The June 1992 election, in fact, proved useless as an instrument for turning public preferences into public policy.

When electoral rhetoric[47] in June 1992 was about the nation, either Czech or Slovak, then the nation was typically presented as a willing partner to a common state. The Movement for a Democratic Slovakia promised national sovereignty and emancipation in the same breath as it claimed to aspire only to an equal common state. The Czech Civic Democratic Party spoke for 'Czechoslovakia' and the best interests of Czechoslovakia, as if the existence of two alternative versions of 'best interest' was inconceivable. Plainly, neither side could go all out for national arguments in the absence of a significant nationalist constituency in either republic. Moreover, neither the Civic Democratic Party nor the Movement for a Democratic Slovakia needed to make 'nationalism' their defining trait since there were other profound and less potentially alienating interests (albeit, in practice, nationally encapsulated interests) that could deliver the powers of the state into their hands.

The results of the Elections, 5–6 June 1992
Election to the Federal Assembly of the Czech and Slovak Federative Republic

	House of the People (150 seats)		House of the Nations (150 seats)	
	Votes (%)	Seats	Votes (%)	Seats
Czech Republic				
Civic Democratic Party and Christian Democratic Party	33.9	48	33.4	37
Left Bloc	14.3	19	14.5	15
Czechoslovak Social Democracy	7.7	10	6.8	6
Republican Party	6.5	8	6.4	6
Christian Democratic Union/Czechoslovak People's Party	6.0	7	6.1	6
Liberal Social Union	5.8	7	6.1	5
Others	25.8	0	26.7	0
TOTAL	100.0	99	100.0	75
Slovak Republic				
Movement for a Democratic Slovakia	33.5	24	33.9	33
Party of the Democratic Left	14.4	10	14.0	13
Slovak National Party	9.4	6	9.4	9
Christian Democratic Movement	9.0	6	8.8	8
HCDM* and Coexistence	7.5	5	7.4	7
SDP in Slovakia	4.9	0	6.1	5
Others	21.3	0	20.4	0
TOTAL	100.0	51	100.0	75

The results of the Elections, 5–6 June 1992 (*Continued*)
Elections to the Czech and Slovak National Councils
Czech National Council

	Votes (%)	Seats
Civic Democratic Party and Christian Democratic Party	29.7	76
Left Bloc	14.1	35
Czechoslovak Social Democracy	6.5	16
Liberal Social Union	6.5	16
Christian Democratic Union/ Czechoslovak People's Party	6.3	15
Republican Party	6.0	14
Civic Democratic Alliance	6.0	14
MSD/SMS**	5.9	14
Others	19.0	0
TOTAL	100.0	200

Slovak National Council

	Votes (%)	Seats
Movement for a Democratic Slovakia	37.3	74
Party of the Democratic Left	14.7	29
Christian Democratic Movement	8.9	18
Slovak National Party	7.9	15
HCDM* and Coexistence	7.4	14
Others	23.8	0
TOTAL	100.0	150

* Hungarian Christian Democratic Movement.
** Movement for Self-governing Democracy/Society for Moravia and Silesia.

The electoral campaigns for June 1992 were not dominated by discussion of constitutional options, or indeed by any specific policy options as such (bemusing details of macro- and micro-economic policy being the exception). Instead political parties competed in two separate competitions, one in each republic, each with a distinct set of parties and issues. In both republics, however, the campaigns consisted of repeated statements of extremely vague ideological beliefs and priorities. The Czech Civic Democratic Alliance (CDA), the one Czech party attempting a Czech secessionist position, hedged its bets and was the most impressively nebulous of all. Espousing the benefits of Czech separatism in the face of Slovak intransigence the party's slogans proclaimed, 'Nationality principle? In life YES – in politics NO!'[48].

With little clarity regarding the practical intentions of each party, the campaigns of 1992 foreclosed the possibility of direct mandates being given to any future government. Such campaigns could not define clear electoral choices but achieved only the minimal endorsement of the electorate and a judgement as to who might most realistically deliver on essentially vague promises. The issue of the common state was discussed either fatalistically, 'it is for the victors to decide', or ingenuously, with parties asserting their own ideal preferences whilst avoiding the *realpolitik* of achievable compromise. For all bar the Czech Civic Democratic Alliance and the Slovak National Party, the favoured state arrangement remained centred on 'federation', a fact which strongly suggests that politicians understood the common state to be popular, even as they avoided the question of how to preserve it. So altogether obscure were the campaigns that President Havel was moved to castigate 'the cowardly inability of politicians to say clearly what they are aiming at'[49].

NATIONALISM IN THE 1992 ELECTIONS IN THE CZECH REPUBLIC

In a strategy that was to prove a hallmark of the party thereafter, Václav Klaus's Civic Democratic Party presented the 1992 election as a democratic crossroads. The electorate was asked, frequently at outdoor rallies and in the most urgent tones, if it wished to go on or be deflected from the course of *democracy* as such. In this way the CDP equated loyalty to democracy with loyalty to the CDP as a political party, the implication being that to vote for others was to vote for democracy's enemies[50]. This strategy may have been brilliant but it was also, of course, contrary to what we might expect in a democratic competition in which it is assumed that every contestant, unless forbidden by the constitution, does at least have the right to participate. For the CDP therefore it was not the nation that was at stake but the nature of the state – the whole, bi-national state – and the Civic Democratic Party, so Klaus claimed, was the one true party of democracy. When he was asked if he was trying to repeat the election of 1990 by threatening the electorate with a renewal of authoritarianism, he replied that the obvious rejection of secret police, fictional surpluses and leading tasks of the party in 1989 was only 'a superficial rejection of one type of common system', and that it was necessary now for the electorate to decide 'in which direction to begin'[51].

The Civic Democratic Party duly portrayed the Civic Movement (its main rival as a pro-market party with strong urban support) as a party of crypto-Communist utopians, regardless of the fact that it was led by some of the most prominent anti-Communist dissidents of the 1970s and 1980s. In an allusion to the dissident philosophy of 'anti-politics', the idea of living in moral truth so as to extricate oneself from the control of the Communist state, Klaus sneered that 'In a functioning parliamentary democracy, non-political politics doesn't have a chance'[52]. Consistent with their liberal belief that the rule of law should preclude the assertion of collective guilt, the Civic Movement had acted through 1991 and 1992 as vocal opponents of the CDP-led legislation to sack Communists, *qua* Communists, from public office. Their stand on the issue, principled though it was, now had the unintended effect of helping Klaus to make the case that the dissidents, many of whom had been idealistic Communists in their early youth, remained somehow deeply sympathetic to the Communist cause. Thus in early April 1992, in an opening electoral shot across the bows of his former Civic Forum colleagues, Klaus stated that together with the Civic Democratic Alliance, the Civic Democratic Party had 'apprehensions of a distinct upsurge of anti-reformist forces, striving to thwart the post-November [1989] development. We are determined not to allow it and strive jointly for a victory of the right-wing'[53]. The implication was that anti-November forces included the dissidents of the Civic Movement, the very nucleus of democratic opposition to Communism for over twenty years.

The main weapon of the campaign against the real political left was the invocation of the ghosts of totalitarianism but also its economic other-worldliness. Klaus spoke scathingly of the left 'fretting and blaming this government because the former Soviet Union no longer buys textiles'[54]. The Civic Democratic Party rejected any 'third way between communism and democracy' (as opposed to between communism and capitalism); indeed Klaus avoided the word 'capitalism', speaking instead of the 'market economy'[55]. The Civic Democratic Party's strongest resource was clearly the absolute association of economic reform with the figure of Václav Klaus. In a series of articles entitled *A short guide to the 'election goulash'*, Klaus was sufficiently confident to conclude with the following advice: 'when deciding for whom to vote, it is enough with economic arguments to use your common sense'[56].

On the structuring of the state, the Civic Democratic Party stuck to its advocacy of what it called a 'functioning federation'. It called for an end to and reversal of the republican erosion of federal powers which it claimed had begun in 1990, and criticised 'experiments', including confederation[57]. Klaus distanced his party from the debacle of the preceding two years of constitutional talks and was outspoken only when explicitly questioned about a Slovak 'third way'. The national question was thus played down, often not appearing at all in party campaign literature. Klaus preferred a strategy of shifting responsibility for the failure to redefine Czech and Slovak relations entirely onto the Slovak side and claimed that it was now 'evident, that votes for the Movement for a Democratic Slovakia are votes for the division of the state . . . Slovak voters, self-evidently, have the right to decide this, but not for all days on end'[58]. Party spokesman Igor Němec apparently concurred that if the party faced 'a choice between a common socialist Czechoslovak state and two independent states, it would choose the latter'[59].

To call this nationalism would be to lose the heart of the matter; before June 1992 Václav Klaus spoke of the nation as his last resort – the Czech state into which he would be forced. Klaus presented himself to his electorate as the most fervent of all federalists, the only man with the full interests and understanding of the common state at heart. Given the nature of Czech national self-identification, moreover, there was an obvious way to finesse a tactical shift toward a state-separation. If Czechs throughout Czechoslovak history had laid claim to a superior rationality, then this was a uniquely post-Communist manifestation of that claim: to appeal to the sentiment and value of the nation *per se* was primitive and barbaric; to appeal to its integrity as the citadel of democratic reform was every good Czech citizen's duty.

In a survey taken in April 1992, Civic Democratic Party supporters more than any others expressed satisfaction with the course of social and political development (86 per cent) and the economy (78 per cent). They were the least afflicted with feelings of 'powerlessness', 'hopelessness' and 'surrender' (33 per cent as opposed to the notably high 55 per cent national average). Civic Democratic Party voters supported the current legal strategy *vis-à-vis* the Communist past and were particularly hostile to the left and Slovak national parties. They were also less likely than average to agree that the Czech right and economic reform might contribute to any splitting of the state. 74 per cent of Civic Democratic Party supporters stood by the view that the Slovak left and the insufficient will of Slovaks as a whole to maintain the state might lead to its division – a result which insured Klaus against losing too great a part of his own constituency should he take it upon himself to end the federation[60].

The Civic Democratic Alliance (CDA) was ideologically almost indistinguishable from the Civic Democratic Party, with which it had an electoral 'non-aggression pact'[61]. Having failed in its repeated attempts to abolish the minority right of veto in the Federal Assembly and seizing on the Federal Assembly deadlocks of 1992 (see Chapter 4), its chairman, Jan Kalvoda, voiced the logical conclusion of the economic right and openly campaigned on the benefits of Czech separatism. The CDA's strategy to render itself visible relied on this more colourful use of the Czech national card and personal attacks against Mečiar, which Klaus avoided. It is striking, however, that even the CDA, the nearest thing to a nationalist party one could find in the Czech mainstream, argued explicitly against using the 'nationality' principle as a political or even a politicising issue. In their electoral sloganeering the CDA called for 'federalism without the nationalistic point of view'[62].

The Civic Movement (CM), despite many months of conciliatory efforts towards the Slovaks, for which it was frequently criticised, had actually shifted its position towards Klaus's by June 1992. The original Civic Forum had split into the Civic Democratic Party, Civic Democratic Alliance and Civic Movement, not least as a reaction to the Czech and Slovak power-sharing talks back in August 1990 (see Chapters 3 and 4), which had distinguished those for whom economic reform was the highest priority from those who felt that the market provided 'only the means to a working state, preferably a federal state'[63]. By June 1992, however, the Civic Movement clearly no longer felt able to campaign on subordinating market ends to the preservation of a common state. What distinguished the CM's electoral campaign was its continuing preoccupation with the integrity of the legal state as a *sine qua non* of democratic development. They thus took the 'legal state' and their opposition to the CDP's legally crude anti-Communist 'vetting' law to election apparently as an act of defiance[64] – popular as vetting was. Though the CM could justly claim to be 'the most consistent advocate for a common state and referenda over its future', the remainder of its programme rang perhaps too resoundingly with noble generalities. It claimed to 'know' that 'the conditions of prosperity and of a dignified life are decency and mutual respect, healthy reason, social responsibility, health, education, culture and clean air'[65]. It also stood for 'radical economic reform which must lead to the resolution of all social and ecological problems'[66].

Although more defensive about the economic costs of federation, the CM still actively campaigned for a common state. It stated frankly that 'jeopardising Czechoslovakia is not only nationalistic, but also the dangerous dream of a unitarian state. We support a referendum as the single legitimate condition of the division of the state or its reshaping with more members'[67]. Federal Foreign Minister Jiří Dienstbier accused Jan Kalvoda of the CDA of irresponsibly playing the Czech national card. Dienstbier in turn appealed not only to emotional and socio-economic reasons for continuing the common state but, for the first time in two years of Czech and Slovak wrangling, raised seriously the issue of international security[68]. Such a late appearance for this issue was extremely unlikely to convince anyone that Slovakia was truly the touchstone of Czech geopolitical stability, however. Undoubtedly more convincing, given its greater currency in the Czech media, was the Klausite innuendo that (as in the 1980s) an economically sluggish and consequently reform-shy Slovakia would arrest Czech development and continue to bar it from its 'European destiny'.

The coalition between the Christian Democratic Union and the Czechoslovak People's Party (CDU/CPP) had a broad manifesto, essentially endorsing current progress, including, with little elaboration, its preference for a federal constitution. The remaining election successes in the Federal Assembly were for the far right Republican Party of Czechoslovakia, led by Miroslav Sládek[69] and on the left. The Left Bloc (LB, a coalition of the Democratic Left and the Communist Party of Bohemia and Moravia) rejected apologetics and hoped that the 'expectations of our citizens from November 1989 are fulfilled'. They supported a 'federation', but, given their lack of internal evolution, it would have all the potentially Marxist-Leninist connotations of their use of the term. The Czechoslovak Social Democratic (CSD) programme varied little from that of 1990. Honest, if lame, on the issue, the party stated: 'we consider a federal constitution the ideal, but at present difficult to implement'[70]. A coalition since 1991, the Liberal Social Union (LSU) represented an uncomfortable alignment of Greens, (urban) Socialists and cooperative farm interests, as represented by the Agricultural Party[71]. There was little common policy ground between rural leftist Agriculturalists and the urban centrist Socialists[72] and other issues dominated their muted claim to support a 'federal state'.

NATIONALIST ISSUES IN THE 1992 ELECTIONS IN
THE SLOVAK REPUBLIC

The range of opinion represented by Slovak parties was ostensibly no less broad than in the Czech Republic. The Slovak electoral scene comprised pro-federal and pro-reform liberal, Christian Democratic parties of two more or less nationalistic shades, a range of minor populist nationalist parties running the gamut of economic preferences, and, finally, a renewed social democratic left. Even Mečiar's Movement for a Democratic Slovakia carried supporters for rapid economic reform. The structure of the state was certainly a dominant electoral issue in Slovakia, but as already stated it combined, in order of concern, with fears over the standard of living, unemployment, health-care, social security, crime and the environment[73]. The electorate was confronted with a plethora of constitutional options, most of them ill-defined and rarely discussed in relation to what was known to be politically acceptable to the other, partner republic[74].

The Movement for a Democratic Slovakia (MDS) claimed to repre-sent 'democracy, humanism, a legal state, human rights and free enter-prise in a market economy' and to aim at the 'all-round elevation of Slovakia'. Thus far it based its claims squarely on 'Chance for Slovakia', the 1990 manifesto of the Public Against Violence. In 1992, however, the MDS also asserted a 'state-legal arrangement on confed-eral principles, the basic social orientation of the economy, complex and sovereign development of the national economy and advantageous linkage to European integration'[75]. The presentation of economic policy, as with elastic discussions of Czech–Slovak relations, illus-trated only how the party projected itself as the natural party of government whilst evading detail.

The Movement for a Democratic Slovakia depicted itself as cham-pioning a transition appropriate to Slovak national specifics but in such a way as to sound both pro-federalist and critical of existing arrangements[76]. It took a typically capricious step just before the elec-tion, calling for the proclamation of the sovereignty of Slovakia as a subject of international law, even though it had up to then effectively blocked such calls from Slovak Nationalists and nationalist Christian Democrats within the Slovak National Council. Within the manifesto the MDS nevertheless hedged by offering to follow the introduction of a Slovak constitution with a referendum on the appropriate form of coexistence with the Czech Republic, to result in a 'treaty'[77]. Crucially the MDS claimed not to be fighting for any 'true Slovak path' so much as for the right of Slovaks to choose that path freely, whatever it should turn out to be. In this sense Mečiar succeeded in making a virtue out of his very lack of programmatic principles. In an equally populist move he announced that he would not support Havel's candidacy for re-election as President. He exploited the sus-picions felt against Havel's clique in both republics and attributed his decision as much to Havel's choice of advisers as to his perceived mis-takes in office[78]. On 14 May Mečiar stated that after elections he would not assume any federal post[79], signalling an intention to maximise the leverage power of the Slovak National Council in post-election talks with the Czechs. According to Mečiar's promises to the Slovak electorate, however, the direction of these talks would depend entirely upon the results of a referendum.

The confident election style of the MDS played upon a clear wave of support. In 1991 the beliefs of those supporting the MDS had still been unclear. By April 1992, however, it was obvious that its supporters more than usually rejected the direction Slovakia had taken since November 1989. More than three-quarters of respondents to opinion polls stated that Slovakia's post-November development had brought great disappointment (as against a high 64 per cent in the whole Slovak population) and 71 per cent judged the federal economic reform too radical or basically misconceived; 84 per cent believed that other conceptions of economic reform would be better than those currently in place. As to the state-legal arrangement, 79 per cent of MDS supporters judged that Czechs insufficiently understood Slovakia and that this was a crucial factor in 'coercing' Slovaks towards independence (68 per cent in the whole population). Less than half, 48 per cent, stated that for the population of Slovakia it was more important to slow the pace of or at least change economic reform than to maintain the common state (41 per cent in the Slovak population as a whole)[80]. Clearly the stresses of post-Communism were highly important in drawing support behind Mečiar. The election, however, demonstrated only that he was a charismatic populist and skilful at pooling as many constituencies as possible.

Having split off from the Czechoslovak Communist Party and changed its name, the shift to social democracy of the Party of the Democratic Left (PDL) and its social orientation had allowed for a resurrection of its fortunes since 1990. Remarkably, by 1992, the Christian Democratic Movement was held in greater suspicion as a potential threat to democracy (by 35 per cent) than Slovakia's former communists (by 20 per cent)[81]. The PDL argued that the election would decide the form of the common life of Czechs, Slovaks and other nationalities, and that it would set the future priorities for the economy and society. For the future state the PDL proposed a 'loose federation with elements of confederation', thus managing to promise flexibility whilst dodging suspicions either of Slovak nationalism or Czechoslovakism.

When Ján Čarnogurský, the leader of the Christian Democratic Movement (CDM), could get beyond defending his views on 'Godless consumerism' – liberalism – he explained that his vision was for a strong, stable and ultimately independent Slovakia and that national consciousness could grow slowly into a stable identity[82]. The CDM was nevertheless embattled by the intense aversion to them of a portion of the population. Of eight negative characteristics pertaining to parties, the CDM scored higher than any other party on six: only pretending to support the common state, use of devious political tactics, poor-quality personnel, elitism, a poor defence of economic standards, and the likely introduction of totalitarianism. They scored positively only in their perceived tolerance of national minorities[83] – in historical terms, a rather paradoxical set of findings.

The Civic Democratic Union (CDU, the liberal 'rump' of the former Public Against Violence) projected itself as a 'liberal and con-servative party of the centre. It stands behind rapid economic reform and the dignified station of Slovakia in the common state'[84]. Any doubts that the affinities of this Slovak party were largely with those on the Czech right were dispelled by their electoral coalition with the Czech Civic Democratic Alliance, the most recognisably 'Czechoslovakist' – indeed, Czech nationalist – of all the Czech parties. Even with low levels of separatist feeling in Slovakia at large, a more electorally suicidal coalition than this one was hardly to be imagined.

The electoral coalition between Klaus's Civic Democratic Party and Slovakia's Democratic Party (DP, a former Communist satellite party) targeted businessmen and the intelligentsia in Slovakia. The Democ-ratic Party supported a common state with the two republics joined in 'some form of common contract'[85] but echoed to a policy the man-ifesto of the Czech Civic Democratic Party. That Klaus assisted in splitting the liberal vote in Slovakia is less significant than the value of this federal coalition in underpinning subsequent Civic Democratic Party claims to have gone to the limit of its powers to secure a common state.

The small Social Democratic Party in Slovakia (SDPS, a party with roots predating Czechoslovak independence) was obscured by the increasing popularity of the Party of the Democratic Left, but received a fillip to its electoral chances by the recruitment of Alexander Dubček as party chairman just before the election. It sought a moderate left image and the political stability of Slovakia within a democratic federation.

The Slovak National Party (SNP) proposed immediate Slovak state-hood, the single other acceptable possibility being a confederation of three regions (Bohemia, Moravia, Slovakia). Even in June 1992 it remained a single-issue party and was the only party (Movement for a Democratic Slovakia included) to clearly attract those against a common state. Where 44 per cent of Slovaks (compared to 57 per cent for the Movement for a Democratic Slovakia) viewed the Slovak National Party as a defender of Slovak interests, another 37 per cent ascribed to them the negative characteristic of inciting racial tensions.

PHANTOM NATIONALISM

These elections may represent many things but not a coherent referendum on the future of the Czechoslovak state, and most certainly not one mandating a divorce. Separatist nationalism as a force capable of seizing power had not yet arrived in Slovakia in 1992. Populist forces quite capable of assimilating nationalist concerns and of mobilising 'soft' nationalist sentiments (i.e. far short of separatism) had nevertheless been elected to government in both republics in June 1992.

Nationalisms as old as those within the Czech and Slovak republics, and as mangled by the Communist experience as we know they were, should perhaps be accepted as sliding beneath the radar of our practical, political definition of nationalism. The very failure to speak out for the separate nations might indicate nationalism so mature as to be beyond protesting itself – commonly understood as implicit in the chosen debates on reform, investment, subsidy and the role of Church and state – the expansive appeals to the good of 'Czechoslovakia' notwithstanding. The problem with trying to account for the persistence of nationalism, particularly separatist nationalism, in this way is that causes and effects cease to be demonstrable in political terms; they can only asserted[86]. To argue that Klaus or Mečiar were 'really' elected as separatists is to argue for a kind of meta-political reality or for a degree of transcendent political foresight on the part of the electorates that is simply implausible in the light of the contemporary evidence.

The evidence so far runs against the 'inevitability' thesis outlined in the introduction to this chapter, the idea that separatist nationalism was just waiting to erupt in post-Communist Czechoslovakia. In practice, strong separatist nationalist movements simply did not exist, and the election results and public opinion polls together suggest that levels of nationalist sentiment in both republics were consistent with continuing cooperation in a common state. The alternative theoretical scenario involving nationalism, the 'relative deprivation' explanation for the break-up, also proves far from satisfying in this light. Although public opinion polls in Slovakia attest to wide-ranging economic concerns, Slovak separatist parties completely failed to co-opt these sentiments to the nationalist cause. Vladimir Mečiar and Vaclav Klaus were far more successful in winning over the economically preoccupied, but, as we have seen, they had married these issues to their own claims to speak for the best interests of the 'federation'.

In one critical respect, however, militant nationalism played a truly vital role in electoral arguments. With the West running in dread of a nationalist wave in post-Communist Europe and Western support essential to the progress of transition, and with the domestic political points to be scored from seemingly defending one republic against the other, both the Czech and Slovak political elites had powerful reasons to portray the other as the seceding, nationalistic, and altogether guilty party. 'Phantom nationalism', with each side accusing the other of separatist ambition, clearly played an essential part in the self-justifying rhetoric of the electoral winners, and, as we shall see, this would develop on a phenomenal scale in the last months of the state.

Clearly the argument that nationalism was wholly responsible for the Czechoslovak split is not sustainable, even though the following chapters will confirm that there were serious rivalries between the two republics, and that these rivalries were clearly exploited. In the absence of strong separatist nationalist movements, however, the more general analytical question should be asked as to what other weaknesses existed in the state and its political structures to have made it unsustainable in its existing form, particularly since the evidence of separatism was slight, and moderate nationalist sentiment was more than matched by evidence for positive, broad-based public support for a bi-national state. Why was it, then, that political leaders were unable – or unwilling – to reach a political settlement? Though it is sorely tempting to stretch the definition of nationalism – to infer a state-splitting nationalist conflict from Czechoslovakia's numerous national conflicts after 1989 – such an argument would have to ignore one of the most striking facts of the separation as revealed in this chapter, namely, that Czechoslovakia separated in the absence of mobilised mass separatist social movements of any kind, in a divorce organised by politicians elected on a platform of the common state's 'best interests', in the Czech case, and on the promise of a 'people's choice' in the case of Slovakia.

The avoidance of explicitly nationalist programmes in the June 1992 election and the fact of the end of the state some seven months later conjures up the perfunctory decisions of a colonial partition or the pragmatism of the post-World War One state-builders. The decision to split amounted to a pre-emptive strike in the treatment of one of

Europe's more manageable quarrels, an approach that is unimaginable in the developed multi-national democracies of Britain, Canada or Belgium. It is to the problems of democratisation writ large that we must turn for further explanation.

3
THE POLITICAL DIVIDE

Democratic federations depend for their survival upon the divided communities involved, and most especially their elites, being willing and able to accommodate one another through thick and thin. The fate of federalism in Africa and Asia has shown that such willingness is extremely hard to sustain, and the evidence from the federations that remain, Canada and Belgium among others, suggests that they have relied for their stability upon sophisticated political party systems managing to operate across the boundaries of their constituent ethnic groups[1]. Even Canada and Belgium have seen a growing 'ethnicisation' of their party politics, however, a development that has prompted numerous gloomy predictions of their imminent demise. In contrast to the First Republic of Czechoslovakia, where state-wide parties dominated but failed to incorporate Slovak grievances, post-1989 Czechoslovakia saw the emergence of two entirely separate and distinct party systems, one in the Czech lands, one in Slovakia. This development alone, if the experience of multi-ethnic federations elsewhere is anything to go by, might have proved fatal.

It is a critical fact, however, that the first non-Communist forces to emerge in Czechoslovakia were not political parties at all but the revolutionary 'civic' movements distinct to the two republics. It was around and from these large political conglomerations that the separate party systems emerged. The national separateness of these two movements, moreover, was not a foregone conclusion. In the midst of the demonstrations in November 1989, a Slovak suggestion that a pan-federal civic movement be formed was rejected in Prague, partly for practical reasons, but also because the Czech dissident leadership was concerned not to be seen to dominate Slovak developments at such an uncertain time – the embattled Communist Party was using the Slovak Party newspaper *Pravda* to raise provocative Slovak claims and to push Alexander Dubček's candidacy for the presidency, in other words, initiating nationalist demands so as to split the Czech and Slovak opposition – a strategy successfully foiled by Dubček withdrawing his candidacy in favour of Václav Havel (Dubček became Chairman of the Federal Assembly)[2]. It was, therefore, a heat-of-the-moment decision to retain organisational distinctiveness, which was subtle and sensitive enough at the time, that confirmed the consolidation of allied but separate opposition groups – the Public Against Violence (PAV) in Slovakia and the Czech Civic Forum (CF).

While there was no open ethnic wound inspiring purely republic-based parties during the revolution itself, the formation of two separate civic movements nevertheless created a new danger, that divided political systems would encourage increasingly nationalistic politics and that, as the all-encompassing civic movements factionalised into new political parties, as they surely had to, political entrepreneurs in the respective republics might thrive upon an exploitation of nationalist arguments. Clearly, the absence of federal parties relieved post-Communist politicians of pro-federal pressures on several levels. Firstly, Czechoslovakia's parties as such did not act as institutions of consensus-building internally, i.e. in uniting their own internal multinational factions. Secondly, in the absence of federal-level competition, the developing Czech and Slovak party political scenes would very naturally be drawn into a political discourse framed in the language of 'us' versus 'them', be it concerning either the 'other' nation or the federal centre, a situation likely to be reinforced by the existence of separate government and parliamentary structures at the federal and republican levels.

An explanation for the separation of Czechoslovakia that heeded the experience of democratic federations elsewhere might highlight this divided 'institutional architecture', and identify built-in party political incentives toward republican conflict – incentives made potentially even sharper by the fact that Czech and Slovak party political contests were only just starting and entrepreneurial parties would necessarily be seeking out new issues over which to fight. The problem with this argument, however, is that the lessons from more stable federations are not necessarily so appropriate to the Czechoslovak case.

As a general principle, although 'institutionalist' arguments have proved powerful in explaining different incentive structures and consequently different policy choices in many countries, the assumption that political actors are developing their strategies according to clear and stable institutional incentives may be inapplicable, in the sense of wildly over-optimistic, in states undergoing a transformation from Communism[3] – i.e. in states that lack precisely the kind of routinised, institutionalised politics typical of established democracies. In Czechoslovakia's case, the lessons to be learned from comparisons with democratic federations may be limited, and so a question for this chapter is whether the separateness of the party systems really did predetermine the federation's collapse, since party competition was still in its infancy and the state itself was ill-defined. As the preceding chapter made clear, nationalists do not inevitably profit when party systems develop only at the national level – indeed, in theory at least, a sufficient political will to a common state on the part of political actors could confront even the most unfavourable, entirely divided institutional environment, and transform it into something coopera-tive and manageable.

Evidence in favour of an 'institutionalist-party system' explanation for the Czechoslovak split would be that the separate structure of the party political system encouraged and deepened the conflict by struc-turing politics toward international/republic level competition. Evi-dence against this thesis would be institutional weakness to the extent that institutional factors clearly failed to structure those political battles that were to prove pivotal to the conflict. (It is also worth noting that politicians might claim that institutions stopped them from achieving a consensus when other interests were demonstrably at work.)

PARTY COMPETITION AND A 'PARTY AUTONOMY' EXPLANATION

If we can accept the possibility that separate party systems as such may not be fatal to a federation so long as party competition has yet to develop (stalled, for example, by a broad political consensus over what is to be done, or because single parties dominate the political scene to the point where other parties are unable to keep up), it is still possible to imagine an alternative theory as to why party systems may yet have proved damaging to the federal project. This second theory is based on the idea of party autonomy resulting from a *lack* of developed party competition (a lack already strongly indicated in the previous chapter).

In the absence of well-defined social divisions (as distinct from the absence of such divisions *per se*, as some of the early literature on post-Communism implied), the most competent parties, so this second theory goes, responded to the lack of reliable or predictable con-stituencies by adopting 'catch-all' or constituency-maximising strate-gies; in other words, they identified themselves with the simplest, broadest and most popular goals of 'transition', in order to win as many votes as possible. Judging by the 1992 election, these entrepre-neurial parties presented themselves as representatives of 'reform' or 'sensitive reform' as such, rather than seeking to find more precise, but also electorally more risky, policy positions. Thus (the explanation continues), even as the nature of predominant social divisions and public concerns became more transparent through 1990 to 1992, political parties persisted in staying vague, avoiding a deeper and clearer competition and preferring to fight on the basis of their credibility as the deliverers of broadly popular public goods, such as 'democracy', 'prosperity', 'security' etc.

One consequence of this electoral strategy may have been that the controversial issue of constitutional design was presented in obscure terms throughout the critical years of Czechoslovak democratisation: 1990–2. Parties may have been particularly wary of clear policy offers on this subject since the public preference for 'some kind of common state' – held by a majority in both republics – was ambiguously divided between different constitutional models. Evidence that political parties failed to address alternative state arrangements with any coherence, not only in 1992, as we have already seen, but also before, between 1990 and 1992, would more completely discredit the subsequent claims of the Czech right that the 1992 election had functioned as a precise referendum on the future of the state. In fact, the contradiction would be absolute; as one observer has pointed out, 'if the options concerning public policy are effectively reduced to one, democracy is reduced to zero'[4]. Given an unwillingness among politicians to compete clearly over alternative state models at *any* stage following the revolution, voters would, by necessity, have based their support for political parties on other issues, leaving the question of a common state as a hostage to fortune. While this may imply some great conspiracy, political elites did not necessarily collude to avoid clarity on the state issue, but since they were unhampered by either grassroots pressures or a fully developed independent media, they may more simply have lacked any electoral incentive to present both realistic and equitable models for a renewed federation. Only at the very crisis point of the state – in the weeks following the election of Vladimír Mečiar in Slovakia and Václav Klaus in the Czech Republic – would it become clear what the full consequences of the 'gagging' of active competition over the state issue might mean, namely that two leaders with irreconcilable visions of the common state might meet as the two respective republic heads and opt *immediately* for separation.

The evidence for or against such an argument would be a significant finding for post-Communist states as such, since one of the preoccupations of early writings on Eastern Europe in transition concerned 'civil society' and its alleged non-existence. According to this argument however, civil society, as measured by associations, clubs and churches with some awareness of their role as public interlocutors to the state, may have been quite alive and increasingly animated within months of the revolution even in Czechoslovakia –

one of the most repressive regimes of the Soviet bloc. The problem may not have been the absence of civil organisations as such after the revolution but the inability of the 'people' or of these organisations to make themselves heard by the state – a lack of means by which to create effective public pressure upon political actors. To rule out one critical explanation for the break-up, namely, that highly democratic and attentive parties failed to deal with practical common state models because the electorate was actually past caring about them, apathetic about a question where the conclusions were foregone and painless, we clearly need evidence of public frustration with the political elite, and a positive demonstration of concern for the fate of Czechoslovakia.

In summary, a second, party-based explanation for the break-up to be explored here is that pro-common state voters failed entirely to impact on state development even in conditions of free elections. Evidence in support of this thesis would be a diversity of public (and, in principle at least, of media[5]) opinion on the state issue and a uniformity of party policies. Evidence against this thesis would be open electoral competition on the constitutional question, involving a variety of clearly articulated alternative models of the state. The 1992 election has already been reviewed in Chapter 2; however, the deeper evaluation of party developments from 1989 continues in this chapter.

POLITICAL PARTY DEVELOPMENT FROM NOVEMBER 1989 TO JUNE 1992

As it turned out, Czechoslovakia's first free election in June 1990 was a poor indicator of public preferences on most issues, the fate of the common state included. The electorate was offered only the plebiscite issue of 'Are you for change?', and only afterwards did the victorious Czech and Slovak anti-regime movements splinter into factions which then constituted themselves as political parties. Those Czech and Slovak parties that attributed a transcendent value to the common state would find themselves politically marginalised by 1992, but not straightforwardly because of their pro-federal views.

In the first three years of multi-party politics there were clearly many rivalries between Czechs and Slovaks, but such tensions as there were proved usable by party agents only in a highly constrained way, stuck as all political parties were in nationally separate, republic-based political systems. From 1990 the anti-Communist movements, the Czech Civic Forum (CF) and Slovak Public Against Violence (PAV), splintered and then competed within their republics over the immediate issues of transition – over the transfer of power from Communism – the completeness of that transfer, and whether or not to purge the Communist *nomenklatura* – over approaches to state-building and democratisation, and over the intensity and scope of the economic transformation. Unfortunately, Czech and Slovak party political scenes developed according to a different ranking of these problems.

GHOSTS IN THE PARTY MACHINE – THE CZECH LANDS

Between December 1989 and the first free elections in Czechoslovakia (June 1990) the country was governed by the supposedly non-partisan Federal Government of National Understanding. This interim government was made up of the Civic Forum and the Slovak Public Against Violence, the pro-democracy civic movements that had mobilised hundreds of thousands of citizens onto Czechoslovakia's streets in November 1989 and forced the capitulation of the Communist regime. A Czech opinion poll in March 1990 placed the Civic Forum second only to the Federal Government of National Understanding as the most trusted institution in Czechoslovakia[6]. At the same time, however, the Socialist Party's youth section launched a complaint that soon became widespread, that the Civic Forum's all-embracing style, its inclusion of virtually all significant Czech dissident organisations[7], its unique mediating role in the revolution and its declaration of principles and objectives for the overcoming of the moral, spiritual, social, political, economic *and* ecological crisis of the country[8] gave it a rather unfair electoral advantage over more conventional political parties[9].

The Civic Forum's chief goal was indeed sweeping. It was, as it had been for the dissidents back in 1968, to 'return Czechoslovakia to Europe'[10], culturally, economically and politically. The Socialist youth also had a legitimate point in that the Forum's rhetoric of non-partisanship had from the beginning obscured a very real political bias. Financial caution – a strong tradition in Czech government, even under the Communists – was now promoted as a call for austerity. As well as advocating the rapid introduction of a market economy, the Civic Forum encouraged the idea that the 'reformed' economic space would thereafter stand entirely beyond 'government', in the sense of 'political' jurisdiction. In other words, the Forum, from the very beginning, sought to carve out truly free-market – liberal – territory.

The June 1990 election campaign evolved around the issues of social justice, democracy, the confiscation of Communist Party assets, the Communist Party's future, and included general statements about the

The results of the elections, 8–9 June 1990
Percentage share of the vote

	Federal Assembly		Czech/ Slovak National Councils
	House of the People	House of the Nations	
Czech Republic			
Civic Forum (CF)	53.1	50.0	49.5
Communist Party of Czechoslovakia (CP)	13.5	13.8	13.3
Christian and Democratic Union (CDU)	8.7	8.7	8.4
MSD/SMS*	7.9	9.1	10.0
Others	16.8	18.4	18.8
Slovak Republic			
Public Against Violence (PAV)	32.5	37.3	29.3
Christian Democratic Movement (CDM)	19.0	16.7	19.2
Communist Party of Czechoslovakia (CP)	13.8	13.4	13.3
Slovak National Party (SNP)	11.0	11.4	13.9
Coexistence and HCDM**	8.6	8.5	8.7
Democratic Party (DP)	4.4	3.7	4.4
Slovak Green Party (SGP)	3.2	2.6	3.5
Others	7.5	6.4	7.7

Percentage share of seats

	Federal Assembly		Czech/ Slovak National Councils
	House of the People	House of the Nations	
Czech Republic			
Civic Forum (CF)	68	50	127
Communist Party of Czechoslovakia (CP)	15	12	32
Christian and Democratic Union (CDU)	9	6	19
MSD/SMS*	9	7	22
TOTAL	101	75	200
Slovak Republic			
Public Against Violence (PAV)	19	33	48
Christian Democratic Movement (CDM)	11	14	31
Communist Party of Czechoslovakia (CP)	8	12	22
Slovak National Party (SNP)	6	9	22
Coexistence and HCDM**	5	7	14
Democratic Party (DP)	–	–	7
Green Party (GP)	–	–	6
TOTAL	49	75	150

* Movement for Self-governing Democracy/Society for Moravia and Silesia.
** Hungarian Christian Democratic Movement.

need to redesign constitutional relations between Czechs and Slovaks. Personalities played a prominent role in the subdued campaign, and this was unavoidable given the few salient differences between the programmes on offer, and the difficulty that parties would have had in defining themselves in any more substantive debate. Even the Communist Party advocated political pluralism and a market economy, albeit without the abolition of state property[11]. The election results are displayed in the table below.

If anything, the Civic Forum's success in these first elections, paralleled as it was by that of the like-minded and equally consensus-seeking Public Against Violence and the Christian Democratic Movement (CDM) in Slovakia, seemed to bode well for the resolution of the national question – all seemed to agree that Czechoslovakia should be transformed into a 'democratic federation'. A threat to stable relations, however, lay in the inevitable disintegrative tendencies of these conglomerate civic movements and the direction such fragmentation might take.

THE DISINTEGRATION OF THE CENTRE: JUNE 1990–SPRING 1992

In the first year after the revolution the status of political parties as such was contentious. For the dissidents the distrust cut deep; it came from the bitter experience of Communist one-party rule and from the concern that decent individuals would again be seduced into dogmatic ideological quarrels, and so fail to realise the potential of the progressive 'civic will' supposedly revealed by the revolution. In the first months of 1990 the reasoning behind anti-party feeling was also based on caution; the civic movements just had to hold together as the only safeguard against the return of Communism. The ambiguous prestige of political parties would continue to be reflected in the two distinctive characteristics of the Czech party system for the rest of the year: the proliferation of single-issue parties (without any hope of scaling the 5-per cent vote threshold for entry to parliament) and the persistence of the monopolising Civic Forum, with its ambivalent attitudes to party competition.

As the events of November 1989 receded in time, however, the imperative of Forum cohesion began to wear off. Having actually achieved power, the considerations of how, in any respect, the Forum should now develop necessarily came to the fore, and this debate brought dissension into the open. To accept the Forum's claim that it was non-partisan – 'a broad church' – would be to ignore the strong factions evident within it and its basic liberal bias, but also the practical difficulty of operating in more 'conventional' political terms after an anti-Communist revolution. In a society where ideas of class had declined in political currency, the liberal dissident and more right-wing leaders of the Civic Forum favoured very different alternatives: the dissidents believed in a hybrid of romantic metaphysics and liberal jurisprudence, a philosophy evolved in resistance to the totalitarian state; the emerging right wing – dominated by only recently politicised professionals – espoused an individualistic, economy-driven and rather more technocratic answer (including radical faith in free markets), to be underpinned by Christian/rightist social values. In 1990 there was little incentive for these alternative views to brave open competition and even when the Civic Forum formally split in 1991 both sides still claimed to represent the interests of the whole society; by 1991, however, these two sides were quite thoroughly divided both by reform philosophy and by political strategy.

The partial clarification of the political scene by the June 1990 election diminished the Civic Forum's appeal as a 'broad umbrella'. It was increasingly accused of opportunism[12] from the outside, and any remaining illusions of 'civic consensus' inside the movement were demolished in October 1990 when Václav Klaus – on the Forum's right, and a firm believer in political parties – was elected chairman. The subsequent emergence of an Inter-parliamentary Club of the Democratic Right, and a parallel group of the liberal centrists and centre left, the Liberal Club, spelled the Forum's end. The liberals protested that the metamorphosis of the Forum into a party, or rather several parties, was illegal and, in transforming the character of the movement, would destroy its popularity. Klaus and the Club of the Democratic Right insisted that the days of loose organisation were numbered. Clearly frustrated by the Forum's unwillingness to embrace his entire strategy, Klaus argued that 'ideological indiscipline' had blocked decision-making and allowed ministers to pursue 'personal policies'[13].

The formal division into liberal and Klausite[14] camps came at the 1991 February Congress. The Liberal Club, led by federal foreign minister Jiří Dienstbier, renamed itself the Civic Movement (CM), while Klaus's group became the Civic Democratic Party (CDP). The Civic Movement retained the core of the dissident movement and the much disputed loose internal structure of the original Forum. The CDP, in contrast, declared a disciplined internal hierarchy and official party registration. Both agreed to remain in coalition until just before the June 1992 election, but as party allegiances settled, the original parliamentary caucuses of the Forum – both federal and Czech – disintegrated[15].

With the Forum finally destroyed its new offspring faced the problem of how to define themselves in the light of an open competition. Personal popularity was uncertain grounds for electoral success at this early stage, and a reputation for being able to deliver on policy was likewise a long-term endeavour – basic design remained the immediate task in practically every policy area. Clarity in priority setting offered some room for contest, but to distinguish the technocratic right wing from the dissident liberals – rather more social liberal in their outlook – something pretty immediate would have to be found: a competitive strategy that was based not so much on performance as on the whole approach to transitional reform.

SETTING THE AGENDA: CZECH PARTY DEVELOPMENT – JUNE 1990 TO JUNE 1992

One commentator on Czech party developments at the time suggested that 'regional, religious and ethnic' and only potentially economic cleavages 'underpinned party diversification in 1990 and 1991'[16]. Though this might broadly describe differences between Czechs and Slovaks, these were not the issues to dominate Czech party evolution. The only regional difference to spawn a political party in the Czech lands was that of greater Moravian/Silesian autonomy. The one Moravian nationalist party, however, having split in pring 1991 over whether to seek republican status or simply greater self-management, looked set to decline altogether in the event of minimal self-administration actually being granted. The Catholic church too was not consistently divisive; Church leaders would go on to fight with Václav Klaus over the restitution of Church property, but it was Klaus, and not just the smaller Christian Democratic parties, who claimed to represent the 'Christian traditions in Europe'[17]. Finally, politicians had little reason to settle on ethnic conflict as a vote winner if opinion polls were anything to go by; ethnic animosity toward Slovakia as such (as opposed to conflicts over a new constitutional arrangement) was consistently discouraged as an electoral strategy by public opinion data that revealed a mutually friendly regard. If there was a problem it was the opposite of nationalist fervour – Czech parties appeared to view the relationship with Slovakia with great complacency. The Czech political right and left set different legal and economic conditions as the minimal prerequisites of a common state, but across the Czech political spectrum, with the exception of the Civic Movement, all substantive difficulties in the Czech and Slovak relationship – economic and constitutional – were assumed to emanate from the Slovak side.

The thorny problem of how to reconstruct the federal state emerged in Czech politics not in the context of heady nationalist rhetoric or passion, therefore, but amidst the pressing post-revolutionary issues that were notable precisely for their lack of pre-Communist roots. Economic reform and questions of anti-Communist retribution were products of the transition and they were problems that lent themselves far more to political polarisation than to compromise – most helpfully for the election-oriented Civic Democratic Party, whose main preoccupation was to distinguish itself from its rival urban liberals in the Civic Movement (the historic political divide between town and country being here of little use to strategists). In the absence of discernible party constituencies, party-builders had a difficult time identifying strategically attractive controversies and, not surprisingly, they gravitated towards the most obvious domestic worries.

NOT SO MUCH A PROGRAMME, MORE A WAY OF LIFE

Economic policy dominated general party development in the Czech Republic in two ways. Firstly, the economy was widely considered the linchpin of political stability and thus of the whole transformation from Communism – some 73 per cent of Czechs *and* Slovaks believed that democracy 'only functions in rich countries'[18]. The question of how to become rich was also, apparently, resolved – Communist oppression in the 1980s had been political and social but also accompanied by the steady decline of living standards, and by autumn 1991 a full 88.9 per cent of Czechs agreed that a market economy was necessary for economic development[19]. The political party with the policy seen as most likely to reverse the negative economic trends of the 1980s thus possessed the most enormous electoral potential; if it capitalised upon this connection between democracy and economic performance it might present itself as the only party capable of delivering all other democratic benefits.

Finance Minister Klaus successfully laid claim to the authorship of an economic reform package that through 1990 to 1992 managed, even during formal privatisation, to maintain exceptionally low unemployment in the Czech Republic – though not, as we shall see, in Slovakia[20]. This claim to authorship gave Klaus leverage to discipline the Civic Democratic Party and the authority to introduce a unique tone into Czech political debate – one that was decisive, confident and pragmatic. In the preamble to a television interview it was commented that 'Václav Klaus functions a little like a man from another world ... He is almost the perfect antithesis of the long-standing picture of a Czech, not genial, but scathing, not idle, but unbelievably hard-working. Not evasive, but direct . . . he alone declared himself to be a conservative. Yet a conservative is he who somehow retains traditions. In this sense Klaus is the most radical revolutionary against the Czech character'[21]. The charismatic appeal of such a personality was not surprising when 72.8 per cent of the population claimed to feel both anxious and insecure when looking into the near future[22].

Klaus's absolute confidence in the efficacy of markets – he claimed to be a 'Thatcherite Conservative' – and the idea that uninhibited markets alone would liberate the Czechs' innate economic genius were evidently well in tune with Czech aspirations – it was, after all, an heroic and inspiring vision, and the lean, square-jawed, 'Western' suit-and-tie wearing, tennis-playing fifty-year-old Klaus looked unusually capable of delivering it (in some contrast, it has to be said, to the heavy-smoking and drink-loving dissidents, who looked like gently crumpled intellectuals even after they had been persuaded out of their jeans and woolly jumpers and into the clothes of 'professional' politicians). Klaus clearly captured a mood that the Czechs should be first in the race back to Europe, and by July 1992, 57 per cent of Czechs over eighteen endorsed and agreed on the meaning of the term 'capitalism' and attributed to it the following, extremely stark features: private ownership should exist without state restrictions; inequality was a natural phenomenon and dependent upon the ability of individuals; poverty was a result of personal inability; the state should intervene only minimally in the economy; unemployment was a consequence of an individual's lack of enthusiasm for their occupation; economic transformation, and privatisation in particular, should be rapid[23].

It might reasonably be pointed out that to be a 'conservative' after forty years of Communism was not so much an ideology as a leap of faith, but Klaus's intention was clearly to claim the heritage of Czechoslovakia's interwar prosperity as his party's own and to wed the philosophical rhetoric of 'preserving what is valuable' to a programme of rapid economic transformation. The ideological allusion helped to distinguish the Civic Democratic Party from other parties of the right, but, perhaps more importantly, this claim to be a conservative apparently persuaded many Czechs that reforms did not have to be as devastating and as fantastically painful as those in progress in Poland. Self-avowedly 'Thatcherite Conservatism' proffered reassurance with the argument that all reform, however drastic or innovative, was fundamentally a return to the 'most valuable social values, formed as the fruit of a thousand-year evolution'[24] – a notable reworking of classic nationalist rhetoric ('a thousand years of the nation') behind a rationalist cause. Klaus's Civic Democratic Party argued that moving forward into reform was the only way to regain the positive aspects of the past (the Czech equivalent of Thatcher's 'Victorian virtues') and to return to the Western path. Such claims, that the process of reform would not only generate the strategy necessary for the present but would also re-invoke what had been known before Communism, simply glossed over the fact of forty years of Communist socialisation, and what emerged was a form of politico-economic mysticism that looked very much like the Marxist-Leninist historical dialectic turned neatly back-to-front.

It may be noted, moreover, that by the critical summer of 1992, Czechs had been led to believe that they had already acquired many of the structures of the 'fully-fledged' market capitalism by which Klaus claimed to set so much store, and yet they still suffered from only the most minimal unemployment and inflation. Economic developments at this vital juncture, therefore, had done very little to temper a 'pull yourself up by your bootstraps' outlook among those Czechs who had chosen to adopt it.

DISARMING THE DISSIDENTS

The electoral benefits of 'looking forward' – of escaping the past – were evidently appreciated by the Civic Democratic Party more than by any other, and, much to the consternation of historians and dissidents (not just in Czechoslovakia but elsewhere), the demands of party competition and the avowed militant anti-Communism of parties to the right of the Civic Movement quickly led them to belittle the events of the Prague Spring – the period during which many of the dissidents had established their dissent. Denying the events of 1968 their status as a popular insurrection, the political right dismissed them increasingly as an irresponsible contest between Communist Party factions, the implication being that not only reform Communists but the dissidents too were essentially 'other' – i.e. bound up in Communist Party intrigues, not 'of' the normal electorate[25] and therefore inappropriate representatives of the people.

While leading this assault on the country's history and collective memory, the Civic Democratic Party at the same time expropriated those central tenets of the '68 platform that expressed the historical aspirations of Czech political culture, the most important being the aspiration to be a part of Europe. In 1968 the novelist Milan Kundera, then a leading cultural voice, had fought for the re-emancipation, the re-Europeanisation, of Czech cultural life. Klaus, playing on his emerging image as the classic 'skilled engineer' – a traditional Czech role model, along the lines of the Czech 'golden-handed craftsman' – promised that the Czechs would 'return' to Europe but this time on solid modern ground and with a thriving economy that abounded with enviable industrial talents. Without such an economy, Klaus threatened, Europe would remain a mirage. The fact that many 1968 reformers had, at one time, been committed Stalinists[26] made it easy for the Civic Democratic Party to espouse the traditions that had underpinned the Spring whilst damning the reformers of the time (among them the Civic Movement's leader, Jiří Dienstbier[27]) as collaborators, unfit for office.

From his platform of economic credibility, and using practical arguments for entry to Europe (rather than relying on dissident shibboleths about the 'European-ness' of 'true' Central European culture), Klaus projected himself as a sympathetic realist whilst satirising the rival, intellectual core of the old Civic Forum. According to Timothy Garton-Ash, he displayed an 'almost comical desire to be taken seriously as a writer'[28]. In practice, however, Klaus's lucid rejection of the priorities of the former dissidents was devastating; he blamed the discursive style of the Civic Forum for delays in economic policy and harped on the intellectual elite's chronic Pragocentrism. By projecting the Civic Movement programme as an apology for the past and a page of metaphysical philosophy in regard to the future, he distinguished the Civic Democratic Party as the most forward-looking and efficient heir of the November revolution. Finally, by taking early to writing articles outlining his policies and beliefs, often in Havel-style state-of-the-nation essays, Klaus pulled a stunt unsuspected by Garton-Ash. Imitating dissident intellectuals proved a most effective way of framing their esotericism. CDP federal deputy Peter Gandalovič could thus make the productive allegation that 'while the inter-parliamentary Club of the Democratic Right concentrated right from the beginning on the drafting of legislation towards more radical reform, one cannot avoid feeling that the Liberal Club rather produced statements suggesting it was the last saviour of democracy, social certainties and culture'[29].

'LUSTRÁCE' – THE DISSIDENTS' LAST STAND

Czech party politics after 1989 were marked by the impulse to exorcise the ghosts of Communism. Though power had been transferred peacefully, battles emerged immediately after the revolution that signalled deep tensions between legal and political remedies to old structures and their influence. When the People's Party was besieged by pre-election scandals, the liberals in the Civic Forum risked their reformist reputation to insist on a fair hearing for this former Communist Party satellite, believing as they did that if the rule of law was to mean anything in the liberated state then equality before the law would have to be upheld from day one. Similarly, when the lack of self-redefinition in the Communist Party[30] led the former satellite parties and Social Democrats to propose banning it, many in the Civic Forum objected that in a mature democracy the Communists and their legacy should be defeated through electoral competition and not legalistically banned[31]. Clearly the dissident liberals, then still dominating the leadership of the Civic Forum, intended to frame their anti-Communism through strict procedurally democratic means. With a population apparently more concerned about the threat of instability than the rule of law, however, such a priority would go on to prove a terrible electoral strategy.

The intense party politicisation of anti-Communist 'screening' (lustrace) in the Czech lands after 1989 resulted from the powerful combination of a demonstrable (though not the main) public desire to escape the past with the intense pressure to find a clear electoral identity within the two-year election cycle. Klaus had won a victory over the drafting of laws for the restitution of property, but this only confirmed his already evident grip on economic reforms. 'Screening', in contrast, provided the Civic Democratic Party with victory in an area previously considered the preserve of the dissidents – that of public morality. As an issue 'lustration' possessed great potential for a display of tough leadership and decisive government, and the evolution of this issue through 1990 to 1992 gives a clear picture of electoral entrepreneurship in the Czech Republic and its attendant costs.

Various commissions, notably one investigating the violent events of 17 November 1989[32], had had access to state security files and had engaged in a process of vetting public officials' records for past collaborations. This initial process had been criticised by parliamentary deputies for its arbitrary application under the People's Party Interior Minister, Richard Sacher. Even after Sacher's departure in June 1990 the vetting procedure remained controversial, becoming the focus of public concern over continuing Communist influence. Public disquiet was mobilised by anti-Communist groups of the right, notably the Confederation of Political Prisoners and the Club of Committed Non-Party Members ('KAN'). These very vocal groups were the heartfelt opposition to continuing Communist power and stood, militantly, for the disqualification of Communists. They found allies in the press[33] and, so it transpired, a champion in the parliamentary right.

Lustration was never out of the press in 1990 and 1991, the implication always being that a coherent Communist force remained, larger and more recidivist than the observable Communist Party. Newspaper stories in spring 1991 centred on the need to screen the administration, particularly on how parliament could acquire the right to dismiss deputies found to have collaborated. In February the Christian Democratic Union and smaller parties of the right had demonstrated for 'universal and legally reliable vettings'[34]. That same month, the head of Prague's Charles University politics faculty, political commentator and member of the Club of Committed Non-Party Members, Rudolf Kučera, made a straight comparison between Communism and fascism and called for Communism to be criminalised and its government members condemned. Kučera warned that another 'victorious February' (as in 1948) waited in the wings[35]. It was thus possible to capitalise on the issue of screening in the name of public safety – rather than revenge – despite liberal appeals for reconciliation. The Czech right claimed that in this case political prudence should outweigh civic and human rights considerations. The threat was animated by figures such as the Christian Democratic dissident Václav Benda, who insisted that 'former collaborators of state security have relatively high representation in the Presidium of the parliament and its Constitutional-Legal Committees'[36]. When Deputy Interior Minister (and former *Respekt* editor) Jan Ruml described changes in his ministry he emphasised the 'dozens of new people, active fighters against the totalitarian regime'[37].

Non-Communist political forces began calling unanimously for a screening bill. The grounds for legislation were strengthened for deputies by leaks to the media and a general increase in the abuse of files for political blackmail through 1990 and 1991. On 27 June 1991, the federal government approved a bill presented by the Civic Movement, and at this point the real disunity among those calling for regulation was revealed. The original draft had intended to disqualify from public office only those proven to have violated human rights. However, on the basis of comments by federal committees under pressure from the right (specifically the Civic Democratic Party), fundamental changes were made that widened the scope of the draft, making endorsement of the bill impossible by any party concerned with liberal legal norms. The bill that emerged in September 1991 covered members of state security, registered residents, agents or holders of 'conspiracy flats', informers or ideological collaborators and other deliberate collaborators[38]. The draft was extended to cover former Secretaries of the Communist Party at district or higher level, members of the Presidium of Central Committees who implemented political control of the National Security Corps, and members of the security departments of the Communist Party Central Committees. By 31 December 1996 these people were no longer to hold elected or appointed positions in state administration bodies, in the army, police force, the President's office, the Federal Assembly Office, the Czechoslovak Government Office, Czechoslovak Radio, Television and ČTK (the Czech press agency) or republican bodies to be named by their governments. The ban was to last for five years, the duration of the law, but by specifying positions it protected the employability, most obviously in the private sector, of much of the old technocratic and political elite[39].

According to objections by the General Procuratory and other ministries, the bill contradicted the Charter of Human Rights, the 1958 International Labour Organisation convention No. 111 on non-discrimination in work; it implied collective guilt; and it intervened in the competencies of the republics. It was also thought profoundly unreliable in that state security files were to be used as evidence[40]. The bill was, nevertheless, approved on 4 October 1991, with a majority composed of the Civic Democratic Party, the Civic Democratic Alliance and the Christian Democratic Party.

In lustration, the Civic Democratic Party had finally found a truly popular issue against the party they perceived as their main rival, the Civic Movement, which had looked likely to dominate government for the foreseeable future after the Forum fell apart. Though the Civic Democratic Party was the larger parliamentary party Klaus was its only federal cabinet member, and from his embattled position among social liberal ministers he quite reasonably feared that his party's control over economic policy-at-large might still be insufficient to secure a CDP victory in the 1992 election. The pressure to manipulate lustration for political gain was considerable. It was only in April 1991 that the Civic Democratic Party had built a public lead over the Civic Movement in economic policy. Moreover, public allegiance for both groups seemed to be waning in the summer. By mid-1991, polls revealed that fewer than half of the Civic Forum's supporters aligned themselves with either party. Before the issue of lustration was raised it was unclear how much value the electorate ascribed to the Civic Movement's dissident roots and civic priorities. As it turned out, the CM's determination to institute liberal legal norms set it at odds with the prevailing public mood[41].

The differences established by lustration were exploited to the full by the Civic Democratic Party, even though for Klaus the need for lustration was scarcely a deeply held belief. Indeed, his neutrality had earlier provoked consternation on the right. The issue was first pushed by the political right at a joint press conference[42] where the Christian Democratic Party's leader, Václav Benda, argued that they wished to change the situation whereby reform Communists still controlled various bodies, not as a result of free elections but because of the undemocratic policy of the Civic Forum[43]. Klaus was thus pressured to endorse wholeheartedly the militant supporters of vettings to retain his right-wing credibility, and the Civic Democratic Party's subsequent shift to the militant sponsorship of lustration revealed, yet again, Klaus's tactical acuity, even as it situated the CDP plainly in what the Polish dissident Adam Michnik scathingly categorised as the 'new Party of the clean and prudent'. Michnik argued that this was a peculiarly post-Communist party, made up of those prudent people who for years had worked in relative safety, inside the official legal structures, avoiding both Party and open opposition activity, only later to express a belated, compensatory aggressiveness toward Communism and toward anyone who had dirtied their hands in the fight for reform[44]. Klaus himself, it may be noted, had never been an open dissident but had benefited from the Prague Spring by studying economics in the West. Although demoted to the State Bank from the Economics Institute of the Academy of Sciences after 1968, he nevertheless returned in 1988 in the new Institute for Prognosis[45], explaining his attitude to open dissent with the phrase 'I have always respected any chair I was sitting on'[46]. What clearly frustrated Michnik was the degree of resentment and unease among the public at large when they were reminded of the heroism of the few. To categorise the dissidents as belonging to the same politically freakish and utopian ilk as the Communists remained, nevertheless, a brilliant tactical move, as Klaus apparently realised.

Lustration, best of all, was an issue where the press had already done the work of stirring up public concern and calling for action. Until now Klaus had wielded the past against the Civic Movement through populist anti-intellectualism, indicting the unbridled intellectual as a dangerously utopian force in politics, but he had lacked the contemporary evidence to drive this message home. The Civic Movement's more prudent attitude to lustration, however, could be made to look like proof, not only of utopianism but even, by implication, of collaboration. In *Why I am an Optimist*[47] Klaus had played down the role of the people at large in maintaining socialist order. Where the Civic Movement's Jan Urban talked of the compromises forced on every individual under Communism, Klaus insisted of the regime that 'it was not "we" who did this. None of "us" would ever have had the audacity, for we do not know this type of ambition. Behind every arrogant attempt to draw up completely new social institutions, there lurks the cerebral and sometimes physical violence of a handful of self-important intellectuals . . . The attempt at socialism . . . was not some "mob rebellion" . . . but rather a revolt by a group of leftist intellectuals'. Such asides about the evils of intellectuals and their obsessive social engineering now underpinned both a popular policy and a direct attack on the ex-1968 reformers within the Civic Movement – all this, it must be remembered, from the man who, in less competitive days, had suggested that 'no litmus test exists which could precisely divide good and evil between Communists and non-Communists'[48].

Lustration proved politically lethal to the liberal ex-dissidents. In crossing the fence from the Civic Democratic Party, the Civic Movement acted anti-pragmatically, as if the responsibility to re-establish basic principles of the rule of law – to bring to an end the habituated abuses by the state of retributive justice based on collective guilt – rested with them. The fact that they were entirely right – that the opportunity (and duty?) to reassert democratic norms existed for government politicians at this stage in a unique way – simply missed the electoral point, and the former dissidents in the Civic Movement evidently stood alone in their preoccupation with procedural principles. The vote-seeking right, on the other hand, had tapped successfully into a vein of public anxiety that was not dependent on economic performance[49] and the Civic Democratic Party capitalised where it could. Deputy Interior Minister Jan Ruml was wooed into the party in the spring of 1992 – just before the elections. During the official election campaign the Civic Democratic Party tied lustration firmly to economic reform (previously linked to the Forum-splitting issue of 'party'[50]). They alleged the fundamentally anti-democratic character of those who could both oppose the government's chosen method of screening and have reservations about reform progress and, in particular, Klaus's extreme faith in free markets. The implication that Klaus's liberal rivals were hidebound by a dissident sensibility proved the Civic Democratic Party's most successful device for destroying the Civic Movement, which failed to retaliate, considering such tactics the lowest form of 'politicking'.

The lustration debate also had a national aspect, though one played out mainly against Federal Assembly chairman Alexander Dubček. The increasingly nationalist Civic Democratic Alliance[51] insinuated much from the fact that the Czech right could not oust Dubček for signing the Moscow Protocols in 1968 only because he was too popular a figure in Slovakia[52]. Dubček, actually a staunch federalist, opposed the vettings procedure for human rights reasons and because it damaged the prestige of the Assembly. According to the Civic Democratic Alliance, however, his popularity originated only in

Slovak preferences for the old regime. Klaus too would eventually join in this accusation, but in a more 'constructive' form. In July 1991, when Dubček left the Public Against Violence, objecting that it had departed the centre ground and had moved rightward, Klaus leapt the hurdle of being too apparently anti-Slovak by pointing out that the Slovak Public Against Violence now also opposed Dubček – Klaus's implication being that 'good Slovaks' would follow such a line. Polls found that Czechs, far more than Slovaks, felt the legislation to be necessary[53].

The vote on lustration thus not only set the Civic Movement apart from the Civic Democratic Party but supposedly aligned it with the forces of Slovak nationalism and the left, who had either abstained with the Civic Movement or voted against the bill. According to Václav Žák, the Civic Movement's opposition to the bill, particularly to the principle of collective guilt, lost it two-thirds of its support[54]. Despite this most dire warning, however, the Civic Movement insisted on running the 1992 election campaign on a platform 'for the rule of law' – electorally falling on their own sword in a manner readily imitated by their liberal Slovak colleagues.

SLOVAK PARTY DEVELOPMENT 1990–2:
LIBERALISM VERSUS 'THE NATION'

'There is a direct conflict between the needs of the Czechoslovak economy and the national interests of most Slovaks'.
Czech Prime Minister Petr Pithart (Civic Movement)[55]

The new Slovak ruling elite that emerged from November 1989 was in fact a combination of dissidents and 'laundered' Communists, the latter split between 1968 veterans and those who resigned in the wake of the '89 revolution[56]. It was, moreover, evident that Slovak preoccupations (at both elite and mass level) centred on matters other than purging the Communist past. This relative absence of retributive impulses has prompted some to suggest that Slovaks were simply unrealistic about democracy[57]. An alternative interpretation, borne out by electoral choices, is that the Slovaks' more favourable experiences under Communism had left them less resentful of its personnel. More generally, Czechs and Slovaks clearly held in common the ambition to defend, if not improve, the socio-economic developments achieved in the last twenty years.

It was to the detriment of their liberal agenda that Slovak dissidents[58] possessed an even greater distaste for party politics than did their Czech colleagues. Led by the sociologist Fedor Gál, the Public Against Violence had been the first non-Communist movement to emerge, but its deep infiltration by 1968 reform Communists and the 'Revival' group[59] soon became apparent – and the PAV had little choice but to make a virtue out of political necessity. The Slovak civic movement had begun to lose support as early as January 1990; the unwillingness of the dissident group to seek parliamentary seats, let alone government posts, had made them seem both in power and yet antipathetic to it. Their reticence enabled the politically less inhibited (and, to the dissidents, unknown) former Communists, such as Vladimir Mečiar, to lead the Public Against Violence in the Slovak National Council, the significant forum of Slovak party development.

Mečiar's rise to the top of the PAV was the most meteoric but hardly unusual, since former Communists, entirely unknown personalities to the PAV executive, would appear protesting their pro-democratic and reformist credentials, and since they were professionals (Meciar was a lawyer) and both confident and competent, there seemed little alternative but to assume that they were as good as their word. Vladimír Mečiar had emerged as a front runner of the Revival group in the aftermath of the revolution and by January had already become Slovak Interior Minister on Dubček's recommendation, an appointment that elicited warning letters to Havel suggesting that Mečiar would misapply his powers[60]. With 9 per cent of public favour at the end of April 1990, however, Public Against Violence trailed the Green Party (SGP), the Democratic Party (DP)[61], the Communist Party, and most of all the Christian Democrats (CDM, under Ján Čarnogurský)[62], and could thus hardly afford to eject the most dynamic political figures emerging on its list.

The Public Against Violence's urgent need to recover lost ground consolidated the pragmatic coalition of dissidents and ex-Party members and eventually prompted the offer of ballot places to the one-time reform Communists Marián Čalfa, Alexander Dubček and Milan Čič, respectively the first, second and third most popular Slovak politicians at the end of April 1990[63]. The most popular non-Communist politician ranked ninth overall in a pre-election poll[64].

Slovak party programmes for June 1990 were no less vague than the Czech – the sociologist and dissident Milan Šimečka feared voters might be overwhelmed by their 'democraticity'[65] – and it would be difficult to discriminate between one list of platitudes and another. At the election a majority of Slovaks divided nonetheless clearly between the Public Against Violence and Christian Democratic Movement (the Catholic Church having constituted the main opposition to Slovak Communism since 1968) – results which clearly confound the Czech

Civic Democratic Alliance's subsequent claims that Slovaks failed to reject the old regime. Turn-out was an impressive 95.4 per cent.

President Havel persuaded Čarnogurský to place the Christian Democratic Movement's 26 deputies behind the federal Public Against Violence/Civic Forum governing coalition, believing that the Christian Democrats were likely to outstrip the Public Against Violence if Slovakia reverted to its pre-Communist clericalism. Čarnogurský himself returned to the Slovak parliament. With only 48 seats out of the 150 in the Slovak National Council, Public Against Violence premier elect Vladimír Mečiar was obliged to seek a Slovak government coalition with the Christian Democratic Movement (with 31 seats) and the Democratic Party (with 7) in order to secure a governing majority. Carnogursky became deputy premier. Coalition rules were established with difficulty, though, as we shall see, a 'first-past-the-post' voting system, rather than proportional representation, would have also run into trouble.

SLOVAK PARTY DIVERSIFICATION 1991-2

The Public Against Violence had responded to the break-up of the Czech Civic Forum by promising to cooperate with all its former associates. By 1991, however, the Slovak civic organisation was itself no longer intact. Even the anti-hierarchical Fedor Gál assumed the PAV's right to approve their premier's decisions and to hold him accountable, yet in this it was frequently frustrated by Mečiar. By March, the Slovak premier had formed a faction, the 'Public Against Violence/Movement for a Democratic Slovakia', publicly splitting the Public Against Violence in half. Fatally for the PAV the real causes of friction were unclear to the broader public until this open conflict.

Mečiar appeared a diligent advocate of the Public Against Violence programme in the public eye but provoked the PAV internally, thus protecting himself from PAV attacks on the basis of policy. In this he was assisted by a nervous media, unwilling to criticise evidently popular political characters. It was obvious to the public that, in contrast to the rest of PAV's leadership, Mečiar believed that among the main pillars of the PAV's agreed programme (September 1990) Slovak national issues should receive priority. Many in the PAV feared that since August 1990 Mečiar had been too confrontational in negotiations with the Czechs, which, combined with his known reservations over and criticisms of Klaus's federal economic policy, could lead to an un-looked-for clash. These 'pillars' were supposed to enjoy 'parity of esteem', but Mečiar believed that the PAV had little choice but to respond to the burning issue of a new national settlement, which he evidently perceived as explaining the growing popularity of the rival Slovak National Party and the Christian Democratic Movement.

At the PAV Congress on 23 February 1991, Mečiar attempted to take over the leadership, only to be defeated by the incumbent, Fedor Gál. Gál not only rejected the proposal to turn the PAV into a party – supported by Mečiar, echoing Klaus – but pointed to the danger of populism, which 'misuses people's national thinking for the narrow power ambitions of individuals'. The liberal economist Jozef Kučerák likewise criticised Mečiar for his rosy portrayal of the Slovak economy's potential under a modified federal reform process[66]. In March, 89 per cent of Slovaks nevertheless cited Mečiar as their favourite politician[67], and, no doubt emboldened by such support, he exacted political revenge, accusing Kučerák of state security collaboration and Gál of censoring his television appearances[68]. When Gál sought to play down the now deep rift in the PAV, Mečiar identified it as professional jealousy[69].

By the end of the first week of March, Mečiar and his colleagues Rudolf Filkus and Milan Kňažko had left the PAV to form the 'Public Against Violence/Movement for a Democratic Slovakia' (MDS). Declaring to the press that it 'starts out from the original base of the PAV movement' they co-opted the June 1990 PAV platform *Chance for Slovakia* as they departed[70]. Mečiar suggested he might collaborate with the rump of Public Against Violence if only it could get rid of its 'undemocratic working methods'. In the same period some 10,000 people demonstrated for Mečiar in Bratislava, and twenty PAV district councils pledged their support[71]. Czech comments, intended to stabilise the situation, promptly destroyed what little chance the rump of the Public Against Violence had of recovering the situation. Czech Premier Pithart quickly endorsed his Slovak liberal colleagues with the unsupported suggestion that Slovaks falling in step behind Mečiar were less apprehensive of authoritarianism than Czechs, a line absolutely guaranteed to antagonise Slovaks[72]. Havel's spokesman, Michael Žantovský, destroyed Gál's last efforts at damage limitation with the comment that a new Slovak coalition had emerged between 1968 reform Communists, present Communists, separatists 'and people who recall the Slovak State as the golden period of the Slovak nation'[73]. In equating Mečiar's tactics and his supporters with fascism Žantovský took the shortest available route to comprehensive Slovak indignation.

The Public Against Violence accused Mečiar of jeopardising reform with an unwarranted nationalist diversion, failing to realise that

Mečiar's support derived precisely from his linking of pre-existing national concerns to a critical economic and social platform. Mečiar claimed a centrist orientation and declared that his goal was only to stop the deviation of the PAV to the right, a claim endorsed by Alexander Dubček[74]. On 22 March it was announced that a new caucus had formed in the Federal Assembly: of the 58 deputies elected for PAV in June, 32 had joined Mečiar. An AISA poll found that 65 per cent of Slovaks replied a 'definite yes' to the question 'Is Mečiar a guarantor of free and democratic development?', and 86 per cent said that the current form of the federation suppressed the interests of Slovakia, with an unusually high 22 per cent claiming to be separatist.

Mečiar's co-option of PAV support was fantastically successful. According to opinion polls, if elections had been held in March 1991, 42 per cent of Slovaks would have voted for the Movement for a Democratic Slovakia and a mere 1 per cent for the Public Against Violence[75]; and, like their Czech colleagues, the Slovak dissidents responded instinctively to confrontation by standing on principle – and in Slovakia, as in the Czech Republic, the result was political suicide. On 23 April 1991 the PAV ousted Mečiar as premier and released him into unfettered opposition at the time of the PAV's lowest ever political legitimacy. From here Mečiar could pursue freely the politics of 'overbidding', of introducing massively inflationary demands into the policy arena – from the state arrangement to the economy – successfully precluding any nascent system of fair party competition.

It has been concluded that, 'when [Mečiar] was forced into opposition, only one path was left for him to fight successfully for a return to power, the national one'[76]. Judging by his subsequent strategy, not playing the independence card but simply bundling constitutional alternatives as the public mood dictated, it is more accurate to argue that Mečiar, having exited on the tide of PAV support, took the nationalist card into his eclectic, populist pack.

Mečiar's ouster inaugurated an unambiguously non-Communist Slovak government, a coalition between the Christian Democratic Movement, with Ján Čarnogurský as the new Prime Minister, and the Public Against Violence rump, now led by Jozef Kučerák. It has been claimed by a former executive member of PAV, with hindsight – and evident disappointment – that the PAV had only ever won in Slovakia because the names of '1968' politicians 'evoked the belief of a continuity of reform socialism among the majority of those 29 per cent of voters'[77]. There were, nevertheless, other significant reasons why the remainder of the PAV, soon to be renamed the Civic Democratic Union (CDU), failed to revive by 1992.

The first reason was that the PAV failed to appreciate the electorate's desire for at least a minimum of continuity and stability. Opinion poll data repeatedly stressed that the public's overriding concern was with declining social welfare and living standards, above all other issues. Having reconciled themselves to a transitional 'vale of tears' – as an article of liberal economic faith – the metropolitan liberals of the Public Against Violence/Civic Democratic Union nevertheless rejected any soothing adjustment of economic reform to worsening conditions. This refusal might not have been so inflammatory had it not coincided with the Slovak electorate's knowledge that the reform's Czech authors governed over markedly different conditions. As it was, most Slovaks did not react to growing national inequality with an equally zealous faith in the free market.

The second reason concerned 'the nation'. The question of Slovak political equality with the Czech lands had arisen spontaneously on the Slovak political scene as an issue requiring attention, and yet the Slovak liberals in what was left of the PAV appeared antagonised by the very raising of the question. Goaded by Mečiar's flirtation with nationalism, Slovakia's liberals insisted upon an ultra-secular, individualistic and a-national image which, though strictly true to their politics, led them to diverge from their constituency quite spectacularly. As with their great faith in free markets, Slovak liberal arguments about the design of the state were widely read as claiming a monopoly on rationalism in public life. By implying that the preoccupation with national equality meant there was a nationalist Caliban at the gate – the supposedly deluded Slovak majority – the Civic Democratic Union actually appeared to sneer at the voters, an unconventional electoral strategy at the best of times.

PARTY FORMATION AND AGENDA-SETTING IN SLOVAKIA 1990–2: THE LANGUAGE LAW

What then were the issues that allowed Mečiar to sustain the kind of support he clearly enjoyed after the collapse of Public Against Violence? The evidence is that whereas his rivals sought to align or root themselves in ideologies and traditions, Mečiar acted from the beginning rather like an ideological property developer, garnering every available coalition with little scruple for consistency. In a nascent party system such behaviour might appear domestically as sensitive – populist though it was – as it appeared to the outside world only and entirely populist.

What is also striking is that Mečiar, like Klaus, was looking for the majority vote and acting strategically. Two alternative language bills had emerged in the Slovak National Council in Autumn 1990. One, drafted by the *Matica Slovenská* cultural organisation and sponsored by the Slovak Nationalist Party and the nationalists within the Christian Democratic Movement, stipulated the exclusive use of Slovak as the official language of the state and clearly discriminated against the sizeable Hungarian minority[78] in Slovakia's south. Mečiar defended the government draft, which made no such exclusionary attempts. On 25 October, after a twelve-hour debate during which parliamentary speeches were relayed to demonstrating crowds, the Slovak National Council approved the latter draft. Mečiar had opposed 'irresponsible nationalism' throughout the dispute, even if many in the Public Against Violence felt his rhetoric changed drastically according to his audience[79]. As with Klaus's pragmatic adoption of lustration, Mečiar took into his armoury only those aspects of nationalism that fitted his needs, and at this point, in the middle of talks on Czech–Slovak power-sharing, his first priority was his image as a responsible national representative. To cultivate this status he had described those provoking student unrest over the language bill as irresponsible, threatened legal action against hunger strikers settled in front of the Council[80], and even berated *Matica Slovenská's* Jozef Markuš on television for his nationalism. Had Meciar sided with the Slovak Nationalists he would have been branded a demagogue. Instead, at the end of the month, alongside Fedor Gál, Petr Pithart, Ján Čarnogurský and Václav Klaus, he signed an avowal that 'we shall energetically withstand all attempts to violate the integrity and sovereignty of our state'[81].

MEČIAR FINDS A PLATFORM

If the Slovaks appeared to be, as Havel put it, the 'motor of the discussions'[82] over the reorganisation of the federal state, this, like the lustration bill in the Czech Republic, had everything to do with the linkage of an issue of observable public concern with looming elections. Constitutional talks between the presidia of the National Councils and the federal government were the formal locus of the federation debate. In party political terms the failure of these talks allows us to map Vladimír Mečiar's switch to a more nationalist rhetoric and to account further for the failing credibility of the Civic Democratic Union–Christian Democratic Movement's governing coalition. For the sake of clarity this account is limited to the four most significant meetings on constitutional reform which took place between 1990 and the June election in 1992, all of which will be discussed in greater detail in the following chapter with their implications for the constitutional debate as such. The first talks, at Trenčianské Teplicé in August 1990, discussed provisional power-sharing arrangements and concluded in December. The second took place in Lány on 10 May 1991 (after preparatory meetings with Havel in February and March). The third occurred in Budmerice on 31 May 1991, and the last in Kroměřiž on 17 June 1991.

Trencianske Teplice

The talks at Trenčianské Teplice in August 1990 set the tone of Slovak premier Mečiar's approach to his Czech federal partners. To their surprise he pre-empted negotiation by arriving with a pre-set agenda that dated back to the Prague Spring. In Mečiar's model, the integration of two national states represented the basic idea of the federation; federal powers were to be delegated from essentially sovereign republican powers. This principle had been accepted by reformist Czechs and enshrined in the constitutional amendment of 1968, although it was later neutralised in practice by the return to 'democratic centralism'.

Though little of the talks was publicised, Mečiar's style made the headlines in both republics, as did his demands that a redivision of competences between the federal centre and the republican parliaments be made as quickly as possible. The Czech response, that Mečiar was practising the politics of the *fait accompli*, and that such serious intervention in the state arrangement would disrupt economic reform, seemed suspiciously evasive of the principle.

The Czechs badly misjudged not only the depth of Slovak expectations but also Slovak party political realities. So long as Mečiar was drawing the national issue into his sphere of influence via the PAV, it would gravitate toward the anti-secessionist and pro-federal political centre, to the position actually accepted by a previous generation of Czechs. Having presented himself as the champion of institutional change while at the same time condemning the impulse toward separatism, Mečiar had warned, in an echo of his Czech liberal detractors, that 'A split in the country must not occur, we see how nationalism develops in the USSR or Yugoslavia'[83]. In August 1990 he had made every show of aiming at a new, more equal relationship with the Czechs, going so far as to concede the frequent – and, in Slovakia, much disliked – Czech allusion to Slovakia as the 'younger brother': a phrase harped on notoriously by the Czech dissident writer Ludvík Vaculík. 'I want to emphasise', said Mečiar, 'that nobody in Europe wants a poor relative he would have to maintain. That would be the case of Slovakia if it broke away from the federation'[84]. Amazing though it may seem with hindsight, Mečiar at this stage clearly represented the Czechs' very best bet as a popular negotiating partner for a new and equalised federation.

By October 1990, when detailed discussion of a new division of competences began to founder, Mečiar's pro-equality stance was backed by demonstrations of over 10,000 people in Bratislava. When agreement was finally achieved the Slovak National Council unanimously approved the resulting draft constitutional amendment. To the public eye (and there were complaints at the secretiveness of the talks), the more nationalist force to emerge at this time was unequivocally the Christian Democratic Movement, whose Second Congress had insisted on the right of the Slovak republic to leave the federation, on its 'full sovereignty', and on its own system of taxes and a separate central bank[85]. Ján Čarnogurský's concept of a separate Slovak 'chair and star' in Europe, a policy of separatism for the propitious moment, seemed bound to be equally irritating to nationalists, federalists – and certainly Czechs[86].

As the first set of talks came to a head, however, Czech federal comment yet again only pushed Mečiar away from the centre ground. When federal Minister for the Economy Vladimír Dlouhý accused him of populism for having evoked the 'so-called economic disadvantage of the Slovak people'[87] the Public Against Violence had the political sense to back Mečiar in all respects, accusing Dlouhý in turn of violating the 'basic principles of coalition partnership'. The federal government, assuming the tone of transcendent Czech/federal authority so opposed in Slovakia, took the moral high ground, claiming that Dlouhý had not only the right but the duty to use professional as well as political arguments to support his views[88] – a hugely inflammatory response, given that Mečiar and the PAV represented at this point not only the Slovak government but also, excepting the diminutive Slovak Democratic Party, the most avowedly pro-federal force existing in Slovakia. When the law on the provisional division of competences was finally passed in December 1990, the Slovak National Party commented scathingly that 'Slovakia clings by such laws to non-democratic Prague centralism which seriously damages Slovak interests'[89].

As news of disagreements between Mečiar and the Public Against Violence filtered into the press, it seemed clear whose faction could manoeuvre with public support[90]. At the end of February, Čarnogurský had made clear to Havel that the two republics should draft their constitutions first and then conclude a state treaty. Thus in terms of Czech–Slovak relations it was again the Christian Democratic Movement that proved the divisive force at the second 'Vikárka' dinner – another round of negotiations – where the Public Against

Violence and Civic Forum positions were close, the dispute within the PAV notwithstanding[91]. Again, Zdeněk Jičínský's claim that Mečiar could only opt to take the nationalist path implies that the PAV split either cut loose a 'really' nationalist Mečiar or steered him irrevocably toward nationalism. I would argue more simply that Mečiar had only to retain his credibility on the national issue already won within the PAV.

From his ouster in April 1991 onwards, Mečiar positioned himself to win on the national and economic front by default. Default in the constitutional arena meant avoiding identification with the increasingly unpopular new Christian Democratic Movement/Public Against Violence governing coalition and distinguishing himself from the already established separatism of the Slovak National Party. Mečiar immediately embarked on the latter by reassuring Havel of his pro-federalism, telling the Czech Press Agency that the numbers against the federation in Slovakia 'are no greater than a year ago ... a small minority'[92]. To position himself in the long term, his new Movement for a Democratic Slovakia adopted 'appealing emancipation rhetorics which aptly blurred the constitutional issue'[93]. Constitutional talks were now entering their most tortuous phase. By the spring of 1991 they were stalemated on the issue of whether a state treaty could be a legal document and not just a political declaration. Both Czech and Slovak governments had managed to reduce the talks to impasse over the very same issues to have emerged already in August 1990. 'Emancipation rhetorics', it is important to note, could not be dismissed as less clear than the statements of the Slovak government, attempting to explain the repeated deadlock in negotiation.

Lány and Budmerice

Before the Lány talks in May 1991, Čarnogurský had reiterated that while separatism was quite unacceptable he would insist on the state treaty[94]. At Lány it was finally agreed, not least through the encouragement of Czech Prime Minister Petr Pithart, that an accord on the principles of the new constitutional arrangement would be signed by the National Councils and that they could thus create an inner-state Czech–Slovak treaty – one based on 'state law' rather than international law, since a treaty with international status would appear to nullify the existing federation. It was thus agreed that legal experts would formulate a text that would allow for Czechs and Slovaks to reaffirm their desire to live together in a federal state.

During negotiations at Budmerice, cross-party representatives completely rejected the results. The continuing ambiguity of constitutional arrangements positively invited the opposition Movement for a Democratic Slovakia into the fray to suggest that Slovakia should be a subject of international law and that the state treaty should be concluded on an international state level. This appeal was typical of several instances of the overbidding to come – interventions that effectively drove the debate into fiasco.

The Movement for a Democratic Slovakia suggested next that the delegation of competences to a higher centre should be such as in negotiations over a confederal Europe[95] – thus pushing the state treaty idea utterly beyond the pale for the Czechs. Within a few days of the MDS's having raised the state treaty stakes, Klaus accused Čarnogurský's position of being 'hysterical', even populist[96]. That Mečiar could so easily drag Čarnogurský down with this sniping from the sidelines (for Klaus managed to cloak Čarnogurský in Mečiar's colours) is testimony to the willingness of Czechs in general to believe that all Slovak politicians essentially shared a vision of independence. This tendency, certainly exhibited by the Czech press, led one Slovak commentator in *Slovenský národ* to object that 'When a Czech identifies with his nation, he is considered to be a great patriot – but if a Slovak so much as identifies himself in a national way, the Czech political machinery labels him a nationalist, chauvinist, clerico-fascist and destroyer of the state'[97].

Kroměříž

In Kroměříž it was finally agreed that a federal commission would draft a legal treaty between the two republics which could then be passed to the federal parliament for approval[98]. This appeared to be a breakthrough, and it was hoped the process would be completed by the end of 1991. In the Slovak National Council, however, Čarnogurský could no longer persuade the nationalists in his party to follow the Kroměříž line, and the Council decided to prepare two parallel constitutions, one with all the responsibility of a sovereign state, the other bound by existing state competences[99] – in effect, a contingency plan.

By December 1991 only the Slovak republic had submitted its constitutional proposals, despite Havel's warnings to the federal parliament that the constitutional process was in danger of foundering. Talks through that summer and autumn had considered the division of competences and had run aground first on the division of economic competences and then again on the state arrangement[100]. The idea of the state treaty had provoked insurmountable opposition among the Czech right wing, particularly the Civic Democratic Alliance. By the beginning of 1992 the talks on the constitutions and those on the treaty arrangement were both stalemated, the one awaiting resolution of the other in the face of the rapidly approaching election. By February 1992, it was again the nationalist faction of the Christian Democratic Movement which helped vote down the final text produced by treaty talks at Mílovy. The governing coalition under Ján Čarnogurský had been beset by disagreement over both the values and interests to characterise the Slovak transition. It has been remarked since that this coalition 'consisted of politicians who looked as if they had come from different historical periods and had spoken political languages of different worlds'[101]. Given the increasing hardships of economic reform in Slovakia the Civic Democratic Union–Christian Democratic Movement coalition, profoundly split on the issue of nation, was extraordinarily badly placed to take a pro-federal package to the electorate by 1992.

A SCHISM IN THE CHRISTIAN DEMOCRATIC MOVEMENT

The issue of statehood had been most dramatically played out in the Slovak National Council and its presidium. Sovereignty, proposed on three occasions by the nationalist faction of the Christian Democratic Movement, was voted down four times between 1990 and 1992. Soňa Szomolányi has argued that Čarnogurský 'unleashed nationalist forces assuming that it was possible to keep them under his control'[102], and certainly he primed the issue that Mečiar deployed more skilfully in the 1992 election and beyond[103]. At the beginning of March 1992 the two factions of the Christian Democratic Movement finally came apart, with the nationalist wing led by Ján Klepáč, deputy chairman of the Slovak National Council, splitting off to form the Slovak Christian Democratic Movement[104]. The Christian Democratic Movement welcomed the split, arguing that it freed the party to present itself as a true right-of-centre Christian Democratic party; the breach came late in the day, however, for the Movement to re-establish its reputation before the 1992 election. By this stage, moreover, Čarnogurský's claim to want to stand once again behind a negotiated settlement, including a referendum on the state's future, had few partners in the Czech republic.

A week after the separation of the Christian Democratic Movement, Alexander Dubček – whose popularity rating, according to an IVVM survey, now outranked that of Mečiar, at 75-per-cent approval to 73-per cent – shifted his allegiance to the Slovak Social Democrats[105]. His move confirmed his pro-federal position, and this, because of the national esteem in which he was held, seemed to represent a blow to the Movement for a Democratic Slovakia. As a condition of his entry, however, Dubček had secured a Social Democrat promise not to enter into a pre-election coalition with the Party of the Democratic Left. Dubček thus split the only realistic competitors against the Movement for a Democratic Slovakia[106].

SOVEREIGNTY – THE ISSUE TOO FAR FOR MEČIAR

Mečiar's manipulation of the sovereignty question represented a simple exploitation of the confusion surrounding the issue. Though he claimed that the Movement for a Democratic Slovakia sought all possible forms of 'sovereign Slovak statehood', with special emphasis on those forms ensuring international legal subjectivity, he consistently opposed attempts to declare sovereignty in the Slovak National Council and consistently avoided the term 'independence'. His strategy was to leave his options open for the post-election negotiations, where, as later talks attested, he apparently believed that the Czechs might ultimately be persuaded into some form of confederation.

Demonstrations for sovereignty and the frequent endorsements from the Slovak National Party, the Slovak national cultural association *Matica Slovenská*, and the nationalist wing of the Christian Democratic Movement had kept the issue as a background pressure throughout constitutional talks, but also as fuel for the Czech press. In April 1990, 20,000 people had demonstrated for an independent Slovakia, and as many demonstrated again on 11 March 1991 and 19 September, always under the auspices of *Matica Slovenská*. Sovereignty, as we have already seen, was one of the most profound barriers to negotiation, with the Slovak desire to possess at some point a moment of entire legal sovereignty – which it would then delegate to a new federation – taken by all Czech negotiating parties as either a devious separatist tactic or as legally nonsensical. To complicate matters further, sovereignty as a term in Slovakia was frequently treated as a synonym for autonomy and was increasingly discussed as if various grades of sovereignty were obtainable[107]. With such elisions in the terminology it was possible for Mečiar to incorporate sovereignty into his agenda but in such a way as to leave Slovakia's potential legal status completely ambiguous. The document with which he stole the whole limelight came with the Movement for a Democratic Slovakia's *Initiative for a Sovereign Slovakia*, launched on 13 September 1991. This promised the achievement of Slovak sovereignty and the adoption of a full Slovak constitution by constitutional and democratic means[108]; 30,000 people demonstrated in its favour[109]. By February Mečiar declared that the two republics would declare 'sovereignty', and then decide through a referendum on alternative state arrangements, but above all Czechs should regard Slovakia as a 'sovereign' subject[110].

THE LAST LIBERAL MISTAKE

On 23 March 1992 the Defence and Security Committee of the Slovak National Council released the second part of a report on the activities of the Slovak Interior Ministry. It revealed solid evidence of Mečiar's collaboration with state security and strong pointers to the abuse of his powers when he was Interior Minister. The report, timed just as the election loomed, stormed into the Czech and Slovak media. The most damaging allegations were that security files kept in state security safe houses in Bratislava and Mečiar's home town of Trenčin had disappeared. Several pages of registration documents concerning Mečiar and his appointees had also vanished. The report concluded that Mečiar had gathered documents on members of the government and the Catholic Church, as well as influential journalists, in order to harass them. His successor, the Christian Democratic Movement's Anton Andráš, had apparently made the mistake of trying to dismiss some of Mečiar's recruits and had suffered accordingly[111].

Mečiar dismissed the report as a smear campaign orchestrated from Prague and the Federal Interior Ministry. A few days later he alleged that the Ministry had a master plan not only to discredit him but also, if necessary, 'to liquidate him physically'[112]. Both the Slovak National Party and Party of the Democratic Left supported Mečiar, while Dubček remained silent. The federal and Czech parliaments, wisely, kept a low profile. Unless stripped of his parliamentary immunity, requiring a simple majority in the House of the Nations, Mečiar could not be prosecuted; and even if he were, the trial would not take place before the election[113]. The timing of the accusation could not have been worse; it came too late to deter those already persuaded by Mečiar's national and economic promises, and, however unfairly, it destroyed the civic credibility of the PAV–Civic Democratic Union as a party above the manipulation of information deemed too common in political life. Mečiar brushed off the affair as being only the first in a series of pre-election slanders[114]; his swaggering indifference to the inevitable Czech censure contrasted sharply with his earlier self-image and immediately with the ultra-Czechophile stance of the PAV/Civic Democratic Union.

The failure of these revelations to dislodge Mečiar led the Civic Democratic Union to take a step that doomed their election chances. The last remaining strategy for 'decapitating' the Movement for a Democratic Slovakia remained lustration. Believing that a strict implementation of the law some time in the near future might finally purge Slovakia of the demagoguery it so feared, the CDU opted for a coalition with the Czech party which was felt to be intellectually sympathetic and most in favour of this aspiration, the Civic Democratic Alliance. Having selected as its electoral partner the one mainstream voice of Czech nationalism, the Civic Democratic Union sealed its electoral fate before the official campaign had even begun[115].

THE POLITICS OF OMISSION

The June 1992 elections[116] created a major barrier against retaining a common state insofar as both election victors appeared to possess greater short-term political incentives to separate the state than to negotiate over the proposals on offer from the other republic. Moreover, since public opinion had consistently rejected a divorce, a referendum was not in the interests of either party, making it impossible to formulate in the Federal Assembly. Even if, by some miracle, referenda had been secured, their likely outcome would have been a demand that the Civic Democratic Party and Movement for a Democratic Slovakia form a federal coalition to secure a common state – in other words, it would probably have changed nothing (although a referendum would at least have made the public's desire for negotiated common statehood explicit, whereas the election left this merely implicit – albeit obviously so). Given the nature of their differences and, in addition, the negative attitudes of CDP supporters toward the MDS and *vice versa*, the damage to the popularity of either party had they compromised would have been considerable, with or without a referendum, and possibly fatal to the party leaders.

An examination of the build-up to the June 1992 elections I think safely confirms the previous chapter's claim that they could not, by any stretch of the imagination, be taken as a meaningful referendum on the future of the state. The political competition had been about state-building – a fight over who would put the results of the revolution at risk, who would take the country into Europe, who would raise living standards. The national issue had been used – and used obscurely – only as a way to underscore those arguments; Mečiar, like Klaus, claimed that their 'federal model' would make these other goals achievable. The Civic Democratic Party and the Movement for a Democratic Slovakia had both always proclaimed themselves 'in spirit' for a common state[117], but the point at which the spirit would be overcome by circumstances was ultimately something the electorate could only guess at since, for each republican electorate, 'circumstances' would be dictated by the votes of the other republic, without chance for redress. Opinion poll data attest to the electorate's exasperation on this point. Feelings behind both Czech and Slovak voting were marked by frustration. By May 1992, 73 per cent of Czech respondents and 86 per cent of Slovaks were either rather or very dissatisfied with the overall political situation[118]. The evidence suggests an elite-level competition hopelessly contemptuous of the public's real aspirations to common statehood.

Those Czechs who valued current economic reforms had little choice but to vote for a party that would turn out to have only the most pragmatic respect for the common state. Those Slovaks who had taken the step of voting for Mečiar, a vote possible under a wide spectrum of motives, were interpreted by the CDP *a priori*, and by the majority of CDP supporters, as having voted for the destruction of Czechoslovakia. This interpretation may have freed Klaus's hand to dissolve the state at his own speed, absolved from responsibility for the separation as the CDP could now claim to be, but with only 16 per cent of the population supporting separation as the best solution in the first week of July 1992[119] the legitimacy of the split was entirely unresolved beyond the borders of Klaus's party.

The limited time available for the development of a truly competitive party system emerges at the root of many of the problems contributing to the division of the state. The two victorious parties outstripped all others in political entrepreneurship to a degree that is hard to imagine in a more developed democratic setting; they were dominated entirely by the charismatic personalities at their head and, in emerging from parliament, rather than from any particular societal constituency, they possessed a quite extraordinary degree of leeway with which to hunt for popular issues. Thus, instead of expressing the interests of some long-established voting base, or of some clear and well-articulated debate, political parties between 1990 and 1992 were defining the electoral agenda *tout court*, and their ability to manipulate electoral preferences was consequently huge. The severe disengagement of public rhetoric from political intention had, of course, been characteristic of the stagnant years of Communism. That new and 'democratic parties' would see themselves as detached elites, with the right to decide crucial public policies behind closed doors once the job of selling the party was over, was a dismaying continuity.

In both republics, party programmes across the board had emerged from the top down – from within parliament – and with little incentive to change the system in which they operated, the Civic Democratic Party and the Movement for a Democratic Slovakia had acted as fledgling catch-all populist parties[120]. Where other parties took the obvious, but high-risk, strategy of co-opting historical, interwar party identities, or acted consistently and according to principle, finding, if they were very lucky, some constituency that agreed with them, Klaus and Mečiar both acted from the very start to maximise their vote; they presented themselves as the only politicians who understood the 'transition' in all its complexity, and they built on the endorsement of voters instead of seeking to encapsulate and articulate anything so narrow as specific interests[121].

In Slovakia, the indeterminacy of the national issue and the existence of the Czech–Slovak relationship as potential scapegoat for many ills had inhibited the development of a realistic party political discourse on internal developments, leaving many problems whose source was entirely internal to Slovakia untreated until the country awoke to find itself independent on 1 January 1993. In the Czech lands the stereotype-ridden images of Slovakia as wishing to pursue a gradualist path, untroubled by the prospect of authoritarianism, and simply as a backward region, cross-referenced into many domestic policy debates. Those Czech politicians – primarily those of the Civic Movement – seeking a more graduated and grass-roots reform, who deplored the draconian lustration law and opposed centralised and strong executive power on principle, found themselves viewed as recidivist – as having entered, in effect, the Slovak political orbit.

It was, as a consequence, possible in the Czech case to offer the electorate the extraordinary (and not explicit) Hobson's choice of most favoured economic/transition path as mutually exclusive of the preferred state arrangement – some form of common state. In both republics (and not simply in Slovakia) the electorate was entirely misled, and most certainly misrepresented, as to the feasibility of the various constitutional choices that were actually available.

The electoral strategies of both the Civic Democratic Party and the Movement for a Democratic Slovakia contributed greatly to the stalling of open party competition. The Civic Democratic Party's demolition of the dissident competition and subsequent re-enactment of the 1990 election in June 1992, this time as the uncontested 'democratic' party, together with Mečiar's well-directed over-promising from the safety of opposition, provoked defensive reactions from other competing parties and successfully blocked debate. To come out against Klaus's position in the Czech Republic had entailed publicly subordinating 'reform' to the common state, according to Klaus, to the point of destroying the potential for reform altogether. Not surprisingly, only the former dissident Civic Movement had dared to even begin such an argument as part of its election campaign; as the party housing the dissident core, the Civic Movement was arguably the most experienced at recognising a false dichotomy – the house style, after all, of Communist Party propaganda. That the Civic Movement's high-principled position was electorally suicidal, on this, as on lustration, was nevertheless clear.

By June 1992 the MDS and CDP seemed elevated beyond reach, a remarkable similarity between them being their optimism. The CDP's rhetoric was not only free-market but essentially about the transition – the market as both 'natural' means and end, all other paths being the 'constructs of ideologists'. Implicitly, the process of liberalising was not only democratic in itself but democratising. The CDP's competitors in the meantime spoke (presciently, as it would turn out) of the necessity of laying firm legal foundations and other preconditions of successful reforms and so, gratingly, echoed the endless 'Jam Tomorrow' promises of the old regime. Mečiar used a similar technique to Klaus. If only implicitly, Mečiar alluded to the release of Slovak national potential as the long-suppressed motive force for transition, most recently suppressed, he argued explicitly, by the policies of the Czech right.

Finally, if one compares the positive rhetoric of Klaus and Mečiar with that of the dissident liberals who faced political extinction after June 1992, a last, crude explanation for the choice of the electorate immediately presents itself. The Slovak liberal elite in particular came too close, too often, to insulting the electorate. One choice phrase amongst Slovak dissidents accounting for fear of reform was 'post-Communist panic'. The 5-per-cent threshold had the effect of eliminating both Czech and Slovak dissident liberals – the moderate centre parties in both republics – thus removing many of the post-November leaders, the core of the pro-federal elite, from both the Federal Assembly and the National Councils[122]. The brief and economically painful experience of liberalism, moreover, was not such as to encourage the Slovak electorate to change its choices.

PROTEST AND SURVIVE

What conclusions can be drawn then as to the two theoretical arguments offered at the opening of this chapter? The 'institutionalist' thesis suggested that the separateness of the party systems in

Czechoslovakia was bound to create electoral incentives for ever-increasing conflict between the two republics, and could thus have contributed to, if not caused, the separation. That the party systems were separate and republic-based is not in doubt. Not only did the civic movements emerge as separate entities, but when, only months later, the Communist Party itself finally federated into Czech and Slovak halves, the party system as a whole was thoroughly and quite manifestly split. At first glance the segregated party system looks to have been deeply destabilising: likely to discourage bargaining and compromise at the elite level and to encourage competitive inter-ethnic relations. Despite the predominance of a republic-centric competition, however, it is evident from opinion poll data that lasting electoral incentives did exist for forging a consensus between the two separate constituencies. The deeper problem of the party system was not therefore the lack of persistent federalist electoral incentives but the ability of political parties to ignore those incentives.

The centrifugal tendencies of separate party competition can only serve as a strong explanation in conditions where representative party competition actually exists. The pre-emptive strategies rather brilliantly employed by both Klaus and Mečiar suggest that applying the argument about separate systems is premature precisely because meaningful party competition had yet to begin. As various sociologists of culture have argued, this shouldn't really surprise us, since it is during the 'unsettled times' that agency or leadership has the greatest impact on social behaviour – and I would add on agenda-setting – while institutional structures exercise their greatest constraint in 'settled times'[123]. The institutionalist emphasis on the hazards of competition in a divided party structure is thus a red herring. In addition, of course, the separateness of the two party systems cannot account for the consequences of the 1992 election, namely that the two victorious parties turned against the known majority preference in their respective republics, indeed against the supposedly pro-common-state 'spirit' of their own electoral campaigns, and proceeded to organise the dissolution of the state.

As I hope is evident by now, the second thesis offered at the start of this chapter far more successfully addresses the failure of the party system to engage with public preferences regarding the state. The party competition argument suggests that in the absence of clearly defined social divisions following the collapse of Communism, the most entrepreneurial parties to emerge from the civic movements sought constituency-maximising strategies (within their own republics), concentrating on reform promises while avoiding over-identification with existing problem areas, the problematic state question being one of them. By sticking to simple claims of 'complete allegiance' to the federal idea when pressed on the issue, political elites preserved an ambiguity as to their real intentions that effectively left them with decisive autonomy.

One of the arguments often invoked to support the legitimacy of the split is that public protest failed to stop it, but against this I would suggest that the party political developments outlined above would have strongly thwarted any impulse to public action in either republic. Political theory would suggest that collective public action – the capacity to get people out on the street – requires the belief that there are actors or institutions out there whose policies or practices can actually be changed, and a shared sense of an available force or constituency that might help to bring that change about[124]. In the Czechoslovak case, however, it was by no means clear whose policies were to be changed, since the electoral system had failed to produce a coherent diversity of opinion over the specific form of the future state. On the contrary, all mainstream political actors claimed to be pro-common-state in principle, and anyway, any threat to Czech–Slovak accord could be attributed to party policies in the 'other' republic. When, and how, in such circumstances would the idea of political protest have seemed worthwhile?

If one consequence of party autonomy from the 'people' in June 1992 was the absence of pressure to respond to existing public preferences on the constitutional issue, then logic suggests that given another full election cycle, Czechoslovakia could not have separated in the manner contrived in 1992. Given another election cycle, or better still two, by which time CDP and MDS corruption and the failures to restructure both the Czech and Slovak economies were beginning to emerge, Czechoslovakia – I would argue – might not have separated at all.

In the light of polls that showed public opinion in both republics strongly split between several state models, and in the light of Klaus's dogmatic depictions of economic reform, democratic reform and common statehood, mainstream political actors clearly felt that other electoral debates in 1992 would prove less risky and more tractable. As far as electoral choices went, it was to other issues that the fate of the state was more or less implicitly tied. While the effective gagging of clear electoral debate thus holds firm as an explanatory component for the separation in general, this argument, like the discussion of nationalism in the previous chapter, cannot explain to what end the victorious politicians adopted, indeed instigated, these gagging practices, other than for the sake of short-term electoral gain. To answer the question of why these leading politicians saw the common state to be worth sacrificing, and how they hoped to perpetrate such an affront to the public will and still hold onto power, we must turn to developments in the law and economics.

4

RENEGOTIATING THE STATE

Czechoslovakia was confronted by a panoply of institutional problems at the beginning of 1990. For the story of the breakup, two in particular were striking: the first was the development of two almost entirely separate party systems located within the two republics; the second was the constitution inherited from Communism, specifically, the inherited right of a minority in parliament to veto any new constitutional legislation. This right of veto in the Federal Assembly was a legacy of the 1968 constitution. The clause was never used under Communism but went live, along with the rest of the inherited legal system, in 1989. Many commentators on the Czechoslovak divorce have seen in this powerful defence against majority rule[1] the key stumbling block in Czech and Slovak constitutional negotiations. Similarly, many of the Czechs involved in the process have blamed a constitutional legacy that could so enable Slovaks, as they saw it, to hold the Czechs to ransom.

The Czech identification of the veto as disastrous is notable of itself since, in theories of conflict resolution at least, the capacity of an ethnic minority to guard against ethnic majority rule – for Czechs outnumbered Slovaks by 2:1 – would be regarded as healthy, indeed as a necessary piece of institutional engineering to pre-empt and prevent ethnic conflict and secessionism. In the last year of Czechoslovakia's existence the eminent political scientist Arend Lijphart duly categorised Czechoslovakia as 'a textbook example of consociational democracy' – in other words, a democracy that had actually institutionalised arrangements for power-sharing and consensus-seeking in order to cope with its ethnic divisions. Lijphart argued that Czechoslovakia's use of proportional representation after 1989 was an integral part of its overall consociational character as a state[2]. 'Proportionality', he maintained, 'is one of the four basic principles of consociationalism, and Czecho-Slovakia [sic] is also thoroughly consociational in the other three respects: (a) it has a power-sharing cabinet including representatives of both the Czech majority and the Slovak minority, as well as a Czech president and a Slovak prime minister; (b) it is a two-unit federal system consisting of autonomous

Czech and Slovak republics with their own governments; and (c) it has a mutual veto in the form of a concurrent majority requirement stipulating that constitutional amendments and major legislation require not only approval by extraordinary majorities but also by such majorities in the upper house among Czech and Slovak representatives voting separately'[3].

The fact that this nominally 'consociational' system was largely inherited from the Communists is a political hiatus Lijphart simply ignored[4], hence the misconception that the existing consociational constitution was new, based on and sustained by a current political consensus. Communist Czechoslovakia, however, had only been as dynamically consociational as it had been democratic. In practice after 1989 the minority right of veto, precisely because it was a Communist legacy and precisely because it had never operated in practice under Communism, was particularly vulnerable to criticism but also to abuse by the new 'democratic' elites. There were no precedents as to how the minority veto should be used, little or no memory among the new parliamentarians of the debates that had produced the veto in the first place[5], and no experience of the antagonism that its use might cause.

It has been argued elsewhere that if power-sharing between elites in divided communities – consociationalism – is to work, it requires three prior conditions. Firstly, rival ethnic units must not be strongly committed to integrating or assimilating the 'other' into their nation or nation-state. Secondly, political leaders must be willing to engage in conflict regulation and to shore up the consociational system with consensus-building actions[6]. Thirdly, the political leaders of the relevant communities must enjoy sufficient political autonomy to manage compromise within their own or constituency territory and to avoid 'outflanking' political manoeuvres from other quarters[7]. This chapter examines whether any one or all three of these conditions were absent in post-1989 Czechoslovakia and investigates the legal deadlocks supposedly central to the separation.

For the divorce to be reasonably attributed to the constitutional inheritance one would expect to find that some or all of the prior conditions for consociationalism outlined above were missing. More concretely one would expect to find that the minority right of veto had been used to block or foil important constitutional reforms and that institutional arrangements more generally had impacted on the various processes of legislation and negotiation, by prohibiting agreement or by adding incentives toward conflict. Evidence against this thesis would be that institutional factors clearly failed to structure those battles which proved pivotal to the conflict.

CONSTITUTIONAL DILEMMAS AFTER 1989

Even Czechoslovakia's most liberal, pro-democratic, legality-obsessed dissident politicians faced real dilemmas of principle when confronted with the question of how to establish a new and democratic constitution. The new parliamentarians faced a triple bind. Firstly, they wanted to avoid a legal 'state of nature'[8], a dangerous legal vacuum where all inherited laws were invalidated as contaminated by Communism. Secondly, they faced the difficulty of employing the morally bankrupted constitutional rules of the past to produce a legitimate constitution for the future. Finally, they discovered a new and persistent dilemma over whether to prioritise immediate political gain over the longer-term and more impartial goals of democratisation. The political scientist Jon Elster captured the frustrations of this risk-laden process with the comment that post-Communist states had no choice but to repeat Baron von Münchhausen's feat of pulling himself out of the swamp by his own hair.

There were other 'transitional' factors encouraging the polarisation of the constitutional debate. It was possible in post-Communist circumstances to argue that a radical transformation to the market also required particularly strong and effective state institutions, if not super-powerful and highly centralised executives[9]. A final difficulty was the elusive nature of constitutionalism *per se*, and to develop this – a culture of abiding by the law – a state requires mechanisms capable of 'ensuring the compliance of the branches of power with fundamental law'[10], the public expectation of the rule of law being among the most important of these mechanisms. Forty years of one-party rule had had, nevertheless, a readily exploitable effect on the electorate's conception of legitimate government. In an April 1992 poll, for example, 69 per cent of Slovak respondents demanded the accountability of members of the government directly to the people and not to parliament. At the same date, moreover, 66 per cent of Czech and 64 per cent of Slovak respondents considered that 'there is too much democracy' in the federation: 'the government and parliament should restore law and order'. The paper presenting these opinions argued that neither republic possessed the consensual preconditions of constitutionalism before 1992[11] – a situation highly conducive to the continuation of strong executive power from the Communist state to the fledgling democracy.

That the transition from Communism would introduce a great temptation to create strong, if not autocratic, executive powers was self-evident to the former liberal dissidents within the Civic Forum (CF) and the Slovak Public Against Violence (PAV/CDU). The liberal dissidents' abiding concern after November 1989 had been that all executive actions henceforth should at least encourage and exemplify the principles of legitimacy and the rule of law. As the monolithic civic movements fractured and the party system developed more fully, however, such principles proved extremely difficult to sustain, most particularly as the reform agenda of the Czech right began to emerge. As Bútora concluded of the dissidents and their fate, '[i]t was not only they and their parties who lost [in June 1992]: a certain political style was also defeated'[12].

AN EARLY CONTROVERSY: THE NAMING OF PARTS . . .

Political rhetoric in the aftermath of the revolution was dominated by the imagery of 'new beginnings', in the economy, civil society, and in Czech–Slovak relations. New constitutions were needed to articulate and to help create a democratic and legitimate state. Political voices in Bratislava stressed that Slovakia had to be made more 'visible' in international relations, not only because of its past humiliations, but because of the competition for foreign economic assistance and investment on which the two republics were now embarked. Visiting the already revitalised Slovak National Council in January 1990, President Havel acknowledged the inadequacy of the Communist federal arrangement and anticipated that major constitutional revisions would follow the first free elections in June. These revisions, he warned, 'must not petrify some outworn structures which exist as the result of an administrative conception of federation. The federation was not understood as a friendly cohabitation of two integral nations in one state but as one of the forms of totalitarian government'[13]. Thus far the redress of Slovak grievances and the creation of a new, non-Communist federal constitution seemed prudently high on the political agenda: the transparent equality of the Czech and Slovak nations was also prominent in Havel's New Year wish list[14].

The event that first signalled that Czechs and Slovaks actually held rather different constitutional expectations occurred only weeks later. On 23 January 1990, President Havel availed himself of his right to propose new legislation and suggested deleting the term 'Socialist' from the state name – the Czechoslovak Socialist Republic[15]. The ensuing disagreement over renaming the state lasted almost four months. The discussion had soon engaged with two alternatives: the original name, 'Czechoslovakia', or a hyphenated version of the same, 'Czecho-Slovakia', which according to the Slovak National Council implied greater parity. Havel's proposed 'Czechoslovak Republic' prompted protests in Bratislava and the objection that the name implied the return of the state to the unitary character of the First Republic. The Slovak National Council's approval of 'Czecho-Slovakia' on the other hand dismayed Czechs who recollected the miserable connection of the same name between post-Munich (1938) Czech territory and collaborationist Slovakia. The rejection of the Slovak proposal and continuing support for Havel's 'Czechoslovak Republic' among Czech deputies prompted a demonstration of an estimated 20,000 people in Bratislava, where a petition was handed to the Council chairman demanding talks on the full recognition of Slovak sovereignty and independence[16].

The 'hyphen-war' appeared to unlock a full Pandora's box of latent grievances and new anxieties. It also revealed how closed the constitutional debate had been for over twenty years; each side greeted the suggestions of the other with utter astonishment. As the Slovak philosopher and dissident Miroslav Kusý[17] pointed out in a Czech paper, 'We have reached the point where we do not even know how to describe this hyphen that the president is slipping into the name of our country. The Slovaks say that it unites, and the Czechs say that it divides'[18]. The interim solution was an unhappy compromise in which Slovakia could use the hyphen internally, while Czech and federal authorities would adopt the unhyphenated spelling[19].

Further negotiations between the republic-level governments at Lnáře on 11 April eventually produced lasting agreement on the name 'Czech and Slovak Federative Republic' (CSFR). The Lnare meeting also agreed that many of the national disputes had their roots in the bureaucratic command system of the past, and that the new federal constitution should 'emerge' from the Czech and Slovak constitutions – an apparent consensus at the republican level that would soon run headlong into federal opposition. Reviewing the meeting, Slovak premier Milan Čič called for an end to the ambiguity surrounding Slovakia's constitutional status and insisted that the decision represented 'a fundamental starting point; we want the federation to be understood as a union of two nations on the principle of their independence and original sovereignty'[20]. For Slovak politicians, evidently, the 'hyphen-war' represented a signal moment wherein the rules of the future constitutional game would be set. In the Czech Republic, however, the broader implications of the debate and the extent to which it indicated deep Slovak anxieties over constitutional equality were clearly unrecognised. The lengthy quarrel had struck Czech press opinion as signifying that Slovak deputies were willing to waste parliamentary time on purely symbolic wars[21] – 'sterile linguistic disputes', according to *Lidové noviny*, whose editor insisted he would use the term Czechoslovak Republic notwithstanding[22].

JUNE–DECEMBER 1990: POWER-SHARING TALKS

The task of constitutional renegotiation began in earnest after the June 1990 elections[23] when the new federal government, composed of the Slovak Public Against Violence, the Czech Civic Forum and the Christian Democratic Movement (Slovak), announced that new constitutions would be drafted for both republics and for the federation before the next election – already fixed for June 1992. The basic mechanics of constitutional redesign looked problematic, however. Each of the three governments had an interest in maximising or at least preserving its own power, and yet the three governments were to undertake constitutional drafting and ratification with no independent arbitrating force between them; the two-year deadline exerted a further pressure upon debate.

To make matters worse, in these early, post-revolutionary months in particular, both National Councils, Czech and Slovak alike, sought an ostentatious decentralisation from federal authority, identified as it was with the centralising instincts of the Communist Party. The post-election programme of the Czech National Council was typical in its impulse to redraw the federal contract with free and 'clean' hands: it declared boldly that 'the federation will have such authority as granted to it by the republics . . . after mutual agreement'[24]. Similar assertions from the Slovak negotiators would subsequently be labelled in the Czech press as secessionist.

In 1990 the only remotely impartial mediating mechanism available to the constitution-building process was the office of the federal presidency: Václav Havel, and his advisers. Not until February 1991 was a constitutional court established, and this avoided political entanglement altogether before being bogged down by its own jurisdictional controversies. As we shall see, moreover, even if the court had been less passive it would have been confronted, as was Havel, by the seemingly endless capacity of the negotiating political parties to generate intractable terminological disputes.

The first constitutional talks were held at a two-day meeting at Trenčianské Teplice beginning on 8 August 1990. The object of these talks was to negotiate a new constitutional law on the division of powers between the federation and the republics pending the drafting of the new constitutions as such. At Trenčianské Teplice the Slovak premier Vladimír Mečiar presented to 'astonished federal government representatives' a plan for the transfer of power from the federation to the republics[25]. According to Václav Žák – a Civic Forum deputy of the Czech National Council at the time – Mečiar proposed 'a really fundamental change to the country's constitution!', derived from the so-called 'dual model' set down in the Public Against Violence election manifesto, *Chance for Slovakia*. In this model the integration of two national states represented the basic idea of the federation; federal powers were to be understood as delegated from essentially sovereign republican powers.

From a historical perspective Mečiar's agenda only reiterated the confederalist founding principles set down in the ill-fated 'Prague Spring' constitutional amendment 143/1968, swept aside by the Soviet-imposed amendment of 1970. This had likewise stated that the relationship between federation and republics was based on cooperation rather than subordination and that this working equality was based upon the recognition of the essential, as it were the 'original', sovereignty of the two republics – a confederalist founding principle. The Slovak proposals in August 1990, that the federation keep defence, currency, foreign policy, the legislative framework and overall economic decision-making power (basic taxation), and that the republics should obtain greater visibility in international-legal jurisdiction, in reality did not amount to a radical departure from the discussions of the 1960s[26]. The Slovak proposals nonetheless struck Czech federal delegates as an assault upon the federal state *per se*.

In the immediate aftermath of the talks the Czech political right responded to Mečiar's proposal with the objection that 'it is only possible to speak of the federative nature of the state if the authority of both national republics is based on the authority of the federation'[27] – as if this was a watertight rejection in legal terms. The political reasons for this rejection were already clear and would not change: the prospect of a renegotiation of power in which the federal authority could make no *prior* claim as the legitimate centre *vis-à-vis* the two sovereign nations – the two original 'contractees' – was irreconcilable with the Czech right's vision of a rapid reform process, under inviolable federal control.

What Mečiar's proposals revealed was that the Czech federal right, still largely subsumed for the moment within the monolithic Civic Forum, adhered not simply to the American federalist vision that the centre must be sovereign in its own jurisdictions – i.e. *in its sphere* – but to a classic view of indivisible nation-state sovereignty, a conceptualisation normally associated not with federal but with unitary states[28]. According to this Czech view, federal authority was prior and indivisibly sovereign not only externally, in the eyes of international law, *but internally, vis-à-vis* the republics. Following the federation's formation, as it were, after the contractual fact (1968) the rediffusion of power to the republics according to this logic was a matter of grace and not of right. This assumption of ultimate, in essence, complete federal sovereignty, however, simply contradicted the first principle of democratic federations, namely that they are based upon the maintenance of divided, shared sovereignty between central and provincial government. Not surprisingly, many Czech and Slovak politicians had assumed that the exact nature of that division was something to be renegotiated and recontracted – but not abandoned – following the collapse of the centralised Communist state.

The only consensus available at Trenčianské Teplice was that negotiations had to continue since deputies from the federal government refused to sign any communiqué. Continuation was proposed in the form of three government commissions empowered to draft principles on jurisdictional problems – by the end of the month. In the meantime, all parties publicly agreed to a mystifying 'strong republics, strong federation principle'[29]. The respective reports to parliament, however, revealed the deeper clash of concepts.

Addressing the Federal Assembly, deputy premier Pavel Rychetský (of the Czech Civic Forum) described the conclusions of the talks as 'both unexpected and problematic'. Slovakia's 'surprisingly' unequivocal proposals had included the devolution of powers over transportation, power generation, telecommunications and foreign trade, and the Slovak government had already established its own Ministry of International Relations in breach of existing federal sovereignty[30]. These Slovak steps, supported by separatists[31], he maintained, drove only to one end: serious intervention in the integrity of the state which would have to be withstood. The economic exigencies facing the country as a whole, Rychetský argued, made this essential[32]. Czech premier and former dissident Petr Pithart (also of the Civic Forum) was more sympathetic to Slovak aspirations. He called the talks constructive and insisted – it is striking that he felt it necessary to point this out – that there was nothing inherently bad in Slovakia holding the initiative[33]. Nonetheless, he assured the Czech parliament that the meeting was purely consultative, a follow-up to Lnáře[34].

In both the Czech and federal parliament the talks were evidently playing a key role in the fight for the political soul of the Civic Forum. Crucially, the right wing's preoccupation with the uniformity of economic reform across the republics could produce an attractive constitutional corollary for the Czech majority nation; a refusal to redefine the federation by its national characteristics, coupled with the assertion of indissoluble federal sovereignty, offered the retrenchment of Czech political and financial power: it amounted in fact to a discreet reassertion of majority rule under the guise of centralist federalism[35]. Klaus's election to the chair of the Civic Forum in October 1990 marked the effective verdict, a decisive shift rightward in the Civic Forum[36].

Mečiar, meanwhile, was buoyed by the commotion: 'the Slovak government went to Teplice with a comprehensive concept, the Czech government with a partial concept and the Federal government with almost no concept at all. From Teplice all left with the Slovak government concept'. Though the talks had achieved little concretely, he pronounced, 'we withstand the resistance of the Federal apparatus, which will lose jobs; of Czechoslovakists who see it as an imperilling of the state's integrity; and of separatists who consider it as not enough'. 'Nothing else than Federation is feasible', he insisted, though his proposals had apparently revealed a definitional conflict of remarkable and, as it were, 'instantaneous' depth. In Slovakia the talks at Trenčianské Teplice distinguished Mečiar as a stronger Slovak champion than the more nationalist-sounding Christian Democratic Movement, which had divided internally on the talks, and at Mečiar's insistence Čarnogurský was forced to choose between observance of the Slovak government resolution – for an 'authentic federation' – and resignation from the coalition. The Christian Democratic Movement eventually withdrew from these power-sharing talks and stayed in the government[37].

It was left to Havel to coordinate some preliminary closure to this initial division of competences between the republics and the federal centre. Meetings duly followed at Piešťany on 11 September (after which Havel criticised the commissions for producing over-detailed drafts), in Prague on 23 October and in Slavkov on 28 October. At these last talks, following nationalist agitation at the Slovak language law debate in Bratislava, Federal Prime Minister Marián Čalfa (of the Slovak Public Against Violence) and republican premiers Pithart and Mečiar together adopted a declaration condemning all attempts to destabilise Czechoslovakia, and pledged to continue the federation[38]. On 5 November, the three met again in Prague and declared that they had resolved most of the issues outstanding from the August talks. They had agreed to maintain the federal government's right to make decisions on economic strategy, defence, foreign policy, banking and federal taxes, and this agreement was submitted, as a draft constitutional amendment, to the three governments for approval. The Slovak and Czech republican governments gave their approval on 6 and 7 November respectively. The federal government agreed 'only in principle', objecting that the draft was too decentralising.

Further meetings, described by participants as 'emergency negotiations', were held in Modra on 10 and 11 November, and in Prague on 13 November. Here it was agreed that defence, foreign affairs, foreign trade, the central bank, taxation and customs and price reforms would remain solely under federal authority. The federal government would establish its budget through direct federal taxation in both republics, and the CSFR economy was defined as based on an internal single market and the free movement of labour, goods and money. The republics would establish their own budgets through a system of local taxation. It was also agreed that all assets originating in the republics, not including natural resources (which would be treated separately in the new constitution), would remain their sole property and would not be transferred to or redistributed by federal authorities. As for international affairs, the *republics* would be permitted to conclude international treaties having gained the permission of the central government. Unilaterally, they could also undertake agreements in specified fields with other units of other federal states. While every clause remained controversial, the last two in particular exposed how the rapid bartering behind the Competences Bill had produced jurisdictional principles on the status of the 'nation' of such incoherence as to make the law inherently unstable[39]. The instability of this law was indeed a necessary characteristic for many deputies in the Federal Assembly, who supported it only very reluctantly[40].

Though the whole package was set to be an interim document and would therefore be entirely superseded by new constitutions, it was still strongly, if not flamboyantly, resisted by the federal Czech right[41]. Federal Economy Minister Vladimír Dlouhý went on the offensive and appeared on state television denouncing Mečiar as a populist[42]. 'The federal government', he complained, 'is under constant pressure to retreat from reasonable principles'[43]. Supported by Klaus, Dlouhý's accusations managed to alienate even the Slovak right wing, a considerable achievement given that many of the former-dissident members of the Public Against Violence were themselves profoundly alarmed by Mečiar's manipulation of nationalist sentiment.

The role of peacemaker again fell to Havel. Sensing an imminent second failure of the Competences Bill he alerted the Federal Assembly to the potential crisis on 10 December[44]. 'The Slovak premier himself', Havel announced, had 'made it quite clear that, if you fail to approve the law in the wording submitted by the Slovak National Council, the latter might declare the pre-eminence of its laws over the laws of the Federal Assembly'[45]. In this way Havel cast Mečiar as the devious state-wrecker, despite the fact that the federal right's assertion of unitary state rights was something no Slovak politician could accept, implying as it did a reversion to Czech majority rule. To ward off such an eventuality Havel proposed that the Assembly pass as soon as possible two proposals aimed at tackling future deadlocks. The first was to form the constitutional court, the second, to provide a law on public referenda. Havel also asked for an extension of his presidential powers. The first two suggestions were greeted warmly, the last, less so[46]. The Federal Assembly finally accepted the Power-Sharing Bill, an antagonistic proposition though it was, on 12 December 1990.

NEW CONSTITUTIONS

Despite the fact that this conflict over power-sharing arrangements had exposed fundamental definitional disagreement between federal and republican players, the presidia of the National Councils had begun to meet at the end of September 1990 to discuss in earnest the creation of new constitutions. Their negotiated agreement was that the federal constitution would be drafted by a commission of ten deputies from each National Council and fourteen deputies from the Federal Assembly[47]. There was, however, no consensus on the most basic issues: the nature of federal power; the number of chambers; the continuation of the minority veto – the existing 'consociational' defence against majority rule in the federal parliament; the need to ratify constitutional changes in the National Councils; the relationship between the federal constitution and some form of instrument to signify a 'fresh start' – agreed as necessary on both sides[48]. Conflicts over the order in which the constitutions might be passed looked every bit as intractable as conflicts over the basic division of authority. Both required consensus on the rights due the present, let alone the future federal centre, an issue around which the republic-centric political party systems themselves were clearly still forming.

When the thirty-four selected deputies proved incapable of allocating a coherent mission to constitutional lawyers, Havel ordered a draft which might be presented to the commissions for discussion. In his next New Year address he appealed for the approval of three new constitutions 'by the end of the year at the latest' to be the basic task of 1991[49]. The continuing failure to proceed with drafting nonetheless provoked the Federal Assembly into taking its own initiative, changing the constitution piecemeal[50], most significantly by producing a Bill of Fundamental Rights and Liberties (emerging from National

Council drafts), passed on 9 January 1991 – formally providing the CSFR with at least a liberal code of civil rights[51]. Even so, the preamble to the Bill entertained 'the right of the Czech and Slovak nations to self-determination'. As soon as Havel, intervening again, convened party talks in February 1991 in an attempt to kick-start the constitutional process[52], the republics duly cited their rights in their claims against 'innate', i.e. inherently sovereign, federal powers.

The issue that can at least be identified as having 'played the lead' in undermining the next series of party meetings, nicknamed Havel's 'touring castles and palaces', was that of a state treaty – the symbolic 'fresh start', suggested by the Christian Democratic Movement chairman Ján Čarnogurský as a precursor to any new constitution. When he suggested the idea to the president in January 1991 Havel commented that it looked more like a confederal than a federal suggestion[53]. Contentious distinctions between federal and confederal principles, a rerun under different vocabulary of the August 1990 dispute concerning prior federal versus innate republican rights, immediately stalemated this next round of talks, intended though they were to be less formal, more flexible pre-negotiations.

THE 'VIKÁRKA' RESTAURANT MEETINGS

Havel's first meeting at 'Vikárka' foundered on its own chaotic informality, leaving the participating government parties determined to formulate their positions in writing[54]. The tensions between the centre and right within the Czech Civic Forum were, in the meantime, institutionalised, as the movement declared its intention to split into two groups, Klaus-ite right and Dienstbier-ite liberal centre/left – the future Civic Democratic Party (CDP) and Civic Movement (CM) respectively.

The next Vikárka meeting ran more decisively into the obstacle presented by the state treaty concept. Ján Čarnogurský had insisted that a treaty would represent merely another incarnation of the preamble to the new (and indeed the old, 1968) federal law. The right wing of the Civic Forum and the Public Against Violence now together objected that a state treaty formulated between the two 'sovereign' National Councils actually necessitated the prior dissolution of the federal state – implying as it did the removal (albeit temporary) of federal sovereignty. A third round of talks at Vikárka (4 March 1991) proved a repeat of the second. Though all participants clearly perceived the public pressure to find some compromise, the subsequent joint statement attempted in vain to portray progress.

It was declared that 'Czechoslovakia will be a federal state consisting of two sovereign and equal republics, linked voluntarily and at the free will of their citizens', that 'the two National Councils will approve the declaration on cohabitation on the eve of the approval of the three new constitutions' and that 'the National Councils will approve the respective national constitutions and the Federal Assembly will approve the Federal constitution. This will happen simultaneously'. It was noted separately, but all-importantly, that while the Christian Democratic Movement agreed that Czechoslovakia would be a federal state, it wished to signal its insistence on the conclusion of a treaty with the proviso that the treaty would be a legal document and not just a political declaration[55]. Such an explicit recontracting, with its demonstration through reiteration of republican sovereignty, remained entirely unacceptable to the Czech right.

THE SLOVAK POLITICAL SCENE FRAGMENTS, AND THE CZECHS EXPECT THE WORST . . .

On 5 March 1991, the next development in party politics came in Slovakia, where Mečiar's faction of the Public Against Violence walked out of the Slovak National Council declaring they would form their own platform of the Public Against Violence/Movement for a Democratic Slovakia (MDS). This event, like the split of the Forum in the Czech Republic, institutionalised the diverging constitutional attitudes of the Slovak civic movement into two distinct streams: the rightist, consensus-seeking view, favouring greater republican equality but conceding a strong centre, led by the liberal Fedor Gál, and a more indeterminate federalist/confederalist view represented by Mečiar. The splitting of the PAV also signalled the end to a stable government majority in the Slovak section of the House of the Nations within the Federal Assembly, essential for passing constitutional legislation.

Havel's reaction was to warn of imminent disaster: the combination of demonstrations, 'the constitutional proposals of the Slovak National Party and *Matica Slovenská*, the approaching anniversary of the Slovak state on 14 March and at the same time the draft declaration on sovereignty [proposed by the Slovak National Party and later rejected in the Slovak National Council]' all added up to 'a very disturbing situation'[56]. More melodramatically still, Havel visited army officers in Mečiar's home town of Trenčin and warned – to their evident bemusement – that 'Our young democracy is experiencing very dramatic movements today . . . I would like to emphasise that our army must not intervene or enter into this complex process in any circumstances or in any way. Nobody should cite such an option as a threat or speculate about it [*sic*] . . . I would like to point out in this place that the Czechoslovak Army will perform any tasks only as a united army'[57]. At this delicate stage, however, with positions forming around the state treaty idea, Havel's grim recitation of Slovak evils was really quite spectacularly unhelpful; in Slovakia he could be interpreted as weirdly deluded or, more generously, as ill-advised, but either way these statements were all too evocative of what could be seen as 'typical' Prague prejudices. A Czech presidential recounting of putative Slovak nationalist sins could only perplex the large majority of Slovaks, given their clear preference for some form of common statehood, and the increasingly 'fringe' political status of Slovakia's separatists.

When finally submitted to the constitutional commission, the adjustments in Havel's draft constitution were derived, not from Mečiar's popular faction, but from Gál's now considerably weakened wing of the Public Against Violence[58]. Mečiar's exit from the PAV was evidently misread in Prague, if only briefly, as having strengthened the liberal rump of the PAV, an interpretation which prompted the most outspoken criticism of Čarnogurský's treaty proposals yet from Dagmar Burešová, Chairwoman of the Czech National Council, and even from Petr Pithart, who declared it a 'legal nonsense'[59]. František Mikloško (Public Against Violence), Vladimír Mečiar and Ján Čarnogurský met Havel at Lány on 17 April in order to try and clarify the Slovak position, but, as Mečiar rightly pointed out, the problem was not so much the obscurity of Slovak desires but an all too apparent disagreement between the Slovak notions of federal rights and those acceptable to the Czech side.

When the Public Against Violence ousted Mečiar as Slovak premier on 23 April, the Czech misinterpretation of Slovak events became more pronounced still. Pithart suggested that 'if the non-functioning of the Slovak economy is the reason for this dramatic change in the Slovak government, then this change is simultaneously a promise for the seeking of one economy, one reform, and that we shall tackle the problem of the state arrangement'[60]. The 'non-functioning of the Slovak economy' was indeed one of the main political forces separating the Public Against Violence, but it was the liberal right and not Mečiar's faction which was held to account for this failure. Moreover, the Christian Democratic Movement's position in the coalition had been strengthened and the populist Mečiar was now completely free to engage in both the constitutional and the economic debate as an opposition member, indeed, as the leading critic of the Slovak government's performance. Following Mečiar's ouster, the Movement for a Democratic Slovakia rallied in opposition with the Slovak National Party (SNP) and the Party of the Democratic Left (PDL) and gathered a growing constituency behind its own eclectic set of arguments for a federation built 'from below'.

The timing of these political developments could not have been worse for the negotiation process. Constitutional talks thus far had achieved only a well publicised deadlock over a treaty of undecided status to introduce constitutions whose actual content had yet to be decided or drafted. A permanent division within what remained of the Slovak governing coalition seemed certain when the Christian Democratic Movement's leader, Ján Čarnogurský, as the new Slovak premier, confirmed that he favoured an independent Slovak state – 'eventually'[61]. His pronouncement that Slovakia should remain part of Czechoslovakia until it joined the EC[62] assisted only in persuading Slovak voters that, of the two would-be champions of Slovakia, Mečiar was the political realist.

LÁNY

At more constitutional talks in Lány, in May 1991, the thirty assembled representatives of all three legislative bodies, governments, government parties and legislative experts seemed to agree that some form of republican-level accord (i.e. not quite a state treaty) on the principles of the new constitutional arrangement would be recommended to their respective parties. Experts would be entrusted to work on the text on the basis of existing proposals. Burešová concluded that both sides had made concessions[63] and indeed they had, but only through the omission of all substantive issues from the talks, postponed, yet again, for future discussion. The Slovak side by now moreover aspired to an inner-state agreement with certain state law characteristics, and this remained in dispute, as did the nature of the authority of the National Councils in signing the document.

Cross-party talks on the state treaty held at Budmerice, attended for the first time by opposition parties, demolished the minimalist consensus of Lány and threatened to lead to a postponement of the upcoming elections. The respective government leaders together emphasised the importance of forming a 'well-functioning state'; they were apparently taken aback by the destructive impact of integrating opposition views[64]. It was at this choice moment that Mečiar intervened with the insistence that the state treaty should be concluded at an international state level. His suggestion, a logical extension of

Čarnogurský's aspirations and a blatant attempt to draw the fire back to the Christian Democratic Movement, succeeded insofar as it provided the Czech right with justification for publicly despairing of the direction the entire talks process had taken since February 1991. Václav Klaus determined to reassert the basic principles of a 'functioning federation' at the imminent cross-party talks in Kroměříž[65].

KROMĚŘÍŽ

With constitutional talks on the brink of collapse, the meeting at Kroměříž seemed to achieve a remarkable breakthrough. A nineteen-point questionnaire prepared by Havel was instrumental in drawing the talks toward consensus, and it was agreed that the National Councils would prepare a treaty on the principles of the future state arrangement. This would formulate the shape of the state, the scope of federal responsibilities, and other basic elements of the constitution. The treaty would then be presented to the Federal Assembly, which would approve beforehand any constitutional law on the approval of constitutions or anything similar. A particular point of breakthrough for the Slovaks was that the federal constitution would be subject to ratification by the National Councils – a one-off event designed solely for the adoption of the new constitution, after which federal decision-making would revert to 'another way'.

In this way, it seemed, the much disputed legal continuity of the CSFR could be maintained and a new federation – subject to the sovereign decision of the National Councils – built on the ground of the existing federation[66]. Under pressure from Klaus, however, it was also agreed that future debates on the constitution would be transferred from extra-parliamentary talks to the parliaments[67], though Klaus was surely aware that neither the parliaments nor their commissions could prove more successful in the absence of a pre-negotiated consensus. As Klaus, of all people, would surely have appreciated, talks within the public chambers of parliament were bound to be even more bedevilled by party political posturing than they had been behind closed doors.

Presenting a draft state treaty to the Slovak National Council on 1 July, Jozef Kučerák, Gál's successor as the Public Against Violence chairman, concluded that 'we have two options – federation or divorce. Musing about confederation or union means disintegration of the common state'[68]. Čarnogurský, however, proved unable to marshal the votes of the nationalists within the Christian Democratic Movement, who joined with the opposition in rejecting the Kroměříž line.

Following the collapse of Kroměříž, the now heavily divided Slovak National Council, which had already formed its commission for the preparation of its new constitution, decided only to prepare two parallel constitutions: one with all the responsibilities of a sovereign state, the second bound by existing legal competences. Contingency planning seemed to have become the only clear order of the day.

In these circumstances it was relatively straightforward for Mečiar to blur constitutional issues still further. Following a Civic Movement 'goodwill visit' (by Dienstbier, Rychetský, Pithart and Burešová) Mečiar found it necessary to 'clarify' his non-separatist position by declaring the Movement for a Democratic Slovakia's opposition to any declaration of sovereignty by the Slovak National Council. Such a step, he said, could have no meaning in the process of the emancipation of Slovakia, which needed, above all, a state treaty with the Czech Republic and its own constitution. At the same time, however, he pointed out that 'sovereignty' should be achieved now and that speaking about it as a thing for the future was dangerous[69] – a phenomenal piece of hedging even by Meciar's standards.

GRIDLOCK

At a joint meeting of the two National Council presidia in Bratislava, the two sides reiterated the points of agreement and disagreement already set out at Kroměříž. Once again they declared that the process of preparing constitutions would be based on maintaining the continuity of the CSFR and on constitutional methods. The Slovak side pointed out that they wished to pursue the principle of sovereignty for the Slovak Republic in the preparation of the Slovak constitution, and the two presidia 'exchanged opinions' on the division of competences. Though they agreed that a common state required a common economic policy, its attributes remained to be specified. To this end they agreed to form commissions comprising experts and representatives of all three governments to prepare proposals on the division of competences – again. These conclusions were once more rejected by the Movement for a Democratic Slovakia and Slovak National Party[70].

Meeting with Ján Čarnogurský, Václav Klaus argued that in the light of the clear stalemate future decisions should be postponed until after the June 1992 elections[71]. A few weeks later, Čarnogurský effectively guaranteed this outcome by proposing to Federal Foreign Minister Dienstbier that the provision on the legal continuity of the Czechoslovak state be deleted from the preamble of the Czechoslovak–German treaty currently under preparation – the continuity guaranteed by numerous international treaties establishing the nullity of the 1938 Munich diktat. Not only did the request horrify Czechs but it drove yet another wedge between the Christian Democratic Movement and its coalition partners, the Public Against Violence/Civic Democratic Union, who objected that only other fascist states had ever recognised the clerico-fascist Slovak state – a situation they hardly wished to alter now[72]. In the first Federal Assembly session of autumn 1991, Havel warned deputies that they faced the choice of a rapid construction of a joint state or dissolution, admitting afterwards that he personally favoured a referendum to decide the issue[73].

From November 1991, the constitutional process entered a period of both intensification and further disintegration as parties set out their positions for the June 1992 election. For Czechs, the Christian Democratic Movement pushed itself further beyond the pale by claiming, quite incidentally – and more than a little strangely – that its attitudes and those of the Communist Party of Bohemia and Moravia were rather close on many questions, not least in their rejection of liberalism and their criticism of the pace of economic reform[74]. Havel resorted to inviting leading government representatives to the 'v peklo' ('In Hell') pub, in a desperate attempt to thrash out a plan for completing negotiations. Havel himself presented a draft treaty, and while his guests agreed to use it as the basis of future talks, and even seemed closer on the substantive division of competences, they remained stuck over the question, yet again, of the shape, legal character and meaning of the state treaty to be concluded between the two republics[75] – sadly for the cartoonists, the 'constitution made in hell' was not to be. Just over a week later, the Federal Assembly failed to agree on the questions that might be put to the citizenry in the event of a deadlock-resolving referendum – a debate broadcast live on state television[76].

On 14 November 1991, the federal government – which for too long, according to its representatives, had been given the most minimal political 'weight' in the constitutional talks – re-entered the fray in some style. It issued a statement on the talks that read: 'The federal government refuses further to sanction the perpetuation of the present state of affairs because it has extraordinarily unfavourable repercussions on economic development, the social situation, relations among people, and the international standing of Czechoslovakia'. The federal government had decided, the statement continued:

- to apply all of its power to halting the destruction of legal and institutional prerequisites of the functioning of the common state;
- consistently to promote the further transformation of society and tackle pressing economic and social problems;

- to prepare draft principles of the new constitutional arrangement in the field of legislative and executive power, using the results of all negotiations so far, and submit it to parliaments;
- to request that all three parliaments discuss those principles as soon as possible in the presence of members of the governments[77].

These requirements were designed not only to force the issue of the common state but also to return the debate, in a public and assertive way, to the argument for reconstructing the state from the top down (i.e. with the sovereign federation delegating new rights to the republics) – as formerly expressed in Premier Čalfa's speech just before the December 1990 vote on power-sharing (see note 39).

HAVEL'S LAST STAND

Despairing of the chances for agreement before full-scale campaigning began for the 1992 election Havel made his last major intervention, declaring on state television his intention to submit five new laws to the Federal Assembly. Resurrecting the role which he had fulfilled to such great effect in November 1989, Havel appealed directly to the people to 'express more loudly than hitherto your longing to live soon in a wisely and justly organised, prospering state, and thus to help our hostile parliaments find a way from the blind alley in which they find themselves'. His first proposal was an amendment to the law enabling the President to initiate referenda unilaterally, if unopposed by the Federal Assembly and supported by 20 per cent of the voters in one republic. His second was an amendment to the constitutional law which would allow the new federal constitution to come into force after ratification by the National Councils. The third proposal concerned the conditions of the disbandment of the Federal Assembly and the declaration of new elections. This would give the President the right to issue laws, after the disbandment of the Assembly, through a form of decree, with the proviso that these would be subject to additional approval by the newly elected parliament. The remaining bills concerned a constitutional law on the new structure of the Assembly and an adjustment to the electoral law[78].

Havel's speech provoked several days of demonstrations of up to 40,000 people in Prague's Wenceslas Square, and brought out in favour of the changes the students – ever faithful to Havel – the anti-Communist Club of Committed Non-Party Members, the Civic Movement, Czechoslovak Social Democracy and the People's Party. Meanwhile the Czech right-wing Civic Democratic Alliance and

Klaus's Civic Democratic Party, though internally split at first, moved within a week into a position of discreet opposition. In Slovakia the death-knell of the proposals' legislative chances was rung by a demagogic Movement for a Democratic Slovakia statement accusing Havel of personal ambition and of only deepening the crisis. After prolonged meetings with the President, Klaus's Civic Democratic Party expressed concern that Havel's efforts had been misunderstood by some as an appeal to civil disobedience. Press commentary foresaw that the proposals would go the same way as the referendum proposals, voted down in the previous week[79].

On 19 November members of the now deeply unpopular rightist Slovak government[80], on the initiative of the Public Against Violence/Civic Democratic Union, the Democratic Party (DP) and the Hungarian Independent Initiative, issued a statement regretting the turn taken by constitutional negotiations. Following Klaus, the statement lamented that the dispute had spilled over into economic management: 'the unsolved questions are concentrated in the budget preparation to such an extent as to make its preparation impossible. In this situation the preparation of state budgets for 1992 can trigger the split of the federal state rather than be an integrating factor', it argued. Consequently, it concluded, 'the Slovak government is of the opinion that the state treaty must not become an extra-constitutional instrument. It rejects any untested procedures and experiments and supports only tested constitutional steps and mechanisms'. The statement was in effect a declaration of loyalty to the existing federal state in Klausite terms, over the heads of their own coalition partners, the Christian Democratic Movement. Not surprisingly, Čarnogurský opposed it as unnecessary and prejudicial to further talks[81].

Amidst this discussion of Havel's legislative proposals it emerged, in the eyes of many Czechs like the visitation of a curse, that the Christian Democratic Movement intended to incorporate the republican state treaty idea into Havel's parliamentary bills. The treaty, Čarnogurský argued, should be concluded first and then the constitution should be approved by the Federal Assembly and later ratified by the National Councils. The problem which the presidia of the National Councils had completely failed to solve thus entered the Federal parliament, even though the Christian Democratic Movement was fully aware that the Czech and Slovak right-wing clubs within the Assembly opposed the treaty in principle[82]. The Federal Assembly eventually voted to postpone the debate on Havel's initiatives until the January 1992 session. By December 1991 only Slovakia had submitted its constitutional proposals, despite Havel's warnings that the process was nearing collapse.

On 21 January 1992, the Slovak section of the House of the Nations in the Federal Assembly threw out the President's proposed amendment on referenda as well as his bill on the method of approving the new Czechoslovak constitution – designed as deadlock-breaking measures[83]. The next day the opposition MDS's Milan Kňažko suggested that 'the treaty between the Czech Republic and Slovakia could replace the Federal constitution', i.e. entirely – a comment timed apparently for the sole purpose of irritating Czech deputies before the Federal vote on the remainder of Havel's proposals[84]. The Assembly meanwhile postponed future votes until February on the basis that this might provide a last window in which the National Councils could reach agreement. The Assembly's statement to the National Councils read 'by interrupting the debate on constitutional changes, the Federal Assembly wants to meet the National Councils in their co-responsibility for the creation of the new constitutional arrangement'[85]. On 28 January the Assembly nevertheless rejected Havel's proposal permitting presidential rule by decree. By February 1992 electoral preoccupations dominated the political scene overwhelmingly, calming the constitutional crisis only by signalling the impotence of further talks. The loss of momentum in the general debate influenced the cool response to talks now held at Mílovy, which months earlier might have represented a real advance.

At Mílovy it was agreed, thanks to a last-minute concession on the Slovak side, that the treaty could be based on the present constitution and could have the form of a constitutional initiative addressed to the Federal Assembly. It was the nationalist faction of the Christian Democratic Movement (the future Slovak Christian Democratic Movement), however, that again chose to vote against the Mílovy text with the Slovak National Party and the Movement for a Democratic Slovakia – two groups which evidently wished to have their hands free for a variety of constitutional promises in the upcoming electoral campaign. This vote closed all coordinated constitutional episodes, a process formally adjourned with some despair by the respective chairs of the National Councils on 11 March. The Slovak National Council chair, František Mikloško, blamed breakdown on the Czech failure to accept the principle of the treaty, whilst Dagmar Burešová of the Czech National Council blamed the Slovak National Council presidium[86]. With this bitter conclusion the issue was left to the mercy of the 1992 electoral campaign, which, as we have already seen[87], proceeded both to distort and to bypass the substantive issues of conflict even more thoroughly than had the actual negotiation process itself.

WHEN POLITICS IS *NOT* 'THE ART OF THE POSSIBLE'

'Forms are likely to be accorded special normative (legalistic) status if a society has experienced a deep break-down in conventional order ... That is, forms matter to the extent that they are needed as surrogates for norms in the conduct of social life'.

Harry Eckstein[88]

It has been argued in several quarters that the rigidity of the legal framework inherited in 1989 aggravated in a systematic way the problem of replacing constitutional legislation[89]. The existence of a minority veto for constitutional legislation is identified in particular as 'the single most important institutional roadblock preventing law-makers in Czechoslovakia from proceeding with constitutional reform'[90].

Though expressing a basic truth of the constitutional crisis, such formal accounts of the vulnerability of constitutional legislation are inadequate on two counts. Firstly, they too baldly identify the Slovaks as the obstructive side in the constitutional process – since it was the oppositionist Slovak bloc that vetoed (among others) Havel's deadlock-breaking bills of January 1992. Secondly, in locating the source of the conflict so cleanly in procedural questions, 'institution-alist' arguments tend to neglect the highly problematic blurring of constitutional and political debates which prevailed between 1990 and 1992. Finally, such arguments also tend to insist that National Council involvement in the talks led to a collapse of federal authority[91], thus accepting the federal government's account of events at face value and ignoring the original reasons for National Council participation (i.e. the desire for legitimacy).

Though it sounds plausible to suggest that the shift in debate to the National Councils was attended by a deepening of the national con-flict, scrutiny of the talks suggests otherwise. At the end of 1990, it should be noted, the disputes in the power-sharing talks between the three governments, the battles in the Federal Assembly, and the lack of progress in the constitutional talks between the National Councils ran *concurrently*. More importantly, the disagreements that dogged presidia, cross-party and inter-governmental talks right through from 1990 to March 1992, did not change qualitatively-speaking – in their substance.

It is this very lack of movement in the issues under discussion and the constant recycling of stalemates in the full panoply of institutional arenas that begs analytical attention. The framework of objections established between the Czech right and Slovak representatives at

Trenčianské Teplice marked out the dispute as it continued, and eventually collapsed, into 1992. Though certain parties attempted to shift the debate onto less intractable issues and into more informal negotiating environments (ending 'In Hell'), the result was a recitation of the fundamentalist and never-resolved positions aired in August 1990.

It is thus unsatisfying to explain the constitutional deadlock merely by looking at the fate of legislative proposals. It was, after all, an essentially political impasse which translated into a procedural impasse. The right of veto in the Federal Assembly is better understood as distinct from the stalemate in every other arena only because it represented a nominally final, institutional closure of debate, though one thoroughly anticipated by the negotiation-paralysis induced by the brewing electoral battle. To attribute to the Slovak veto the prime role in having prohibited new constitutions is to ignore the profound failure of the negotiation process that went before it. The substantive causes of stalemate were political[92].

The semantic 'black hole' that constituted Czechoslovak constitutional terminology after 1989[93] has been exaggerated, implying as it does a hopeless terminological confusion on the part of the political actors involved[94]. The evidence argues rather the contrary, that what did exist was a straightforward and very well understood deadlock over terms and, on the part of Klaus's Civic Democratic Party and Mečiar's Movement for a Democratic Slovakia, a transparent manipulation of Czech–Slovak friction. Though there was indeed a proliferation of terms that supposedly denoted actual 'types' of federation – 'true', 'dual', 'authentic' and, perhaps the most consistent, 'functional federation' – it nevertheless seems unsafe to infer that this snowballing of obscure constitutional forms derived from the inexperience of the politicians concerned or even, as Mathernová does, from their wilful adoption of arguments as a 'pretence, a playground for political ping-pong'[95].

Rather than assuming either non-comprehension, pure cynicism or entrenched, increasingly nationalist conflict, the stalemate was exactly as it appeared: a narrowly politically motivated stalemate over constitutional terms which brooked of no obvious compromise. Though any party may consistently claim to be both federalist and peculiarly concerned with the needs of energetic governance, with that extreme of the federal continuum represented by concentrated unity at one end and a diffusion of powers at the other, there is little evidence that the Czech federal right felt themselves to be speaking from within such a continuum, with any need to recognise the equal claims for a diffusion of authority at the other extremity. Václav Klaus's term 'functional federation', which first appeared in the Civic Forum manifesto of June 1990, was a concept ever more clearly elucidated; it denoted a federation with a sovereign and sufficiently strong centre to legislate and administer unhindered a radical economic reform package, requirements laid out frequently and ever more bluntly. For two years Klaus argued that he and his party were uniquely realistic about the new democratic federal state, that anything less than his arrangement would not be a federation at all, and in the run-up to the 1992 election the Civic Democratic Party platform made explicit a position which had been implicit throughout. Unless such a federation obtained, the optimum solution would be the cessation of *all* constitutional ties. In the light of such a statement, accepting that federalism is a system designed to 'prevent tyranny without preventing governance'[96], one is hard-pressed to recognise a federalist in Klaus. The idea of committing to a system of open bargaining and institutionalised power-sharing proved entirely alien to him.

By 1991 the position on the Czech right, moreover, clearly underpinned all basic deadlock concerning 'sovereignty' or state legal personality, including that over the state treaty. This development could only deepen the stereotypical assumptions on the Slovak side, that the Czechs remained Czechoslovakist, and on the Czech side, that the Slovaks would sacrifice nothing to a common state. As Jan Kalvoda (Civic Democratic Alliance) had insisted at the end of yet another failed meeting of the National Councils, the existence or non-existence of the Slovak wish to live in a common state was the cardinal question of the state treaty. He also observed that Slovak politicians who favoured an independent Slovakia had simply not yet dared to say it publicly[97]. It is the fusion of such national stereotypes with highly politicised perceptions of the requirements of democratic stabilisation, which we may call state-building arguments, that holds the key to understanding the legal deadlock.

THE PROBLEM WITH NEW INSTITUTIONS

In an institutional landscape in which ultimate conflict-regulating power had rested with a single party for over forty years, political representatives after 1989 were faced by a relative wealth of potential institutional environments for resolving their differences: parliaments, inter-governmental meetings, inter- and intra-party meetings, inter-parliamentary executive meetings and so on. Through 1990 it was also already evident to parliamentary insiders that political affiliations and the political constellations in each republic were shifting and unstable entities, providing further scope for future coalitions of consensus just

as shifting negotiating environments might provide more or less conducive conditions for problem-solving. That the main political actors
of the constitutional debate could be observed repeating themselves
to the echo through almost two years of negotiations, in various
combinations of negotiating forums, is, from this perspective, less
surprising.

Rather than indicating persistent misunderstandings of the law, the
repetitiveness of the debate reflected the initial aspiration to legitimacy
and the relative unchartedness of the new institutional landscape
facing the negotiating parties. It also reflected the reasonable expectation that bargaining positions should be sustained and the modification of claims resisted given the reasonable prospect of shifting
coalitions and the imminence of a second election. Far from merely
'touring castles and palaces', what we can see is that the question
of constitutional redesign went on a full round-the-institutions
exploratory trip; it also engaged phenomenal numbers of political
representatives. Together these tendencies ran entirely counter to
the lessons of successful negotiating processes elsewhere in the
world, which typically minimise the number of actors involved and
rely on the ability of these actors to win support for their compromise position in their respective constituencies once a full negotiated
consensus has been reached. In the Czechoslovak case the one major
misconception throughout the process, indeed one prolonged by the
process itself, was the republican deputies' under-estimation of the
persistence of federal government self-interest and the identification
of the Czech public with their position, implicitly majoritarian as it
was.

The federal government's exasperated restatement of the basic
'minimum conditions' for the continuation of the state represented a
'reality check' for the negotiation process. It is clearly from this period
in late 1991 onward that the realisation finally dawned that institutional adjustments (i.e. negotiating environments and the stabilising
constellation of political parties) were unable to take the dispute
further. If the electoral term had been longer, it is arguably *at this point*
that fruitful negotiations, as opposed to position-taking, would have
begun. Instead, from this point on the federal government, the Czech
government, and lastly the Slovak government finally conceded that
the issues would have to wait on the ultimate shift in political distri-
butions already widely expected: the installation in the June 1992 election of the Czech right and Slovak national populists (Movement for
a Democratic Slovakia) in government – that is, until after a new and
potentially decisive *vacuum* of consensus had been created at the
federal level.

'SOVEREIGNTY' – A SLOVAK CONSPIRACY TO
DESTROY CZECHOSLOVAKIA?

What then was the substance of these recycled deadlocks between 1990 and 1992? The issue of sovereignty was obviously a focal point of conflict. The opposition Slovak Nationalist Party clearly aspired to full international recognition for Slovakia as a fully independent state. The Christian Democratic Movement meanwhile visualised some form of transitory relationship with the Czech Republic, leading eventually to the full flowering of sovereign Slovak statehood within the European Union – an aspiration that divided it utterly from its coalition partner, the Public Against Violence/Civic Democratic Union (not to mention the vast majority of Czechs and Slovaks, who understood that this scenario was a pipedream like no other). The less nationalist majority of Slovak deputies on the other hand were preoccupied not so much by *suverenita* (sovereignty) as by *zvrchovanost'* – a right to pursue one's own national life, a cultural imperative theoretically consistent with a federal common state. Those Slovaks who sympathised with the latter aspiration endorsed the pursuit of symbolic signifiers – of terms and agreements which would indicate the essential 'equality' of the two nations. It was for these rather than for secessionist reasons that the state treaty idea had resonated favourably with many Slovak deputies – a fact that would be borne out by their behaviour during the negotiations to separate the state after June 1992.

The majority of Slovaks conceived of constitutional reform as an opportunity fundamentally to redraft the federal contract, this time by two equal, consenting nations in conditions of political freedom. To the Czech right, the authority of the established federation, however flawed in its constitutional detail and however coerced its formation and structure, already existed and was, as embodying the international sovereignty of the CSFR, superior and binding. Any attempt to assert republican sovereignty (the sovereignty of national 'peoples' as against the invoked sovereignty of 'the people'), if only momentarily and symbolically, destroyed the 'sovereign rights' of the federation. A state treaty, moreover, appeared to leave open even confederal options, in which sovereign republics would cede power to the federal centre. This was not, however, a purely legalistic objection on the part of the Czech right but an objection inspired by (and dependent upon) the assertion that federal powers had to be maintained, uninterrupted, for the purposes of continuing Klaus's state-wide, state-building economic reform, massively resented in Slovakia though this was.

Indeed, the extent to which treaty discussions remained mired in formal legal argument and abstracted from their underlying political agendas on both sides is one of their most remarkable aspects. In this respect, moreover, stereotypes played a crucial part, fortifying the driest of legal arguments – the status of the treaty in international law, for example – and keeping purely party political motivations under cover. Such a prejudiced legal discourse proved a particularly effective method of keeping policy positions stable whilst affecting to enter into an argument. The recital of stereotypes among Czechs emerged as follows: the Czechs – tolerant, conciliatory, but finally robust in the face of legal ignorance and absurdity; the Slovaks – irrational in regard to their 'best interests' (at best romantic), nationalistic, parochial in outlook and inexperienced in the art of the possible.

It was clearly a formal and symbolic expression of equality which motivated Čarnogurský in his bid for a state treaty. Such a treaty, formally delegating republican power to the centre, would have represented a lasting legal caveat to the age-old assumption of top-down federalists (and Czechoslovakists before them), that the highest legislative body, the Federal Assembly (previously the National Assembly), was *a priori* and indivisibly sovereign. Slovak suspicion of the centre, however, was interpreted in Prague (despite the fact that it had been mirrored in the Czech National Council) as a function of nationalist hostility, and not as deriving from their unhappy experiences under Czechoslovakist and pseudo-federal practice. The state treaty was thus an opportunity missed on the Czech side, and their hostile response forced the pace in Slovakia's internal political development, greatly to the benefit of Vladimír Mečiar. What resulted was an ever-sharper polarisation of debate. The main body of Slovak representatives argued that the new state should be built 'from the bottom up', and the Czech right in both the Czech Council and the Federal Assembly insisted that if the new state was to survive at all, it could only be built from the top down – as it were by grace and not by right.

HAVEL'S UNEQUAL STRUGGLE

One final question posed by deadlock was whether there existed outside forces capable of moving the political impasse to more profitable ground, if not ending it altogether. In theory at least, either the constitutional court or the presidency might have fulfilled this role. The passivity of the constitutional court throughout these two years, however, proved damaging in two respects; not only did it ultimately fail to insist upon the constitutionally required referendum to ratify the dissolution of the state, but it also failed to intervene with clear definitional rulings when the negotiating parties, virtually from day one, became ensnared in tortuous terminological disputes. As for the presidency, Václav Havel's most significant power, apart from his own standing among the political community, was his independent right to introduce legislation. In this, however, he was as much subject to the unfavourable weaknesses of the Assembly as any other legislator – a real obstacle at the point where it was attempted. Havel's other resource, his prestige, was nonetheless always more vital; and had he been able to represent a vision more favourable to the Slovak side he might conceivably have mediated more than a pre-election stand-off.

Havel's failure resided in his own political fears, and his growing allegiance to (indeed, given the prospect of an independent Czech republic, his dependence upon) the Czech right. In practical terms Havel's efforts were unceasing and heartfelt; he convened some twenty meetings between federal and republican representatives in the space of two years, encouraged the Assembly to introduce referenda, and offered his own draft constitution. When it seemed the federation was dying on its feet in 1992 Havel intervened with an assertive referendum bill and proposals for rapidly completing a new federal constitution. Any reading of Havel as the tragically ignored, lone reasonable man, however, carries an erroneous assumption that his avowed pro-federalism amounted to an ability to act as a tactful and disinterested arbiter.

A series of major diplomatic mistakes thoroughly doused Havel's reputation in Slovakia, damaging enough to break the aura of impartiality that had crowned his election to the presidency[98]. His failure to consult over the naming of the state back in 1990 (following his first official visit – to Germany, not Slovakia) was particularly alarming to Slovak deputies, though his tribune style annoyed Czech deputies for different reasons. In many cases Havel also appeared to veer toward the *laissez-faire* posturing of the Czech right, siding early with the defence of solid central powers over macro-economic policy coupled with non-intervention at the micro-level. In relation to the state treaty, Havel had accused the Christian Democratic Movement of adopting a position that endangered federal institutions, the implication being that the stability of the state as a whole was not a Slovak priority. Such an accusation was too readily reminiscent of the Vaculík view, that Slovakia would typically put parochial national interests before those of the state; and the impression that Havel too believed that Slovaks – once again – might not scruple to let all hell break loose was confirmed absolutely by his extraordinarily ill-judged warnings to the Slovak military. The loss of confidence in Havel's impartiality undermined his capacity to act as 'third force' even while his attempts to bring the two sides together continued to be appreciated. It was unfortunate, in the view of many non-Public Against Violence Slovak representatives, that 'by and large, Havel . . . used his authority to support the [federal] government rather than compete with it'[99].

PLACING THE FEDERAL IDEA UNDER SIEGE

Economic radicals, notably those on the Czech right, the Civic Democratic Alliance and Václav Klaus's Civic Democratic Party (with the support of the Slovak right of the Public Against Violence), framed constitutional choices not between centralisation and non-centralisation or between unity and liberty – critical concerns when framing a legitimate constitution for a bi-national state – but between an 'optimal' and a 'sub-optimal' future. The optimal future was deemed achievable only by strong government implementing radical economic and state reform. The economically sub-optimal future would allegedly arise out of a decentralised federation. The preconditions for the optimal path were a sovereign and highly responsive centralised executive and a strong administration, and for purposes of legislative efficiency the absence of disruptive constitutional conflict – as if that were possible in the chosen multi-reform conditions of transition – if not a consolidated unitarian constitution. The ascendancy of the Czech right's political agenda (victorious in splintering the Civic Forum and decisive in the June 1992 elections) successfully 'froze out' Slovak demands for a deeper federalisation. This never-challenged but simplistic depiction of entirely conflicting economic and state-forming constitutional requirements created irreconcilable goals as perceived by the two republics' political leaderships.

The dichotomised character of the discussion produced the main 'transition effect' on the constitutional dispute. The backlog of state and economic reforming legislation accumulating in 1990 certainly required an efficient legislature, more or less immediately, depending on one's appraisal of the role of reform and the stability of the state. It nevertheless remained particularly unlikely that Slovaks would be persuaded of the importance of economic reform so long as they lacked the most basic sense of the legitimacy of the system in general, and of the dogmatically presented economic reform in particular.

It has been argued that the bi-national nature of the dispute 'over-politicised' every constitutional issue and that no swing vote or third force existed to break the impasse[100]. The point is well taken but underplays the very particular 'transition effects' of attempting to reform the state and the economy simultaneously. I would argue the reverse, namely, that the constitutional debate was 'under-politicised' because the party political, as opposed to the supposedly 'objective reformist', motivations behind the Czech right position of federal 'realism', of 'functioning federation' and 'federation or bust', were accepted uncritically in the debate over the proper constitutional structure of the state – a conflation of interests compounded by the still underdeveloped party system.

Far from 'the centre' being too weak, which has been so widely claimed as to have become the accepted wisdom, the right wing in the federal executive retained both the political will and the authority to force and define the entire issue of common statehood, as it did with its declaration of 'minimal conditions' for the continuation of the state in late 1991. As is observable in another, but this time relatively stable, democratic state, suffering simultaneous difficulties with resource distribution and national relations, i.e. Canada, far greater clarity exists here as to the relationship between constitutional and political interests – a fact which, while it may not make the problems more tractable, has at least cautioned Canadian politicians against framing constitutional arguments in strictly dichotomous and dogmatic terms. More importantly still, the perceived relative stability of both the economy and the democratic institutions in Canada has tended to mitigate the sense of time pressure felt so acutely in Czechoslovakia in 1989 – a sense on which the Czech right largely depended. A strong case can be made that English-speaking Canadians and Quebecois have not had, and do not have, even in more fraught times, high expectations of a full or decisive 'closure' of their own constitutional wrangling, however desirable this might be in opening opportunities for radical governance closed to a necessarily consensus-seeking centre. 'Closure' in Canada would anyway have been achievable up to now only by the top-down imposition of a solution – something politically inconceivable in a stable democracy.

The many crises of 1990, particularly as defined by technocratic notions of rapid economic reform, installed a profound stalemate of perceived state-building interests at the earliest point of constitutional negotiation: a stalemate not fully comprehended until the second election in 1992. Though significant decentralisation was conceded at the end of 1990, the evident desire of the federal government to retrench its power clearly divided Slovak perceptions of Czech goodwill. Slovak pessimists certainly had reasonable grounds for suspicion. As Klaus made clear in November 1991, 'the meeting of governments at Trenčianské Teplice last year began the disintegration of our state in which the legitimate federal bodies (both the Federal Assembly and the federal government) were in principle isolated and, step by step, pressed away from their constitutional rights and responsibilities. The participants in those talks [implicitly Klaus's political rivals from the liberal Civic Movement] began to spread a false opinion that this process of weakening the federation represents the only means for its preservation. Petr Pithart (CM) cannot rid himself of the responsibility of having been one of the initiators and chief protagonists of that process', Klaus argued, though he himself had participated at the close of these talks at Hrzan palace in December 1990[101]. The missing (or rather unspoken) logic in Klaus's continuing advocacy of a uniquely sovereign and uniformly reforming federation unfortunately was that no Slovak partner existed for such a practically unitary state. When stalemate in negotiations translated so seamlessly into parliamentary deadlock at the federal level, the Czech federal right could nonetheless claim to be provoked.

WAS THE CONSTITUTIONAL INHERITANCE TO BLAME?

An assessment of the opportunities lost through the exercise of the veto in the Federal Assembly – an 'institutionalist' argument – apparently only scratches at the surface of the conflict in its observable dynamic. An oft-cited opportunity lost through the use of this veto was that of holding a referendum. However, we know that when a referendum was proposed, it would have revealed only a highly problematic array of preferred models of a state: an array of preferences at least in part moulded by the party political debate that had gone before (i.e. through 1990 and early 1991) and that had precipitated the 'conflict'. The obstruction of Havel's legislation by the veto likewise represented a significant revelation of failure in the process of constitutional reform, but it did not produce any sea-change in the substantive conflict over alternative state forms as such, other than signalling the elevation of this conflict from the parliamentary to the electoral level. The electoral level, however, turned out to be decisive, given the willingness of Klaus and Mečiar to administer the separation once in power, but that development is hardly to be explained by a purely institutional argument. Finally, even if Havel had succeeded in strengthening the presidency, he would not have been capable of realigning the governing elite with the preferences of the public. Havel's reputation as a disinterested arbiter was irreparably damaged by the time of his legislative interventions, a fact which had very little to do with institutional constraints.

An alternative institutionalist analysis might focus on the absence of those prior conditions required for consociationalism to work, namely elite support for the principles of power-sharing. Evidently the damaging effects of the minority veto went far deeper than those resulting from its actual employment. To many on the Czech right the perception of a perpetual 'national' constraint on government seems to have been at least as antagonising as its impact[102]. The Czech Civic Democratic Party under Klaus had pressed for the minority veto to be modified, the Civic Democratic Alliance for its abolition. Both argued that the veto was an instrument solely of (Slovak) leftist and nationalist recidivists, who wished to hold the state to ransom, using the veto to 'suspend' parliament. The climactic quality of their rhetoric was most effective, and that Vladimir Mečiar was aware of the strategic value of Slovak blocking power in the Federal Assembly is certain. That the Czechs were given justification for their anti-veto position is nevertheless an argument from hindsight. Even after two years of persistent deadlock and disagreement over the very basis of the state the federal state had legislated for comprehensive economic reform, the privatisation of small and large-scale enterprises, an adjustment in power-sharing (blocked initially by the Czechs) and a new constitutional law establishing a civil code of liberal human rights. Contrary to the claims of the Czech right, the post-1989 federal state, although its jurisdiction remained unclear, was by no means under siege.

The Czech federal right's concern was the prospect of a persistently successful Slovak intervention against legislation perceived to run against the Slovak national interest, however defined – the right of veto was of course instituted (and recommended during the Prague Spring of 1968) for this very purpose. The Czech federal right viewed the Slovak veto as unacceptable and provocative from as early as August 1990. To Slovaks, this public objection naturally called into question the Czechs' desire for a common state of equal nations, and yet, despite this, the Slovak secessionist nationalist parties failed to thrive. The rejection of the veto demonstrated the federal right's antipathy not only to one of the basic tenets of consociational governance but to the underlying principles of consociation – power-sharing and the protection of the interests of the minority nation against majority tyranny. The impact of the use of the veto was that it exposed established elite assumptions about the validity of a minority veto as such, and so benchmarked a deeper conflict. It is to the economic dimension of this conflict that we can now turn.

5

A LENIN FOR THE BOURGEOISIE

As we have already seen, economic reform dominated the more general democratisation debate to a remarkable extent. In this chapter the aim is to investigate federal and republican economic policy and changing economic conditions in greater depth. With public opinion and leading political parties together apparently predicating democratisation as such upon economic success, the fate of the Czech and Slovak economies and the management of economic divisions was clearly going to have a major political impact. In the absence of significant, well-respected constraints such as a unifying presidency and given the existence of two quite separate party systems it looked highly likely that major tensions over how to prioritise reform and how to divide economic powers between the republics and the federation could of themselves provoke a state-dissolving clash of interests. The story that emerges is one of clear-sighted purpose from the federal centre and the overwhelming dominance of Czech economic interests.

If Czechoslovakia separated because of irreconcilable understandings of economic reform and democratisation then one might expect to find the following evidence. First, that the observable tensions between centre and periphery, and, indeed, between the two republics, were formulated as democratising or reform arguments (as contrasted with programmatic nationalistic arguments for the nation-state as the vehicle for national realisation). Secondly, that those forging dominating state-building arguments were primarily pro-democracy/reformist elites, and, thirdly, that the latter elites argued that democratic reform was potentially incompatible with a common state. And finally, one would expect to observe the prioritisation of 'reform' in public opinion polls. Evidence against this argument would be that pro-democracy/pro-reform elites supported the continuation of a common state as an overriding public good, that there was consensus on constitutional reform among pro-democracy/reform elites and that common statehood was prioritised in public opinion polls.

ECONOMIC REFORM: FEDERAL = CZECH

The authorship of the federal economic reform programme from the very beginning looked distinctly Czech. Supported by the Civic Forum, the key economic positions in the post-revolution (federal) Government of National Understanding had gone to the Czech staff of Prognost – the Forecasting Institute of the Czechoslovak Academy of Sciences. Václav Klaus, never a Party member, had become Federal Minister of Finance, whilst Valtr Komárek, returning his Communist Party card, had become a Deputy Premier, with overall authority for reform[1]. Vladimír Dlouhý, who would soon become one of Klaus's most important allies, headed the State Planning Commission before becoming Federal Minister for the Economy following the June 1990 election.

The Slovaks' relative lack of such an economics team, educated and skilled in liberal theory, would reduce their bargaining power from the beginning. Jozef Kučerák of the Public Against Violence was a liberal economist isolated in too many ways. When the issue of republican power-sharing emerged in the summer of 1990 Kučerák was so concerned that economic factionalism might paralyse the reforms from Prague that he too, along with Mečiar, supported devolution of significant reform powers – a pragmatic impulse that his Czech federal colleagues interpreted simply as nationalism. The liberal credibility of Jozef Markuš, the new Deputy Premier of the Slovak government, responsible for economic affairs, was similarly tarnished not only by his real nationalist sympathies but also by his 'positive vetting' after the June election[2].

After ten years of effective economic stagnation, the Czechoslovak economy in 1990 saw a switch from positive to negative Net Material Product[3] of 1.1 per cent and an overall drop in industrial output of 3.7 per cent. Compared to her neighbours, post-Communist Czechoslovakia was in an enviably stable macro-economic situation and relatively unburdened by international debt. Major economic disruption at every level had nevertheless followed from the disruption of Soviet-bloc trade and in anticipation of the shift from plan to market.

Although Czechoslovakia in 1990 was hardly in dire need of the radical stabilisation packages already in place in Poland, Valtr Komárek's strategy for economic transformation still seemed worryingly half-hearted. In the charged atmosphere of early 1990 Komárek's preoccupation with egalitarianism in the economy made him appear Luddite. The public was clamouring for immediate change and this was ably amplified by the Czech political right, who equated all ideas of gradualism – incremental and more interventionist reform – with a foolhardy nostalgia for the false dawn of the Prague Spring. Komárek quickly lost the confidence of his cabinet colleagues, even of those opposed to Klaus's radicalism, and he was replaced in April 1990 (after the intervention of the President) by Václav Valeš, a veteran of the 1968 reforms and a prison colleague of Havel's. The overall initiative for reform, however, shifted effectively to Václav Klaus and the boldly presented macro-economic reform line he had already partially developed before the 1989 revolution.

As a neo-liberal, Klaus believed that the market was a self-regulating system based on the price mechanism within which any government intervention was a source of unwanted distortion[4]. The secret of reform lay in the macro-economy, and according to Klaus it was possible to bring supply and demand into equilibrium in all the most important markets by using macro-economic tools. As he told *The Times*, 'we are the monetarists of Eastern Europe'[5]. The abolition of central planning and the dismantling of price and wage, exchange rate and foreign trade controls would be combined with a change in ownership, resulting in a transfer of property rights that in theory at least would usher in the culture and incentives of the market itself, the profit motive in particular. In this scheme the market was king.

Neo-liberalism, of course, is an idea that came into its own under Ronald Reagan in the United States and Margaret Thatcher in Britain, and, as anyone living under either of these governments will recall, it is a political philosophy that ascribes a truly radical role to the market. Where classical free-market economics works on the basic assumption that we are all rational and profit-seeking individuals in our economic decision-making, neo-liberals extend the logic of personal utility max-imisation, costs and benefits, into all aspects of public life, and from this logic they derive an extremely deep antipathy to the state and all notions of state 'engineering'. With individual 'freedom' their core value, neo-liberals go one step further than plain liberals or conserv-atives and positively argue that economic freedom and the absence of state control or intervention in economic affairs constitute the main-stay of political freedom in all its dimensions. Appealing to the social sciences for support, neo-liberals would point to the pathologies of bureaucracy, welfare abuse and growing government interventionism and cronyism as the lasting legacies of rival ideologies with more faith in the state. According to von Hayek – one of the pre-eminent philosophers of this line of reasoning – markets are mechanisms that allow us to discover human abilities and needs, and thus to control the market must inevitably lead to the suppression of individual choice and, with it, individual liberty. In post-1989 Czechoslovakia neo-liberalism seemed to provide not only decisive-sounding strategies for reform but also a coherent explanation for Czechoslovakia's problems. State intervention, according to neo-liberals, has the terrible effect of politicising aspects of societal operations previously accepted as natural outcomes of impersonal forces – be they market forces or civil associational forces. In this sense Klaus offered not only marketisation but also an appealing critique of the whole socialist experiment with state control. He argued pointedly that it was not for the dissidents to lecture society about civic imperatives; individuals in this new order could decide for themselves.

It followed from this logic that in terms of economic reform strategy the questions of industrial restructuring and growth were essentially secondary; they would follow on from a combination of general liberalisation and re-acclimatisation into the market, as day follows night. On the question of privatisation the change of ownership, rather than the structural advantages of new capital or expertise, was the key shift. The mass distribution of share vouchers to the public, according to Klaus, would offer the widest and quickest way of dispersing ownership into the society, and with it, he argued, would flow the principles of private agency. The formal freeing of industry from state control was thus the first objective, and one with obvious political advantages. According to Klaus, much would follow from the removal of 'easy money', i.e. state subsidy. As he and his colleague Thomáš Ježek agreed, 'As true liberals, we should start with a very heavy dose of monetarist medicine – with economic policy measures, not with formal institutional reforms – because with "easy money" no real changes can be achieved in economic behaviour of any agents, private or public'[6].

The federal government produced an outline reform strategy in May 1990, together with a detailed timetable for implementation. There were, however, reservations within the government over Klaus's chosen form of 'voucher' privatisation, even from Vladimír Dlouhý, since the more or less free distribution of share vouchers to the population seemed incapable of bringing in the much-needed capital investment to revitalise industry. The pace and ordering of price and import liberalisation were also contentious and together these doubts held up programme approval until after the June 1990 election. Klaus's reform draft duly became the basis for parliamentary debate following the Czech CF/Slovak PAV/CDM election victory.

Following the elections Klaus not only survived Havel's hopes to have him kicked sideways to become head of the state bank – a position that would have used his skills but effectively neutralised him politically, curbing his growing dominance over the liberal core of the Civic Forum – he also weathered continuing criticism of his reform package from economics departments. Klaus was, indeed, uniquely confident regarding the merits of his strategy and persuasive in defending it, and he emerged from June in an eminently stronger position[7]. Klaus had gone on record as saying that he saw no benefit in broad public discussion[8], and the final debate in parliament was handled as a confidence vote. Criticism was tantamount to outright opposition – a strategy clearly intended to expose the doubters as faint-hearts, or worse. At this stage there appeared to be very few opponents in either republic.

Klaus explained his position to the public in the purest neo-liberal terms. His 1990 programme seemed clear in its purpose; it started from the establishment of equilibrium (quantity of supply equalling quantity of demand) on all markets, to be followed by demonopolisation and steps to define ownership – after which prices could be freed[9]. Competition was to be encouraged at the macro-level by an abolition of restrictions on imports. The dominant themes of reform were the need for a restrictive fiscal and monetary policy at the republican and federal levels and the need to avoid inflation – 'a socio-economic evil, which must be prevented at any cost'[10]. The latter agenda formed the basis for deflationary policies. Most importantly, the uniform reform preconceived of the federal state as a fully integrated single market, an already homogeneous entity implying uniform reform measures and, as far as possible, a nationally undifferentiated strategy, and it was always presented this way. Institutional changes such as price liberalisation, privatisation, exchange rate and foreign trade reforms were all necessarily federation-wide. The *a priori* requirement of a strong and absolutely decisive federal centre, however, meant that economic reform was left a hostage to fortune as far as federal–Slovak relations were concerned, and *vice versa*.

The government's Scenario for Economic Reform, finally accepted in September 1990, comprised seven sections. The first four represented Klaus's strategy, the remaining three were concessions to his colleagues; the latter would never be fully implemented. Klaus's first policy concerned the absolute priority of preventing inflation – to be secured by a further tightening of monetary and fiscal restraint in 1991[11]. The second section covered denationalisation and privatisation, with the full plan to be approved in October 1990. A commitment to 'commercialise' large enterprises by the end of 1990 and some variations permitted within the voucher privatisation system represented the main concession to Klaus's liberal rivals[12]; given the neo-liberal domination of the Federal Finance Ministry and both the Czech and Slovak Ministries of Privatisation (after June 1990 the former was under the authority of Klaus's colleague from Prognost, Thomáš

Ježek, the latter, from 1991, under the Slovak liberal, Ivan Mikloš), Klaus's view of privatisation would nevertheless prevail in many respects. The Federal Ministry of Economy under Klaus's ally Vladimír Dlouhý similarly dominated its Czech equivalent[13].

The third section of the Scenario related to prices. The date set for price liberalisation and the establishment of internal convertibility was 1 January 1991. Monetary and fiscal policies were to restrain price rises, as would a restrictive wages policy and some regulation of particularly sensitive prices[14]. The fourth section, probably the most controversial at the time, covered the internal convertibility of the currency, with a proposal that enterprises could buy foreign currency but would be forced to sell all their foreign currency earnings. Although accepted as a reasonable measure in the longer term it was feared that immediate internal convertibility – effective devaluation of the currency – would both be inflationary and would have highly uneven effects on industry, favouring exports of low value-added raw materials and semi-finished products and pressurising those manufacturing and industrial sectors more dependent upon imports. The main criticism of the policy was that enterprises and entire industries that were actually viable in the long term would be placed under unsustainable pressure in the short term, either being forced under or requiring substantial government interventions and subsidies[15].

The remaining three sections, brief and apparently of little interest to Klaus, concerned agriculture, the social aspects of the transition and structural policy, which also drew some criticism. Structural policy at this stage consisted of cutting armaments production and the mining of uranium and some other ores. Academic criticism pointed to the inconsistency of including an ill-defined (interventionist-sounding) structural policy that contained none of the more usual 'mixed' economic policies for export promotion or technological advance. The latter section had also anticipated a regional development policy, an instrument that might have been used to great effect in Slovakia, if only in the political selling of reform; financial support, however, was never forthcoming[16]. The Federal Ministry for State Planning (Slovak-led as Dlouhý acceded to the Ministry of Economy) likewise became an ever more moribund and persistently under-funded organisation[17]. These last three policy areas would in effect discreetly 'wither away'; nevertheless, their disappearance ensured that later, pivotal conflicts in economic policy were by no means simply between Slovaks and Czechs, but between more moderate social liberals – such as Václav Valeš and Petr Miller in the federal cabinet, Vlasák, Kouba and Šulc in the Czech parliament – and the monetarist Klausite team of the Federal Finance ministry[18].

Consistent with Klaus's reform priorities the new Scenario – the blueprint of Czechoslovak economic reform – failed to mention specific Czech and Slovak conditions in any form. Such specificities were considered factually negligible, providing no grounds for special treatment in a neo-liberal scheme. There were, moreover, practical problems facing anyone who did wish to draw a distinction between these two economies, most critically, a basic absence of economic data disaggregated by republic (not available until mid-1992). As Czech and Slovak economic performance began to diverge, this basic lack of statistics would leave Slovak explanations as to the causes of their decline straightforwardly lacking in evidence, and vulnerable to accusations of 'political' motives. It soon became clear in addition that there was a deep-rooted assumption among Czech economists that similarities between the two republics were more significant than differences[19]. As a result, Klaus would not only consistently defend the right of the federal government to control macro-economic policy, but would claim it as a transcendent necessity that all three government policies should remain as determined within the Scenario's monetarist strategy, despite an increasing divergence in economic performance.

With the Scenario secured, Klaus turned to the political front within the still ill-defined Civic Forum and argued for three fundamental changes: a total commitment to his economic strategy; a total opposition to socialism 'in all its forms'; and the conversion of the Civic Forum into a properly organised party – thus decisively manoeuvring the split of spring 1991. Following the Forum's collapse Komárek joined the Social Democrats in April; Dlouhý, despite his previous Party membership, was welcomed into the neo-liberal Civic Democratic Alliance (CDA) in March; and the former liberal club of the Forum, including many of the dissident core, and the federal ministers, Jiří Dienstbier, Petr Miller, Pavel Rychetský and Luboš Dobrovský, became the core of the Civic Movement (CM).

The neo-liberal assertion that people's economic conditions should be in the realm of the market rather than the state was, fortunately for Klaus, a belief that cohered well with the re-emerging Czech entrepreneurial self-image – the Communists had always encouraged the traditional Czech pride in their craftsmanship and engineering skills – to which Klaus hastily began to appeal. In Slovakia, however, as federal economic reforms began to kick in, the confluence of declining conditions through 1990–1 to a far harsher degree than in the Czech Republic, combined with similar aspirations to improved status – 'an explosion of nationalist tendencies', according to Dlouhý's former adviser, Jan Klacek[20] – cast an early frost on neo-liberal politics.

MEČIAR VERSUS THE LIBERALS: SETTING UP SHOP

Whatever conclusions can be drawn regarding the parity of Czech and Slovak economic performance in the 1980s, significant differences were once again apparent in 1989. In the Cold War world Slovakia's position might have been interpreted as unusually secure. Her proximity to the Soviet Union had pushed her bias towards heavy industry and towards armaments production in particular (some 80 per cent of Czechoslovak production, according to the *Financial Times Survey*[21]), making her heavily dependent upon Soviet oil and raw materials[22]. As the economic compass shifted West in 1989, however, Slovakia's industrial structure went from economic asset to political liability, and the Czechs found themselves with the geographical upper hand. Slovakia was, for many reasons, unequally equipped to ride out the external shocks engendered by the collapse of the Soviet trading bloc – the Council for Mutual Economic Assistance – and the corresponding exposure to world markets and the shift to hard currency for Russian fuel. Slovakia's relative structural vulnerability made the republic all the more susceptible to the internal shocks likely to emanate from a rapid and anti-interventionist reform process.

Klaus's insistence that supposedly existing economic parity between the two republics stood as the solid basis of the Federal Reform Scenario clearly put Czech and Slovak relations at the mercy of a controversial interpretation of the Communist past. The federal claim of parity harked back to official assertions through the 1970s and early 1980s that economic equality between the republics stood as one of the lasting achievements of socialism. By 1990, however, it flew in the face even of recent Communist economic policy. It was hardly surprising then that as Slovak conditions worsened through 1990, Mečiar quickly reoriented his initially pro-market rhetoric to a reassertion that Slovakia laboured under particular difficulties, and that adjustments should be made to the basic assumptions underpinning federal reform.

The economic issue played a key role in the political divisions within the Slovak Public Against Violence as early as the latter half of 1990. Through 1990, radical reform was backed wholeheartedly by the Public Against Violence's Jozef Kučerák, but many other self-proclaimed liberals in June 1990, such as Jozef Markuš, Rudolf Filkus and Michal Kováč, veered increasingly toward Mečiar's clearly popular arguments for the greater adaptation of reform to Slovakia's distinct conditions. Even Augustín Húska, the Minister for Privatisation, who had advocated rapid reform at the June 1990 election, joined Mečiar in his exit from the Slovak Public Against Violence within a year.

Though the Public Against Violence's eventual split in 1991 was unambiguously due to Mečiar's struggle for power, he apparently understood that his championing of economic adjustment represented the most effective platform by which to distinguish himself from those liberals he now wished to leave behind. Mečiar would later describe the climactic divisions within the Public Against Violence as having been between two factions holding different views on future constitutional arrangements and on the means of economic reform, in which he cited the problems of armaments conversion and unemployment as particularly close to his own heart. Though the ex-dissidents understood his motives as somewhat less public-spirited, the liberal Kučerák had in a sense obliged this version of events by lambasting Mečiar for his rose-tinted presentation of economic alternatives during his ouster as Prime Minister. Mečiar revealed his political acuity when he described the platform of his new Movement for a Democratic Slovakia as supporting 'full self-determination of the Slovak nation expressed by a common democratic federation with the Czech nation and support for social policy'[23].

Jozef Kučerák had co-led the executive move to oust Mečiar in April 1991, and of itself this helped set the right-wing economic stall apart from the Movement for a Democratic Slovakia's still rather ambiguous, but apparently more sensitive, alternative[24]. Mečiar's Slovak government executive was duly replaced by a new selection from the Public Against Violence/Christian Democratic Movement coalition headed by Ján Čarnogurský. Čarnogurský's aspirations to an independent Slovakia within the European Union did not prevent him from supporting common economic reform, but he clearly did so without the secular market-liberal convictions of his Public Against Violence colleagues. This ambiguity, in particular Čarnogurský's distaste for consumerism and self-interested individualism, brought him into constant disagreement with Václav Klaus, adding to the popular perception within Slovakia that Čarnogurský lived on an ideological island of his own. Kučerák went on to lead the liberal rump of the Public Against Violence (which became the PAV/Civic Democratic Union in October), identifying that party once and for all with neo-liberal policy. The Civic Democratic Union and the Christian Democrats thus found themselves sitting together somewhat uncomfortably on the radical, rightist side of a superficially more polarised debate ranged against the Slovak Nationalist Party, the Party of the Democratic Left, and, situated perfectly in the middle, Mečiar's new Movement for a Democratic Slovakia.

As Čarnogurský's government launched the Slovak side of privatisation, the Christian Democratic Movement became associated with what quickly became an unequal distribution of state property, a process referred to by Mečiar at the time as 'the biggest swindle in history'[25]. Now in opposition, Mečiar thus positioned his party with surprising ease to thrive on the progressively more painful impact of reform in Slovakia, already set by spring 1991 to pay out reliable political dividends[26]. The now slimmed-down, ultra-liberal Public Against Violence answered perfectly the Slovak nationalists' picture of an 'alien' reform formulated at the Czech and federal level, and 'imposed' on Slovakia by co-opted so-called 'federal Slovaks'[27] or, as the insinuations also emerged, by Jews such as the PAV/CDU's Fedor Gál. Mečiar too, as would become ever clearer, was not above recycling haggard anti-Semitic myths of international financial conspiracy against Slovakia's 'better' interests.

CULTURAL DIFFERENCES

That federal neo-liberals overlooked the possibility of adverse Slovak reactions to their economic policy would be less surprising if the economic parity argument had ever held water. In the chaos of transition, it would seem reasonable to ask, who would have known the consequences of any major reform? That Czech neo-liberal economists swallowed the Communist declaration of parity seems curious, to say the least, and as Slovak unease about the progress of federal reform began to develop, what can only be called nationalist cultural assumptions among the Czech economic intelligentsia came rapidly to the fore. One of the most striking aspects of Czech commentary on economic issues at the time is that, rather than considering the measurable impact of reform, analysts frequently and openly operated under a form of cultural determinism. By presupposing that the Slovak reaction to reform reflected a more 'interventionist' political economic culture *per se*, Czech analysts routinely discounted or trivialised Slovakia's experience of federal policy, misinterpreting their political adaptation to it.

The implications of such widespread assumptions – that Slovak national responses to economic reform were more historically and culturally than economically determined – were clearly serious[28]. The prevailing idea seems to have been that Slovakia's political culture had been irrevocably affected by its developmental history under Communism, contrary to the 'ancient' and thus supposedly more stable and resistant cultures of Moravia and Bohemia. That Slovakia had enjoyed substantial development under Communism and that this might reasonably have predisposed Slovak voters to a more favourable view of the left is not to be gainsaid. It is also obvious, however, that to account for scissoring economic conditions as a matter of cultural maturity amounted to an intensely provocative interpretation of Slovakia's increasing economic misery. In practice, Slovak disenchantment resulted from conditions that Czech ministers, including Klaus, worked assiduously to avoid imposing on their own constituency[29].

The working assumption of relative cultural maturity among Czech economists guaranteed the addition of insult to injury. The persistent refusal of federal authorities to adjust federal economic strategy and the increasing pressure that this refusal would place on liberal Slovak politicians when evidence of divergence became blatant is an outstanding aspect of the separation of Czechoslovakia. In Slovakia, the neo-liberals around Kučerák (Public Against Violence/Civic Democratic Union) and the pro-reformists in Čarnogurský's Christian Democratic Movement found their defence of the federal economic scheme, particularly after April 1991, increasingly untenable.

Slovakia suffered the four major negative consequences of economic transition – decline in living standards, inflation, unemployment and collapsing industrial output – to a greater extent than the Czech Republic. Perhaps more pertinent to the tolerance of such divergence was the fact that Slovakia's prospects of improvement were also significantly worse. Despite some devolution of economic authority to the republics after the power-sharing agreement of December 1990, the crucial differences in performance were already discernible by the beginning of 1991, before the creation of the Movement for a Democratic Slovakia in Slovakia. Crucially for later political developments, conditions deteriorated seriously in Slovakia when a relatively strong federal centre and the neo-liberals within the respective governments could be perceived as responsible for introducing the change. The privatisation process was implemented after Mečiar's ouster in April 1991. Henceforth Mečiar would depict his dethroning as a coup by a club of jealous intellectual liberals defending their economic dogmas against the 'man of the people'. By 1991, Czech GDP per capita was already 24 per cent higher than Slovak[30].

THE IMPACT OF REFORM

Swords to . . .

The federal government curb on arms production in Czechoslovakia is an example of a government policy tailor-made to sour national relations. Armaments production was a prominent pillar of the Slovak economy. In 1989, more than two-thirds of approximately 70 state armaments factories were situated in Slovakia, employing (inclusive of connected enterprises) close on 100,000 workers. Of the 29 billion crowns of arms production in 1987 (3 per cent of total industrial output), some 19 billion was produced in Slovakia[31].

In 1990 the federal government, through the Scenario for Economic Reform and various spokesmen[32], declared the intention to curb arms production and export, in particular of heavy armaments, Slovakia's main preserve. The policy, a preoccupation of Dienstbier's and Havel's, was justified in high ethical terms, on the basis that arms production was an indefensible legacy of antiquated Soviet militarism, morally inexcusable and, given the state of the technology, economically unsustainable. Perhaps a further selling point, though never alluded to explicitly, was that the Slovak's post-'68 dominance of the arms industry and the wealth it produced in the 1970s and '80s was an oft-heard Czech resentment. Political motivations aside, within two years the federal government action had cost more than 35,000 jobs in Slovakia and those conversion projects that existed lacked funding. Zdeněk Lukas points out that while the estimated costs of conversion in Slovakia were about 26.3 billion crowns, the federal government had made no more than 1.3 billion available by 1991[33]. The federal government would in fact renege on the policy piecemeal and favour continuing Czech production first[34]. Vladimír Dlouhý's U-turn on the principles of production was completed after two years, i.e. just prior to the June 1992 election, by which time the job losses, the considerable publicity accruing to them and the neglect of conversion had proved weighty arguments in Slovakia against the Czechocentrism of federal policy.

Industrial policy, specifically, policies aimed at small-business start-ups and restructuring existing industry generally, had been sabotaged from the right by 1991[35]. The resulting policy vacuum in this area until 1992 seemed particularly ill-attuned to Slovaks' anxiety over their relative ability to gain foreign investment and Western markets. Though the contentious data on industrial performance provide some basis for assessing policy, arguably a more telling account of the state of the industrial sector across the two republics can be gleaned from Aleš Bulíř's survey of 'expected production'. According to Bulíř, Czech firms were more optimistic, apparently with good reason, about both stability and increases in total demand and expected external demand. As far as production was concerned, over 55 per cent of all firms in the Czech Republic expected an increase in output, by comparison with less than one-third in Slovakia[36].

Privatisation

In 1991 the private sector did little to compensate for the general decline in economic activity, least of all in Slovakia, which accounted for only 23 per cent of all private businesses[37]. Though both the Czech and Slovak Ministers for Privatisation were committed to comprehensive privatisation, for Ivan Mikloš (PAV/CDU), installed after Mečiar's ouster in April 1991, this commitment spelled increasing political isolation. Indeed, by December 1991, Mikloš was even opposed by the future Slovak Christian Democratic Movement deputies within the Christian Democratic Movement, causing Kučerák to threaten withdrawing the PAV/CDU from the Slovak coalition altogether[38].

Slovak objections to Klaus's original voucher scheme for the privatisation of large enterprises (known as 'large privatisation') had led even the basically sympathetic Slovak government to work out a modified strategy, abandoned only after some minor alterations to the federal scheme were secured by pressure from Czech moderates. The enabling law of 26 February 1991 conceded that vouchers should be bought at the nominal price of 1,000 crowns. More importantly, vouchers could be used together with alternative forms of privatisation within schemes worked out by enterprises themselves and approved by the responsible ministry, i.e. the Czech or Slovak ministries of industry, agriculture or internal trade – an apparent cabinet victory for the Civic Movement. This legal flexibility appeared to imply some initiative in the hands of the privatisation ministries, which processed plans approved by the responsible industrial ministries; however, this nominal flexibility came within the context of an extraordinarily short time-scale for processing voucher privatisation. The list for the first wave – 1,436 Czech and 573 Slovak enterprises – was to be completed by the end of October, with transfer to private ownership ready within five months[39]. If the problems of processing were marginally less severe in Slovakia this was for the problematic reason that Slovak enterprises were less desirable – average profitability of those on offer was half the Czech level – and on average only two (enterprise) proposals came forward for each[40].

In 1991 the federal government had earmarked approximately 6,000 large enterprises for privatisation, about 4,400 in the Czech Republic and 1,600 in Slovakia. The privatisation process was divided into two waves, with each wave consisting of several rounds of bidding for the firms that entered voucher privatisation. By late 1992 it was evident that Slovak companies had been priced lower than the Czech, despite their relatively low indebtedness, and that they had attracted relatively little interest from Czech investors, who assumed them to be poorer investments, in great contrast to Slovak interest in Czech firms[41].

Certainly the Slovaks had reason to be concerned by the relatively poor progress of the privatisation process as a whole, especially as a method for reinvigorating the economy. Slovakia saw poorer participation of foreign capital (few firms were seen as internationally competitive), less impressive returns on vouchers and thus relatively greater difficulties in implementing the federal programme as a whole. There was a significantly lower share of private firms in Slovakia[42], with the gap narrowing in retail, but widening in both construction and industry. By the summer of 1992, Czech private firms accounted for one half of all construction works and more than one quarter of industry output whilst the same figures for Slovakia were 20 per cent and 4 per cent respectively. When looking at firms of over 25 employees, medium and large private firms had an almost seven times bigger stake in output in Slovakia.

Another significant feature of the voucher privatisation process in political terms was that it tended to produce extremely uncertain outcomes[43]. It was an intrinsic part of the working theory that officials (of the federal coupon privatisation centre) would be able to induce market equilibrium between bidding rounds by adjusting prices proportionately to excess demand. Final share prices were thus unpredictable. Officials also increased this uncertainty by leaving undetermined the number of bidding rounds and securing for themselves discretionary powers to alter share prices and to remove firms with excess demand out of the privatisation process as a whole[44]. Although no doubt intended to introduce the logic of the market, this procedure could not but add to the Slovaks' perception that their relatively poor performance was at least in part the result of a process designed and administered, with apparently harmful interventions, from Prague.

Next to price liberalisation and currency convertibility, privatisation was probably the most visible pillar of the federal reform programme. Its success in the Czech Republic thus served to bolster the federal package as a whole there. Even in the Czech Republic, however, the methods had been controversial, with the hell-for-leather speed of the whole process breaking the partnership between Klaus and his old colleague from Prognost, the Czech Minister of Privatisation, Thomáš Ježek, who tired of being scapegoated for all the difficulties on the Czech front, complaining that Klaus sacrificed proper administration of privatisation to electoral showmanship. In Slovakia, however, even with privatisation emerging as a relative failure, the politicians responsible remained faithful to the programme; the Public Against Violence's Ivan Mikloš sided with Klaus against Ježek and in so doing became thoroughly identified with a programme failing to address Slovak difficulties: relative lack of domestic capital, uncompetitiveness, unattractiveness to foreign capital etc. This impression only deepened as Mikloš struggled to consolidate the existing reform before the by now inevitable defeat of the PAV/CDU in the June 1992 election.

Václav Klaus's signature as Finance Minister appeared on every privatisation voucher, thus clearly associating him personally with the programme. In the Czech Republic it has been remarked that 'it did much to mark him as the father of an economic reform programme that was at once relatively fair, popular and effective'[45]. Others have concluded that 'the consequence of the voucher privatisation was not to make popular capitalism but to make Václav Klaus popular', pointing out that the June 1992 election followed just weeks after millions had registered their investment points[46]. In Slovakia it seems safe to infer, however, that the omnipresence of Klaus's signature in connection with the relative devaluation of Slovak industry and investment would have had something of the opposite political effect.

Living conditions

Already in early 1991, various factors in Slovakia were signalling a decline in living standards and a sense of relatively greater caution and anxiety among the Slovak population. Slovakia's retail turnover was, and remained throughout 1991–2, below the federal average, a consequence of lower average monthly wages and higher unemployment[47]. Slovak consumers were clearly less optimistic, and consumer demand was effectively flat. In the Czech Republic, meanwhile, the rate of saving was increasing[48], in contrast to Slovakia, where household bank deposits were diminishing even as more money was going into circulation. In 1990 dissaving occurred in Slovakia for the first time since 1970[49]. Bulíř suggests (though admitting such behaviour is unobservable) that Slovak conditions might have resulted from Slovak households hoarding goods from the better supplied Czech Republic[50]. Horakova suggests more broadly that the Slovak population remained sceptical of further economic developments and sought to rid itself of domestic currency, in contrast to the Czechs, whose trust in the currency had apparently been restored. Consumers in the two republics evidently began to behave as two different populations after 1990, with Czechs spending a higher proportion of their household budget on durable goods and less on food than Slovak households[51].

Inflation in 1991 stood at 61.2 per cent in Slovakia and 56.6 per cent in the Czech Republic, and Slovak purchasing power declined by some 27 per cent. However, according to Bulíř[52], the inflationary trend was reversed in 1992 thanks to the Slovak government unilaterally beginning to introduce more expansionary fiscal policies and to lower aggregate demand accompanied by the preservation of some subsidies to specific goods and public services. Where the Czech government liberalised 95 per cent of all prices in 1991, or at least relaxed price controls and cut many subsidies, the Slovaks preserved some of the latter, namely on transport, paid medical services, rents etc. Though this served partially to offset other growing pressures to social peace in the republic, it was clearly a costly divergence from the federal reform line which drew accusations of irresponsibility from the Czech National Council.

Unemployment

According to an intuitively reasonable, if sweeping notion, 'people' are willing to sacrifice much for the sake of economic reform, but become restless at the point where their work and future are threatened by unemployment[53]. According to this view, the development of Slovak unemployment alone could well have accounted for Slovak political disenchantment with the federal agenda. Factors frequently cited for the success in keeping state-wide unemployment low during transition are a boom in the private sector, active labour market policies and an unwillingness of directors to lay off workers before privatisation. Disentangling the relative importance of structural factors as against government policies in countering unemployment is always a difficult task; nevertheless it was clear that most new employment in the Czech Republic was in the private sector and in particular in small businesses effectively replacing jobs lost in the state sector. Unemployment in Slovakia, however, rose disproportionately, most obviously because of difficulties on two fronts: fostering a new private sector and implementing proactive employment measures. By the end of 1991 unemployment stood at 4.1 per cent in the Czech Republic but 11.8 per cent in Slovakia. In the first quarter of 1992, the unemployment rate fell from 4.1 per cent to 3.7 per cent in the Czech Republic but increased from 11.8 per cent to 12.3 per cent in Slovakia, falling back to 11.8 per cent by the end of April[54]. The upshot of this divergence in unemployment trends was that the share of Slovak jobless in the total number of unemployed in the CSFR rose to 57.7 per cent[55]. Both the rate of unemployment and the total number of unemployed had increased more quickly in Slovakia.

In the Czech Republic, active employment measures (1.7 billion crowns worth in 1992[56]) proved adequate. Without them, Mitchell Orenstein argues, the unemployment rate in the Czech Republic would have been 80 per cent higher by May 1993. Such policies were, moreover, an important condition of the 1991 General Agreement in the Czechoslovak tripartite council. According to a PHARE report commissioned and submitted to the federal government at the beginning of 1992[57], however, there were significant imbalances of provision for active employment measures, with insufficient provision in the Slovak Republic and even an excess in some parts of the Czech lands. In particular, Slovak offices were significantly under-staffed compared to their Czech counterparts: when set against the level of unemployment, a single member of staff was responsible for 57 clients in the Czech Republic and 149 in Slovakia[58]. Significantly, the Federal Budget Act for 1992 and adjustments to the benefit system would, rather than rectify (as advised by the PHARE report), continue the scissor-like divergence of performance between the republics, specifically by *reducing* the proportion of money available to Slovakia for pursuing active employment measures. The federal reduction came despite Slovakia's demonstrated relative difficulty in creating jobs and its greater problems of long-term unemployment, in contrast to the Czech Republic, where the number of job vacancies rose steadily[59].

Noteworthy also in this respect was Slovakia's receipt of significantly smaller flows of foreign direct investment – the proportion of direct investment being roughly 1:9 (Slovak:Czech) by 1992[60], the massive investment of Volkswagen in Czech Skoda making the significant difference[61]. The lack of investment in Slovakia was crucial in the relatively sluggish development of the Slovak private sector. In the eyes of politicians such as Carnogursky it stood as evidence not only of their relative structural disadvantages but also of their lack of international visibility. A highly practical economic justification thus clearly existed for Slovak concerns over her constitutional and international status, a case never considered by the Czech press when assessing the unilateral foreign visits of Vladimír Mečiar, which were typically written off as expressions of his personal and nationalist egotism.

Budget and finance

The area of fiscal and other transfers between the two republics and the federation between 1990 and 1992, as well as being politically charged, was also fraught with a basic disagreement over estimates, even of purely budgetary transfers. The main source of difficulty in calculation was that there were in fact no explicit transfers between the Czech budget and the Slovak budget (though some from federal to republican budgets). Transfers rather occurred implicitly, and thus controversially, through four main channels: through the allocation of tax revenue to the different budgets; through spending programmes with heavier commitments to one republic than another; through non-market pricing of some commodities and services; and, finally, through the commercial bank refinancing operations of the State Bank of Czechoslovakia[62]. The latter, though not included in formal budget data, represented significant sums[63]. Calculation of the level of subsidy between the federation and the republics thus remained an expression of the basic state-arrangement arguments stalemated elsewhere, with estimates ranging from a transfer of 10 per cent of Net Material Product from the Czech lands to Slovakia throughout the 1980s to Slovak arguments that among other transfers, taxes on wage bills from Slovak subsidiaries of Czech enterprises had made the Czech lands the net gainers. A second major problem in analysing distribution arose from the lack of systematic data on the allocation of expenditure, with the overall expenditure of the federal government the significant unknown[64]. In Slovak eyes, moreover, the location of the federal administration in Prague represented a constant and significant transfer of resources that was never acknowledged.

With so little budgetary transparency every alteration in budgetary responsibility was open to controversy[65]. According to the OECD, for example, the disproportionate strain of higher unemployment expenditure (and other related social payments) on the Slovak budget and the resulting switch of responsibility for unemployment payments to the federal level in 1992 represented a new transfer to Slovakia[66]. Because of the unfavourable adjustments in benefit entitlement that followed, however, this transfer was extremely politically sensitive, implying a practical loss of Slovak autonomy over a critical aspect of its population's welfare, placing Slovak liberals in a terrible predicament when federal responsibility failed to resolve the continuing divergence in unemployment rates.

Raphael Shen argues that the most 'delicate sensitivity' was applied to the question of federal–republic jurisdiction and general fiscal reform after 1989[67]. Under Communism the federal budget had overwhelmingly dominated the republican, despite a debate in 1968 over the assignment of revenues to their origin. The essential requirement of any budget revision was thus the introduction of the basic principle of self-sufficiency in the respective budgets, taking into account the transition to the market. The new law of December 1990 pursued the aims of containing inflation and reducing the government role *per se.*

Sources of revenue and jurisdiction were redefined, and, given ground rules for the three governments' revenues, it was eventually agreed that each state budget, including the federal budget, would have its own revenues, defined exactly in the law on budgetary rules[68] – the decision which marked Klaus's victory over the republican proposals of Lnáře, back in April 1990.

These ground rules were based on three main principles which in the existing situation were largely impossible to administer with any precision, discrediting the arrangement as soon as it was established. Firstly, governments on different levels had to determine *ex ante* their respective incomes, with fiscal independence from other levels of government: an objective assuming a jurisdictional clarity which did not exist. Secondly, regulatory functions of the federal budget had to be assured on all levels, integrating fiscal practices into a market-oriented structure for the state's economy as a whole. In essence this corresponded to the principle that federal government should be restricted to the level where functioning federalism could be maintained. Unfortunately, the definition of minimum federal government as reflected in the legal division of competences remained uncertain and impossible to agree. Thirdly, for practical purposes, existing subsidies to state enterprises would remain the responsibility of the federal government[69].

Revenue shares, and also the revenue sources to be shared, were supposedly renegotiated annually and formalised in the budgetary law – another major source of dispute. In practice, the process more resembled a rolling negotiation, as often proposals agreed at the advisory council were rejected by the republican governments or National Councils, and were duly returned for renegotiation[70]. Each year nevertheless saw a shifting proportion of the three budgets in the overall shared revenue on principles 'inspired by a policy of aligning of the expenditure per capita level in both republics'[71]. In effect the 'minimal federation' was something thus practically redefined at each budget negotiation and each budget Act, but on each occasion toward the abandonment of the redistributive functions of the state, a development following impeccable neo-liberal logic but one that absolutely called into question the political will behind a consensus-seeking federation. Had it not been for the fact that the budget was negotiated by the three Finance Ministers (republican and federal), politically and intellectually behind Klaus, the loose legal definitions of their relative competencies and the aforementioned difficulty in defining real transfers would have made budgetary agreement impossible. As it was, budget negotiation was not a clearly bounded process and was accompanied by far less consensual non-official positions. While Klaus managed to retain both the reins and the whip hand on an extremely technical debate, the conflict over allocation was played out vicariously in the continuing conflict over the constitutional division of competences – that is, until the two debates converged dramatically in November 1991.

By the end of 1991 the federal government had a 6 billion crown surplus, the Czech Republic, a 14 billion crown deficit, Slovakia a 9 billion crown deficit[72]. Tax collection had proved a disappointment in 1991 and Klaus tried, unsuccessfully, to blame the high spending of the Czech and Slovak governments for the shortfall in the 1991 budget. According to Shen, much of the latter deficits resulted from unplanned subsidies to weakened enterprises, problems in securing tax payment and increased government expenditure on active employment measures[73].

Though the latter governments could not adjust their commitments for 1991, the federal government reacted by substantial cuts in entitlement to state benefit for the 1992 budget, its solution to an emerging stand-off between the Czech and Slovak National Councils over budgets through late November–early December 1991. In a negotiated compromise between the three Finance Ministers in Bratislava on 20 November the Financial Council agreed that the existing ratio of the division of turnover and profit tax would stand at 41.5:23.5 (1.77:1) – a concession from the Czech Republic, which had originally demanded a division proportionate to the number of inhabitants (1.95:1). The Czech National Council, however, reacted to the previous weeks of constitutional controversy by opposing Czech Finance Minister Karel Špaček's agreement as a climb-down, acceptable only if the maintenance of the common state could be guaranteed. 'We must not', said Petr Pithart, 'buy the federation for a couple of weeks only'[74]. Klaus opposed what he saw as the Czechs breaking ranks, and Anton Vavro, Slovak deputy premier, pointed out that the Czechs were playing into the hands of Slovak separatists by insisting on proportionality at a time of disproportionate economic difficulty[75]. Though agreement was finally reached on 5 December via a one-off subsidy to both republics from the federal budget, this was secured by drastic inroads on social benefits, and, as we have already seen, on unemployment benefits in particular.

In 1990 Klaus had had the foresight to sell proposed public expenditure cuts in the yearly state budgets as an effective way to reduce his own powers: 'because the market understands the division of restricted resources far better than the most democratically elected parliament, though it had in its hands the [reform] foundations of the most genial finance minister in the world'[76]. By 1992 the electoral issue was not so much the reduction of federal power as such, but the popular, budget-led impression that the Czech and federal governments (apparently incensed by Slovak gestures toward independence) were withdrawing responsibility for the decline in Slovak conditions emanating from federal reform[77]. While the federal budget had a relatively stable surplus in the first three quarters of 1992, both republics' budgets were often in the red. Slovak prospects appeared relatively worse at the end of the year owing to low profits and flat retail sales. After the June 1992 election both budgets were kept relatively balanced through prudential expenditure policies and cuts. In the case of Slovakia this behaviour was in clear contradiction to Meciar's pre-election promises[78].

REFORM IN THE NAME OF THE 'STATE'

The post-Communist aspiration to 'roll back the state' held serious implications for Czech–Slovak relations. According to constitutionally enshrined rules, the task of the Communist federation had been the balancing of economic and social differences between the two republics. Democratic Czechoslovakia had duly inherited a constitutional injunction to create the same conditions and opportunities for the creation and utilisation of national revenues (article 4, paragraph 4 of Act 143/1968). While many accepted that such a clause had to be replaced as part of the dismantling of the central plan, for the professed market purists, amongst others, material subventions to Slovakia and the 'financial engineering' of national relations were unacceptable in principle. Starting from the view expressed discreetly in the Civic Forum June draft election manifesto, that 'both nations are at equal levels of economic development' and that the federal state should not in future redistribute to Slovakia any part of the national product originating in the Czech lands[79], the position of the right marked out an essential stumbling block of the ensuing conflict.

Five months after the revolution Klaus wrote, apparently addressing the entire population, 'we must sign together what is termed in the expert literature a 'social contract', one which will differ a great deal from the last'[80]. Such a contract was nonetheless upheld only in the Czech Republic. Moreover, the frustration with existing conditions that led Slovaks to reject their rightist government and the subsequent parliamentary upheaval were apparently interpreted by federal neo-liberals as a constraint on 'imperative' economic policies rather than as a dispute of any transcendent cultural or historical importance –

indicating a peculiarly dogmatic, 'post-Communist' manifestation of neo-liberal politics.

When one looks at Klaus's statements during the dispute over competences in late 1990, their most striking feature is the belief that there existed an unassailable realm of the economic, and that politics, or what Klaus termed 'classical political disagreement', was subordinate to achieving economic success, or even inhabited a separate realm entirely. Though Klaus was deeply pragmatic in his approach to attaining reform, 'politics' for him remained a technocratic art. The politics of the national dispute represented something else entirely: compromise, inefficiency, a potentially fatal threat to market reform – the unattractive prospect of, at best, sub-optimal economic and political returns.

In November 1990 Klaus was asked if he had any ideas on how to formulate Czech policy in relation to the federation. Again his main aim seems to have been to distinguish the economic from the political debate, but also to set out the ostensibly reasonable condition that unity was feasible only within specific economic parameters. 'The absence of Czech policy is an objective concern', he replied. 'That is to say that Czech parties never had the need to work out an actual policy. Whether it is a big mistake will only reveal itself . . .'. He concluded that 'it would be preferable first of all to straighten out economic relations. I believe that it is then in the political realm to clear anything up'[81]. Once economic relations had been 'straightened out', it was implied, they should not be permitted to re-enter the political or national debate. The experiences of other federations and the history of Czech and Slovak relations together show plainly, however, that these realms cannot realistically be separated.

It has been argued elsewhere that three sets of attitudes were important in determining Czech acceptance of the economic reform programme: optimism about the eventual success of reforms and future increases in living standards; expectations about how long the period of sacrifices would last, how great the sacrifices would be, and how quickly the benefits would come; and, finally, perceptions of fairness[82]. However, what clearly passed for interventionist, even social democratic/corporatist, forms of intervention in the Czech economy proved woefully inadequate in Slovakia, where intervention was at disproportionately lower levels and unsupported by a macro policy anticipating the Slovaks' relative lack of foreign investment and adaptable industrial structure.

It has also been argued that one can identify divergent republican economic policy and macro-economic results from the beginning of 1992[83], implying that scissoring conditions created a mounting pressure to adjust policy only months before the June election mandated such a change. I would argue instead that the federal reform had already done its worst by April 1991, when Mečiar departed from the Public Against Violence. Thereafter, though the prudent policy of the Czech government was accompanied by positive macro-economic response, even with the mild stimulative attempts of the Slovak government, aggregate demand in Slovakia continued to fall. Moreover, it had become clear by 1992 that the faltering process of privatisation in the Slovak Republic could neither absorb unemployment nor lead to a significant rise in output[84].

It was little wonder that many Slovaks sought adjustments in the pace of reform and greater powers of decision when these conditions emerged. Slovakia's 'relative deprivation' was, by 1992, indisputable. Yet at the federal level the logic of radical economic reform was relentless: a functioning free-market economy was a given end-state of radical reform, to be reached via certain essential measures, most importantly by tight monetary policy and the avoidance of state intervention and 'regional' policy. According to this logic, Slovak failures, given the facile presumed starting point of parity, must have emerged from a mismanagement of the economy within the administrative parameters afforded the republican government prior to 1992. The implication was that Slovakia was erring from the path not as a reaction to an intolerable style of reform but because of irrational Slovak nationalism, administrative incompetence, and a prior preference for a different end-state – i.e. some form of etatist, interventionist economy – throughout the Slovak administrative and political structure.

We are left with the difficult question to what extent Klausite reform can really be held up as having precipitated a political backlash in Slovakia against the political right. Demonstrating absolutely that economic conditions motivated the voting behaviour of 1992 is not possible, and yet opinion polls consistently revealed living standards and declining economic conditions to be top on the Slovak electorate's list of concerns. It is also impossible to separate out absolutely those latent Slovak attitudes to the federal centre from those produced or even consolidated by federal practice between 1989 and 1992. From what we know of federal relations before 1989, however, it is clear that for many Slovaks democratisation represented the first real opportunity for a redress of national grievance. We also know that Slovaks had willingly put their support behind the reform package in mid-1990 and that, as conditions deteriorated, remarkably, support for militant Slovak nationalist movements remained extremely low.

What we may assess with relative ease is the degree of

accommodation to Slovak national concerns forthcoming from the federal centre and the likely impact of federal behaviour on the reputation of pro-federalist Slovak political representatives. If lurking in such a question is the awkward counterfactual – was any other policy route possible, politically or economically? – it is perhaps a question to be asked only after considering whether the exigencies of state-building as understood in neo-liberal terms *in themselves* put an intolerable strain on national relations.

In his discussion of the characteristics of 'big bang' or radical reformers, the political economist Gerard Roland suggests they concern themselves more with *ex post* than *ex ante* (feasibility) political constraints, i.e. those that refer to the danger of backlash and the reversal of reform after outcomes have been observed. In effect this means that such reformers have to build irreversibility into their reforms, or the nearest approximation to it, which normally, though not described so explicitly as such, takes the form of a strategy of *fait accompli* to constrain a successor government by increasing the costs of reversal of policies adopted today[85]. If, for the sake of argument, we step into Klaus's self-confessed school of thought, and apply this to federal government reform in Slovakia, thus referring this theory to a partner, rather than a successor, state, we can conclude that discontent in Slovakia would have been maximised by two facts. Not only did reform disregard initial feasibility constraints (economic specificity); it aggravated the situation by attempting to create the irreversibility of programmes many of which had been greeted with disquiet in the first place.

The coincidence of pressured public finance with continuing output and revenue falls looked set to destabilise Slovakia's macro-economic situation further. While conditions in the Czech Republic improved, in Slovakia a critical mass of privatisation was not achieved, collapses in industry and output were not offset, aggregate demand did not rise, and the costs of unemployment escalated.

As we have seen, Klausite reform as applied in the Czech Republic looks to have been conscientiously state-building. By fulfilling the social contract of low wages in return for low unemployment (aided by the tourist boom in Prague) the Czech reform gained the characteristic of social sensitivity – assisted in no small measure by the moderate Civic Forum ministers in the federal and Czech governments – allowing time to build support behind existing measures before moving on to others[86]. The result was a peculiarly post-Communist hybrid of radical neo-liberal philosophy, conservative rhetoric and practical *sozialmarktwirtschaft* strategy.

The sense in which institutional reforms and strategy appeared unequivocally radical was in Klaus's outright opposition to attempts at modification, even in the face of growing Slovak political hostility. The ostentatious rejection of policy modification by the federal government *maximised* the impression of Czech–federal suzerainty over the Slovak economy; the curb on arms production succinctly illustrated this point. If one agrees that it is politically prudent under a new federal democratic framework to begin with reforms which are advantageous for both constituent units, then the prioritised decommissioning of one of Slovakia's major industries could not have been more provocative.

Could a greater decentralisation of reform, even a rhetorically greater federal sensitivity to Slovak conditions, have activated political constraints in quite the same way? Gerard Roland suggests that if one assumes the transition to the market economy represents a 'Pareto improvement' – i.e. a ratcheting-up of efficiency – it should be possible to compensate losers with the efficiency gains of reform . . . Thus if political constraints play a role in designing the programme, this should be related to the difficulty of compensating losers[87]. The problem with Roland's suggestion is that it presupposes national homogeneity, since arguably any degree of compensation will be viewed as inadequate if a central package of reform is seen to systematically damage one national economy within a federation more severely than another – as Slovaks reasonably perceived to be the case. In addition to this basic perception, social compensation was, in many instances, both less available and less effective in Slovakia than in the Czech Republic. Thus, while Slovak voters may or may not have paid attention to the technicalities of macro- and micro-economics, they could certainly glean both from the newspapers and from their relatives and friends in the Czech Republic that the federal economic vision had less to recommend itself to Slovaks. That the federal government managed to protect reform in the Czech lands from the damaging political effects of failure (and here Klaus was indebted to his more moderate colleagues) is testimony at least to the fact that these effects were not underestimated. Why then were they allowed to flourish in Slovakia, and, more importantly, not only not recognised and accommodated (even rhetorically) at the federal level, but actually compounded by budgetary allocations and unmodified reform?

The federal government was not above reacting to maintain the social peace, as demonstrated by its continual postponement of the implementation of the Bankruptcy Law – a signal that prompted more generous bank credit in the Czech Republic, thus sustaining enterprises with high inter-enterprise arrears. If the neo-liberals were thus adequately sensitive to Czech pressures, as we observe they were, the thesis that economic dogma as such prevented federal adjustments for Slovakia is rather weak. Klaus, however, had often emphasised the importance of a pragmatic and instrumentalist strategy for achieving neo-liberal goals. As he and his colleague Thomáš Ježek wrote in 1989, 'There probably exists a critical mass of reform measures, but we do not pretend to know the location of this point. We try to be led by pragmatic flexibility rather than by moralistic or ideological fundamentalism'[88].

Back in 1989, contemplating the problem of the credibility of reform in a 'forecasting' pre-revolution issue of *Politické Ekonomie*, Klaus had cited rational choice theory to bolster his claim that the attainment and retention of social consensus 'depends to a decisive degree on the integrity of the whole society, on the effectiveness of the social mechanisms which facilitate the achievement of an operable consensus forming the basis of any long-term positive social activity'[89]. Such a belief in operation could only leave federal neo-liberals with the second best available option, in the event of a society split in two: that is, given the republic-centric political party structure, a strategy of deliberately (for credibility required visible commitment) opting to please only one constituency. Given the pervasive presumption of technical, if not cultural, superiority among Czech professional economists (and others), it proved a straightforward task to explain away Slovak difficulties. Slovak oppositionist objections to current economic policy, particularly those raised by the Movement for a Democratic Slovakia, were *a priori* assumed to come from populist and etatist, rather than instrumentalist, impulses. Publicly, Slovak objections were dismissed as the musings of inept and nationalist economists. They were thus rejected. Though reform was presented in the name of the 'federal state', Klaus's Slovak neo-liberal colleagues were left to fend for themselves, with their support averaging below 5 per cent throughout the second half of 1991 and until their defeat in June 1992.

It seems reasonable to conclude that Klaus, in light of Slovak economic disadvantages, applied the neo-liberal logic of reform and decided that eliminating Slovakia from the Czech process was more prudent than any attempt to prioritise national relations over economic reform. As he and Ježek had also written in 1989, 'the only reasonable reform is a "negative reform", based on the elimination of different kinds of distortions and obstacles to the ever-present human action (in the sense of Ludwig von Mises), whereas an ambitious dirigistic reform blueprint based on rationalistic constructivism and on social engineering is bound to fail'[90]. In the June 1992 election the logic of neo-liberalism required that voters choose *between* short-term economic interests (in terms of prospects of distribution) and a common state.

A LENIN FOR THE BOURGEOISIE

While Mečiar's skill lay in positioning the Movement for a Democratic Slovakia most profitably between the early-established fault-lines of the Slovak political scene, Klaus's party acted as the issue-defining motive force of the entire Czechoslovak post-Communist transition. One of the most remarkable aspects of this story is the Civic Democratic Party's assumption, before and after June 1992, of the status of a sovereign administrator in whom the public interest was somehow innately invested, as opposed to that of a government in which the public had momentarily placed its trust. Klaus's conception of his party's role brought about two further developments, both of them perverse in the light of a transition from Communism. Firstly, Communist-style 'Leading Role of the Party' claims were now marketed in liberal capitalist terms. Secondly, Czechs were once again demanding that Slovaks subordinate their particular (national) claims to the 'higher interests of the state', i.e. state reform.

The pre-eminence of economic reform underpinned Klaus's preferred model of the state. Its neo-liberal principles carried a distinct constitutional corollary: the economy was the engine from which all social transformation, including democratisation, would follow. If technocrats typically believe that there exists an unassailable realm of expertise to which politics is necessarily subordinate, what is extraordinary in the Czechoslovak case is the presumed scope of the technocratic realm and Klaus's willingness to place all other values accredited to the common state – historical, metaphysical, economic or strategic – beneath it. While this may imply a tacit, perhaps unconscious Czech nation-statism on Klaus's part, all the available evidence points to his reasoning being predominantly economic. The constitutional corollary of this technocratic model was that the 'functioning federation' would have to be designed first and foremost as an *instrument* of reform. In practice if not in intention, Klaus's reform agenda 'captured' the entire state debate. His vision, however, was evidently a unitary state; though it was frequently referred to as a 'unitary federation', the repetitive coupling of these two contradictory terms alone could never give the phrase meaning.

When Slovak claims for higher national recognition formed the backbone of the entire Slovak party political scene, Klaus's electoral call for a 'unitary federation' or 'bust' was a fabulously disingenuous message. A 'unitary federation' begged the question of why a 'federal' state had been formed in 1968 in the first place, and, of course, entirely ignored Slovakia's seventy-odd years of national claims. For the Slovaks to have wanted less than the fulfilment of their legal rights established back in 1968 would have amounted to the unprecedented step of a European nation in the late twentieth century actually retreating from its historical national status – a *kamikaze* position for any Slovak politician to endorse.

What emerges from this and previous chapters is some points of truly remarkable kinship between the structure of the Czech Civic Democratic Party's arguments for state reform – as it were their sociology of state reform – and that of the former ruling Communist Party. This is not in any way to imply that the CDP enjoyed or asserted anything even remotely resembling the pervasive and vicious authority of the Communist Party – it obviously did not, nor did it aspire to. The points of similarity were not in the degree of state control but in the CDP's insistence on the scientific and absolute validity of one ideology – and only one – and an extreme instrumentalism in the achievement of political goals. In this respect it was truly a great political blessing for the Czech Republic that a critical part of Klausite ideology was the principle of a minimal state! Pluralism in that state, however, and press freedom were evidently aspects of democracy that Klaus could frankly take or leave. He clearly considered the CDP to be an essentially vanguardist party, uniquely suited to the task of defining the democratic future by virtue of its scientifically superior vision of state development. The construction of the future state was projected as a priority – an imperative which might be secured at the cost of the state's immediate democratic functioning. No value was to be ascribed to inherited constitutional norms, as the knowledgeably charismatic qualities of the party's vision were considered adequate guarantees of the state's proper administration. The administering state's definition of public goods was deemed superior to those prevailing among the public themselves – and again this was axiomatic in that it was backed by scientifically defined 'facts of transitional necessity'. Klaus's understanding of nationalist conflict was blankly materialistic insofar as he apparently presumed that prosperity – market prosperity – would suffice for the neutralisation, if not the withering away, of national sentiment.

Finally, the prevailing ideology was legitimated as historically determined (determined, that is, by the developmental path and economic culture of the First Republic – only momentarily sidetracked by

Communism) and was also defined 'negatively', i.e. as a 'defence' against an exaggerated external threat, not Western imperialism in this case, but Slovak nationalism. When we look at Klaus in the mirror of history, we see, to a remarkable extent, a vanguardist of the market – a Lenin for the bourgeoisie.

6

THE SHORT GOODBYE

A 'realist' explanation for the break-up of Czechoslovakia – one that assumes that politicians everywhere are purely self-serving and power-mad by nature – is that Czech and Slovak political leaderships colluded to produce it. In the absence of a potentially legislation-blocking rival, Klaus and Mečiar could steer their 'own' states more completely along their own desired paths and remove significant threats to their continuation in power[1]. As has been commented, 'the economic and political interests of the two leaders, while opposed, were nonetheless easy to reconcile'[2].

The most plausible line of argument accounting for the strength of political leadership is not that these two political entrepreneurs brought a strong state to heel, but that they effectively redefined the conflict over the state in a way that served their own ends. Having persuaded others in authority of the validity of their state visions they brought effective decision-making power under their personal control. In this they would have been assisted by the atmosphere of imminent instability prevailing in all post-Communist countries in the aftermath of the revolutions. An apt Czech cartoon of the time showed an opinion pollster accosting an anxious-looking citizen only to be told: 'I would give you my opinion – but I don't want to cause a government crisis'[3].

Previous chapters have already lent support to a 'realist' argument about the strength of political leadership insofar as we have already identified the opportunities uniquely available to political actors in the conditions of top-down party development and generally rapid institutional change. It has also been established that the policy-defining and policy-making processes were dominated by these two leaders before June 1992 and that opinion poll data looked likely to develop into endorsement of the separation – to the benefit of the Civic Democratic Party in particular. To consider a realist explanation in full, however, we need to apply a final question to the post-election 'endgame', namely, is there evidence of collusion between Klaus and Mečiar? Evidence against the realist argument might include examples of pro-common-state consensus-seeking behaviour on the part of either Klaus or Mečiar, seemingly irrational risk-taking on their part, or, lastly, strong attachment on the part of either leader to the common-state idea.

'ENDGAME'

June 1992

The new Slovak leader, Vladimír Mečiar, insisted, as talks began in Brno on 8 June 1992, that Slovak independence was 'not a point in the MDS programme'. Vaclav Klaus had campaigned against a republican erosion of federal powers and for a return to a recentralised *status quo*, arguing that a vote for the confederalist-sounding model touted by Mečiar in Slovakia would amount to a Slovak vote for the division of the state. The Civic Democratic Party position of centralised 'federation or bust' duly emerged in post-election negotiations as an absolute, and before June was out Mečiar admitted 'if we talk about independence it is not because we want it, but because we must'[4]. Mečiar's apparent belief that the Czechs might be strong-armed into a confederation proved baseless.

The post-election agenda consisted of the appointments for federal and republican governments, ministries and institutions on the one hand, and negotiations over the future state structure on the other. Klaus maintained that his Civic Democratic Party saw 'scope for negotiations' with the Movement for a Democratic Slovakia and argued that 'manoeuvring space exists on both sides'[5]. He also warned that the country would split if negotiations failed, implying that both parties would, indeed, manoeuvre. In fact, as throughout the constitutional talks that had begun in 1990 and continued in various forms until their collapse in February 1992, two issues put these new post-election negotiations into instant gridlock: the recognition of Slovak sovereignty and the indivisibility of economic policy across the republics.

Immediately after the election Mečiar proposed a delay in the formation of a new federal government in order to attain two 'structural changes'. In the first, an interim government would be formed to function until a referendum – promised by the MDS as part of their election campaign. In the second, new bodies would be constituted on the basis of the referendum's results. 'The crucial thing', Mečiar determined, 'is whether Czecho-Slovakia will become two states or not. We insist on a treaty of cooperation which would respect the existence of the two legal entities from the viewpoint of international law'.

Underlining this demand for an apparently loose confederation, Mečiar also suggested that a provision for the post of Slovak president should be included in a Slovak constitution to be approved by the end of August[6]. The Civic Democratic Party, with no stomach for any such unprecedented state re-engineering, even as an opening gambit, dug in its heels and waited.

Mečiar's Movement for a Democratic Slovakia, the (Slovak) Party of the Democratic Left (PDL) and Jozef Prokeš' Slovak National Party (SNP) took the most obvious path and cooperated in the Federal Assembly, provoking full-blown conspiracy-theorising in the Czech press. Czech commentary insisted that a Slovak leftist/nationalist government would give Mečiar the upper hand in negotiations, where, as one commentator put it, he could 'dictate the conditions' with a 'broad smile', warmed by the 'admiring glances . . . from Czech left-wing forces, mainly the Communists'[7]. Another commentator, Jiří Leschtina, warned that MDS, PDL and SNP unity in the Federal Assembly was intended to 'assure left-wing control over Parliament', an invocation of old demons in the light of the expected Slovak veto of Václav Havel's re-election as Federal President[8]. Klaus in turn engaged the Czech right, unlikely to retreat in the event of any show-down between a common state and the continuation of unmodified Klausite economic reform[9]. He appealed to 'constructive' prejudices and stressed the cost of protracted negotiations. He also observed that while the Czech right struggled for consensus the Communists exploited the situation to recover power[10].

The details of the first round of Civic Democratic Party–Movement for a Democratic Slovakia talks in Brno on 8 June emerged acrimoniously. Mečiar's spokesman announced that the CDP had demanded either a federation with a uniform economy or a state split and 'sanctions against Slovakia'. 'A complete lie', according to Klaus, who nevertheless insisted only that the term 'sanctions' was never used and that the Slovaks had dropped the term 'confederation' for 'economic and defence community/union'[11]. Undisputed differences had centred on Klaus's definition of a recentralising 'functioning federation', the continuation of uniform radical economic reform across the federation and the re-election of Václav Havel as federal President. The only agreement was on the need to reduce the size of the federal government and the powers of the Federal Assembly Chairman[12]. According to the pro-CDP Czech newspaper *Telegraf*, the Movement for a Democratic Slovakia had proposed an interim federal government to transfer responsibilities from federal to republican bodies, with parity membership and without executive responsibilities; two independent states with a common leadership of two independent armies; the continuation of a common currency with two issuing banks; the declaration of sovereignty at the first session of the Slovak National Council (23 June); approval of a Slovak constitution, and finally, election of a Slovak president – in sum, a division of the state, according to Václav Klaus[13].

As it turned out, the MDS was ill-prepared to be taken literally on any of the above. If its agenda is interpreted as an opening strategy, a starting bid for the highest possible stakes, Mečiar had acted on a fatal miscalculation of Klaus's interest in anything but Slovakia's full capitulation. On the question of forming new governments, the Civic Democratic Party's Jan Stráský had assured that his party would wait on the outcome of 'at least' two rounds of talks before distributing its forces. With this minimal commitment, however, he had also delivered an unambiguous warning message: 'In the case of a partition [sic] of Czechoslovakia, Václav Klaus will lead a strong Czech government'[14].

Before the next round of talks, in Prague on 11 June, the Civic Democratic Party's Miroslav Macek maintained that 'we are due to discuss a full federation or the division of the state. Not a third way'[15]. These negotiations nevertheless stalled again on the possibility of an international legal personality for Slovakia (permitting membership in international organisations such as the United Nations, a point much cited by the Czech side as proof of Slovak secessionism – reasonably enough), and also over the deadline for the formation of a federal government and Czechoslovak presidential elections. The second session had become further mired in a discussion of separate central banks and a single currency, rejected by Klaus as leading inevitably to economic and currency collapse.

As this round of talks concluded Klaus lamented the lack of progress, while Mečiar remained uncharacteristically silent; MDS Vice-Chairman Michal Kováč only reiterated that his party programme had made no provision for splitting the state and did not aim for that end. The Movement for a Democratic Slovakia, according to Kováč, wanted a free union of two 'sovereign' states and demanded a referendum to decide the matter – a referendum which would ask citizens if they wished to live in the federation, a free union, or an independent state. Klaus's response was to claim concerns about 'continuing uncertainty' and to suggest that a referendum be held in Slovakia alone, making it potentially the seceding nation; he even offered to assist in hastening the deadline for its declaration. The Movement for a Democratic Slovakia retreated, fearing for the successor rights that Slovakia could forfeit if identified as the unilateral secessionist; it duly objected that a referendum could not be rushed but was being considered for the end of 1992[16]. Despite Stráský's warning, Mečiar's Movement for a Democratic Slovakia had thus squandered the last purportedly 'open' round of talks.

Having had his opening terms dismissed as preposterous Mečiar stressed that his party's interests were to find a form of coexistence beneficial to both republics, claiming he 'did not understand' Klaus's doubts as to whether the Czechs would wait for the results. In Bratislava Mečiar again declared to journalists 'neither the Civic Democratic Party nor the Movement for a Democratic Slovakia has a mandate to divide the state!'[17]. Backpedalling swiftly on the prerequisites for forming a federal government Mečiar claimed that the MDS now agreed with the CDP in the sphere of central monetary policy but differed on tax, customs and pricing policy, which it maintained should be implemented at the republican level[18].

Both sides had agreed to continue negotiations on the following Sunday – 14 June – but the Movement for a Democratic Slovakia cancelled, broadcasting their confusion. Mečiar told his party's presidium that if the Czechs continued to seek the *status quo* he would favour partition, a stand he later vociferously denied. Though Mečiar clearly preferred to aim for high stakes, this strategy carried enormous risks, indeed, given Klaus as an opponent this strategy would make divorce inevitable, and the Movement, as Mečiar himself had pointed out, possessed no mandate for separation. In addition to public dismay, the prospect of a split appalled many of Mečiar's own most able and senior colleagues within the Movement. The MDS presidium nevertheless instructed its deputies to oppose Vaclav Havel's re-election. They also issued an open letter to their 'fellow-citizens', thanking them for their support in spite of 'slanders, crude invectives and intimidation spread in pro-federal and some foreign media . . .'. The letter promised that talks would lead to results acceptable to both sides[19].

Only days after the second round of talks the Slovak Party of the Democratic Left retreated from its alliance with the Movement for a Democratic Slovakia, despite its long-stated interest in a federation with confederative elements. Balking at Mečiar's already obvious inability to 'manoeuvre' without performing a *volte-face*, the Democratic Left declared that it had quite different opinions on tackling mutual relations with the Czech Republic and that a full confederation did not constitute a common state. As it transpired, Mečiar was determined to form a government alone (with 74 seats in the Slovak National Council he was only two votes short of an absolute majority), confident as he remained of the basic support of both the Democratic Left and Slovak National Party[20].

The Czech Left Bloc (LB) meanwhile expressed the state of general bewilderment among the Czech opposition and protested to President

The People's Militia rallies in Prague for the 'Glorious February Revolution' – the Communists complete their coup d'état.

The end of 'Socialism with a human face' – Prague, August 1968.

Alexander Dubček votes for the declaration of the Czechoslovak federation, 27 October 1968, knowing that it will not be the state he had dreamed of.

October 1989 – a blind man walks through a cordon of the Czechoslovak police. ('For the real question is whether the "brighter future" is really always so distant. What if, on the contrary, it has been here for a long time already, and only our own blindness and weakness has prevented us from seeing it around us and within us, and kept us from developing it?' Václav Havel, *The Power of the Powerless*, 1978.)

The November 1989 revolution: for a democratic federation.

Relief! The regime starts to crack when members of the Central Committee of the Communist Party resign, 24 November 1989.

November 1989: Havel to the Castle!

CDP negotiators during the split of the state, Bratislava, 22 July 1992 (from left to right, Jiří Schneider, Josef Zieleniec, Václav Klaus and Miroslav Macek).

HZDS negotiators during the split of the state, Bratislava, 22 July 1992 (from left to right, Milan Kňažko, Michal Kováč, Vladimír Mečiar and Augustín Marián Húska).

Václav Klaus and Vladimír Mečiar negotiate the break-up of Czechoslovakia, the Villa Tugenhadt, Brno, 26 August 1992.

Mečiar and Klaus sign an agreement on future cooperation between the independent Czech and Slovak Republics, 29 October 1992.

Taking it on the chin – Václav Klaus declares his resignation at CDP headquarters, Prague, 29 November 1997, after an 11-hour meeting with the party leadership.

Fighting back in the June 1998 election campaign: 'If you give me your paw, if you give me your paw, then we will say, that we really do care ...'

What Next Mr Prime Minister? (singing) 'Farewell, I did not hurt, I did not hurt, any of you ...'
Vladimír Mečiar announces his resignation, 30 September 1998.

Havel that the Civic Democratic Party and the Movement for a Democratic Slovakia had exceeded their electoral and constitutional mandates[21]. The President met with Mečiar on 15 June, and though Mečiar expressed his party's willingness to tackle economic issues, he refused to compromise on Slovakia's international legal status, the cornerstone of the loose confederative arrangement. Dismayed, Havel promoted the calling of a referendum in both republics as soon as possible, maintaining that this was an issue for the citizenry[22].

The third round of talks took place on 17 June at the Civic Democratic Party's Prague headquarters. Before the meeting the CDP declared itself in favour of an unambiguous decision either to create a federal coalition or a caretaker federal government to oversee separation. The CDP also proposed that the week's meetings should constitute the final political negotiations[23].

In the midst of the talks on 17 June, Klaus is reported to have reproached the Slovak side for seeking 'Czech finance for Slovak independence' and to have asked '[a]re you a proud nation or are you not?' Mečiar is said to have replied 'Each for himself'. This retort is supposed by many commentators to have been Mečiar's ultimate admission of separatism[24] and the motivation behind Klaus's subsequent decision to become Czech premier. This interpretation, however, confuses real Czech decisions with the opportune moment for their announcement. The Rubicon had clearly been crossed before the meeting, arguably before negotiations had even begun, since compromise in these talks depended not only on the Slovaks' but on the Czechs' willingness to soften their demands[25]. It must be borne in mind that those Slovak (as opposed to Hungarian minority) parties of the centre right that had *accepted* Klaus's course of recentralising constitutional reform had failed to secure a single seat in the recent election in either of the chambers of the Federal Assembly or the Slovak National Council. It had been made abundantly clear in the June 1992 election that Klaus's vision was unsustainable in Slovakia. For a Slovak party to have accepted it now would have been political suicide.

Following the announcement that Klaus would take up the Czech premiership Mečiar called the decision 'a wise step which will lead to good cooperation between the Czech and Slovak governments'. He, as expected, took up the Slovak post. The subsequent agreement on government formation resembled the Movement for a Democratic Slovakia's earlier proposals: a federal government of ten members with five members from each republic. It survived, however, at crossed purposes; Mečiar described the future interim federal government as a 'working one', likely to last a minimum of one and a half years.

In talks with President Havel the Party of the Democratic Left now declared itself for a 'loose federation', and Alexander Dubček's Slovak Social Democrats appealed for the transfer of talks to parliament. Together with the Czech left, Slovak federalists now began to comprehend the need to array themselves appropriately in the light of a potentially lengthy and unpopular dissolution. Federal trade union representatives meanwhile clearly recognised that Klaus had the upper hand and, presumably with an eye to the future, endorsed the CDP's strategy wholeheartedly, asserting that 'a prospering economy was the best social guarantee for employees'[26].

The fourth round of negotiations began in Bratislava on 19 June. These fourteen hours of talks confirmed that the new federal government would consider its mandate temporary and would seek to 'prepare, if it is empowered to do so, conditions for the smooth functioning of two sovereign states with international personality'[27]. It was also agreed in writing that 'the government will support a quick solution of the constitutional problem on the basis of an agreement between the two National Councils' – a startling conclusion in that it raised the authority of the National Councils above that of the Federal Assembly and was thus unconstitutional. A CDP recommendation that agreement should be reached by the end of September 1992, 'at the latest', was also included[28]. Both parties agreed that in the event of separation the National Councils would approve laws on the incorporation of members of the Federal Assembly into the legislative bodies of the two republics[29]. Clearly Klaus's CDP had done its homework on the schedule of a rapid partition, in this case pre-empting any objections that might arise from federal deputies acting to slow a separation for reasons of their own job security. Klaus's persuasive case was that the Movement for a Democratic Slovakia had 'refused CDP compromises' by persisting in the demand for international legal personality. As he insisted, 'a Slovak compromise on this point would be to withdraw it. Non-withdrawal means the split of the state into two'[30].

The Civic Democratic Party's budgetary policy now prevailed, and the redistribution of finances through the Federal Budget was set to end from the beginning of 1993[31]. Though affirming that the Slovak National Council would declare sovereignty at an early (though no longer the first) session, Mečiar insisted again that 'this should not mean the split of the state'[32]. President Havel endeavoured to count the blessings of the talks during his regular Sunday broadcast. The process toward divorce, he argued, would at least be civilised[33]. The federal government line-up was leaked to the press on 24 June. Jan Stráský (CDP) – known as a skilled and tough-minded mediator – was to be Federal Prime Minister, Rudolf Filkus (MDS) Federal First Deputy Prime Minister, and Miroslav Macek (CDP) with Antonín Baudyš (Christian Democratic Union/Czechoslovak People's Party) Deputy Prime Ministers. Jozef Moravčík (MDS) was to be Federal Minister for Foreign Affairs[34].

When Havel next met with Czech parliamentary party leaders his already faltering resistance to the idea that political elites would decide on the state was further weakened. Though referenda were supported as the valid, constitutionally required method of separation, most parties, according to Václav Benda (Christ.DP), emphasised 'other forms of possible split, not dictated by the constitution, which would be suitable for a quicker and problem-free split', i.e. parliamentary agreement. One-sided steps, such as a Slovak declaration of sovereignty, Benda insisted, would also render referenda superfluous since 'there would be nothing to decide'[35]. On 25 June President Havel tried for the last time to convince the Federal Assembly that referenda remained the only constitutional option. The appeal was half-hearted, however. Fatally, Havel conceded that the Assembly as the highest legislative body could invent another method which he would respect. In admitting this, the President exploded the notion of profound constitutional constraint, resolving in a sentence any fears the government may have had that he might again take his cause to the people[36].

As June drew to a close, the former Czech premier, Petr Pithart, concluded that the 'basic problem of Slovakia is that it does not know what it wants'[37]. While this was hard to verify, Mečiar evidently saw a pressing need to manufacture some version of Slovak desires, and instructions were apparently sent to Slovak state broadcasting organisations to this purpose. Slovak television introduced its own current affairs programme on the national channel at 7 pm on 27 June, having reported to Czechoslovak Television that it could no longer process shots from federal television, including the weather[38].

Despite the facade of free choice, however, Slovakia's bold advances toward increased autonomy within a common state had been thoroughly corralled. The very predictability of the impasse between the conflicting visions of Klaus and Mečiar had lent, under Klaus's direction, a great momentum to the Czech and federal governments' decisions. It was already settled that the federal system would be shrunk to the working minimum necessary to oversee the divorce: the number of federal ministries would be reduced from twelve to five (Finance, Defence, Interior, Foreign Affairs and Economy), and the Movement for a Democratic Slovakia could only briefly attempt to portray this as a victory against the centre and the beginning of a drawn-out process of compromise. Changes such as the preclusion of a federal budget for 1993 made it clear that a separation was already decided, whatever the legitimacy of the process.

Mečiar's tactic of overbidding, of asking for confederation from a Czech government that others appeared to have recognised as resolutely centrist, afforded the very alibi Klaus would need for hastening the split of the state. Klaus's CDP could charge that Mečiar's vision of confederation flew in the face of political realities, that the Czech parliament could never endorse such a misalignment of administrative rights and financial liabilities, and that, far from a Yugoslav scenario, Czechs preferred to aid and abet the Slovak leader, Mečiar, who was currently only mismanaging both the Slovaks' and his own secessionist impulses. To avoid censure, Klaus, citing Czech subsidy of the Slovak economy (estimated at 25 billion Czechoslovak crowns in 1992), could plead the political insanity of his Slovak opponents.

July

At the beginning of July the now nervous Slovak government pursued placatory measures at home. Government members offered their May salary increase for charity purposes and Labour Minister Olga Keltošová suggested changing the Slovak budget to the advantage of social benefits[39] – only to admit a fortnight later that funds for unemployment benefits in the 1992 Slovak budget had already been exhausted. On 1 July the Czech coalition partners – Civic Democratic Alliance, Christian Democratic Union/Czechoslovak People's Party, Christian Democratic Party and the Civic Democratic Party – signed their consent to the transfer of federal responsibilities to the republics and urged the establishment of a Czech constitution and constitutional court. Agreed on the indivisibility of Czechoslovakia's legal personality they concluded that questions of alternative union would be solved post-independence[40]. The level of consensus on the Czech right is striking in the light of Slovak dismay, but also in the light of an opinion poll of the time, which reported that more than two-thirds of Czechs felt themselves to have good or very good personal relations with Slovaks and *vice versa*[41].

Premier Stráský (CDP) was characteristically proactive in keeping federal deputies to Klaus's agenda, as was Milan Uhde, the CDP Chairman of the Czech National Council. When a dispute arose over whether the Council presidium should be formed on the basis of party proportional representation, Uhde objected that such a 'forum' would be too discursive to represent an effective 'head of state' at this stage[42]. Addressing the Council Klaus declared that he considered building the 'firm foundations of Czech statehood . . . a positive and creative task', adding 'we do not only want to adopt a defensive position, as the former government often did'[43].

Two interviews illustrated how differently the two leaders depicted the motivation to separate. In *Mladá Fronta dnes* Klaus claimed to have opted for the Czech Premiership on 17 June. 'At that time I understood that the efforts of [our] Slovak partners to attain independence for Slovakia were final and irreversible . . . that it was not simply pre-election rhetoric' but the profound aspiration of 'all MDS representatives'. He claimed to see the symptoms of the split most visibly 'in the economic sphere . . . The already existing non-homogeneous economies in Bohemia and Slovakia have been irreversibly moving away from one another. I cannot imagine a political force which would manage to thwart this process' – a statement completely at odds with his previous, positive assessments of economic parity. Acknowledging that 'public opinion polls among citizens do not speak unequivocally about the split', Klaus nevertheless described developments as if observing a meta-political process beyond help; 'I am only afraid that the dividing processes about which I have just spoken are beyond the hands of Mr Mečiar'. Personally, he said, 'I define a viable nation differently'[44].

Interviewed by the French daily *Le Monde*[45], Mečiar claimed: '[w]e do not want independence, we are being pushed into it', and dated this pressure from the first meeting in Brno. According to Mečiar, Klaus's delegation had decided on state dissolution after a forty-minute debate, yet since then Slovakia had withdrawn its request for a central bank and had admitted that Slovakia was unprepared to form its own currency. 'Slovakia wants to continue the economic reform but with a new strategy, heeding regional specifics, and on the basis of more advantageous distribution of foreign investment. The Czechs keep rejecting this', he explained[46]. Unfortunately for the Slovak cause, the credibility of Mečiar's claims was instantly undermined by his appraisal of Hungarian ambitions in Slovakia. In the same interview Mečiar identified a 'badly masked' Hungarian scenario wherein the minorities would gain territorial independence and be annexed by Hungary with appeal to the right of self-determination – a lunatic piece of demagoguery even by Mečiar's flamboyant standards, and one hastily amended by Jozef Moravčík, the MDS's luckless Foreign Minister.

On 3 July the Federal Parliament failed to elect the new Czechoslovak President, even in repeated rounds of voting. Vaclav Havel, the only candidate, was rejected by the House of the People and the Slovak section of the House of the Nations; the repeat round elicited only reduced support in the chamber of the Nations. A second election with new candidates was scheduled for 16 July. Klaus concluded that the 'Czech public will interpret the non-election of Mr Havel as a further step toward questioning the common state'[47]. Later he added that, in the event that no one was elected as Federal President, Havel would become the logical and CDP-endorsed candidate for the imminent Czech Presidency[48].

Only days after considering the threatening deep disruption of the Slovak economy[49] the presidium of the Slovak National Council discussed two draft declarations on the sovereignty of Slovakia in the expectation that one would be approved on 17 July. The first draft declared a national-cultural sovereignty – a statement of principle – the second, the state-legal sovereignty of Slovakia, i.e. international legal personality. Despite the far weaker first alternative the Civic Democratic Party responded only by reciting its policy that relations with Slovakia were no longer at issue until after independence[50].

The assumption of injured innocence was one of the few remaining postures available to Mečiar, and at a Slovak press conference he called on the Czech government to publish its 'secret' timetable of separation steps. While admitting that Slovakia was not prepared for a split in the common market, currency and even in the realm of human rights, Mečiar also compared the present coverage of Slovakia in the Czech and world press to a cold war determined by the Prague view[51]. Something of a cold war atmosphere had indeed developed. Mečiar resorted to the most blatant conspiracy-mongering (by now a staple of commentary in both republics), whilst the Czech *Telegraf* reported the beginning of 'political purges' in Slovak ministries. Representatives of the Association of Slovak Journalists, meanwhile, together with the Congress of Slovak Intelligentsia and the Slovak cultural organisation *Matica Slovenská* declared that celebratory bonfires would be lit across Slovakia if sovereignty were declared[52].

The Slovak National Council debate on the government's policy statement revealed Meciar's growing political isolation. The draft was criticised by MDS allies and opponents alike. The Slovak National Party reproached it for the lack of comment on the market economy. The Democratic Left criticised the statement as too dirigist; 'one cannot wish for a common currency and draw up a policy which rules this out', complained PDL leader Peter Weiss. Further disagreement came when the Movement for a Democratic Slovakia and the Slovak National Party proposed that the vote on Slovak sovereignty be by roll-call. František Mikloško (CDM) objected that the proposal positively invited the nationalistic harassment of parliamentary deputies; the Party of the Democratic Left, the Hungarian Christian Democratic Movement (HCDM) and the latter's coalition partner, Coexistence, agreed[53]. Continuing the debate the next day, Ján Čarnogurský (CDM) called the government policy statement 'the vaguest set of intentions submitted by post-November governments', and noted that while the actions of the government tended toward the state's separation the statement disregarded this completely. Mečiar closed the debate with a bizarre and epic plea. Present world changes amounted not only to the collapse of Communism but the birth of a new civilisation, he said, and 'adaptation to [this motion] means the struggle for survival'. The speech degenerated further into the grandiloquent when Mečiar again claimed to have read a 'horrific secret report' outlining retaliatory steps against Slovakia, prepared by the Czech presidium. These steps, Mečiar railed, amounted to racism 'as a programme'. 'If the new governments do not collect enough courage to disassociate themselves from the positions of the former government, the Slovak government reserves the right to make the whole affair public internationally. Let people know how an exodus of Romanies to Slovakia on the occasion of the split was prepared'[54]. He continued, now appealing to the deputies' increasing sense of fatalism, 'you do not have to express confidence in this government. But I ask you – have you got a better one? . . . Please, give your confidence to this government. The citizens have already done so'[55].

Klaus too had turned to domestic issues, instructing the Czech government to submit a draft constitution[56]. His tactics, however, revealed a political leverage far superior to Mečiar's. As before the election, his preferred strategy was to harass the Czech left with accusations of 'disloyal opposition'. Though the left claimed that the government was acting unconstitutionally, Klaus described their approach as 'incomprehensibly negative' and indicative of 'the fragility of our democracy'[57].

The second round of presidential elections followed with only one candidate, the extreme right Republican leader Miroslav Sládek, but he remained un-elected in either of two ballots. A third round was planned, again with new candidates. The Federal Assembly nevertheless approved the federal government's policy statement and, the vote secured, President Havel announced his intention to resign on 20 July[58]. On the same day, Friday, 17 July, the Slovak National Council approved a Declaration of Sovereignty. To Czech media eyes this was a coincidence of calamities that signalled the end of all hope for Czechoslovak statehood. In his resignation letter Havel had explained that he feared becoming an obstacle 'to the emancipation efforts of the Slovak Republic, which found political reflection in the Declaration of Sovereignty approved today'[59].

In fact the vote for Slovak sovereignty – by roll-call, 113 of the 147

Slovak National Council deputies – was a vote for the milder version of the declaration: *zvrchovanost'*, Slovakia's right to pursue its own national life – a definition still compatible with the principle of an 'originally sovereign' nation about to re-enter a new federal contract. All deputies of the Christian Democratic Movement and seven of the allied Hungarian Christian Democratic Movement/Coexistence voted against the declaration. All deputies of the Movement for a Democratic Slovakia and Slovak National Party voted for it. In a speech notable for its relative dignity, Mečiar concluded that: 'The Declaration expresses the level of intellectual and social maturity of a Slovakia which is able to take its destiny into its own hands. The Declaration is a political and not a constitutional act, it does not mean an independent state but it is a clear signal for those abroad that we are taking into our own hands the intention to form our own statehood. The development so far means that the Federal Constitution will become invalid in Slovakia on the day when the Slovak constitution comes into force'[60]. Members of the Christian Democratic Movement asked for protection, and were flanked by police on leaving the parliament[61].

Unlike his coalition colleagues, Klaus considered the Slovak move insignificant. It could hardly change the situation created by the 'absurdities' of the 1968 constitution, he commented[62]. It presented nevertheless a good opportunity to reconfirm Slovakia as secessionist (the ambiguity of the declaration notwithstanding), and Klaus duly pointed to 'the fact that the Declaration . . . does not mention the word "Czech" as very surprising and significant'[63]. The Czech government waited to consider the Slovak declaration in its normal session; when the Czech National Council met on 20 July the presidium announced itself 'convinced of the necessity for accelerated negotiations' toward two independent states[64]. In his broadcast from Lány Havel considered separation a now irreversible development[65].

At the fifth round of MDS–CDP talks, in Bratislava on 22–23 July, the two delegations agreed that, having preliminarily confirmed the split of the federation into two independent republics, they would henceforth focus on what Klaus called 'the optimal course' for its demise[66]. The talks thus shifted significantly away from substantive decisions toward procedural issues. Mečiar and Klaus told journalists 'we shall together initiate, in the Federal Assembly, the Law on the Manner of the Dissolution of the Federation and on the settlement of property and other matters'. In case their proposals failed they pledged 'to maintain peace and regulate alternative processes for the dissolution of the Czechoslovak federation'. Klaus expressed the hope that 'all of this process will be discussed, approved and developed in the

National Councils by 31 August', i.e. one month earlier than already timetabled.

In connection with tax and monetary policy the two sides had spoken only of the potential for coordination – an ambiguity that now raised Slovaks' fears for their future financial stability. Klaus had commented that 'we are not sure whether it is possible or even purposeful and necessary to assure unity between the budgetary, tax and financial policies of the two republics. It would be irresponsible to say whether we will be able to maintain a common currency'. Mečiar professed uncertainty when asked to name a date for the final dissolution, but Klaus reckoned on 31 December, when the 1992 budget would cease to be valid. 'It is an important moment', he said, 'irrespective of whether we wish it or not'[67].

Mečiar had argued that the republican presidents should be elected before the federal one, a scenario which looked increasingly likely since none of the three federal candidates gained the requisite votes in the third round on 30 July. A Civic Democratic Party/Movement for a Democratic Slovakia amendment allowed for presidential elections to be postponed by eight weeks if the next round, the fourth, was again fruitless[68]. So it proved, since no candidates stood[69]. At the close of the month Čarnogurský's Christian Democratic Movement submitted a bill to the Assembly demanding a referendum with the question, 'are you for the continuation of the common Czechoslovak state and for the declaration of new parliamentary elections?' A Civic Democratic Party spokesman (J. Schneider), however, rejected out of hand the idea that 'with the help of the referendum it is possible to return life to the concept of a federation'[70]. A poll at the time, however, revealed that only 16 per cent in each republic positively favoured a dissolution of the state. A full 85 per cent of voters said they would participate in a referendum[71].

August

Mečiar's obsession with the appearance of victory was by August pulling the MDS executive apart. At the Movement's presidium meeting, Federal Foreign Minister Moravčík warned that 'full disintegration has no meaning for us'. Federal First Deputy Prime Minister Rudolf Filkus protested the serious economic impact of continuing on Mečiar's course; on the question of common currency and monetary policy he pleaded 'a compromise must be found. We could make an agreement with the Czech Republic on cohabitation and define common interests'[72]. Mečiar, however, was not to be contradicted. Within days these more forceful ministers were outflanked, not only in negotiations but within their respective portfolios, and Mečiar turned increasingly to favour those whose priorities were only to entrench MDS power. This increasingly autocratic strategy could also be seen beyond the party. Answering public complaints about the lack of media coverage of the talks, Mečiar said that 'the Slovak government does not place sufficient confidence in the media to inform them about its most confidential activities'. Newspapers, he said, behaved like 'money-makers' with information[73].

Mečiar's colleagues resorted to meeting with the Czech opposition to try to secure a referendum; but they too were seen as culpable, if only for seeking a marriage of convenience[74]. According to the right in both republics, the consensus-seekers within the Movement for a Democratic Slovakia and in the Czech left saw in a sustained deadlock or a less than heavily centralised federation only a tactical lever for softening Klaus's reforms. Moreover, as things stood it was highly uncertain that a referendum would do more than confirm the conflict of interests established by the election.

The next meeting of the Federal Assembly dissolved in chaos as the Civic Democratic Party coalition and the Movement for a Democratic Slovakia locked horns over candidates for committee chairmen. CDP and MDS deputies together continued to obstruct the Assembly by non-attendance, sabotaging the second joint meeting of the Assembly; the third was not scheduled until 22–5 September. The quarrel had erupted when Klaus's ally, Václav Benda's Christian Democratic Party, had accused both the Czech and Slovak left – the MDS at its head – of attempting a *coup d'état*[75]. Klaus had then escalated the debate by attacking with unusual ferocity Mečiar's reference to CDP 'hawks'; what did exist, he countered, was 'the understandable impatience of CDP deputies' intent on progress and disquieted by 'the limitless arrogance and aggression of deputies from left-wing parties'[76]. The signal of Klaus's dwindling patience had the desired effect; fearing that he may have pushed Klaus too far again, Mečiar re-emphasised the importance of the MDS–CDP agreements for future developments. He even asserted that on the question of state dissolution he himself had warned the left that whatever its actions, the federal parliament would still cease to exist[77].

Addressing clubs of deputies, Klaus emphasised that no alternatives existed to separation since these would only thwart Slovak desires, souring relations still further. Answering comments that the Slovaks had clearly been retreating in their demands, inviting the renegotiation of the common state, Klaus insisted that 'Slovak representatives ... started to realise there were concrete problems and became more realistic. They do not [however] change their basic standpoints and we must respect them'. To the opposite view, that Slovakia had withdrawn and should reap the consequences, Klaus replied 'it seems to me impossible to push Slovakia into the role of unilateral liquidator. It would be unwise from the viewpoint of our future coexistence and our own interests'[78], the amicable appearance of separation being one of the those interests. The first draft of the Bill on Dissolution of the Federation was thus duly prepared, but was objected to by Klaus's CDP for the *faux pas* of not including all those conditions agreed between the CDP and the MDS, namely the four official options for a split: a referendum, agreement between the National Councils, a Federal Assembly law and the withdrawal of one republic[79].

In the Slovak National Council, meanwhile, the MDS's Milan Kňažko rejected complaints that time pressures would impair the quality of the Slovak constitution[80]. The MDS's desperate haste was nevertheless palpable and won little sympathy in either republic. The Slovak government was particularly unwilling to admit what was already lost, that they had failed to secure a single currency to bind the two economies in the future. It was left to the Czechs to reveal that divergent policies precluded agreement on tax or budgetary coordination, the necessary conditions for a long-term monetary union. The MDS's explanation was suitably incongruous; Slovakia, claimed Slovak Finance Minister Julius Tóth, had moved too far to the right for the regressive Czechs. 'The policy of the Slovak government, when you take its orientation and acts, is more right-wing than that in Bohemia'[81], he argued. Mečiar again tried to switch his role to that of the persecuted hero of common statehood: 'with three more voices they [the CDP] could block the whole parliament', he declared, claiming that the MDS had prevented a division of the federation no fewer than six times in the last two months[82].

The Movement for a Democratic Slovakia avoided the meeting scheduled for 27 August. Having cited among other grievances the Civic Democratic Party's failure to carry out certain personnel changes, notably in the FBIS (the security services), Mečiar concluded that negotiations could continue only when these agreements were fulfilled. To Klaus he nevertheless wrote, 'you are the only politician in the Czech Republic in whom the Slovak side can place trust'. Klaus replied that these matters were too trivial to justify delays. He rejected Mečiar's claim that the Czechs were resolving Czech party battles at Slovakia's expense and listed his agenda for discussion, including clearing up 'our attitudes over the draft principles of the Law on the Manner of Dissolution of Czechoslovakia'. Mečiar reiterated his letter and continued to call off the meeting. After speculating publicly that

Mečiar aimed at a unilateral Slovak secession, Klaus secured an earlier meeting date of the 26th with one further phone call[83].

The sixth round of MDS–CDP talks took place in Brno. Mečiar and Klaus met face to face for two and a half hours, mending party relations. 'The Czech and the Slovak Republics should come into existence as independent states on 1 January 1993', declared Mečiar to the assembled press. The timetable was brisk; by the end of September the Federal Assembly should have approved the Law on the Manner of Dissolution of the Federation, and in October it should approve the division of property. By November the National Councils should have discussed a basis for the future cooperation between Czech and Slovak Republics. In December the MDS and CDP would 'tackle their mutual problems'.

The Federal Assembly's agenda was almost entirely that of the CDP. Among their pre-talk grievances the MDS secured only the right to propose a nomination for the head of the Federal Information and Security Service – and the CDP's Miroslav Macek could hardly resist pointing out that proposals to abolish the entire federal security service would be submitted at the Assembly's next session[84]. The MDS had also agreed to a programme for ensuring 'transparency and cooperation'. This stipulated that deputies from the two parties would only submit to the Assembly matters already discussed by club representatives. Secondly, they would prefer questions concerning the constitutional arrangement. Thirdly, important agreements would always be recorded in writing, and party chairmen would meet before important institutional meetings, including those of the policy committees of both parties. Lastly, uninhibited by conventions of parliamentary opposition, both agreed that these principles should be applied by all other political parties[85].

In another proposal bearing the hallmarks of the CDP Klaus explained that a common currency would continue to exist in Czechoslovakia after 1 January 1993, and that a 'crown zone' would be introduced from that date, controlled by a pared-down version of the current State Bank. In the second stage the Czech and Slovak currencies should become independent with a firmly fixed rate of exchange set at a ratio 1:1 to begin with, though this could not be maintained permanently. Klaus suggested that cooperation should start from agreement on a customs union and this transitional model of monetary union. After the split, he insisted, there would be many common policies. Even so, the MDS's subsequent comment, that Slovak citizens would be glad that they had retained all rights in the other republic bar that of voting, was patently misleading, as we shall see[86].

September

The Slovak constitution was passed on 1 September, after Mečiar rejected all Hungarian amendments as resulting from a failure to understand the text[87]. Of the 134 deputies present in the Slovak National Council, 114 had voted in favour, 16 deputies of the Christian Democratic Movement voted against, and four Hungarian deputies from the Party of the Democratic Left abstained. The Slovak half of the Czechoslovak national anthem was sung and a festive programme was announced for the following evening. Remarkably few papers commented on the event, though Czech columnist Ivo Slavík ascribed to Mečiar a 'wantonness . . . bordering on contempt'[88]. The occasion was overshadowed by the news of a road accident involving the Slovak Social Democratic chairman, Alexander Dubcek, an obvious candidate for the Slovak presidency. Mečiar had recently turned against Dubček for his federalism, and the suspicion that the still popular champion of 1968 might have been 'silenced' hung heavily in the air. A poll taken a week later, between 8 and 14 September, revealed that more than 80 per cent of those polled in both republics now considered a split inevitable[89].

The Slovak constitution was signed on the evening of 3 September, attended by the CDP's Jan Stráský and Milan Uhde but not by Václav Klaus. Though the CDP was content not to see the signing as a violation of CDP–MDS agreements, their coalition partners, the Czech Christian Democratic Union/Czechoslovak People's Party, were purportedly outraged. Deputy Chairman Jan Kasal argued that Slovakia had withdrawn from the federation and should face the consequences[90]. The signing certainly heralded a new belligerence in Mečiar's tactics. Journalists were lectured on the rules of 'ethical self-regulation' and the liberal politician Fedor Gál was singled out and threatened with a section of the penal code prohibiting the 'spreading of inflammatory news'[91]. The Hungarian Christian Democratic Movement and Coexistence movement in the National Council accused the MDS leadership of a similarly escalating hostility toward members of the Hungarian minority and its leading politicians[92].

In great contrast to Slovak events, Klaus was now embarked on a conciliatory co-option of the parties arrayed against him in the Czech Republic. Meeting with Left Bloc deputies, Klaus lobbied for a joint decision on separation by the two republican National Councils. His confidence apparently unbounded, he publicly rejected any accusations that the left might be non-democratic (his own allegation before June 1992) as 'pre-election rhetoric'[93]. To avoid controversy over the economy Klaus had announced that the Bankruptcy Law would come into effect not on 1 October but six months later and in a weaker version. Despite his efforts, however, the Czech opposition still held out for a referendum on dissolution and the inclusion of Assembly deputies into the negotiation process. CDP Federal Prime Minister Jan Stráský objected that a referendum was unrealistic and likely to draw the state nearer to a Yugoslav-style crisis. Klaus also adopted an argument against chaos, accusing pro-referendum politicians of adopting the principle 'worse is better'[94].

When the draft Czech constitution was rejected by committee, however, even Civic Democratic Party deputies complained that it had vested excessive powers in the hands of the premier – Vaclav Klaus – which would be justifiable only in a state of emergency[95]. Legislation was also delayed in the Federal Assembly. The Bill on the Manner of Dissolution of the Federation was stuck at the committee stage while opposition parties insisted that draft amendments of the Law on Referenda and the carefully entitled 'Bill on the Division of Property if the Federation Becomes Dissolved' be discussed first[96]. As a legislature the federal parliament was in fact buckling under the strain. The bill on changing the structure of the state administration (dissolving ministries) was approved purely by chance; opposition deputies had walked out in protest before the vote – an effective move because of the supermajority requirement on constitutional legislation – and the necessary quorum was provided only by two opposition deputies taking minutes and another who returned to the meeting room to fetch his briefcase[97].

Preparing for October's legislation negotiators had agreed the ratio 2 : 1/Czech : Slovak as a guiding principle governing the division of federal property; another was the 'territorial principle' for the division of real estate, whereby buildings became the property of the state in which they were situated[98]. Klaus had rejected the Slovak ideas for a defence union and common army, but Federal Defence Minister Imrich Andrejčák had asked the premiers to leave this issue until later[99]. As it transpired, the more the CDP cut the ties that the MDS had assumed would bind the two republics, the more the MDS resorted to obstructing property agreements, in the hope, presumably, that Klaus would then offer further concessions to keep the process on schedule[100]. Federal First Deputy Prime Minister Rudolf Filkus (MDS) objected that the intention to divide the army was a change from the original CDP–MDS accords. Mečiar called for a middle version: two armies and two ministries which would agree on common services. He also echoed Andrejčák's belief that the division would take years rather than months[101].

The Czechs' response to this Slovak 'challenge' merely re-emphasised their superior leverage, however. The CDP's Miroslav Macek announced that the army was 'behaving as a third force in the state' and that its division was becoming the most difficult problem in the separation[102]. The accusation was pitched to call the army to order, and in little over a week Andrejčák had revised his agenda and publicised his hope that the army would be divided according to the 2:1 ratio, or the territorial principle when the ratio could not be applied[103]. Chief of Staff General Karel Pezl suggested that forces could technically split even before 31 December, revealing that he had at his disposal a document in which all three Prime Ministers had earlier expressed consent to the ratio 2:1 for dividing army property[104].

At the end of September, Presidential election time had come around yet again in the Federal Assembly. This time Jiří Kotas was not elected as President of Czechoslovakia (only 16 deputies of the House of the People and 24 of the House of the Nations voted for him). A sixth round was scheduled for 2 October, the day after the Slovak constitution would come into force[105].

At a meeting of the State Defence Council Meciar rejected the territorial principle for *any* property under negotiation and then walked out, despite the MDS's prior agreement to the principle earlier in September. He told journalists: 'if they want to play children's games I have no time for them, so I apologised and left the meeting'[106]. His headline-grabbing actions took on the quality of farce the next day when Jiří Pospíšil, First Deputy Federal Minister of Defence, pointed out that the Council had rejected Mečiar's proposals for a joint defence institution and a non-aggression pact because it had no mandate to accept them; both were constitutional issues subject to the talks, as was the division of property. Briefing the exasperated Slovak government, Mečiar denied that he had caused an uproar, insisting that he had in fact saved Slovakia billions of crowns. He also attacked Filkus's property proposals and the MDS's federal ministers in general as in error in abandoning the idea of a financial settlement, though this had long been flatly refused by the Czech side[107].

When Klaus again intervened, phoning Mečiar and announcing that 'I have mixed feelings on whether we shall succeed in discussing the Bill on the Dissolution of the Federation by 30 September, as originally agreed', his doubts were evidently calmed. The Federal Assembly opened its debate on 29 September[108]. Mečiar's rejection of the property principle was nonetheless practically disruptive. The federal government had been preparing the Bill on the Division of Federal Property for three weeks and was bemused by Mečiar's last-minute rejection of its basic premise[109]. Next – for he was clearly closing the month with a campaign – Mečiar queried the exchange-rate projections, the fixed rate of 1:1 which he had already publicly endorsed, and proposed a floating rate. Slovak Finance Minister Tóth broadcast that Slovakia had no means of introducing her own currency soon and was 'not preparing to do so', suggesting that the introduction of a Slovak currency would need a 200-million-dollar subsidy to maintain its convertibility[110].

October

Though Klaus had chosen to disregard Mečiar's protestations and queries in late September, there was a brief moment in early October when it seemed Mečiar might railroad the Czech Civic Democratic Party into more radical concessions. The Federal Assembly failed to pass the Bill on the Dissolution of the Federation but passed instead, by one vote, a motion requiring the preparation of a commission to draft a bill transforming the Federation into a Czech-Slovak *Union*. With opposition deputies, the MDS had voted for the motion, proposed by Miloš Zeman of the Czechoslovak Social Democrats.

Reacting in the Assembly, Klaus condemned the support of the MDS for a motion submitted by the Czech left as a violation of CDP–MDS cooperation (and he noted that Czechs could likewise rescind all settlements) and a threat to post-November (1989) changes. As for the process of separation, Klaus left no doubts. 'The existing division of tasks, according to which federal institutions manage the split of Czechoslovakia and republican institutions are responsible for the new arrangements, has been seriously questioned. We shall have to seek alternative solutions . . . For three years we have been resisting almost constant Slovak pressure for the destruction of the common state of Czechs and Slovaks. We sincerely deplore the actual split but we repeat that we shall not allow any farcical transformation into a semi-detached house or Czecho-Slovak union. Such a form of state is not in the interests of the citizens of the Czech Republic and we shall not create it under any circumstances'[111].

The Assembly had been shown its place; when Klaus had designated the federal government a caretaker role he had expected the legislature to consider itself temporary. If federal deputies now rejected dissolution he would describe them as instruments of leftist recidivism or Slovak nationalism and would write them out of the process altogether[112], and nationalist appeals to Czech national interest could be used in the name of self-defence. Federal government members were given until Wednesday, 7 October, to submit their final opinions[113].

The Slovak government now postponed the joint meeting under preparation for Židlochovice and informed the Czechs that it should be held only after the Federal Assembly had passed the amendments to the Laws on Responsibilities – laws devolving competences that the Slovaks needed urgently. They also proposed that the MDS and CDP delegations meet at Židlochovice as parties. Though not ruling this out Klaus commented: 'the Slovak side is putting itself in a complex situation as it is developing several games and will have problems in keeping them under its control'[114]. This was undoubtedly true. Mečiar, it appeared, was attempting to hold the state to ransom. Klaus and Mečiar agreed to meet on 9 October, but before then Mečiar expressed his regret that '[t]he arrival of Mr Klaus at the Parliament resulted in the cancellation of all agreements, i.e. between the CDP and MDS'. Mečiar also claimed to have warned the CDP that, without compromises, the Dissolution Bill would be blocked, that the preservation of a union remained an issue prior to the manner of state dissolution, and that an MDS-led coalition existed to defend this idea. Lastly, Mečiar had suggested that the MDS might overcome its reservations about property division with mutual agreement, explaining: '[w]e do not care whether we lose a billion or 5 billion, but we are not ready to lose everything'[115].

Klaus's sense of credible threat clearly remained unmoved, and his public reply exuded resolve. 'At this moment', he maintained, 'decisions are made about our future, the cards have been given out and the slightest hesitation, slightest weakness on our side, could have catastrophic consequences for the future of the Czech state and the Czech nation'. He had, he said, the document necessary for the declaration of Czech independence 'in his drawer', and could use it at any time. In suggesting that Czech independence was an obvious, if complex, solution[116], Klaus made it plain that Mečiar's powers of obstruction were at most an irritant. The Czechoslovak Social Democrat chairman Jiří Horák swiftly dissociated his party from the union idea, which they had previously supported so keenly[117].

At Jihlava it was reconfirmed, after eight hours, that the federation would be dissolved on 1 January 1993. Klaus said the talks had opened the way to making the Assembly and other federal bodies 'operative' and treaties would be discussed between the two governments within the week and passed to the National Councils. Asked if the Movement for a Democratic Slovakia still supported a union, Mečiar replied that the CDP had refused to accept either confederation or union and the MDS had decided to 'respect' this fact, as it had also abandoned thoughts for a 1993 budget. Klaus confirmed that the Assembly might now pass the Competence Law. Both sides had agreed to support the Bill on the Dissolution of the Federation in the Federal Assembly and, on the CDP's initiative, both had signed a communiqué:

'Against its original viewpoint, CDP had come to respect, during the first post-electoral negotiations, MDS disagreement with the continued existence of the Federation of the Czech and Slovak Republic, and has expressed its disagreement with transforming the federation into a confederation. Therefore it did not, and does not adhere to the existing federal arrangement. Similarly MDS respects the fact that CDP disagrees with the formation of a union of the Czech and Slovak Republic, and with efforts to transform the federation into a confederation. Both sides have assured one another that they will only proceed further in this matter on the basis of mutual agreement. MDS and CDP will promote the conclusion of partial agreements such as a customs union, a monetary and payment agreement, etc. which should come into force on 1 January 1993'[118].

How had Klaus persuaded Mečiar of the futility of attempts to form a Czech–Slovak union, so soon after he had staked CDP cooperation on the opposite? Before the Jihlava meeting Klaus had told journalists 'nothing can be agreed upon unless the Slovak side completely changes the approach it has been following in the past few days . . . [a]n elementary honesty is needed on the part of the Slovak side'. The CDP had then handed the MDS the communiqué at the beginning of the meeting, together with a written pledge to desist from promoting a union, and had explained that they, the CDP, would leave the meeting unless the MDS signed. Anticipating, correctly, that Mečiar would resist, Klaus had been careful to offer him a way out, even though the communiqué excluded the word 'Union' – the chief term of the MDS election campaign. The communiqué's final sentence permitted Mečiar to say with satisfaction that 'one union with a capital U has been replaced by several unions each with a small u' – his expressed and, as it turned out, prescient fear being that Václav Klaus would renege on these later[119].

The communiqué had not, however, mentioned property, and Mečiar hung on to this bill as still unacceptable – Slovakia would demand financial compensation. Property, he confided to the press, was the real cause of the current dispute and, putting the show right back on the road, he offered asylum to any Czechs fleeing that republic when the situation there 'got worse'[120]. Czech Finance Minister Ivan Kočárník reminded Mečiar of the gravity of his economic situation, pointing out that on 5 October the Slovak deficit had reached 5 billion Czechoslovak crowns and that the situation was becoming critical; foreign banks had ceased lending money to Slovakia and government bond sales had collapsed. 'Arguments over each crown are a dangerous game', he said, emphasising the generosity of the 2:1 ratio still being offered by the Czechs[121].

The Bill on the Devolution of Responsibilities was passed on 8 October. This stipulated that in the interim there would continue to be only six federal ministries, the Ministry of Inspection being added to the original five[122]. Defending himself against charges from his own party that Jihlava represented a betrayal, Meciar once again promised a referendum[123]. On a television panel discussing the first 100 days of the Slovak government Mečiar again protested that the CDP had stepped beyond their original agreements, explaining: 'I managed to claw at least two months back, otherwise the Czech and Slovak Federative Republic would not have been in existence now'[124].

The two republican governments met at Prague-Koloděje castle on 10 October. Within only six hours the elementary principles of cooperation between the two independent republics had been agreed, including the establishment of a customs union. Some 90 per cent of the drafts had been submitted by Prague. As for future monetary arrangements, they came out in the familiar three stages first promoted by Klaus, Mečiar even echoing that the duration of the crown zone would depend on financial conditions. The debate foundered this time on new citizenship rules[125].

The federal government issued an extended policy statement, its agenda and priorities. These were entirely economic, true to the fixedly pragmatic role it had been assigned. The federal government considered 'as its main priorities the maintenance of macro-economic stability throughout the entire territory, a continuation of quick privatisation and the prevention of a deficit in the state budget'. In its only allusion to the public's interest, the statement promised to settle constitutional questions without jeopardising the savings of citizens, their property, or the property belonging to enterprises. Until completion of the constitutional arrangement the government pledged to ensure united action on foreign affairs and in international relations generally[126]. In response, Federal Assembly Chairman Michal Kováč (MDS) asked only that the government should submit to the parliament a programme of the legislative activity of the Cabinet, and that the national legislatures should meet more adequately the needs of the Assembly in evaluating Bills.

In Slovakia Mečiar permitted himself another breach of the federal constitution. Though under the Slovak constitution the premier would inherit presidential powers in the absence of an appointee, the Slovak government conferred on Mečiar the immediate right to represent Slovakia abroad, to conclude and ratify international treaties, to receive and appoint ambassadors, to declare amnesties and, most ominously, to appoint the General Procurator and members of the Constitutional Court. Federal Premier Stráský confessed himself surprised[127]; Klaus dismissed it as 'a unilateral act which is about as important as the approval of the Slovak constitution'[128].

In a memorandum for presentation to European Community President John Major, the two governments pledged at a meeting in Javorina (25–6 October[129]) to maintain a high level of economic integration and to apply the principles of the free market and pluralist democracy. At the same time Klaus hedged as to the duration of a Czech–Slovak single currency, stating that conditions would 'not only be implemented by states, banks or governments, but by all citizens in their handling of the Czechoslovak crown'[130].

Only limited demonstrations, for and against the separation, marked the state-founding anniversary. During his speech following the presentation of the T. G. Masaryk Orders, Jan Stráský regretted that 'in intoxication from newly-acquired freedom and renewing democracy, the common state has gradually been questioned and dismantled with excessive ruthlessness' – by the Slovaks – and he appealed for Czech 'grandeur' throughout the divorce[131]. Klaus told journalists that to hold a post-independence election for the proposed Czech second chamber, the Senate, implied a huge waste of time, confirming that the 'CDP is in favour of designing a method of transferring Federal Assembly deputies'[132]. In a poll from the second week of October, 90 per cent of respondents in both parts of the country considered the split of Czechoslovakia certain[133]. In an early November poll 50 per cent of Czechs and 40 per cent of Slovaks considered the dissolution of the Federation 'necessary', and 43 per cent of Czech and 49 per cent of Slovaks 'unnecessary'[134].

November

November was dominated by assertions of republican government authority and by horse-trading over legislation. Government authority in Slovakia was both less assured and more arbitrary than in the Czech Republic. Representatives of the Party of the Democratic Left and even of the Slovak National Party stated publicly that Slovakia was not prepared for independent existence and that legal chaos loomed[135]. After meeting with Coexistence the Democratic Left's Pavol Kanis announced that both considered Slovak conditions anti-democratic[136]. 'The government does not respect the decisions of Parliament and the Slovak National Council is pushed to the wall', said Kanis, claiming that all parties bar MDS had 'been raped'[137]. Alexander Dubček, the one broadly respected pro-federal voice in Slovak public life, died of his injuries on 8 November, aged 71[138].

The fifth joint meeting of the Federal Assembly failed to approve the Bill on the Dissolution of the FBIS (secret services) and also the policy statement of the Czechoslovak government – both blocked by the Slovak part of the House of the Nations. Those MDS deputies present had voted for the statement (those from the Christian Democratic Movement, Party of the Democratic Left and Social Democratic Party of Slovakia were against), but almost a quarter were absent from the vote[139]. Federal Premier Straský was concerned: the rejection of the policy statement signalled a potential delay to the major bills of separation.

The republican governments meeting at Židlochovice in the meantime had agreed to sign a framework treaty on friendly relations and cooperation, valid for fifteen years and, unless renounced by either party, automatically extended for another five years. Klaus described it as a 'standard treaty' which 'resounded more as a friendly pact' than a treaty between two foreign states. The two sides continued to disagree over a defence treaty but expressed their desire for the early discussion of the Constitutional Law on the Division of Federal Property[140]. Even so, both the Dissolution and Division of Property Bills were supported only by government parties and the Slovak National Party. Deputies of Czechoslovak Social Democracy, the Left Bloc, Left Social Union, Party of the Democratic Left, Christian Democratic Movement, Communist Party of Bohemia and Moravia and Coexistence continued to insist on a referendum as a condition of their consent to the law on Dissolution.

On 13 November the Federal Assembly, after the third vote, approved the law on the Division of Federal Property, to come into force after the endorsement of dissolution. Of an estimated total of 633,700 million Czechoslovak crowns, the Czech Republic would get 430,000 million and the Slovaks 202,000 million. The law was opposed by the far right Republicans, Coexistence, a substantial part of the Left Bloc, the Party of Democratic Left and several Czechoslovak Social Democrat and Left Social Union deputies. The Assembly also approved the dissolution of the federal information and security Services and an amendment to the Law on Large Privatisation, separating a further round of coupon privatisation[141]. During a telephone conversation on the same day Mečiar and Klaus reconfirmed that the mandate of the federal deputies would vanish with the federal state and that the National Councils would decide these deputies' future. Thus the job transfer to a new second chamber in each independent state was offered to the federal deputies as a bribe for the ratification of the divorce. J. Horák objected that this was both legally and politically impossible. More of a realist, the Communists' J. Svoboda described it as 'a form of corruption'[142]. Three days later Havel announced his candidacy for the Czech presidency with the words 'we must by all means strengthen the culture of mutual relations, the civic culture, the culture of a free economic life and of course the political culture'[143].

Meetings of the National Councils passed concurrently and without delay the Constitutional Bill on the Dissolution of the Federation. The Czech National Council passed it by 106 votes, with 67 opposition deputies against. Two draft amendments, one from the right-wing Civic Democratic Alliance, giving the republics the right to conclude treaties before the dissolution, the other from the Czechoslovak Social Democrats, providing that the dissolution should be confirmed in a referendum, were rejected. In the Slovak National Council the bill was passed by 73 to 16 votes, with 42 abstentions. The council rejected Carnogursky's (CDM) amendment calling for referenda but passed that tabled by the Slovak National Party's J. Prokeš, which insisted that those states succeeding the Czech and Slovak Federative Republic must not use its symbols. The version of the Bill going to the Federal Assembly included a provision that legislative power in the two republics would belong to legislative assemblies consisting of deputies elected to the Federal Assembly and the respective National Councils[144]; the bribe to the federal deputies thus remained intact. On the anniversary of the November revolution (17 November) there were public demonstrations in Prague by two groups cordoned off from one another – one advocating independence, the other federation[145].

In the Federal Assembly the government Bill on the Dissolution of Czechoslovakia was approved on 18 November but only by the House of the People and the Czech section of the House of the Nations. In the Slovak section, where 45 votes were needed, 42 voted for, 18 against, and 11 abstained[146]. The Bill was rejected on the grounds of the government's unwillingness to compromise over a referendum. A committee was elected for further negotiations and a revote on 24 November. The Czechoslovak Social Democrats' Ivan Fišera again put forward a referendum amendment which Klaus resolutely opposed; 'none of those proposing a referendum mean it seriously', he protested[147].

Having reminded journalists that the decision over dissolution could fall to the National Councils, Klaus stressed the importance of the Constitutional Bill on Measures Connected with the Dissolution of the Federation, already approved by the Czech government. Though it was formally dependent on the Dissolution Bill, Klaus suggested that this Czech legislation was applicable for any form of constitutional division. The Bill on Measures enabled the Czech Republic to function practically as an independent state while maintaining its existence within Czechoslovakia. Besides continuity in the legal system it tackled the responsibilities of the basic state institutions, the transfer of rights and obligations and continuity in foreign policy and succession. If approved in the National Council, this Bill would come into effect on the day of promulgation and not on the first day of independent statehood[148]. Klaus thus made it clear yet again that if the Assembly was going to cause delays, its authority would simply be hollowed out through transfers of critical powers to the Czech parliament.

On 19 November, the Czech National Council approved a resolution echoing Klaus's point: 'The Czech National Council is motivated by an effort to ensure calm progress in the constitutional situation, particularly progress which is orientated towards forming an independent Czech state from 1 January 1993. Aware of its responsibility to the citizens of the Czech Republic, the Czech National Council has declared that together with the Czech government, it accepts full responsibility for continuing state power throughout the Czech Republic and for the protection of the interests and the needs of the citizens of the Czech Republic'. It was approved by 109 votes (from a government coalition of 105 in a chamber of 200). Their 'mandate' confirmed, Czech Deputy Premier Kalvoda (the nationalist-leaning leader of the Civic Democratic Alliance) insisted that from now on the Czech National Council and the Czech government had the right to approve, irrespective of the views of federal bodies, laws and measures which would ensure the full functioning of the independent Czech Republic from 1 January 1993[149].

A highly contrasting scene was being played out in Slovakia, where the eighth meeting of the Slovak parliament finally approved the government bill on referenda. According to the law, Slovak radio and television would give ten broadcasting hours to a referendum campaign, divided equally among parliamentary parties[150]. The Chairman of the Constitutional Committee of the National Council, M. Sečánsky, then declared it impossible to call a referendum by the end of 1992, since it would cost Slovakia 100 million crowns[151]. The long-promised law was thus provided along with instant justification for its delay[152].

When the fifth joint meeting of the Federal Assembly reconvened it became clear that the negotiations committee for the Bill on the Dissolution of Czechoslovakia had failed to produce a consensus. Government parties now needed one more vote in the Czech section and three votes in the Slovak section of the House of the Nations, and two more in the House of the People. The Slovak opposition in particular continued to block the Bill through several negotiating rounds, until all were confronted by a version of the Bill which lacked the bribing clause transferring federal deputies to their new national second chambers[153]. Presented with this ultimatum, eventually all three chambers approved the Law on the Dissolution of Czechoslovakia on 25 November, including the decision that there would be no referendum on the dissolution.

The vote was met by stormy applause from the gallery and deputies. Klaus observed that it was an important sign to other countries who had feared a Yugoslav-type collapse; 'I believe that the voting represents a gesture of calmness to the whole world'. Václav Havel approved of the endorsement of the highest legislative body. Mečiar commented that when Parliament had appeared on the brink of its self-destruction, it became aware of its importance and approached the vote reasonably[154]. Federal Premier Stráský concluded dryly that it implied the 'maintenance of a political culture'.

With dissolution assured, the Czech side hardened its stance on property negotiations and threatened to bring coupon privatisation into the equation if the Slovaks continued to question agreed principles[155]. The Czech government meanwhile met 27 November and approved the draft budget for 1993[156]. At a press conference Kočárník announced that 'the first budget of the independent Czech Republic will be balanced' and reported that Czech inflation was the lowest among the post-Communist countries and would not exceed 12 per cent by the end of the year[157].

The sixth meeting of the Federal Assembly was inquorate owing to absentees in the Slovak section of the House of the Nations. Terminal fatalism had finally set in. The Assembly recommended that yet another round of presidential elections could now, at last, be cancelled[158]. Asked whether any new complications had arisen in the Czecho-Slovak Commission for the Division of Federal Property, Strasky said no, 'no new complications ... The Czech side resolutely insists on the territorial principle of the division of federal real estate, without any further financial settlements. Slovakia reacts as always by playing the card of yet another enterprise which should be reassessed and have its division adjusted'[159].

December

In the last month of the federation the republican governments faced the domestic issues sidelined over the previous months. The need to ratify a new Czech constitution demanded much of the CDP's attention, since the proposals were causing friction even within the governing coalition. The Federal Assembly meanwhile continued to dissolve the administrative centre – when it was not made inquorate by absentee deputies[160]. In Slovakia the political situation degenerated as the government sought to prosecute journalists hostile to the Mečiar regime[161]. In a statement lifted verbatim from the Communist era, Mečiar warned that 'anyone who attacks the government attacks the whole Republic and its citizens'.

Despite Klaus's calls for a smooth transfer of power, the Movement for Self-Governing Democracy/Society for Moravia and Silesia, the Republicans and Left Bloc deputies in the Czech National Council still opposed the transfer of federal deputies. They also had sympathisers, though they were overruled, in the coalition Civic Democratic Alliance. Alive to such problems, however, the Civic Democratic Party had carefully separated the transfer issue from ratification of the draft constitution[162]. Having first approved the reception law enabling the smooth transfer of federal legislation and powers[163], the Czech National Council approved the Czech constitution on 16 December. Of 198 deputies present, 172 voted for, 16 against, and 10 abstained. Klaus described the endorsement as the 'logical result of the whole political development since the moment when the Czech public rejected the Communist regime'[164].

The Federal Assembly marked the end of its activity on 17 December by singing the Czechoslovak anthem. In his closing speech Stráský declared that Czechs had regarded Czechoslovakia as the state which could fulfil their ideas about democracy, whereas the attitude of the Slovaks had always been different, and since 1989 they had shown their dissatisfaction. He congratulated the Czechs for their recognition of Slovakia's natural right to independence, concluding that 'Czechs owe nothing to Slovaks, and I venture to claim that Slovaks are aware of this fact'. Federal Assembly Chairman Kováč (MDS) confirmed that Czechoslovakia had indeed fulfilled the idea of Czech national statehood but pointed out that 'Slovaks could only start to fulfil their aspirations after the 1992 elections'. He emphasised the considerable achievement represented by the peaceful and 'constitutional' end to the state[165].

The Czech National Council approved the law on state symbols on 17 December but, with some emphasis, broke the Slovak National Party's constitutional amendment in the process. Having apparently hearkened to Stráský's sentiments it was decided that the Czech Republic would continue to use the current federal flag without any change to the blue ('Slovak') wedge, along with other traditional symbols[166]. By their decision the Czechs had 'confirmed that they had regarded Czechoslovakia as the Czech lands and that Slovakia had always been playing second fiddle', concluded Ivan Gašparovič, chairman of the Slovak National Council. In retaliation Slovaks could also declare the Czechoslovak state flag as the Slovak flag, he suggested, though he added that they would not[167].

In these last weeks the Slovak government appeared harassed from all sides by the secretive manoeuvres of its own leader and by a near collapse of official information. Slovak ministers learned belatedly of Mečiar's meeting with Russia's Victor Chernomyrdin. They also found themselves considerably beneath the Czechs in the estimation of international organisations. The majority of states did not reckon with opening diplomatic missions in Bratislava; ambassadors accredited to Slovakia would reside in either Prague or Vienna. Pavel Bratinka, Czech Minister of International Relations, told the European Parliament that the Czechoslovak federation was dividing solely because most Slovaks had felt no loyalty towards the Czechoslovak Republic[168]. When Klaus announced that the International Monetary Fund (IMF) quotas would be divided in the ratio 2.29:1 and not 2:1, (the quotas affecting the granting of credits), Hvezdon Koctúch, chairman of the Slovak Budgetary Committee, complained that they had not received the IMF Special Report at all. Koctúch's objections must have provoked wry comment in the Czech Republic; the document, Koctúch complained, should have gone to the Federal Premier, since 'Czechoslovakia still exists'[169].

A meeting of the Federal Assembly presidium agreed that the mandate of federal deputies would not end following the dissolution of Czechoslovakia, since mandates could be abolished only by elections and not by the National Councils. They also decided that deputies' legal immunity should be dissolved by elections in 1996, though they conceded that their material benefits were a matter for the successor states. Stráský responded to these federal musings with an abrupt letter to the presidium declaring the Assembly's autumn session closed[170]. With the ultimate fate of federal deputies still in Czech government hands, it was agreed that National Council Chairman Milan Uhde could invite them to the planned gala meeting in Vladislav Hall on 1 January 1993, as a mark of the public's appreciation of their work[171].

The celebrations for independence were to be sedate, with speeches from Uhde and Václav Klaus, an ecumenical mass at St Vitus's Cathedral and a gala concert of the Czech Philharmonic Orchestra at the Dvořák Hall in Prague, all to be broadcast on television and transmitted to screens in Jan Palach Square[172]. In Slovakia the Slovak National Council agreed that, together with the diplomatic corps and government, they would attend a gala meeting on independence day, with speeches from the Council chairman and Premier Mečiar[173]. On

18 December, moreover, the Slovak government released 25 million crowns – 5 crowns per capita – for the celebrations of the first day of Slovak independence. These finances would be covered by government reserves, set for extraordinary expenditures[174].

NATIONALISM – OR RATIONALISM?

Slovakia might splash out for a national holiday, but this was more an act of defiance than of exaltation. The negotiations had progressed inexorably toward separation; Mečiar, with no electoral mandate to split the state, had attempted to postpone the public disclosure of the decisions being made and to adjust and delay their execution. Klaus's Civic Democratic Party had indulged the Movement for a Democratic Slovakia only insofar as this smoothed the selling of separation to a disappointed Slovak population, but it was the Czech and not the Slovak will to state separation that proved implacable. To undermine Czech claims that the Movement for a Democratic Slovakia had always been schemingly secessionist, the reincarnation of prewar Slovak separatism, one need only observe the pantomimic state to which the Slovak party was reduced when confronted by Vaclav Klaus more fully in power. As Theodore Draper observed, 'it was as if Mečiar pounded at Klaus's door without really wanting to knock it down; to Mečiar's surprise, Klaus opened the door, and Meciar fell in'[175].

LEADERSHIP – THE USES AND ABUSES OF PUBLIC FATALISM

That Klaus and Mečiar were skilful political entrepreneurs is clearly not in doubt. That they did not positively collude on the divorce, however, is apparent from their behaviour during the last seven months of negotiations – behaviour that contradicts the 'realist' account of the break-up. Though Mečiar had raised the political stakes enormously high for the purposes of victory in June 1992, if he could win *no* confederal privileges for Slovakia he could deliver neither on any of his election promises nor on his own ambitions. Mečiar accepted being coerced by Klaus's strategy *only* when it became clear that the odds on maintaining the state without a full Slovak capitulation had collapsed.

Following the June 1992 election, Czech and Slovak voters looked on with frustration but also a palpable lack of surprise as their new leaders assumed an electoral mandate to sever the state. Opinion polls as early as January 1991 showed that more than 80 per cent of Czechs and Slovaks believed that political parties' interest in the electorate was limited to winning their support in elections, and that this attitude was unlikely to change[176]. Havel was right to observe that the state effectively 'belonged' to the political parties[177]; parties perceived the state as their property – a clear continuity from the Communist period.

Whatever the true state of opposition to the split, 'society' as a protesting, voting or even legislating force was kept largely at bay. Whether this was because of the obscurity of the source of the separation, of the 'it' against which the public could gainfully protest, or because of low public expectations of government accountability, can hardly be distinguished. Klaus for his part was relatively safe in the knowledge that 74 per cent of his own supporters considered that the Slovak left and the insufficient will of Slovaks as a whole to maintain the state might lead to its division. As we also know from the last seven months of the state, however, Mečiar's path to a decent excuse was unclear. His subsequent zigzagging in search of political justification cost him not only the support of several of his most able ministers, but also, once and for all, his credibility as a democrat.

Klaus's and Mečiar's evaluations of the political risk of divorce should also be viewed in light of the second-order preferences expressed in public opinion poll data. Widespread resignation to the split or something akin to it in fact drove support for separation as 'necessary' steadily upward after June 1992 – if not to a majority, then at least to a few percentage points short of a majority by the time of separation[178]. This remained in contrast to first-order preferences (i.e. most-preferred options) over the state arrangement, which we might reasonably assume to have stayed stable or to have shifted more gradually toward positive support[179]. By November 1992, politicians could observe that 90 per cent of both populations considered separation 'inevitable', even though in July only 16 per cent of respondents in either republic had 'preferred' two independent states[180].

According to the polls, both leaders had reasons to hope that a majority of their supporters might eventually be convinced of the sad but 'objective necessity' of splitting the state, and it had clearly been in these terms that both Klaus and Mečiar had justified their actions between June and December. For Mečiar more than Klaus, however, this would be an uphill struggle; in February 1993, 45 per cent of Czechs saw a short-term worsening of the general situation arising from separation, against 18 per cent of Slovaks. In contrast, 54 per cent of Slovaks foresaw a long-term degeneration as against only 18 per cent of Czechs, implying that a majority of the latter remained essentially unperturbed by events. As for the dawn of independence, 29 per cent of Czechs anticipated rapid general advancement, compared to 1 per cent of those supposedly deluded secessionists, the Slovaks[181].

STATE MYTHS

Klaus's peculiar genius as a leader lay in making the Czech partition look like Slovak secession, despite Slovak protestations to the contrary; concessions were made only when the process looked in danger of succumbing to domestic pressure for broader political inclusion – inclusion that would only have slowed, if not sabotaged, the march toward divorce. Throughout the negotiations Klaus projected the looming split as the realisation of a historical Slovak craving for emancipation, while projecting national optimism at home with deft signals such as the prediction of a balanced Czech budget for 1993. The Movement for a Democratic Slovakia had more clearly broken its election promises and had this to overcome, quite apart from the immediate economic impact on the Slovak economy in massive loss of subsidy and the loss of international confidence so crucial to foreign investment[182]. If this was a victory for the Movement for a Democratic Slovakia it was entirely conditional on Mečiar's ability to develop a state-founding myth strong enough to overcome Slovak disappointment – or state power strong enough to suppress it.

MDS–CDP agreements prohibited recreation or renegotiation of a common state for a minimum of five years, and Mečiar's capitulation forced him to become the deliberate all-out nationalist in the independent Slovakia that the Czechs had long supposed him to be. By the same token, the more nationalistic Mečiar's rhetoric would become, the more credibility would accrue to Klaus's explanation of the separation as the inevitable result of irreconcilable politics: liberal-democratic politics versus nationalist and demagogic rule. As the nationalism scholar Walker Connor has noted, 'while myths of unity have a capacity for engendering harmony they also have a capacity for accentuating division. And the myths are invoked more often for the latter'[183].

The full implications of Klaus's basically nation-state model suggest an interesting question. Would Klaus have moved to break up the inherited federation even if Mečiar had failed in the June 1992 election, beaten perhaps by Čarnogurský's Christian Democratic Movement, or Peter Weiss's Party of the Democratic Left? In the first case, that of a Christian Democratic victory, the answer is almost certainly 'yes'. Čarnogurský's calls for Slovak independence at the propitious moment 'some time in the future' supported Klaus's depiction of

Slovak desires more convincingly than Mečiar's constant hedging and pure populism. Čarnogurský's nationalism was personally heartfelt and articulate, and his party's dependence upon the votes of ageing Slovak L'udáks provided ample basis for dire warnings of a creeping return of 'black' Slovak clerico-nationalism. A victory for Čarnogurský in Slovakia would not have fitted Klaus's projection of the future liberal-democratic state.

A victory for the Party of the Democratic Left, the reformist Slovak wing of the former Czechoslovak Communist Party, was for Klaus potentially the most problematic of all the realistic electoral outcomes. For though the Democratic Left was plagued by its past, Weiss had succeeded in dragging it towards a recognisable Western European social democratic position by 1992. Though he was determined that Slovakia should achieve some improvements in its status, Weiss was unwilling to see the common state forfeited and would have declared Slovakia's federal allegiance both loudly and coherently not only in Slovakia but also in the Czech lands, where he might have persuaded the still influential former Party paper *Rudé právo* to come to his aid. The dissident opposition would again have entered the fray on his side. Would Klaus have dared a necessarily more explicit partition of the state in these circumstances? One can but speculate. The bottom line, however, is that the conflict between an implacable Slovak 'threat' to Czech national reform interests was hardly going to be avoided with Václav Klaus in power in the Czech Republic. Mečiar's unrelenting personal ambition and egotism thus made him Klaus's ideal candidate. That the rhetorically outrageous and ideologically unhinged Mečiar was the only Slovak politician spared the Civic Democratic Party's withering campaign assaults in 1992 was always a curious omission. In this light Klaus's frequently expressed and highly publicised expectation of Mečiar's election victory in Slovakia makes perfect sense; he had found the perfect 'fall guy'.

TECHNOCRATIC AUTHORITARIANISM

To explain how it was that these two leaders could be elected and then so extraordinarily dominant it is essential to remember their respective visions of the state, and the nature of the charisma that proved so successful. The separation was not marginally affected, but quite observably caused, by the distinctive politics of the transition; the main barrier to consensus in the constitutional debate derived from the Civic Democratic Party's ideological assumptions regarding transition and its insistence upon a 'unitary' federation. The second major barrier emerged from the structure of political opportunities, in particular from the difficulties facing public and party political opposition to the separation. Pro-common-state forces were thwarted by the absence of legitimate and well-functioning political institutions of any stripe – a defining trait of the post-Communist condition. These two issues are in fact deeply connected; the story of the separation is one of a distinct form of technocratic authoritarianism, dependent upon the conditions of transition. This is best illustrated by instances where the Civic Democratic Party deliberately and directly suppressed opposition to the separation.

Two of the most important assessments made by a frustrated citizenry would have concerned, firstly, the extent of the public protest required to adjust CDP–MDS behaviour, and secondly, the extent of protest necessary to adjust the supposedly dichotomous relationship between economic prosperity and continuing coexistence as framed by the party system as a whole. As explored in previous chapters, the prospects for adjusting the latter looked poor. Klaus's policies were perceived by Czechs as both successful and desirable, and yet by Slovaks as incompatible with harmonious national relations[184].

As regards public protest, the early failure to call a referendum sent a public message to those 2.5 million citizens active enough to have signed the referendum-supporting petition back in 1990–1. The message was that concerted public bids for government accountability would not be heeded by government – a sense that would have been compounded the more adversarial the parliamentary atmosphere became. In addition, though a majority of citizens opposed separation, no obvious majority shared a common view of an alternative feasible state; opinion was divided between the options of a unitary, confederal, land-based republic or a federal state. It was thus possible for the governments of both republics after June 1992 to insist that separation was the (popular) second-best solution, made necessary by the reprehensible actions of the 'other' republic. It was correspondingly electorally unappealing for parties, but also basically problematic for would-be pro-federalist protesters in general, to unite and mobilise public opinion on a clearly agreed alternative strategy. Thirdly, fear of the loss of state order, whipped up by the Civic Democratic Party, and consequent fears of losing the achievements of the post-November 1989 years, may have acted as strong disincentives against meaningful protest. Important barriers to representation existed at the state level, as we have seen. That over 2 million people signed a petition, moreover, argues for the basic fact that while civil society was alive and kicking, little connected it to the political elite. The dissident Civic Movement had always been acutely concerned by this. Klaus's Civic Democratic Party, on the other hand, exploited it to the full.

Following the 1992 election there were only a handful of demonstrations for the federation in either republic, promoted in the main by opposition parties and attended more often by hundreds rather than thousands of protesters. Those who would conclude that there remained a strong continuity in Czechoslovak political culture from the Communist to the democratic period might point to several important legacies: society's lack of vital representative structures, articulated common interests and identities, organised interest groups, a critical press etc., and the supposedly habituated tolerance of authority (as compared to Poland) etc. An argument about the continuity of low public expectations could certainly point to the short-lived trust in democratic political institutions after 1989. The flaw in these culture- and psychology-based accounts of 'passivity', however, remains the lack of compelling evidence. The fact that 90 per cent viewed the split as 'inevitable' does not tell us that the electorate was 'fatalistic' any more than it tells us that they were highly realistic and rational observers of the events unfolding before them. Similarly, the apparent failure of public opinion to translate into persistent protest may tell us that the electorate struggled to overcome some inner, psychological passivity, but it may equally tell us that they took any number of reasonable decisions that persuaded them that protesting would be either pointless, too time-consuming, given other pressures, or impractical in the light of the failure of previous attempts and the location of the adversarial opponent in the 'other', politically untouchable republic – a dichotomy fully established by political party behaviour.

PARLIAMENTARY OPPOSITION?

In the sixteenth-century dispute between the English crown and parliament the new and diffuse opposition had looked to parliament as a means of organising and expressing itself, and parliament had come to provide both an ideological and an organisational function – one which came to inform, in a reflexive way, the English national consciousness[185]. In contrast to sixteenth-century England, Czechoslovak federal parliamentarians had little by way of recent historical encouragement to believe in parliament as either a unifying or an intrinsically authoritative force, capable of countering an assertion of authoritarian power. The newly animated rights and powers of the federal legislature after 1989 had been almost immediately called into question[186]. One of the few concrete achievements of the constitutional wranglings of 1990–2 had been to cast doubt upon and bring into disrepute the most basic principles of the existing parliamentary structure, in particular its strong minority right of veto which had surfaced when the Communists' paper tiger legislature had come lumbering to life.

Excluded from the last six months of negotiation over the separation of the state, the Federal Assembly suffered fatally from the lack of precedents that might have dictated to Klaus the need to put negotiated settlements to a meaningful parliamentary test – one without the threat of a total loss of authority to the National Councils. On the contrary, it followed from the Civic Democratic Party's assumed electoral mandate to create two new sovereign republics that the Federal Assembly's one remaining role was to legislate itself and other federal institutions out of existence. For the Civic Democratic Party to have entered into a dialogue with the federal parliament, however, would have been to admit to the existence of alternative feasible agendas, something the Party had never done. This exclusion of the Federal Assembly from more than an administrative (as opposed to a representative) role in the dissolution was of course essential to the separation, as well as being a throwback to the Communist era. In its single most explicitly nationalistic move, the Civic Democratic Party argued that the imminent cessation of the federation removed from the Assembly any profound parliamentary responsibility to uphold the federal state, the oath of loyalty for the swearing-in of federal deputies notwithstanding. Within the CDP logic it followed that the reformist Czech right possessed a unique grasp of the interests of the Czech people as a whole – a stereotypically 'nationalist' assertion. From this line of reasoning the CDP felt itself entitled to assume parliamentary responsibility for the future of the Czech people before the legal fact of Czech parliamentary sovereignty had been established.

In late August 1992, the CDP–MDS agreements on deputy behaviour in the Federal Assembly insisted that the two parties table only those questions pertaining to the constitution. The two parties had agreed in addition that the principle be applied to all other political clubs. This last extension of the agreement represented an explicit attempt to limit the legislature as well as the temporarily mandated federal government. The Civic Democratic Party clearly saw that it was now possible to manipulate the growing insecurity felt by federal deputies as to their legitimate legal/political powers. In the same vein, opposition initiatives to prevent separation were portrayed as practically *ultra vires* by the CDP, by virtue of its assumed mandate to separate the state. In a throwback to the election tactic of imputing anti-democratic credentials to parties critical of the CDP programme, the parliamentary opposition were accused not merely of a political opposition to the CDP stance, but of a 'legal' misdemeanour. The need to rescue Czechs from Slovak economic (or, by now synonymously, 'socialist') sabotage was invoked in a manner implying that obstruction to divorce amounted to a treasonable negligence of the interests of the future Czech state.

The language of crisis was all-important to the weakening of parliament, invoking as it did the dangers of a helpless government in the face of threat and the terrible internecine conflicts of twentieth-century Central Europe, though the threat was fundamentally bogus. An atmosphere of an only-just-avoidable-crisis characterised much of the Civic Democratic Party's rhetoric throughout the final process, a skilful strategy for eliciting shows of cross-party consensus where none, in more routine times, would have existed.

The fact that the Federal Assembly was confronted by the 'bottom line' of its own fragile existence immediately after the election only deepened its already questioned efficiency as a legislature. It was given little time to ponder major legislation and was disrupted by frustrated and disillusioned attendance, and an unsteady, intimidatory flow of information about government intentions. Klaus had contended that a Slovak Declaration of Sovereignty could hardly worsen 'the absurdities of the 1968 constitution', but if parliament was beleaguered by ambiguously grounded constitutional authority, it is also clear that the executive disregarded it, showing a contempt strongly reminiscent of the previous regime. Klaus acted under the vanguardist assumption that his 'mandate' permitted the hollowing-out of the Federal Assembly as a representative institution, if this ensured the smooth creation of a new and ideal state. As even Havel had asked himself, what was to be conceded to the representatives of a country that would soon be non-existent? Nothing more, it seemed, than what was required to secure their legalising rubber stamp. Those who insisted that by ratifying dissolution the Assembly had chosen to uphold 'political culture' expressed a great historical irony – ratification was a practical admission that real power had followed the CDP to the Czech state long before the Czech state had been legally or legitimately created.

As we have seen, the inglorious demise of the Federal Assembly did not amount to a pragmatic blip in the Czech right's respect for constitutional law. The punch-line to the story of the dissolution, a study in political co-option, was that in the independent Czech Republic the promised second chamber, the Senate – the combined carrot and stick that had persuaded federal deputies to abolish the state – remained un-established until 1996, when the electoral mandate of the federal deputies finally *expired*. In effect, Klaus never paid his bribe to the federal deputies, and they were rendered parliament-less. In accordance with the agreement by the Federal Assembly Presidium, however, these soon-to-be phantom federal deputies retained their parliamentary immunity from prosecution and their mandate for the full term – to serve the federation.

THE PRESIDENT

Finally, the co-option of Havel – the charismatic leader of the revolution and the tie that bound a significant network of emotionally pro-federal groups – can be seen as having greatly weakened the prospects for opposition. President Havel's early decision to place his fate in Klaus's hands can be seen as having greatly bolstered the CDP's ability to pressurise Czech federal deputies into believing hitherto unsuspected versions of parliamentary responsibility. To many Czechs President Havel had represented a defender not only of the federation, but also of the right of citizens to be consulted through a referendum on the specific issue of the state's future. Slovaks on the other hand had long had cause to be irritated by Havel's patrician attitude to Slovakia, and by the uncensored musings of his adviser Michael Žantovský, seen by many close to Havel as responsible for his leaning ever nearer to Klaus's more pragmatic views. According to Czech National Council deputy Václav Žák, Mečiar hammered the last nail in the coffin of the idea of transforming the federation when the MDS blocked Havel's re-election as president in July 1992[187].

More fateful than the end of his presidency, though, was Havel's removal of his own tremendous moral authority from behind the federal cause. His acceptance of the separation left the opposition marooned without a popular champion. Without Havel, Klaus could point more easily to a conspiracy of Czech leftists delaying separation only in order to hang on to Slovak gradualism as a bulwark against federal economic reform. '[N]one of those proposing a referendum mean it seriously', he had said, after the Dissolution Bill was defeated on 18 November[188], the implication by then being that a pro-federalist deputy was a deputy with a dubious ulterior motive.

Asked under what circumstances he would not wish to become President of the Czech Republic, Havel made a statement back in September 1992 that would haunt him as the powers of the new Czech presidency were steadily removed in the independent state. 'I would not', he had declared then, 'like to be a president who is doomed to wear a tie from morning till evening, to lay bouquets on memorials, make festive speeches on anniversaries and attend innumerable lunches and dinners . . .'[189]. Despite his claims that he had no desire to be a 'paper' President and that he regarded the collapse of the federation as a personal failure, Havel had acted to maintain office rather than stand up (or rather stand down) for his belief in a federal Czech and Slovak state, and the relationship, as he put it, 'bound together by thousands of historical, cultural, and personal ties'[190]. In line with the arguments he employed against continuing parliamentary dissent we may view Havel's adherence to a common Czech front as following perceptions of his own historic destiny, in particular, his belief that an (inevitably) independent Czech Republic would fare better with his blessing than without it. In that thought he may well have been right; his switch, however, came within weeks of losing the presidency, and for Czechs who still believed in the federation it represented a surprising capitulation from the principle. It was a signal of the public's disappointment that long after independence it was commonplace to hear Czechs single out Havel as the individual most responsible for the separation. With Havel lost to the Klausite line, the role of a state-protecting, state-nurturing federal president disappeared. Following Havel's departure, the highly symbolic post was utterly discredited by the failure of parties to put forward respectable candidates, let alone elect them: a lack of capable political personalities which not only demolished the presidency months before its official abolition but which characterises the Czech transition even today.

Policy debates about ethnic/national conflict are conventionally focused on the possibilities open to elite action in mediating profound, mobilised and disruptive societal crises[191], such crises being the usual repercussions of state separatism in an otherwise peaceful international environment. It is a key observation of this case, however, that despite the absence of significant nationalist movements, the last governing elite in Czechoslovakia acted as if wrestling down a crisis, adopting measures with a haste and rhetoric appropriate to a society on the brink of real civil turmoil. In the history of separatism, therefore, the Czechoslovak case represents a departure. The choices of the June 1992 election in Czechoslovakia created, uniquely in the history of modern separatism, a crisis more of governance than of ethnicity. Where the inherited institutional structure and party competition acted episodically upon the dispute – by structuring sudden shifts in the prevailing rules of the game – the issues of leadership, reform philosophy, and democratisation impacted constantly and pivotally.

THE DECOLONISING POWER

The speed with which the final dissolution of Czechoslovakia was settled and the entirely behind-closed-doors nature of the decision-making process suggest not so much a nationalist separatist struggle as the logic of a decolonisation, with the Czech Republic acting as the colonial power, Slovakia, the reluctantly unhooked colony. The end of the Communist system has been described not only as the end of the Soviet empire in Eastern Europe, but as the end of the 'internal empires' of the Soviet Union, Yugoslavia and Czechoslovakia[192]. Relative to conflicts in the past, and in comparison with conflicts elsewhere in Europe that have not led to separation, we might also suggest that Czechoslovakia between 1990 and 1992 hardly experienced a period of 'exceptional' conflict. Similarly, '[i]nside Africa', it has been noted, '. . . it was hard to find turbulence enough to explain why, having earlier seemed so resolved to keep the continent, the colonial powers . . . now, after the war [World War II], seemed so preoccupied with how to get out'[193].

This argument must clearly retain its proper scope – the idea that Czechs had *always* 'colonised' Slovakia, and that what we were seeing in 1993 was the end of seventy years of imperialism, would be a gross distortion. Though the First Republic under Masaryk may have carried the overtones of colonial rule – Czech administrative structures and personnel were imported into Slovakia, the Slovak economy was exploited for its raw materials and labour, and the underdeveloped Slovak elite was thoroughly divided by pro- and anti-colonial feeling – it should nevertheless be remembered that Czechoslovakia was a complex multi-national state born in a difficult, indeed, in many ways, hostile, international environment. Despite its shortcomings the First Republic was arguably a rather enlightened solution – and there might certainly have been more divisive alternatives. As the beginning of this book made clear, Czechocentrism and Czech nationalism were most certainly a problem, but to speak of this as 'imperialism' would be a-historical and an exaggeration (and an acceptance of the Leninist view that 'the chauvinism of the dominant nation is the worst by definition' – an argument severely undermined by Slovakia's political preferences during the Second World War). Even if the claim that this was 'an end of imperialism' is unsustainable as such; it nevertheless remains striking that the Czech right after 1989 appeared to conceive of the state in so many respects in colonial terms. What was so remarkable about the CDP's politics was its willingness to ignore Czechoslovakia's more complex history, adopting a distinctly imperious attitude to the value of the state as if that were a fair reflection of the state's past – as if a Slovak desire for substantive equality must now render the state redundant.

The peculiar outlook of elite actors in the colonising and decolonising condition is thus instructive to our case. 'Decolonisation is almost always viewed as resulting from metropolitan calculations, usually belated, that because of unrest in the colony, changing international circumstances, or shifting interests or economic conditions, the military, political, and/or economic costs of controlling the possession outweigh the perceived benefits'[194]. As has also been noted of Africa, imported institutions notwithstanding, 'the colonial system functioned in the conviction that the administrator was sovereign; that his subjects neither understood nor wanted self-government or independence; that the only article of faith on which administrators could confidently depend was that all problems of "good government" were administrative, and that disaster would follow from attempts to conceive of them as political . . .'[195].

This description might equally be applied to the Czechoslovak Communist system in its last years. Highly constrained administrative tinkering was all that remained to Czechoslovak Communism, ideologically bankrupted by the Warsaw Pact occupation of 1968, and what we appear to see is a profound continuity in the technocratic assumptions of the Civic Democratic Party: 'Decolonisation was a move to shore up "stabilising" forces in restless regions, rather than a recognition of the right of peoples to the independence and the freedom that the phrases of the UN so eloquently embodied . . .'[196].

The decolonising analogy above all captures Klaus's geopolitical interest in effecting the uncoupling of the Czech lands from the more slowly reforming Slovakia and the 'Asiatic' and Balkan world beyond and below. The geopolitical risks of such a strategy were not negligible, but they fell disproportionately upon the Slovak side. Czechoslovakia in 1989 found itself in a period of unique strategic vulnerability. The collapse of the Warsaw Pact meant that in the early 1990s the state belonged to no alliance other than the institutionally weak and unwieldy Conference on Security and Cooperation in Europe. The CSCE (now the OSCE) was nothing more than a timetable of meetings backed by a skeletal administration – an alliance possessed of no military capability whatsoever, and in which *every* member state had the right of veto. With the collapse of Czechoslovakia's satellite status, diplomatic relations had to be built from scratch via bilateral agreements. Both the European Community and NATO offered the most fraternal congratulations in 1989 to the liberated 'other Europe' but insisted then that until 'democracy and the market' could be achieved, Western Europe would in no way presume to be its 'brother's keeper'[197].

It was in these precarious conditions that the state was partitioned, leaving Slovak Hungarians particularly vulnerable to the now hegemonic Slovak majority, and Slovakia in turn, an island of instability bordering on a still more chaotic Ukraine. Under Klaus's guidance the Czech Republic effectively unhooked itself from 'the East' to become a German peninsula, leaving Slovakia to find its putative 'natural home' in what the West perceived, and arguably still perceives, to be the pre-democratic backwater of Eastern, no longer Central Europe. Czechs were encouraged to believe that they had partitioned their way into an uninhibited liberal existence – away from the primitive and nationalist Slovaks – an argument, ironically enough, that Klaus would develop into a destructively parochial nationalism in the independent Czech Republic. This justification for partition, moreover, was straightforwardly wrong about the aspirations of the majority of Slovaks and also completely deluded about the liberal-democratic values of the CDP. The uncoupling of the state, moreover, did a terrible disservice not only to the unprotected Hungarians in Slovakia's midst but also to the majority of Slovaks, who identified themselves far more consensually and democratically than Mečiar, after 1993, would allow.

7

THE NEW STATE BUILDERS: 1993–2000

The Czechoslovak divorce gave Václav Klaus and Vladimír Mečiar the opportunity to build two new states in their own image. In Slovakia Mečiar proved more interested in building party power than in establishing either effective democratic institutions or legal norms. By 1994 his government had opted for a self-serving rule that would grow increasingly kleptocratic and authoritarian in its abuse and monopolisation of state power; and for several years, with the party political opposition in disarray, there seemed very little that anyone could do about it. In Klaus's case, as a neo-liberal with a deep antipathy to the state in principle, an ideological rather than entrepreneurial explanation might be offered for his party's continued unwillingness to build productive state institutions; however, neither an automatic shrinking of the state, nor the flowering of a Czech civil society, nor the creation of transparent markets followed from these beliefs.

THE INDEPENDENT CZECH REPUBLIC

Klaus's Civic Democratic Party dominated the governing coalition of the Civic Democratic Alliance and the two Christian Democratic parties throughout its first term of office, from June 1992 to June 1996. The coalition persisted with the previous economic reform programme, completing the implementation of the second and final waves of voucher privatisation in March 1995. The Czech economy continued to grow, with unemployment remaining incredibly low at just above 3 per cent through the mid-1990s and inflation declining steadily to 8 per cent by 1995 from a high of 52 per cent in 1991. Already in the spring of 1994 Klaus declared that the Czech 'transition' was complete. 'We have created a standard system of political parties', he claimed, 'which function in a pluralistic, parliamentary democracy'[1].

In practice, however, the transition was far from over; low unemployment and inflation masked a deeper failure to restructure the economy that would take the country deep into recession by 1998. As for pluralistic democracy, four opposition parties – the Social Democrats, the Liberal Social Union, the Left Bloc and the Republicans – had been elected to the Czech National Council in June 1992, the LSU and LB themselves unstable coalitions of smaller groupings. Reeling from the split of the country the opposition remained fractured throughout this first Czech parliament and was quite unable to project anything resembling credible political alternatives. A combination of uncertain parliamentary powers of review, a constant process of parliamentary caucus splitting, merging and political 'tourism' (with deputies changing party as many as three times a year) left the governing right-wing coalition unchallenged. The dissolution of the Federal Assembly had meant that the majority of government and party leaders were not even members of the Czech parliament – as their mandates had been for the federal parliament – another factor that increased the opacity of executive power in the new Czech Republic.

With so little pressure from the opposition and such self-confidence within the leadership the Czech government seemed to feel few incentives either to explain or to justify its policies, and as the dust on the divorce settled, the coalition lost its reforming zeal. By 1995 the government's show of a collective right-wing mission had been swamped by intra-party bickering[2]. The growing awareness of government complacency brought with it public criticism, and the fortunes of the Social Democrats began to rise; 1995 saw significant labour unrest, with public-sector workers protesting at the stagnation of salaries and conditions[3]. The last parliamentary session before the 1996 elections was aborted as the coalition failed to agree even a basic legislative agenda.

The 1996 electoral campaigns were criticised by the media for their abstraction from the concerns of ordinary Czechs, and the '96 competition was dominated by internal coalition squabbles. The Civic Democratic Party's campaign was based almost entirely on previous accomplishments, with Klaus running on the slogan 'We have shown we can do it'. Despite an overall increase in the vote for the governing coalition, it lost parliamentary seats, and in 1996 Klaus became leader of a minority coalition with the Civic Democratic Alliance and the Christian Democratic Union/Czechoslovak People's Party[4].

The Social Democrats, having concentrated on the growing problems of corruption, crime, and deteriorating social conditions, in particular on the growing crisis in the health and education systems, gained 26 per cent of the vote, only three points behind the CDP and a massive improvement on 1992, when they had gained a mere 6.5 per cent. Klaus's coalition subsequently controlled 99 seats in the

200-strong legislature, with the remaining 101 divided between the Social Democrats, the neo-fascist Republicans and the barely reformed Communist Party.

The divisions between the new parliamentary opposition parties were sufficient to make the new minority government sustainable with ordinary luck, but weak. As the profound lack of restructuring in the Czech economy began to take its toll, however – some eleven banks collapsed between 1994 and 1996 – Klaus finally became vulnerable to attack over economic strategy. The climate following the first Senate elections[5], in November 1996, was one of wary and defensive coalition partners actively looking for opportunities to undermine Klaus, a newly assertive Social Democratic opposition under Miloš Zeman, and an increasingly imperious CDP.

The Senate elections failed to break the emerging parliamentary stalemate. Although the CDP won seven more seats than the Social Democrats, the electoral turn-out was so low it could claim no strengthening of its general mandate, and within parliament it looked increasingly embattled. By the end of 1996 Klaus's coalition partners were growing more assertive and two Social Democratic MPs defecting from their party were required in mid-December to pass the 1997 state budget – a balanced budget that, given rapidly deteriorating welfare provision, was unpopular all round. The CDP party conference in December confirmed Klaus as party chairman but amidst criticism of his 'dictatorial style', not least from Milan Uhde, the leader of the CDP's parliamentary caucus.

In 1997, Czech illusions about the completion of their transition were steadily shattered. The year began inauspiciously when President Havel, recovering from lung cancer surgery, contracted pneumonia, and Czechs were forced to realise that were Havel to die the Republic would have no successor of equal stature. By spring the Czech economy was struck by a balance of payments and exchange rate crisis and in May the government was forced into emergency measures, widely criticised internally as cosmetic. In June 1997 the CDP government hung onto a confidence vote by one voice – again – that of a Social Democrat, Jozef Wagner[6], the vote revealing how little love remained for Klaus even within his own governing coalition. The chairman of the coalition party CDU/CPP Josef Lux led the most effective attacks, clearly hoping that Klaus would not make it through the economic storm. He survived, however, and the now thoroughly fissiparous coalition faced the daunting task of creating a social consensus to cope with what had become essential austerity measures as well as recruiting sufficient parliamentary cooperation to face up to structural economic reforms. Years of government disparagement of organised labour and aggression in parliament meant there was little hope for either. In July, prolonged floods devastated Moravia and Eastern Bohemia and the Western media shone a spotlight on an 'exodus' of persecuted Czech Roma to Canada – phenomena that conspired to create a sense of disintegrating confidence in the country as a whole.

In October 1997 the CDP's foreign minister and co-founder, and an emerging rival to Klaus, Joszf Zieleniec, resigned from the government at the height of NATO accession talks[7], invoking irregularities in party finances as his reason[8]. The resignation released a spectacular coalition cat-fight and by November the weight of accumulating scandals threw the CDP into crisis. As it turned out, massive loans had supposedly been given to the CDP by two donors: a Hungarian who had died in 1982 and a Mauritian who denied any such connection. Klaus had boasted about the donations back in 1995, saying, 'Even people who aren't Czech and don't live here feel that what we are doing is important enough to support us financially'[9]. In November 1997, however, the 7.5 million kcs were reported to have come from a Czech, Milan Srejbar, a former world-ranked tennis player and then head of Moravia Steel. The donation had fallen just prior to the privatisation of one of the country's largest steel-makers, subsequently awarded to Srejbar. The media went into a frenzy of investigation, and was soon alleging that the CDP also had at least $5 million secreted in a long-established Swiss bank account. Jan Ruml and Ivan Pilip – the former Minister of Interior and the current Finance Minister – resigned, arguing that the credibility of right-wing politics was at stake. Having declared that their own leadership certainly knew of the alleged Swiss bank accounts they called on Klaus to join them. On 29 November the coalition partner Christian Democratic Union/Czechoslovak People's Party resigned their ministerial posts, followed shortly by the Civic Democratic Alliance, thus pulling the plug on the government. On 30 November 1997, thoroughly isolated, Klaus resigned.

In a move reminiscent of the days when the Communist Party used to wheel out the sons of men in prison to call for their harsh punishment, Klaus's wife led a demonstration on St Wenceslas Square in which she read out a letter from her son to his father. It said: 'Your conscience is clear, and in this you differ from all the others. In short they couldn't stand the fact that you were more capable and intelligent than they. They used disgusting practices to further their careers ... You were the winner, morally and humanly, and I am proud to be your son'[10]. On 9 December, however, Havel, just released from hospital, delivered a state-of-the-union address to the Parliament and

Senate in which he excoriated the inadequacies of the Klaus administration and of neo-liberalism as a solution to transition. 'The declared
ideal of success and profit was defiled because we permitted a state of
affairs in which the most immoral became the most successful and
the greatest profits were made by thieves who stole with impunity',
he declared. 'Under the cloak of an unqualified liberalism, which
regarded any kind of economic controls or regulations as left-wing
aberrations, the Marxist doctrine of the structure and the superstructure lived on, though paradoxically it was hidden from view. Morality, decency, humility before the order of nature, solidarity, concern
for future generations, respect for the law, the culture of interpersonal
relationships – all these and many similar things were trivialised as
"superstructure", as icing on the cake, until we realised that there was
nothing left to put the icing on: the forces of economic production
themselves had been undermined'[11]. CDP senator Jan Kramek suggested that 'the president is not only physically sick, but mentally sick
as well'[12].

Following the collapse of the Klaus coalition, President Havel
presided over talks that produced an interim government led by the
central banker, Josef Tošovský. The new administration was largely
dependent upon the Freedom Union, a breakaway faction of the
CDP[13]; it also included CDA and CDU/CPP ministers – among them
Josef Lux and, much to Klaus's disgust, CDP rebels, Ivan Pilip,
Stanislav Volák and Michal Lobkowicz. The new interim government,
combining party men and experts, gained parliamentary support on
condition that it introduce early elections, and these were called for
June 1998. For a brief moment, with Klaus snubbed and with the parliamentary club of the CDP voting to support the Tošovský cabinet –
against Klaus's declared wishes – the CDP leader looked about to enter
the political wilderness. According to *Factum* polls Klaus stood as the
fifth-least popular politician in the country, and his party trailed
behind the Social Democrats, despite the latter's still unclear programme, by some 7–10 per cent. In early 1998 prospects for a stable
coalition emerging out of the June elections looked poor, with the
right splintering over corruption scandals and the possible coalitions
with the Social Democrats an unknown quantity. By February, the
Civic Democratic Party, the Civic Democratic Alliance *and* the Social
Democrats were all subject to police investigations, a tidal wave of
scandal further reducing public expectations of political integrity –
even if they did indicate a more assertive press.

The humiliation of the CDP laid bare the weakness of the Czech
party political system. In the absence of another charismatic leader
– Zeman came across as passionate but temperamental (and not

always entirely sober) – Klaus's star fell, only to rise again as the June 1998 election approached. On 13 May the CDP published an advertisement in national newspapers apologising for the party's corruption in the past and assuring that they would respond in full to a self-imposed financial audit by Deloitte and Touche – concluding that 'For these mistakes, CDP has already paid a not-insignificant political price. To our members, sympathisers, and the voters, we apologise for all of these past problems and mistakes' – a confident *mea culpa*[14].

The rest of the political scene looked chaotic; the Freedom Union[15] found themselves thwarted not only by their late arrival into the contest but also by their leader, Jan Ruml, who not only expressed his reluctance to become premier but bore such personal animosity to other party leaders that he dismissed the Union's most obvious coalition prospects. As the election neared, a Pensioners Party arose from nowhere to grab early support in opinion polls of up to 10 per cent (pensioners constituting a third of the Czech voting population) and the far right Republicans and the Communists together seized some 20 per cent of polled support, though both remained untouchable in coalition terms. Public opinion polls suggest that voters were bewildered; people changed their minds by massive margins from one week to another, being particularly anxious about the true potential of the Czech Social Democratic Party, which saw the most violent swings in support. The level of expressed voter disaffection was also markedly high, and particularly so amongst the young, who felt themselves to be thoroughly ignored by the party system as a whole. Of the 20–29-year-olds polled in May 1998, only 37.5 per cent said they would certainly vote[16].

The campaign for June 1998 – another mobilisation for democracy . . .

The idea of the state under siege had characterised CDP rhetoric in 1992, and with the economy in recession in 1998 Klaus again invoked this threat. This electoral strategy aimed, yet again, to shift party competition away from policy criticism towards pseudo-revolutionary politics, the logic being that if Klaus's CDP had only had a majority in 1996 the Czech economy would never have gone astray (thus distinguishing Klaus as the only economist in modern Europe to have factored in himself as the critical variable in a model of economic growth). The CDP effectively ran two campaigns: one of almost hallucinatory cheerfulness for its own supporters ('Look ahead', Klaus declared to a Prague crowd, 'we have had enough of this bad mood!'), and another, for the undecided voter, that raised the spectre of the imminent demise of democracy. Both campaigns focused upon Klaus the individual and to both audiences he depicted a flourishing country dragged from the true path by a recidivist left wing – this time in the guise of Social Democracy. As in 1992 and 1996, Klaus presented the election as *the* crossroads to democracy, the CDP as the one true path, and every other party as a slide backward to the Communist abyss. The positive campaign of the CDP, moreover, was populist. The posters that adorned many benches, walls and tram-sides throughout the Republic stated 'If you believe in yourself – vote Klaus', an essentially pre-political slogan of some brilliance, playing upon the idea that confident, self-reliant and well-balanced voters were the CDP's natural constituency. CDP rallies likewise resembled family entertainment more than political meetings, with small children being brought to the stage to concoct party slogans and to win prizes – among them videos of Klaus, together with an assortment of Czech pop stars, including Karel Gott, a star of the Communist era, swaying to a crown in Prague's Old Town Square and singing the CDP's campaign song:

> When I drove to the studio this morning, so I choked in the car
>   three times,
> [second voice] And I even had a similar experience
> And so we said to ourselves, that we can't carry on like this.
> If you give me your paw, if you give me your paw,
> Then we will say, that we really do care.
> If you give me your paw, if you give me your paw,
> After the long night, the dawn will come.
> I am a man like any other, only perhaps I have something of a
>   higher voice,
> We breath only poisons, and yet it is enough, four, three, two,
>   one,
> If you give me your paw, if you give me your paw,
> Then our words will change into acts.
> If you give me your paw, if you give me your paw,
> Then the ozone gap will close.
> One person is always terribly little: two may often be more than
>   one,
> Three will certainly be more than two, and four without doubt,
>   is more than three.
> If you give me your paw, if you give me your paw,
> Then our paw-ey paw-eys will change everything.
> If you give me your paw, if you give me your paw,
> After the long night, the dawn will come.

If you give me your paw, if you give me your paw,
Then our paw-ey paw-eys will change everything.
If you give me your paw, if you give me your paw, then
After the long night the dawn will come.
'"Why should we not look forward if God blesses us?"' (From
Smetana's *The Bartered Bride.*)

As for the recent scandals, Klaus shrouded the November 1997 events
in a mist of quite astonishing conspiracy theory, depicting himself as
a martyr to the democratic cause. His eviction from the premiership
was presented as a *coup d'état* by jealous rivals – the CDP manifesto
went so far as portray the months following November 1997 as the
'Road from Sarajevo'[17], comparing Klaus's political assassination to
that of the Austrian Archduke Franz Ferdinand. The inference was
that his former coalition partners and colleagues in the Freedom
Union represented a new 'Black Hand Gang', and that his defeat might
pitch Europe, not just the Czech Republic, into turmoil. On the last
legal day of campaigning the CDP produced fliers across the country
proclaiming 'MOBILIZACE'; they read, 'I am calling upon all who
want to live free. I am calling upon all who are not indifferent to the
fate of our country – vote CDP' – the implication being that, as in
1938 or 1948, 1998 represented for the citizens of the Czech Republic a last chance to protect democracy.

Television advertisements for all political parties avoided substantive issues. As in 1992 and 1996 the Civic Democratic Party ran the
best-orchestrated and most visible all-round campaign. The CDP's
television placement consisted solely of the ghastly 'Give us your
paw' song. The Freedom Union and the Christian Democratic
Union/Czechoslovak People's Party claimed the moral high ground
and donated their allocated television time to Czech charities, a pointedly noble move – in the light of recent scandals – which did
absolutely nothing to increase the voters' ability to define their
choices. The Pensioners Party and the Communists left no stone
unturned in terms of promising improved social conditions for every
imaginable section of society, with the Pensioners Party committed to
lowering the retirement age, though the existing threshold was already
well below the European average and crippling to the public budget.
The neo-fascist Republicans overstepped democratic boundaries,
cutting their campaign film from footage of the 1989 mass demonstrations in St Wenceslas Square to footage of the leader, Miroslav
Sládek, intoning on a platform, to Sládek being dragged down by
policemen. The film was clearly meant to depict mass public support
for Sládek and the state victimisation of the Republican cause – a tale

that well reflected Sládek's former life as a Communist censor and propagandist.

The Freedom Union had trouble in establishing a distinct electoral profile so soon after its foundation; indeed, it never succeeded in distinguishing itself from the party it had first tried to scuttle and then abandoned – Klaus's CDP. The Civic Democratic Alliance, defunct under the weight of finance scandal, only dared go so far as to encourage voters to choose other right-wing parties. The long-established Social Democrats meanwhile were split between an old guard with traditional pro-state socialist views and younger social liberals. Though they emphasised the well-targeted themes of anti-corruption, a rejection of 'arrogance in power' and 'social investment', the practicalities of these issues remained ambiguous. In their manifesto the Social Democrats argued for investment in education, health, housing construction, public services and the protection of living standards, particularly for vulnerable groups such as young families and the elderly. The main thrust of their campaign was the promise of social cohesion, civic society and solidarity – in other words, the very same goals as the Civic Movement back in 1992.

One of the most notable aspects of the 1998 election was the vitriolic intensity with which every party declared that it could never work with at least one other named party, to the point where any coalition capable of gaining a majority had been categorically – and I mean scathingly – rejected by at least one key party. The result in June was a narrow victory for the Social Democrats, with the CDP a close second. 'We have suffered a victory', moaned Social Democrat deputy Jaroslav Basta – well aware that his party was now in for weeks and possibly months of coalition talks, with a thankless agenda of austerity measures and economic reform to ensue. Klaus, for his part, declared that 'we managed to convince the voters not to allow a turn to the left . . . We are still on the true path'[18]. The one unambiguously excellent piece of news was the terrible performance of the Republicans. With below 5 per cent of the vote they were at last ousted from the Czech Parliament[19], and their departure represented a note of optimism in an election that otherwise seemed to resolve little by way of regaining impetus for the Czech democratic project.

True to their pre-election quarrels, Jan Ruml of the Freedom Union ruled out working with Zeman of the Social Democrats; and both Ruml and Lux of the CDU/CPP recoiled at the prospect of another coalition with Klaus, once again the undisputed leader of the CDP. Personal differences among the various leaders thus prevented the most logical coalition formulas; they also revealed the continuing superiority of Klaus's instincts for gaining power.

After protracted coalition talks during which Zeman made reasonable offers to every conceivable partner, the solution that emerged was a 'toleration agreement' between none other than the Civic Democratic Party and the Social Democrats, in which the CDP committed not to bring down a new, minority Social Democrat government in return for constitutional changes and powerful positions in parliament, the economic sphere and, so it would appear, in the media[20].

This development was astounding; the CDP electoral campaign had depicted the Social Democrats as a party peddling 'a mixture of untruths, semi-truths, blatant lies and facts expediently extracted from context'[21]. In *realpolitik* terms, however, it was a brilliant step; a Social Democrat/Civic Democratic Party alliance would provide 137 seats in parliament – enough to change the constitution and thus the electoral law. Such a prospect was perfect for Klaus in every way; it was both intolerable to the Communists (lined up as future allies to the Social Democrats) and deeply threatening to the survival of both the CDU/CPP, which now lost its proposed cabinet seats, and the new Freedom Union, which had rejected cabinet participation. As Klaus had clearly realised, all might be kept out of government for good with a new, strongly majoritarian electoral system.

Several parties, including the Freedom Union and the Christian Democrats, condemned the 'opposition agreement' as unconstitutional[22]. President Havel too was unhappy; 'I feel it is my obligation', he said, 'to express my fears over this very unusual solution, which is an agreement between a left-wing party that has for years fought against a government of alleged right-wing embezzlers and a right-wing party which has called for mobilisation against the left that is supposedly attempting a return to socialism'. He particularly feared 'ideas such as deliberately changing the Constitution for the benefit of the two large parties under the pretence of political stability'[23]. Several commentators alluded to the beginnings of Mečiarism in the Czech Republic. Mečiar, ever gifted in the art of aggravating Czechs, complimented Klaus on his 'proven ability to strike compromises'. The main efforts of the smaller parties turned to convincing the electorate that the Senate was now the last line of defence for plurality in Czech politics, since the CDP and Social Democrats would need a two-thirds majority here too to pass constitutional legislation. This they signally failed to do.

In the run-up to Senate and local elections in mid-November 1998, the CDP slogans were 'We think differently', 'Just say no to socialist experiments' (as if these could be afforded in recession) and 'With us, against the danger'. As the political monthly *Nová Přítomnost* ('New Presence') commented, the casual political observer could be forgiven for forgetting that the Social Democratic government only existed due to the CDP's support[24]. The Social Democrats meanwhile declared 'Yes, a new Politics!' The Senate campaign, like the June election, was cabalistic in the extreme. On the very spot where a vast statue of Stalin had towered across Prague until it was reluctantly torn down by Antonín Novotný, Klaus raised an image of himself, with the shadow of Zeman behind him. The turn-out in the first round of the Senate elections was 42 per cent, but 20 per cent in the second round – the lowest figure in any election in the Czech lands, indeed in any major election in any country in Central Europe, since 1989.

The post-1998 Social Democratic government under Miloš Zeman – a 'suicide government', as he called it – had little choice but to get to grips with the legacy of the previous government, albeit with only 74 seats in the Lower Chamber and therefore at the mercy of the CDP. The Social Democrats faced a major headache given victory; the economically advisable privatisation of banks would practically guarantee bankruptcy for massive and uncompetitive industries, which in turn employed tens of thousands of workers. While bank privatisation might restore growth, it would also guarantee a rise in unemployment – a result that would split the Social Democratic party between its socialist and social liberal wings and lose it support. The Social Democrats nevertheless started to move on bank privatisation, effective bankruptcy procedures and a 'revitalisation programme', in which a politically independent agency, under an international manager, would be established to help restructure enterprises and prepare them for strategic investors. Politically, however, the government appeared to take on wholesale the CDP attitude to patronage and *ad hoc* administration, and it has been dogged from the outset by the deep divisions between its own irreconcilable factions. The pro-Social Democrat paper *Právo* reported that voters who had seen Zeman's first three months in government were disillusioned by the pragmatic agreement with the CDP and by 'unfulfilled promises', 'lack of direction', and 'nepotism'[25].

Most controversially, the CDP continued to press the Social Democrats for a change in the electoral law to a more majoritarian system. In June 2000, legislation was passed changing the type of proportional representation used (to D'Hondt), raising the electoral threshold for parties within an electoral alliance and raising the number of electoral districts to 35, thus making it far harder for small parties or electoral alliances to gain representation. Since the principle of proportional representation – stipulated in the constitution – was maintained, the CDP insisted that this was not a constitutional amendment, despite the fact that it would critically reshape the Czech political landscape; the bill thus required only a simple majority in the Senate to pass, and it scraped through with one vote. Even though a larger majoritarian component in the Czech lower chamber might be beneficial in principle, the new law reeked of a deal to stitch up mainstream politics at the very point where a more moderate right wing was finally developing and when the public's sense of political accountability was dismally low. Although the press attacked the measure there was little that could be done – a presidential veto of the legislation could, in turn, be outvoted and the Constitutional Court was stuck with the vagueness of the Czech constitution, which speaks only of 'the principle of proportional representation', not naming the system to be used[26].

Despite the 'Opposition Agreement', the CDP continued to act as an opposition party, voting against major Social Democratic proposals on many occasions. It thus secured for itself the enviable position in which it kept the Social Democratic government weak, even as it extracted significant patronage and legislative favours – tarnishing the Social Democrat record after scarcely two years in government. Opinion polls through 2000, moreover, consistently placed the CDP first, with the Social Democratic government trailing third behind the barely reconstructed Communist Party. In these circumstances the significant factor keeping the Social Democratic government afloat was that Klaus had little interest in returning to government until the Czech economy escaped recession and the new electoral law and further self-interested constitutional legislation had been passed: the Czech Republic's first social democratic government has been, therefore, a suicide government indeed.

State intervention in the economy – the extraction of rents

In the early 1990s it was possible to see in the Klausite reform project a sincere, if dogmatic, attempt to transform Czechoslovakia into an assertive neo-liberal society. Klaus's economic vision went sour for many reasons, many of which were clearly no fault of his government but a direct and inescapable Communist legacy afflicting every country in the region. However, some of the most chronic problems of the Czech economy can be directly attributed to four aspects of Klausite policy and neo-liberal ideology. The first is the basic problem of state administrative capacity; the second, the insistence on rapid privatisation at all costs; the third, the perverse and entirely counterproductive hostility to market regulation; and the fourth, resulting from the previous three, corruption: the abuse of the market by asset-managers, and the abuse of state power by ministry officials and party politicians. If the radical neo-liberal reformers under Klaus's leadership ever began with some sense of their limited rights as public servants, by the mid-1990s these had apparently disappeared. By 1997 the governing coalition was caught feeding out of the trough that it had, whether deliberately or inadvertently, created.

Executive autonomy

Klaus had conceded in his writings that in the period of transition 'it is necessary to grant a large "constructing" role to the economic centre, to the institution whose role at a time of normal conduct of this conceived system must otherwise be minimal'[27]. The idea that reformers should build a strong administrative and regulatory state more generally, however (as opposed to retaining whatever form of state intervention seemed expedient at the time), remained anathema to Klaus, and he condemned it both in theory and in practice as a delusion held only by socialists.

Under Klaus's leadership the Civic Democratic Party showed little interest in establishing a state 'capable of formulating and enforcing, impartially and universally, the framework of rules and institutions necessary for a functioning market democracy . . .'[28]. Constructing such a state is arguably the hardest task for every post-Communist country; however, simply to abdicate this task, to reject it as a foolish aspiration, as the CDP effectively did, was to introduce new barriers to both economic and democratic developments. The condition of the Czech Republic by 2000 suggested a strong counter-argument to the Klausite model; with the state retaining a significant stake in the economy but failing to provide either market regulation or impartial public administration, the conditions for official corruption become ideal.

In keeping with its philosophy, the CDP blocked all attempts through the 1990s to professionalise the civil service, the first necessary step towards strengthening the state and allowing for the possibility of high-quality administration. In addition, Klaus endeavoured only to guarantee party, rather than legal or parliamentary, review over the administration. To this end the CDP coalition politicised the top-flight civil service to the extent that the allocation of party posts in the senior civil service was among those written into governing coalition agreements. Ministries were left subject only to the normal criminal law and their own, internal departmental audit committees. In effect, Klaus was attempting to 'safeguard' executive autonomy from the parliamentary accountability anticipated in the purposeful reformist days of the early 1990s. In practice, the ministries emerged as a collection of party political fiefdoms, in many instances losing all reformist ambition. The impact in terms of administrative capacity was serious, causing constant delays in the legislative programme, exacerbated by major personnel changes in the second half of 1998 following the appointment of the new government[29]. Administrative weakness was not confined to ministries, moreover, but also affected the investigative and judicial structures of the state. The state's persistently low capacity for discovering economic crime, establishing due title and organising redress over time had several serious consequences, the discouragement of foreign investment and disillusionment with the equity of the reform process among them.

Rapid privatisation

After five years of privatisation the most powerful beneficiaries of voucher and standard privatisation – barely regulated Investment Privatisation Funds[30] (IPFs) and the Czech state[31] – frequently maintained an at best passive and often venal control over enterprises. Far from becoming 'active owners', keen to embrace the market and to restructure their newly acquired assets, many IPFs used the lack of legal protection for minority share holders[32] and the general lack of regulation in capital markets and commercial law to asset-strip, or, as the Czechs call it, 'tunnel' out, their newly acquired enterprises – frequently to the point of endangering previously viable industries.

The state, meanwhile, in the form of the National Property Fund, the subject of numerous corruption scandals, was effectively indifferent to restructuring, without the manpower or expertise to organise it, and anyway politically biased under Klaus's direction toward the idea that the state should refrain from meddling until residual state holdings were privatised. The fact that these significant residual state holdings, particularly in strategic industries, were public assets, whose revenues might be essential to public services, was ignored. Together, the state and the IPFs kept out more active owners, particularly foreign owners, after the CDP opted for an increasingly nationalistic antipathy to foreign investment, its free-market protestations notwithstanding. The insistence on rapid privatisation in many cases led to highly convoluted ownership, leaving many enterprises without majority shareholders.

Czech industry was already highly indebted and undercapitalised as a legacy of the Communist era, and voucher privatisation was duly criticised for bringing no capital for industrial restructuring. In the absence of a flourishing stock exchange, however, the Czech banking system stepped in to fill the need for continuing credit, but in an extraordinarily under-regulated environment. Thus, if enterprises promised favours, or were already so indebted that they might bring down their bank (many IPFs were themselves owned and capitalised by banks), then banks themselves held considerable political leverage on the state, which wished to see neither bank collapses nor rocketing unemployment. The emerging government policy of recapitalising and relieving banks of bad-loan debt – at the expense of the Czech taxpayer – in turn perpetuated the ability of banks to extend expensive loans to already indebted companies, by 1997 resulting in a major banking crisis and a crisis in the public budget. In 1997, non-performing loans accounted for over 25 per cent of Czech GDP – compared to less than 5 per cent in either Hungary or Poland. With practically unsupervised powers to decide to whom to lend, how much and on what terms, Czech banks were self-regulatory for a sufficient period to dig themselves into a situation described by *The Economist*[33] as 'a deadly cocktail of mismanagement, orgiastic lending (often to the bank's own shareholders) and, more often than not, fraud'. As the guarantor of 'last resort', the state effectively maintained its Communist role as the source of soft credit – the ultimate disincentive for any profound change in the Czech economy.

Non-regulation

'We have no doubt it is the new owner, not the government, who will find ideas, time, and resources for the necessary restructuring'.
Václav Klaus[34]

There were two clear reasons why the Klaus government fought against market regulation. The first reason was electoral; the extraordinarily rapid mass privatisation of the economy had been the flagship of the CDP's economic reform programme, and arguably the key to that party's electoral success from 1992 to 1996. The drafting and implementation of an effective regulatory regime, by contrast, would have taken years and would have meant the loss of quick political credit. It would also have meant loss of patronage and state power through the depoliticisation of the civil service and the empowerment of the judiciary.

The second reason for opposing market regulation was purely ideological. Despite having parliamentary power to pass roughly 90 per cent of its legislation until the 1996 elections, Klaus's coalition prevented the legal regulation of the privatisation process, banking and capital markets on the basis that regulation of any kind was a socialist abomination. Dušan Tříska – a 'lustrated' CDP member reappointed by Klaus, Deputy Finance Minister supervising voucher privatisation preparations, a member of the price commission setting voucher share prices and eventual head of the RM-system, one of Prague's two stock exchanges – declared capital market regulation an anachronism of 'American socialism'[35].

The CDP coalition not only opposed regulation but did much to destroy or confuse the regulatory frameworks carried over from the federation, inadequate though they were. It blocked legislation that would have provided for shareholder rights, investment fund regulation, laws on conflict of interest[36], and disclosure requirements. In December 1993 the government abolished the state prosecutor's function of general supervision over the state administration. The possibilities of external audit were also minimised. In July 1993 a National Audit Office (NAO) was established whose president and vice-president were both CDP appointments. The new NAO was stripped of previous powers to audit where it chose, and now depended on initiatives from parliament, government or the president. Given that the NAO was only permitted to audit a company until the property was transferred into private hands, the NAO President Lubomir Volenik pointed out that it was no longer worth auditing privatisation at all[37].

Klaus had long insisted that a change in ownership would induce the competitive laws of the market. In this quaint understanding of the market, 'good' market actors would themselves regulate the 'bad', by being more successful than other market actors who might act corruptly[38]. What the Czech economy went on to prove, however, is that market actors, given the chance, will collude instead of compete, if this is patently the fastest and easiest way of getting rich. A total failure to regulate many aspects of privatisation – in particular, the failure to regulate new Investment Privatisation Funds and banking – provided excellent conditions for collusion and non-competitive behaviour.

Capital market regulatory authority was vested in the Ministry of Finance and directed by officials with little or no experience of capital markets, who anyway did not believe in the state's right to intervene. Czech capital market regulations placed minimal disclosure requirements on enterprises or Investment Privatisation Funds, even over issues as basic as ownership, changes in ownership or intentions to change ownership. The regulations also omitted provisions governing insider trading. Those violations that did appear were punished by minor penalties – a weakness of regulation that joined with gaping holes in the tax and commercial codes to create a legal open season. Ultimately, moreover, the Ministry of Finance delegated regulatory authority to the stock exchanges, and since the Prague Stock Exchange[39] in particular was dominated by bank and Investment

Privatisation Funds, the stage was set for influential owners to manipulate and corrupt the capital markets – which they duly did[40].

Corruption

By the mid-1990s the unwillingness of the CDP government to regulate the economy looked less ideological and more and more self-serving[41]. As the party finance scandals of the late 1990s revealed, the abuses resulting from the lack of regulation of privatisation were not limited to state bureaucrats and asset managers, but had touched upon practically the entire political scene. Through 1996 and 1997 Czech newspaper headlines were dominated by a massive banking crisis involving privatisation scandals and increasingly aggressive behaviour by Investment Privatisation Funds. All of these cases carried the strong implication of government or bureaucratic collusion and incompetence. The transactions leading to the demise of the C.S. Fond, one of the largest investment funds in the country, having been approved by government regulators, amounted to a humiliation for the Finance Ministry, which eventually led to the resignation of Finance Minister Ivan Kočárník and Deputy Finance Minister Vladimír Rudlovčák. When in the spring of 1997 the Czech Republic was struck by a balance of payments and exchange rate crisis, the coincidence with investment fund scandals shook public and foreign investment confidence in government economic policy to the core. By November 1997, public trust in state institutions – parliament and government – had sunk to 16 per cent[42].

A leading commentator on corruption in the Czech Republic, Quentin Reed, has made the acute point that 'any theory in which politics is *determined* deprives its actors of autonomy and therefore makes it difficult to conceive of them as being corrupt'[43]. As Klaus had asserted back in 1994, the citizen was the only basic element of democracy, and 'everything that is above the citizen is derived from him'[44]. If politicians, a mere four years after the revolution, were already selling themselves as the neutral (if 'chosen') executors of the 'public will' then to condemn them was implicitly to condemn the society – a great, indeed revolutionary, step. It is clear from the statements and behaviour of coalition politicians since 1993 that, just as the late Communist system depended upon corruption and informal networks, so prominent members of the Czech governing elite in the 1990s also saw little contradiction between private interest and state administration. When Jaroslav Lizner, head of the Ministry of Finance Centre for Voucher Privatisation, was arrested in October 1994 after taking an 8,334,500 kcs bribe in return for a controlling share in Klatovské mlékárny – he claimed that he took the money as a 'commission'.

The evolution of Klausite politics

In defeat in November 1997 Klaus was 'certain that I did more than a little for the transformation of the Czech economy, the formation of our democratic political system, the birth of the Czech Republic and its promotion on the international scene and for the transformation of the entire ideological climate in our country. And I am sure all that will be appreciated in more sober times than these'[45]. On reflection, however, Klaus's genius as Czech prime minister was that of reinstating – using the language of capitalism and the minimal state – some of the more effective political tricks of Communism. Politics in any democratic country is to some degree about myth-making or vision-creating – it being the vision of a better future that persuades society to accept the compromises and trade-offs in any given plan. There is a degree of myth-making that steps beyond conventional democratic campaigning and into the *culture* of authoritarianism (though certainly not its physical reality in this case), however, and this is arguably when the vision becomes an incontrovertible 'truth', or more blatantly, when the vision is said to have already arrived, and to be in need of protection. Even though there is, of course, a huge gulf between the Communist party-state with its omnipresent secret services and its grotesque abuse of the citizenry and the merely anti-pluralistic electoral strategies and political *rhetorics* of the CDP (the neo-liberal vanguard leading to a bright market future), the cultural continuity is nevertheless striking. Just as the Communists attacked critics as class enemies or suffering from false consciousness, so Klaus attacks those who disagree with him as either 'crypto-Bolshevik' or 'hopelessly deluded'.

The feeling of deep pessimism in the Czech Republic in 2000 was in stark contrast to the high expectations and almost euphoric sense of progress typical to Czechs in the mid-1990s. The disillusionment of recent years is apparently the comedown from the dizzy optimism of before – an optimism that had sprung from the reassuring replacement of one all-explaining politico-economic orthodoxy with another. As Milan Šimečka wrote, in his classic critique of the post-1968 regime, '[t]he restored order creates a false picture of reality, chiefly because it has placed an ideological straitjacket on all representations of it . . . once out of the bottle, the lying genie is hard to control. Day after day it invents fresh absurdities and clothes reality in a rosy smoke screen which has the power to render impossible even attempts at rational government of the State. So long as propaganda is only intended to deceive citizens, it is not so bad, because they do not believe it anyway. But it is dangerous to the State when political leaders become captivated by their own propaganda'[46]. In seeking to portray itself – whether in government or in opposition – as the party carrying a faultless, scientifically 'proven' agenda, the CDP, without doubt, had become entranced by its own vision.

Milan Šimečka concluded that 'In order to integrate into the new society, all the citizen had to do was to come to terms with a few very basic notions; that there is only one party of government; that there is only one truth . . . that the world is divided into friends and foes; that assent is rewarded, dissent penalised'. As it happens, Klaus has been extremely frank about his party's co-option of this old formula. Addressing the Heritage Institute in Washington in October 1993 he argued that 'To be successful, political leaders must formulate and "sell" to the citizens of the country a positive vision of a future society. The first task is formulation of the vision; it must be positive (not just negative); it must be straightforward (not fuzzy); it must motivate; it must speak to the hearts of men and women who have spent most of their lives under a spiritually empty Communist regime; it requires clear words, biblical yeses and nos; it must be stated in an ideal form (which needs "extreme" terms, because compromises belong to reality, not to images or visions); it must explicitly reject all "third ways", which are based on incompatible combinations of different worlds . . .'[47]. It is perhaps the last phrase that is the most telling – the 'incompatible combinations of different *worlds*' – as if any given country can only cope with one ideology at a time.

By the late 1990s, under pressure from a failing economy, corruption scandals and a loss of policy direction, the Civic Democratic Party was using in everyday politics the Bolshevik culture of 'vanguardist' arguments that it had previously reserved only for elections. The vanguardist assumptions of the CDP, used in every election since 1992, are, of course, a perfectly circular argument for the party's authority to control the state. As the CDP ideological line now runs, more shrilly and consistently than during the life of the federation, it represents the one 'true' pro-market party, standing as the unique voice of the pro-democratic Czech people. Whatever it has done, therefore, it has done as the exact and valid expression of the will of a free society. As with the Communists before, this is as solipsistic a political idea as can be imagined – exactly illustrated by the CDP's campaign slogan for June 1998, 'If you believe in yourself – vote Klaus'. By the late 1990s, however, the political scene was clearly divided between a pseudo-revolutionary CDP on the one hand and defensive and still strikingly imitative 'European' mainstream political parties on the other.

This may make Klaus a brilliant neo-liberal politician, but is there really anything more sinister to be laid at his door than that he fought his political corner with more hard-nosed political talent than anyone else? It might be argued that the CDP's arrogance provided the necessary force for change, 'snapping the dead wood of Europe's social democratic conventions', to city the ball-breaking phrase of the American Enterprise Institute's Michael Novak[48]. The CDP's coalition partners speculated in 1997 that a purged CDP under Klaus would actually move to the far right; one CDP deputy, under conditions of anonymity, said when the more moderate Freedom Union had broken away from the party that 'the CDP is finished as a large liberal-conservative party representing a third of Czech voters. Klaus will turn it into a libertarian, isolationist, anti-European party'. The CDP's own Labour and Social Affairs Minister, Stanislav Volák, predicted that it 'would experience something like a Bolshevisation . . . of the 1930s'[49]. As yet these views remain over-pessimistic, but they are correct insofar as Klaus, since 1997, has taken the CDP to a new and far more alarmingly populist, nationalist and isolationist political threshold to retain the air of activist fervour that was the party's signature in the early 1990s.

In August 1999 a Senate by-election was held in the city district Prague I, a traditional stronghold of the CDP. The election was crucial, since the CDP had to maintain its mandate to retain the Social Democrat/CDP two-thirds majority in the Senate, essential for passing constitutional legislation. Partly in protest against the opposition agreement, however, an independent candidate, Stanislav Fischer, stood for election. A right-wing multi-millionaire entrepreneur and Czech émigré, Fischer was in many ways the personification of the Klausite ideal Czech – a self-made man. The CDP, however, to the astonishment of the media and many CDP voters alike, ran the most vitriolic and personal campaign seen in the Czech Republic since 1989. The newspaper *Mladá Fronta* refused to publish a CDP campaign advertisement it judged defamatory. In it Klaus complained that 'just because the Romans saw fit to elect a horse to the Senate, Fischer seems to think the same can happen in the Czech Republic'; he also alleged that Fischer was backed by the Communists. Fischer won the vote with a landslide of 74 per cent.

More recently, there have been other indications of a Klausite move toward populism: vocal criticism of the EU whenever it issues its reports on the condition of Czech reform (the EU has tended to blame delays in the Czech accession process on Klaus's reform strategy, thus making itself a barn-sized target); immediate and outspoken opposition to NATO intervention in the Kosovo war – one week after the Czech Republic officially joined the Alliance; Klaus's outspoken defence of Austria's sovereign right to elect who it wished, after the formation of a government including Jörg Haider's far-right Freedom Party in February 2000; and the unwillingness of the party leadership to muzzle CDP mayors making overtly racist statements about the Roma minority, to name but four. It seems increasingly likely that Klaus will run on a pro-sovereignty and possibly even an openly anti-EU platform in 2002, or whenever the next elections are held. The CDP's shadow foreign minister, Jan Zahradil, recommended, somewhat surreally (and before Turkish entry to the EU looked plausible), a 'Turecka cesta' – or Turkish way – for the Czech Republic in Europe.

In 2000, one of the most striking features of the Czech political scene was its stagnation. The political leaders were the same faces from 1992, though many were already associated with policy failures, or, worse, corruption scandals – and Zeman and Klaus looked like the gatekeepers of a sorry *status quo*. The remainder of the Czech right, in the form of the CDA, the Freedom Union, the Christian Democrats and the diminutive Democratic Union, formed a four-party alliance which did well in the November 2000 Senate elections, but their success was viewed widely as a protest vote against Zeman and Klaus, as these parties too were deeply implicated in the failures of the 1990s. While the four-party alliance's ideas – a brand of more 'compassionate' and certainly more normal conservatism – remain popular, their leaderships look far from fresh, and the alliance, depending on its eventual political form in 2002, when the next elections for the lower chamber will be held, may be severely hamstrung by the new electoral legislation. Zeman's Social Democrats were punished in the 2000 November Senate elections, gaining only five seats in the aftermath of a spate of corruption scandals and inner-party intrigues.

The CDP's strategy for the future is apparently to switch the party's constituency from a reformist to a purely populist base, and there is clearly potential for such a strategy in a country where support for EU entry hovers ambiguously at 50 per cent. By blocking EU pressures for the Czech Republic to restructure its civil service, judiciary, regional government, human rights and legal structure, however, the CDP in power might next time spell a real tragedy for democratisation in the Czech Republic. By 2000 Czech commentators were discussing the 'Haiderisation' of Klaus's CDP – the transformation of the great neo-liberal leading light of Central Europe into an increasingly radically xenophobic and parochial party, an imitation, in fact, of the Austrian far right.

The cost of the Czech experiment with neo-liberalism has been fantastic. From day one Klaus proved willing to be instrumental about those barriers that stood in his path – whether these barriers took the form of constitutional law, the common Czechoslovak state, the liberal dissidents, or the very notion of fair party competition. That he managed to remove these barriers without inaugurating an authoritarian state is testament to his skills. Indeed, these skills remain in excellent working order; according to CDP Deputy Chairman Ivan Langer, the party is contemplating promoting a radical constitutional change as part of the 2002 election platform: a recommendation that the Czech president be popularly elected and given the powers of a 'chancellor', i.e. pre-eminent executive powers[50]. Klaus has professed to oppose this idea; having thoroughly neutered the presidency under Havel, he would have to. It seems likely, though, that Klaus would not be averse to becoming the first Czech Chancellor.

There is an epilogue to the Czechs' first ten years of post-Communist change – a political event at the close of 1999 that seemed to parody the Czech political troubles of the previous ten years. As part of the Czechs' November 1999 ten-year anniversary celebrations of the 1989 revolution a student movement calling themselves 'Thank you – Now leave!' demanded that all existing party leaders stand down – by reason of their alleged ineptitude and corruption. Far from being ignored as youthful radicalism, the petition for this particular demand quickly drew 150,000 signatories and in December 1999 the cause provoked mass demonstrations of up to 50,000 people – a level of public mobilisation not seen since the days of the revolution itself.

Extraordinarily, and possibly even extra-constitutionally for a ceremonial president, Havel appeared to endorse the group, echoing, yet again, the deep exasperation of the people at large with their unimproving political leadership. Prime Minister Zeman, meanwhile, described the whole idea of 'Thank you – Now leave!' as 'a pubescent step'. Jan Ruml, head of the Freedom Union and ever a man of dissident culture, actually abided by the students' wishes and stood down – thus depriving one of the few forward-looking parties in the country of its leader even earlier than expected. One opinion poll in the first week of December revealed that 25 per cent of the population would vote for a new political party formed out of the student radical body – even as the movement's leaders expressed their great disgust with politics and their intention never to go near it in a professional capacity. In a spectacular protest vote, the Communist Party moved into first place in public opinion polls that month.

The 'Děkujeme, odejděte!' movement suggests that after ten years the political elite of the Czech republic was widely regarded as a three-ring circus. Far from the younger generation coming to the rescue, moreover (the expressed hope of many, many Czechs of all ages), young people of integrity, only ten years after the November revolution, regard 'democratic' politics as a school for thieves and do not see how they can participate, in Havel's long-cherished terms, as citizens.

THE INDEPENDENT SLOVAK REPUBLIC

Looking at the confidence of the Meciar regime in the mid-1990s it is easy to forget how shaky the Movement for a Democratic Slovakia's hold on power had been in the first two years of Slovak independence. Meciar appeared to be in the ascendant but only because the reformist opposition was in tatters and the Slovak National Party and the Party of the Democratic Left, the former Communists, continued to hedge their bets with pragmatic cooperation. Following the break-up Slovakia was in political disarray. The 1992 parliament – a single chamber with 150 seats – ranged 99 former Communist Party members against a demoralised opposition. The Christian Democrats had 18 seats and the liberal Hungarian coalition 14. The 1992 election had seen the small Slovak liberal vote split and wasted as neither the Democratic Party nor the Civic Democratic Union – the liberal remnant of the Public Against Violence – had made it into parliament[51].

Neither the ruling Movement for a Democratic Slovakia nor the Slovak National Party could escape the fallout from administering an unpopular separation for which the Slovak economy was ill-prepared. In March 1993 Milan Kňažko, rebellious during the last months of the federation, was finally sacked as the Movement's pro-Western Foreign Minister, and in April he founded the Alliance of Democrats of the Slovak Republic (ADSR) – reducing the MDS's 74 parliamentary seats to 66. The floundering Movement for a Democratic Slovakia only survived in government thereafter with the peripatetic support of the Party of the Democratic Left and the xenophobic Slovak National Party; the latter re-established a coalition with the MDS in November 1993, having extracted the education and European integration portfolios, among others.

Mečiar's policies through 1993 seemed to echo the floundering mode of the separation talks. In the first month of Slovak independence he warned that economic difficulties and austerity measures would be the price to pay for independence. As conditions deteriorated – foreign investment continued to fall from its already low rate, bankruptcies loomed, banks withheld credit, trade with the Czech

Republic practically halved by spring 1993 and inflation and unemployment continued to rise – support for the MDS fell to 18.6 per cent. By March 1993 an overwhelming 78 per cent of polled Slovaks believed members of the government to be 'incompetent'[52].

Mečiar's tendency both in rhetoric and in policy to lash out against internal and external 'enemies' began to grow through 1993, and to deepen the divides within his own party. Over allegations of corruption the MDS split again at the top in February 1994 and MDS Foreign Minister Jozef Moravčík and Deputy Prime Minister Roman Kováč formed a new faction – the Alternative of Political Realism (APR). The APR was eventually reconstituted, along with Kňažko's ADSR and the National Democratic Party (a splinter group from the Slovak National Party) as the DUS, the Democratic Union of Slovakia, latterly known as DU. Following its success in the 1994 election the DU would take over the liberal pro-democracy space in parliament vacated by the first liberal politicians of the PAV – DU members effectively repenting their part in establishing the Movement for a Democratic Slovakia in the first place.

For the electorate the post-divorce political scene was an unedifying sight – a party too weak to govern without opportunistic opposition support, an opposition too pedantic and divided, particularly over Hungarian participation in government, to oust the man they agreed had brought Slovakia to an impasse. Only after Slovakia's new President, Michal Kováč, established himself as a gate-keeper of the reform process and launched a highly critical 'Report on the State of the Slovak Republic' did the opposition finally succeed in passing a no-confidence vote against the Mečiar government in March 1994. At the point at which the painful process of economic reforms clearly needed relaunching the MDS was briefly pushed into opposition, pending fresh elections in September.

For the spring and summer of 1994 an ideologically disparate, essentially anti-Mečiar coalition came into government made up of the Christian Democratic Movement, the Party of the Democratic Left (in historical terms, the CDM's strongest rivals) and the new Democratic Union, under the leadership of Jozef Moravčík[53]. In the September 1994 election, however, these coalition parties fought as separate entities, having been fractious during their brief term in government. With these parties and every other anti-Mečiar group standing alone and splitting the vote, Mečiar's MDS again campaigned as the most confident political force in the country. The whittling down of the MDS leadership through 1993 to a less scrupulous and more loyalist core had freed Mečiar's hands. Even more than in 1992, he ran a fabulously populist platform.

By claiming that the MDS would have 'policies on' full employment ('for everyone who wants it'), prosperity, minority rights, protection of Slovaks in mixed nationality areas, a flourishing economy and an efficient state that would aim at full integration westward, the Movement promised everything to everyone. Mečiar stuck to his previous insistence that Slovakia 'should' – i.e. in a just world – flourish and that it could only do so under his leadership. As the MDS's 1994 manifesto argued, 'The citizens will decide if the state remains in the hands of those who didn't want it, or to allow those who established the state to continue its development. The Movement for a Democratic Slovakia wants to solve problems resulting from the creation of the new state. It acknowledges the Christian value system. It wants to achieve recovery and the renovation of society's growth. It wants to give jobs, prosperity, peace, order and opportunity for everybody.' The Movement's 1994 campaign declared: 'Slovakia – go for it – and trust yourself!'

The broad claim that the opposition had demonstrated their lack of patriotism back in 1992 was useful to Mečiar in framing attacks against the Moravčík coalition, and he tarred them as intrinsically anti-Slovak by their supposed usurpation of Mečiar's post-divorce government. Despite facing internal divisions and thankless policy tasks, the Moravčík coalition had been bold in practice, pledging a re-acceleration of economic reforms, launching a second wave of voucher privatisation, winning IMF approval and loans worth $263 million and, to counter the best efforts of the Slovak National Party, finally improving relations with the Hungarian minority (the Moravčík government enacted favourable Hungarian language rights and thus gained the parliamentary support of the Hungarian party, Coexistence). Mečiar duly accused the reformers of selling out Slovakia to the West and to Hungary.

The Moravčík government paid the price of introducing tough economic legislation and controversial reforms without the time in which to prove their worth. The six-month anti-Mečiar coalition was duly defeated in the September 1994 election, with the liberal DU winning barely 9 per cent. The Movement for a Democratic Slovakia, with financial aid from Berlusconi's Forza Italia party[54], won 35 per cent of the vote in coalition with the tiny Peasant Party, making the MDS yet again the single strongest party in Slovakia. When the Christian Democrats and the Party of the Democratic Left made it clear they would not work with Mečiar an alliance of the 'anti-pluralists' became the clear alternative. Eventually, on 11 December, Mečiar formed a 'red-brown' coalition of the MDS, the Slovak National Party (SNP) and a radical, supposedly far-left splinter group from the former Communists – the Association of Workers of Slovakia (AWS). The AWS took the critical portfolio of privatisation; the SNP gained defence and again education[55]. Together the post-1994 election coalition had 83 of the Slovak National Council's 150 seats.

It was during this second term in the independent Slovakia, from 1994 to 1998, that the Movement for a Democratic Slovakia adopted an increasingly authoritarian style in government and used government intervention more as a resource for developing clientalistic networks and government cohesion than as an instrument of anything resembling reform. Even before the new cabinet had been formed the MDS legislated through the night of 3 November to undo the privatisation legislation of the Moravčik government, cancelling over 4 billion crowns worth of privatisation projects, and purging three critical institutions. In one night the Special Oversight Board, monitoring the Slovak intelligence services; the National Property Fund, which would subsequently be given powers to make direct sales of state property; and the councils supervising public broadcasting services, were all taken entirely into government hands.

Mečiar's aspirations for the legislature in the mid-1990s were clearly that it should fulfil the theatrical function established by the Communists – its purpose was to provide a rubber stamp for the decisions of the powers that prevailed. As the forum of 'the people', parliament was to provide the veneer of 'due process'. With only one legislative chamber in Slovakia and an executive constituted by a prime minister, a cabinet of ministers and the president, the development of strong institutional checks and balances on majority rule was always going to be a necessity for the consolidation of democracy. After 1994, however, Mečiar could rely on an essentially stable majority of 83 in parliament and effective control over the legislative timetable, allowing the regime to present incoherent legislative packages and vague *ad hoc* proposals that in practice left the government considerable discretion. Legislation was subsequently railroaded through packed committees and a woefully under-informed and under-consulted house[56]. The two effective bulwarks against the abuse of process under the Mečiar regime were the President – in the person of Michal Kováč – and the Constitutional Court. Both attempted to constrain the government and to return legislation at odds with the constitution throughout the period of Mečiar's rule. In Kováč's case Mečiar's response was to launch a radical campaign of intimidation and media attacks. In the case of the Constitutional Court, its rulings on breaches of constitutional principle were frequently simply ignored, as we shall see.

The political opposition thus found themselves pushed aside – excluded from oversight in parliament and from influence over an increasingly politicised civil service. As after the 1989 revolution, the defensive and fragmented nature of the opposition in 1994 had allowed Mečiar to rise again against the odds. Remarkably, it was not until 1996, when legislation to curtail democracy became less *ad hoc* and more systematic, that the Slovak opposition would learn the painful lessons of divide and rule and evolve into an effective anti-Mečiar force. In the autumn of 1996 the Christian Democrats and the Democratic Union, averaging around 12 and 10 per cent of public support respectively, formed the 'Blue Coalition' with the smaller Democratic Party – the indication of political learning being not just in their acknowledgement of the proximity of their centre-right policies but also in their declared willingness, given the frictions of 1994, to work in the future with leftist parties and the Hungarian coalition. Further rationalisation, however, did not occur until Mečiar made two major tactical mistakes that not only galvanised public opposition but literally forced the opposition parties to pool their resources. The first provocation came with a crisis over how to elect a new president, since Michal Kováč was due to leave the post in March 1998. The second provocation, only a few months before the 1998 election, came in the form of an electoral law.

By the end of 1996 the non-governing parties realised that the President's term would end in March 1998. Without the required three-fifths majority to elect another, Slovakia would find itself without a president, and according to the constitution (Article 105) the powers of the presidency would fall to the government and to Mečiar. Specifically, Mečiar would inherit the post of Commander in Chief of the armed forces and the right to declare a state of emergency by means of a constitutional statute – two extremely alarming additions to his already considerable authority. In order to stave off such an event the opposition proposed a constitutional bill to introduce the direct election of the presidency. When the coalition refused to schedule the bill for consideration the opposition launched a petition for a referendum on direct election that gained the required 350,000 signatures. The resultant cross-party Joint Initiative for Referendum at last created cooperation and a common effort among opposition parties and highlighted their mutual interest in forging a more democratic political process.

In the short term these efforts were rebuffed, but so crudely as to only add momentum to both the civil and political opposition. In May 1997 the Mečiar coalition passed a resolution directing Kováč to call a separate referendum on NATO entry, a move aimed both at deflecting attention from the question of direct election and at producing a scapegoat for an imminent foreign policy failure. When Kováč decided to place four questions on the same ballot – the three loaded government questions on NATO entry and a single question on direction election of the presidency – Mečiar instructed Interior Minister Gustáv Krajči to withdraw those ballot papers with four questions and to replace them with the NATO questions alone, thus sabotaging the referendum[57]. After an opposition campaign for a boycott, scarcely 10 per cent of registered voters went to the final polls, and the Central Referendum Commission declared the poll invalid. Despite a Constitutional Court ruling that the Interior Minister's actions were unconstitutional, however, the government blocked any new referendum.

Though a debacle on the issue of the presidency, the referendum would nevertheless prove a hugely beneficial event for Slovak democracy writ large. It acted as the loudest signal yet to the Slovak population that the struggle for political power was not only undermining Slovakia's institutional order as such but also reducing her reputation abroad to the condition of farce[58]. Following their cooperation in the Joint Initiative the 'Blue Coalition' grew, as the leaderships of the Christian Democratic Movement, the Democratic Union, the Democratic Party, the Social Democratic Party of Slovakia and the Greens agreed in July 1997 to form a coalition for the 1998 election, which they duly named the Slovak Democratic Coalition (SDC).

January 1998 opinion polls showed support for the government at only 36.4 per cent and at 54.8 per cent for the opposition – with over 30 per cent going to the new SDC – and with general elections due in September, there were growing fears that Mečiar would resort to entirely extra-constitutional measures to win. When Kováč's term expired in March 1998, the Slovak parliament was indeed unable to muster the required majority to elect a new president, and presidential powers, including that of accepting the resignation of an incumbent government after defeat in an election, fell to Mečiar. Speculation grew that even if defeated at the ballot box the MDS would refuse to step down and Slovakia would experience something akin to a *putsch*. As if in early answer to these growing fears the MDS duly changed the electoral law.

Before the formation of the Slovak Democratic Coalition the MDS had shown interest in changing the electoral law to a majoritarian or first-past-the-post system of election – from which it would obviously benefit. Mečiar's solution to the new-found coalition strength of the Slovak Democratic Coalition – and a solution at last acceptable to the SNP and AWS – was to add an amendment to the existing (proportional representation) law whereby every party within a coalition had to achieve 5 per cent of the vote. The law also made Slovakia a single electoral district, thus enabling Mečiar's name – the most prominent in Slovak politics – to appear as a candidate on every ballot in the country.

The electoral law for the 1992 election had stated that a coalition of two parties needed 7 per cent of the vote to enter parliament, that a coalition of three parties required 9 per cent, and that those of four or more required 11 per cent. In the old law only single parties had had to gain 5 per cent to enter parliament – a prohibitively high threshold as it has turned out, which in 1992 had led to the wasting of 24 per cent of the Slovak vote as such. One aspect of the new MDS amendment, passed on 20 May 1998, just three months before the registration of electoral parties, was to demand that each party even *within* a coalition still had to clear the 5 per cent threshold – a clause designed to prohibit the formation of coalitions comprising a mix of large and small parties – in effect, to debar the Slovak Democratic Coalition and the Hungarian Coalition, which was made up of the Hungarian Christian Democratic Movement, the Hungarian Civic Party and Coexistence. The real impact of the legislation, however, was to finally push the opposition to such a high level of cooperation and realism that it would finally manage to organise Mečiar's downfall.

The two main opposition coalitions differed in their response to the new electoral law, but both significantly consolidated themselves in preparation for a showdown against the MDS. The Hungarian Coalition, spurred by their long experience of cooperation, the similarity of their platforms (conservative/liberal), and their obvious interest in consolidating the Hungarian ethnic vote, opted to merge into one single party: the Party of the Hungarian Coalition (PHC)[59]. The parties of the Slovak Democratic Coalition, meanwhile, decided to form a new 'election party' that would organise a joint candidate list for members of the Christian Democratic Movement, the Democratic Union, the Democratic Party and the Slovak Green Party and the Social Democratic Party of Slovakia, who together decided to abandon the unpredictable Party of the Democratic Left. Candidates were nominated for the electoral list in proportion to average voting preferences through June 1996–1997, and the question of ideological differences between the parent parties was dealt with by establishing separate and corresponding platforms within the SDC. The five parent parties meanwhile continued to exist, but refrained from competing in the elections. Although this arrangement would clearly require clarification after the election (indeed would plague the coalitions when in government), the reorganisation of the SDC into an electoral party cleared the immediate electoral hurdle of Mečiar's gerrymandering electoral law[60]. The parent parties, meanwhile, had maintained their essential freedom, and with that, their respective constituencies.

The second Slovak revolution

By 1998 the use of force in Slovakia had been widely expected, and it was a happy shock for the democratic opposition that it did not come. In the September elections, on a wave of mass civil mobilisation and an extremely high electoral turn-out, Slovakia celebrated, in effect, its second revolution. It had still not been clear in 1994 that fully-fledged Mečiarism could represent a one-way departure from democratic reform, and the combination of tough economic reforms and disunity within the Moravčík coalition parties had ushered Mečiar back in. The Slovak electorate in September 1994 had split decisively between urban, better educated and younger voters, who on the whole voted for pro-democratic opposition forces, and the relatively less well educated, rural and older constituencies, who had voted overwhelmingly for parties emphasising economic and 'national' security over pluralism, such as the MDS, the AWS and the SNP. After four years of increasingly authoritarian rule, however, the significance of the electoral choice by 1998 had become stark as it had not been even back in 1994; to vote for the re-establishment of the democratic project – or to capitulate to an increasingly arbitrary political rule. Not only did the opposition finally manage to unite on this theme, but in articulating the deeper consequences of this next electoral choice the so-called 'Third Sector' – Slovakia's civil society – came into its own. Through non-partisan campaigns aimed at bringing out the vote and educating the public in their electoral choices, a wide range of non-governmental organisations calling themselves 'Civic Campaign OK '98' contributed to an exceptionally high electoral turnout of 84.24 per cent – an increase of almost 9 per cent on 1994, gained primarily, and crucially, in Slovakia's large towns[61].

The campaigns

A notable feature of the 1998 campaign was the role played by the private – and politically relatively independent – media, particularly by Radio Twist and by TV Markíza, in combating the blatantly pro-government stance of state radio and, in particular, of Slovak State Television, STV[62]. The election law prohibited either public or private electronic media from 'making public any information which promotes the candidate political parties', allowing in practice for a state media monopoly on campaign party broadcasts. State radio devoted a massive 82 per cent of its broadcast time to the governing parties[63], while almost 80 per cent of STV's evening news was given over to politicians of the ruling coalition[64]. Slovak TV council member Jerguš

Ferko's explanation was that the government required more time as it was 'building the state'[65].

Perhaps as instructive as this media bias was the battle over the ownership of TV Markíza. The station was seized twice during the electoral campaign by security officers working for the station's alleged new owners – once on 18 August and again on 15 September. In response some 5,000 protestors arrived to protect the station from what was widely perceived to be a state-led attempt to shut it down[66]. What began as a call for people to protect immediate broadcasting turned into a rally for 'freedom of expression and the right of citizens to receive information'[67].

The election campaign of September 1998 marked a turning point in Slovak political life. The public debate about the nature of democracy was far better informed in 1998 that it had been nine years previously. As if to emphasise the split between the democratic and the Mečiarite paths, Mečiar ran a campaign that stood as an unwitting epitome of his previous years in government – emotive, expensive, manipulative of the law and state media and lacking both policy content and direction.

The MDS's party conference back in April had declared the party's aim of winning a full majority in parliament, and Mečiar announced that 'the MDS was formed as a non-ideological movement of citizens, standing on three pillars: national values, Christian values and social justice'. He concluded that 'we can proudly announce to Slovakia and others that the basic tasks of a national-democratic revolution, emancipation and freedom for Slovaks have been accomplished'[68]. The tone of the September campaign was triumphalist in ways strongly reminiscent of 'really existing socialism', emphasising public investment and major developments such as road-building and the controversial hydroelectric power plant in Gabčíkovo Nagymáros. MDS billboards showed Mečiar in the foreground of these epic projects and declared 'We have managed it together' and 'Together we can manage more'. The MDS also brought in international stars such as Gérard Depardieu, Claudia Cardinale and Claudia Schiffer to attract younger voters[69] and to evoke the image of Mečiar – photographed waltzing with Schiffer – as an international mover and shaker[70].

The MDS's campaign motto, appropriately enough, was 'Vote with your hearts', but the emotional appeals were essentially, if emptily, nationalistic. The MDS used the imagery of a heart mown into meadows beneath a mountain and Mečiar leaning on a five-bar gate, coffee mug in hand, under the slogan 'Country of Our Heart' (the country behind him was actually Switzerland, as the opposition revealed). The Movement also sponsored radio ads that stated 'it takes long years of care until a mighty linden tree grows from a little seed, but its crown will protect us . . . Let's plant our Slovak tree of justice' – continuing with 'MDS Chairman Vladimír Mečiar has a linden seed for each of you'. As in 1994 the MDS played on Mečiar's role as the founder of the independent Slovak state; however, in 1998 the attempt was made to lend Mečiar iconographic status by a clever series of unattributed billboards that ran in series through major figures in Slovak national history: the first depicted the national awakener Ľudovít Štúr, the second showed the monument marking the grave of Milan Rastislav Štefánik, a Slovak co-founder of the Czechoslovak Republic, and the third carried a quotation from and depiction of Andrej Hlinka – the charismatic priest of the interwar period whose fascist legatees had founded the Slovak wartime state. The fourth billboard depicted Mečiar – the obvious implication being that he was the modern father of the nation – only then revealing this historical line-up to be an MDS campaign[71].

The MDS also attempted to use the law to thwart the opposition. In August 1998, a month before the election, the MDS filed a protest with the Supreme Court questioning the organisational status of the Slovak Democratic Coalition. By insisting that the SDC remained a coalition rather than a party the MDS intended to prevent it from running. The Supreme Court, however, dismissed the case[72]. MDS attempts to use a referendum on the non-privatisation of the strategic gas and energy companies to raise privatisation as an electoral issue also backfired, as the turn-out for the referendum was insufficient and the opposition more successfully seized on privatisation scandals involving MDS leaders and their relatives[73].

Not to be outdone by Mečiar's reference to the Hungarian coalition parties as 'irredentists'[74], the Slovak National Party also ran a highly nationalistic and anti-Western campaign, differing from that of 1992 most obviously by its increased religiosity; in 1998 the SNP sought to present itself as the unifying force of Slovak Christian and national values. Back in July the party convention had endorsed a merger with the small and nationalistic Christian Social Union as well as the Slovak Green Alternative[75]. The SNP's campaign focused on family, nation, God and racism, with slogans such as 'The family – the core of the nation', 'For God – for the nation' and, nearer the end of the campaign, 'Let's vote for a Slovakia without parasites'. The SNP's main policy themes, apart from building a 'social-market economy', rendered it unequivocally extremist, as it promoted Slovak neutrality, the reintroduction of the death penalty and the rejection of ethnic Hungarian participation in Slovak government[76].

Again, as in 1994 and 1992, the SNP set itself entirely against both the Roma and the Hungarian populations and, as before, it placed itself unequivocally within the heritage of the Slovak wartime fascist state. On the fifty-ninth anniversary of the foundation of the Slovak state the SNP had declared that '14 March 1939 was a clear demonstration of the Christian values from which the Slovak Nation must draw'. SNP vice chairman Viliam Oberhauser's rhetoric in the party's manifesto came close to Ján Čarnogurský's fears of a godless Slovakia back in the early 1990s, but with an additional note of derangement; 'If you don't vote SNP', he declared, 'the people who lead us will sell us out for a cup of lentils, and turn Slovaks into atheists and servants in our own house'[77].

The opposition parties were less innovative and professional in their use of television and billboard advertising than the MDS[78], but their campaigns were also cheaper and conveyed a strong and constant theme – that the 1998 election represented not merely a choice of government but a truly democratic crossroads for Slovakia as a whole.

The campaign of the Slovak Democratic Coalition concentrated on direct presidential election, the electoral law, the democratisation of society writ large, the corruption of the privatisation process and the need to revive Slovakia's chances of European integration. At its founding conference in July the SDC's new leader, Mikuláš Dzurinda, had announced that the SDC would contemplate a future governing coalition with the Party of the Democratic Left, the new Party of Civic Understanding and the Party of the Hungarian Coalition – thus confirming the potential for a grand anti-Meciar coalition, should the election results allow it. The SDC also capitalised on its status as the main party of opposition to the MDS by convening six round-table discussions that included not only other opposition parties but also the civic sector – the Union of Towns and Municipalities of Slovakia, the Council of Slovak Youth, the Confederation of Trade Unions and the Gremium of the Third Sector – thus firmly linking the party to the civic campaign for a democratic election, 'OK '98'[79]. Through these meetings, planned to coordinate the role of these bodies in ensuring a free and fair election, the opposition parties built a far stronger basis for post-election cooperation than had existed in 1994. The SDC was not above using negative and populist campaigning, however, relying heavily on satire and negative campaigning and also making quite unrealistic promises, such as doubling real wages within four years – a pledge endorsed by the SDC's election manifesto, 'Agreement with the Citizens'[80]. The SDC also brought in Slovak stars, actors and sportsmen to endorse it. The party's criticism of the MDS government, however, was trenchant – it posted a website outlining corrupt practices in the privatisation process and highlighted the dirty tricks campaign of the secret services to discredit the opposition[81].

The Party of Civic Understanding (PCU) was established only at the beginning of 1998, essentially as a future presidential platform for the popular mayor of Košice, Rudolf Schuster. The PCU's line in the early months of 1998 was that it was meeting a public desire for a consensus-seeking force in the confrontational Slovak political scene, and it duly got off to a flying electoral start even before it had indicated any kind of party programme[82]. Schuster – a former Communist – promised that the PCU would never form a coalition with the MDS, and he went on to clarify that the party desired to work closely with the Party of the Democratic Left, the Slovak Democratic Coalition and the Party of the Hungarian Coalition. Following strong attacks from the pro-MDS newspaper *Slovenská Republika* and STV, however, the PCU quickly abandoned its positive rhetoric and went into a highly critical campaign. Its emerging programme was for Slovak entry into the European Union, 'all forms of direct democracy', and the development of small and medium-sized businesses. The campaign also featured an original song, performed by one of the party's candidates, international opera star Peter Dvorský, and by party Chairman Rudolf Schuster[83].

The Party of the Democratic Left started its campaign and presented its programme early – in late spring 1998. As former Communists in Hungary and Poland had done so successfully in 1994 and 1993 respectively, the PDL presented itself as a party of experts – young technocratic reformers who would secure a higher standard of living, the return of Slovakia's status in Western Europe, security, investment for young families, a legal state and an end to corruption, improvements in health and education, higher pay and lower unemployment. In other words they alluded to their past as the party of social care, and at the same time presented themselves as a modernising force for democratisation and pro-Europeanism. The party's youth organisation was highly active, and the PDL benefited from the presence of young and popular political stars like Róbert Fico – of whom more later. The PDL produced a document called 'Coalition with Young People' emphasising the need for apartments, loans, free university education, the right to a first job and abolition of compulsory military service[84].

In terms of Slovakia's social and political developments the line of the Party of the Hungarian Coalition was close to that of the Slovak Democratic Coalition, namely conservative/centre-liberal – the main concerns of the PHC being to represent the interests of the

Hungarian minority in Slovakia and to fight against what they felt to be the steady erosion of Hungarian minority rights during the Meciar years. In an attempt to counter the polarising rhetoric of the SNP the Hungarian Coalition also used an ethnic Slovak party supporter, Juraj Hrabko, in some of their advertising, who emphasised that he voted for the Hungarian Coalition as the most consistently constitutional party of them all.

The result of the 25–26 September elections was a victory for the Slovak Democratic Coalition, the Party of the Hungarian Coalition, the Party of Civic Understanding and the Party of the Democratic Left; together they garnered 58 per cent of the vote. This pro-democracy alliance was truly an anti-Meciar coalition, involving ten parties of varied electoral strength. The Party of the Hungarian Coalition had won 9.1 per cent of the vote, the Party of the Democratic Left 14.7 per cent, the Party of Civic Understanding 8 per cent, and strongest of all was the Slovak Democratic Coalition, which had achieved 26.3 per cent – a whisker behind the Movement for a Democratic Slovakia, which still remained the single strongest party, with 27 per cent of the vote. The turn-out had been particularly high among urban and first-time voters, a critical factor given the by now clear rural–urban divide in voting for Meciar regime parties. There were few wasted votes due to the electoral threshold and practically no wasted anti-Meciar votes, significantly increasing the truly representative nature of the 1998 parliament as a whole[85]. Two of Meciar's supporting parties failed to enter parliament – the former coalition partner Association of Workers of Slovakia and the Communist Party of Slovakia. Meciar's room for manoeuvre in terms of coalition building was now thoroughly constrained – not only by the loss of the AWS, but because the party had so clearly put itself beyond the pale for a significant proportion of the electorate that only the SNP – which achieved 9.1 per cent of the vote in 1998 – could countenance cooperation with it.

The post-election ruling coalition under Mikuláš Dzurinda put its government in place on 29 October 1998, after overcoming teething troubles during coalition talks when the Party of the Democratic Left objected to the participation of the Party of the Hungarian Coalition as a strategy for increasing its own strength in the coalition[86]. The new government proceeded to abide scrupulously by parliamentary regulations ensuring opposition representation on parliamentary committees, offering the chairmanship of six of the total of 18 parliamentary committees to the opposition[87]. The government's programme declaration was accepted in the Slovak parliament early in December; however, the SDC's new Justice Minister, Ján Čarnogurský, head of the Christian Democratic Movement, voted against the document for its failure to recommend pro-Catholic legislation in education. The new coalition government carried 93 of the parliament's 150 seats – a constitutional majority and so sufficient in theory to begin to undo the Mečiar legislation of the previous years, and to attempt to kick-start the Slovak reform project.

This anti-Mečiar governing alliance nevertheless remained in many ways an unnatural grouping, united in their opposition to Meciar but divided ideologically. The coalition, as in 1994, brought together uncompromising Christian Democrats – with Ján Čarnogurský chief among them – and former Communists and Hungarian liberals who had quickly discovered that the former Communists would play the nationalist card at the drop of a hat. With hindsight, a central Slovak political problem has become extremely clear – that throughout the 1990s Vladimír Mečiar had acted as a dead-weight on more coherent Slovak political developments and alliances. In erecting a populist, clientalistic and increasingly authoritarian state it was as if the independent Slovakia had been forced through another semi-authoritarian era, requiring another democratic revolution – in effect, the election of 1998. The new Dzurinda government, as a result, still represents the full Pandora's box of Slovakia's non-Mečiarite political forces and, without doubt, only Mečiar's departure from the political scene altogether will open the way to a rational realignment of the Slovak political scene.

The evolution of Mečiarism

Following his defeat in the 1998 general election Mečiar made a special broadcast on the show *What next, Mr Prime Minister?* in which he performed a short Slovak funeral dirge. Waving slowly and with tears in his eyes he sang:

> Farewell [literally, 'With God, I am going away from you']
> I did not hurt,
> I did not hurt,
> Any of you.

Like Klaus, Mečiar's dominance of Slovak politics throughout the 1990s was phenomenal. By electing a brilliant opportunist to a state that needed redefining, Slovaks, it transpired, had awarded themselves not so much a clear-sighted and statesmanlike father of the nation as 'The Godfather'. Having been given the opportunity, Mečiar consolidated and established a clan state, resorting to a personalised and ideologically neutered version of the more decadent Communist practices of the 1980s, right down to the co-option and reactivation of the interior security services, reporting directly to him as Prime Minister. Examining the various aspects of state- and nation-building required in 1993 what emerges is not only the vast scale of the opportunities presented to the MDS government, but also the failure of any ideological or programmatic vision to emerge. The isolationism, pan-Slavism and economic centrism and protectionism evolving through 1997 and 1998 in Mečiar's hands looked less like some quasi-nationalist/socialist state-building ideology than the sorry consequences of a deeply erratic foreign policy, a falling-back upon old Communist networking and lobby interests, and a persistent uncertainty about the nature of Slovak identity beyond the insistence that whatever Slovak identity might be it was endangered by foreigners.

Following the break-up of Czechoslovakia the Mečiar government had to reassess reform on every front on its own terms. Having spent the previous three years claiming that Slovakia should be 'equal', Mečiar now had to define a Slovakia that stood alone. If the divorce was not to be experienced as pure humiliation, Mečiar in 1993 had three major tasks. Firstly, he had to define the independent Slovak nation so as to shed the Johnny-come-lately tag so successfully ascribed to it by the Czechs. Secondly, he had to try to rescue the Slovak economy from its exposed position at the break-up. Finally, he had to establish a functioning state, having exited the Czechoslovak federation entirely ill-prepared both constitutionally and administratively. On all three fronts the Mečiar regime's subsequent actions were characterised by a mimicry of democratic language and process that scarcely concealed both an instrumental use of the state for party interest and a sheer lack of ideas.

While opportunities unimaginable in the federation arose for patronage, network-building, cronyism and generally opaque government intervention in the economy, the task of nation-building emerged as an undertaking that paid ever diminishing dividends. Perhaps more than any other aspect of his rule, Mečiar's lack of national vision over time laid bare as grotesquely fraudulent his claim to be the liberator of the nation's potential. The supposedly nation-building nationalism that emerged, defined in essentially negative terms, could not but tend toward authoritarianism, intrinsic in any banal insistence that 'we are together because – we must be together'. It also led to Slovakia's almost complete isolation abroad.

'Slovakia of Our Hearts'

After 1989, Slovak party politicians, both entrepreneurial and sincere, adopted what they had hoped would be the resonant attributes of

Slovakia's past, only to find themselves outmanoeuvred by a political movement more interested in electoral psychology than history. Throughout the post-1989 federation Mečiar had kept his nationalism populist, occasionally even 'civic' and inclusive (with the emphasis on citizenship rather than ethnicity) – in keeping with the post-revolutionary aspirations of the time – and simple. Contrary to the platforms of some of his rivals, the early Movement for a Democratic Slovakia maintained that Slovaks were neither peculiarly Catholic, Slavic (even if they would continue cordial relations with the Russians) nor racially 'pure', but good and reasonable people who had not despised the economic security and prosperity brought to them by Communism. Mečiar's argument after 1989 was that Slovaks now looked for equality of treatment and respect both politically and economically – a claim notable for its essential moderation – the odd bout of personal political slander notwithstanding. So long as Slovakia stayed within the federation, an identity of misunderstood Slovak reasonableness was more than enough, and provided considerable political mileage at home, allowing many people of an essentially liberal bent to remain happily even within the MDS itself.

Following the 1994 election, however, when every aspect of the Mečiar regime shifted into a more authoritarian gear, the MDS began to define the nation in consistently negative terms – as that which was victimised, under threat, misunderstood and underestimated. Mečiar occasionally sounded positive and invoked familial cohesion, suggesting that Slovaks, like Mečiar himself, were always undaunted. The scapegoats for Slovakia's ills were the Roma and the Jews, as they had been under Communism; but now, with increasing frequency, the Hungarians too became Mečiar's open target, as illustrated by legislation such as the Slovak Language Law of November 1995[88]. The law's preamble stated that 'The Slovak language is the most important characteristic of the Slovak nation, the most valuable part of its cultural heritage, an expression of Slovak sovereignty, and the general means of communication of its citizens, guaranteeing them freedom and equality in dignity and rights on Slovak territory'[89]. The effect of such a law could only be to increase ethnic antagonism. The regime's 'vision' for the nation was to select something already existing that was undeniably Slovak and to insist that *this is really important*', whipping up ethnic tensions that the regime might then, in turn, exploit.

The response among the majority of Slovaks to this form of ethno-centric nation-building was actually one of consistent immunity, and indeed growing concern at the authoritarian practices being ushered in under the guise of national interest. The language law restricted the use of anything other than Slovak in various aspects of public life and demanded the use of Slovak in official communications – in contradiction to Article 34 of the Slovak constitution[90]. As it transpired, surveys suggested that after the law was passed the use of Hungarian by ethnic Slovaks living in southern Slovakia actually increased[91]. Similar evidence of growing popular disquiet over the government's abuse of nationalism emerged by 1996 when Mečiar's culture minister, Ivan Hudec, launched a clampdown on culture, most notably by merging theatres, sacking directors, and attempting to install regime loyalists in the Slovak National Theatre. Hudec decried the insufficiently 'Slovak' programme of the National Theatre, and the loyal media produced articles slandering the independent arts with slogans lifted straight from the 1950s, claiming 'Whoever is not with us is sick and manipulated'[92]. Hardly troubled by a still deeply divided parliamentary opposition, the Mečiar coalition had clearly not anticipated the public response – that entire companies of actors would rebel against government sackings and that some 30,000 people would sign a petition entitled 'Save Culture!'[93].

As with Mečiar's evolving definitions of Slovakia's needs within the federation, the MDS's definition of nationalism in independent Slovakia remained opportunistic, emerging from the basic short-term need to find electoral space and to capitalise upon it. Throughout the mid-1990s Mečiar's room for manoeuvre with the nationalist card was constrained on two fronts. On the one hand the MDS needed national imagery distinct from that of the liberal, pro-Western opposition, and on the other hand the MDS's credible policies on 'the nation' were clearly bounded by its coalition with the Slovak National Party. Although the SNP had adopted more Catholic rhetoric and imagery into its armoury than it had attempted under the federation it remained an extremist party of the far right. In February 1994 the brief and relatively moderate leadership of Ľudovít Černák was replaced by that of Jan Slota, who over the years heightened SNP rhetoric to constantly frenzied levels. He frequently invoked the glories of the Slovak fascist state and the iniquities of the Roma, whom he argued deserved 'a small courtyard and a long whip'[94]. Reputedly while drunk at a rally in Kysucké Nové Mesto in March 1999, Slota urged MDS and SNP supporters to get into tanks and attack Budapest. He was ousted from the leadership in September 1999 by the scarcely more moderate Anna Malíková. These constraints encouraged Mečiar's negative definition of the nation at home, but they also conditioned what evolved into a disastrous Slovak foreign policy.

Coalition with the Slovak National Party would appear to have doomed a 'Westward-looking' Slovak foreign policy from the start (the SNP, apart from its sheer extremism, followed a foreign policy of

Slovak neutrality – in flat contradiction to the coalition's professed desire to join NATO), but Mečiar's foreign policy proved more convoluted than simple isolationism. In attempting to come up with a national image at home that could not be easily co-opted or better represented by the opposition, i.e. by being something other than simply dotingly pro-Western, Mečiar got into such confusions over Slovakia's international orientation as to lose effective steerage of foreign policy altogether.

It would clearly be a mistake to believe that without the SNP, the Movement for a Democratic Slovakia would have acted purely according to EU accession guidelines. For Mečiar to have steered the independent Slovakia on a consistent path towards NATO and European Union entry would have meant reforming the state and conducting public political debate in ways that would necessarily have ended his own political power, or at least severely constrained it. Instead Mečiar, as ever, hedged his bets, creating such vagaries in foreign policy that Slovak policy Westward ceased to carry any credibility whatsoever.

After the break-up of Czechoslovakia Mečiar continued to support European integration, going so far as to make Slovakia an active participant in NATO's Partnership for Peace programme after February 1994 and signing, albeit belatedly, a controversial and, at home, unpopular Slovak-Hungarian state treaty in March 1995, pledging the implementation of United Nations and Council of Europe norms for the protection of and respect for minority rights. Despite appointing pro-Western foreign ministers, however, Mečiar also attempted to position Slovakia as the 'gateway' between East and West, forging MDS party links with Milosevic's Serbian Socialist Party, Forza Italia, the Union of Ukraine and the Polish People's Party. Already in the first months of Slovak independence, Mečiar's foreign policy pronouncements had seemed to signal Slovak ambivalence towards the West; his New Year's Day 1993 address emphasised relations with Russia and Ukraine, and he had claimed to favour a 'third way' between capitalism and socialism[95].

The aspiration to make Slovakia a bridge was predicated economically on the continuation of significant trade flows with Russia and on Slovakia remaining Russia's main Central European partner for transporting natural gas and oil to Western Europe – neither of which have been sustained in practice[96]. The grand delusion of Slovak foreign policy under Mečiar in the 1990s was that the closer Slovakia's relations with Russia were, the more of a foreign policy linchpin she would be for the West[97]. Over time, however, Slovakia's benefits from cheaper Russian oil notwithstanding, Western concern over the Slovak–Russian alliance proved negligible and the Mečiar regime found itself having embarked upon commitments East and West that were simply incompatible, for example, calling for pan-European security structures and supporting Russian opposition to the enlargement of NATO even after Slovakia had stated its aspiration to join it.

Mečiar's attempts to play multiple foreign policy games landed Slovakia in a diplomatic vacuum. As Slovakia's credibility in the West dwindled, moreover, he cut his losses and introduced the European Union into the language of anti-Slovak conspiracy and persecution – as one of the many international and internal enemies of the fledgling state. This strategy and the growing authoritarianism of Slovakia's domestic politics inevitably led to her increasing international isolation through the late 1990s. At the EU Luxembourg summit in December 1997 it was announced that Slovakia was relegated to the second wave of accession countries – a double blow since NATO's Madrid summit in July had rejected Slovakia's application. In the case of EU entry, Slovakia, of all ten East European applicant countries, was the only one barred for political, as opposed to economic, reasons.

In the last years of Mečiar's rule it became clear that foreign policy – where Mečiar's pronouncements were so totally at odds with Slovakia's official agenda of goodwill abroad, presented by Mečiar's own hapless foreign ministers – had no other function than as a vehicle for whipping up support or creating a sense of crisis-needing-to-be-mastered at home. In 1997, for instance, Mečiar made an impromptu proposal to the Hungarian Prime Minister Gyula Horn for a mutual exchange of ethnic populations. In its last years the Mečiar regime clearly abdicated the prudent representation of Slovakia's national interests abroad, exposing it as content to lead Slovakia into international isolation by default. At first the international community seems to have found Mečiar's theatrical Messianism genuinely alarming; eventually, however, it was simply viewed as crass.

The strategy of defining Slovakia as that which unites against enemies both at home and abroad can be understood as a straight-forward strategy of conspiracy-mongering, but also as an attempt to internationalise discussions from the early 1990s about the arrogance and misconceptions of the Czechs regarding valid Slovak grievances. To this end, the Czechs too were consistently invoked as attacking and victimising Slovakia, and ongoing disputes between the two republics over the post-divorce division of property, the customs union and immigration were all used as grist to this mill. By March 1998 Czech–Slovak diplomatic relations, frosty since the break-up, dropped below freezing point when President Havel commented on the worsening state of Slovak democracy with the statement that 'free-minded Slovak citizens struggling for democracy will sooner or later say "enough"'[98].

Through a combination of confidence-boosting hyperbole and rampant conspiracy-theorising Meciar hit upon a recipe for often charismatic but essentially content-free nation-building; he discovered how to make many people feel good about themselves without purporting to tell them who they actually were. For the vast majority of Slovaks the vacuity of this approach to nation-building was unacceptable, however. By October 1997 a mere 13 per cent of Slovaks polled were proud of Slovakia's international status and by April 1998 a considerable 79 per cent favoured Slovak entry into the European Union. Despite this high level of aspiration to align Westward, as many as 43 per cent said they felt they did not know where Slovakia was heading, and 25 per cent expressed the fear that Slovakia might be moving towards a military and political alliance with Russia[99]. Asked in May 1998 'in which direction is Slovakia heading' more generally, some 69 per cent of Slovaks answered that it was heading in the 'wrong' direction, 20 per cent that it was 'right' and 11 per cent did not know[100].

Carving up the economy – goulash nationalism

The second, clear task in which Mečiarism proved its own undoing was that of economic reform. Although opportunistic, Mečiar's 'Godfather nationalism' was at least consistent with other aspects of Mečiarism. The empty language of 'us' could run alongside the reorganisation of the economy and state along patronage lines, giving clear signals as to how to belong and the benefits of belonging: a phenomenon Slovak sociologists nicknamed 'goulash nationalism' (after the 'goulash Communism' of the Kádár era in Hungary). Darina Malová termed what followed between 1994 and 1998 as 'party-state corporatism'[101]. In other words, politics in Slovakia in the mid-1990s became less about the development of a reform path for Slovakia and more about the creation of powerful positions both in the state and in the economy that might be monopolised and exploited by their incumbents. The new web of sinecures ranged from positions in the governing executive, in the institutions managing the privatisation of state assets – the National Property Fund was constituted entirely of members of the three-party ruling coalition, with the MDS holding six out of nine seats, including the executive chair – and in the security services, state television and radio. The governing parties established close links to industrial associations – the successor managerial networks of the Communist era – which effectively captured the Ministry of Economy, and to important financial groups and business lobbies, which in turn provided party funding; party leaders became direct members of the supervisory boards of major enterprises. As the regime became more confident, this party state corporatism also involved attempts to re-establish the Communist practice of creating transmission belts – cultural, media, educational, professional and labour organisations – for the co-option and monitoring of public support for the ruling party[102].

In essence the new governing alliance of the MDS, AWS and SNP emerged as built upon clientalism, with MDS the dominant, 'hegemonic' party amongst them[103]. With entrepreneurial politics their common feature, the AWS and SNP inevitably found maintaining any kind of electoral image distinct from that of the dominant MDS difficult; indeed, the AWS saw its electoral support slump after 1994, and it was really the SNP that would go on to be the more significant coalition partner. The period 1994–8 saw sporadic bouts of opposition within the coalition, ostensibly for electoral reasons but typically over quarrels with a significant impact on the distribution of either power or resources[104]. To imagine that parties ostensibly of the far left and far right might be incompatible in government would be to vastly overestimate the ideological as opposed to pragmatic motivations of any one of these three parties, as a mild coalition hiccup in 1996 illustrates. Through early 1996 it looked as though coalition objections to the latest MDS proposals on privatisation might finally pull the alliance apart. When it became apparent that the MDS would simply supplant the old coalition partners with an apparently eager Party of the Democratic Left, however, the AWS and SNP simply hurried back and the quarrel was ended[105].

Purely in macro-economic terms, Slovakia by the mid-1990s appeared to flourish under Mečiar's rule, growing at one of the highest rates in the region (6.9 per cent in 1996) and maintaining low inflation. As in the Czech Republic, this ostensibly potent combination thwarted any sweeping criticism of the government's economic policies for many years[106]. In fact, the eventual development of problems similar to those of the Czech economy was not coincidental. Notwithstanding the MDS's rhetoric, the Mečiar and Moravčík governments had until the end of 1994 essentially retained the basic reform strategies – liberalised prices, restrictive fiscal and monetary policies – they had inherited from federal Czechoslovakia. The first and most significant departure in Slovak economic policy was the area of privatisation, the introduction of an interventionist industrial policy and an explicit shift to an expansive fiscal policy[107].

Slovakia's apparent macro-economic success was achieved by sacrificing the long term to the short. As in the Czech Republic, Mečiar's economic management meant avoiding bankruptcies and with that came the failure to promote restructuring either of the industrial or banking sectors[108]. Moreover, Slovakia had never managed to improve its attractiveness to foreign investors, already low in the early 1990s and blighted further by the break-up, and so the economy lacked this alternative stimulus.

Most seriously of all, however, the Mečiar regime effectively halted privatisation in 1993 (although during the first twelve weeks of 1994, just prior to the end of Mečiar's second term in government, three times as many assets were privatised as during the whole of 1993[109]). Privatisation was restarted and accelerated after November 1994, but from now on it was mainly processed through direct sales from an entirely politicised and unscrutinised National Property Fund – a form of privatisation that economists, putting it mildly, would describe as suffering from 'moral hazard'. Through the mid-1990s Slovakia saw levels of corruption in the process of privatisation[110] and increasingly unrestrained public spending that by the late 1990s had left the Slovak economy in a potentially critical state. The hijacking of the privatisation process and the wild public-sector borrowing for state-funded projects together left the incoming reformist government of 1998 with a crisis – a massive public budget deficit[111], a record trade deficit and an increase in unemployment to almost 16 per cent and rising. According to the corruption-rating agency Transparency International, corruption in Slovakia by 1998 was the highest in Central Europe; indeed, Slovakia was ranked roughly equal with Belarus[112].

As in the Czech Republic, the Slovak press by 1996 was beginning to expose some of the more blatant aspects of the state carving up of public assets. The parliamentary opposition too kept the issue in the limelight through 1996 by repeated calls to allow parliament to scrutinise the privatisation process – efforts consistently refused by the governing coalition until Ivan Mikloš was finally allowed on to a powerless supervisory board in 1997. Minister of Economy Ján Ducký (assassinated in 1999, three days after it was announced that he was under investigation for financial mismanagement of the state gas company he led from spring 1997 to November 1998[113]) admitted back in 1996 that 'every government gives in privatisation to those groups that cooperate with it'[114]. Perhaps most blatantly of all, Vít'azoslav Moric, SNP honorary chair, told the Council for Economic Development of Slovakia that 'a just privatisation does not exist; we all know that the only criterion was loyalty.' He also added that those who carry the responsibility of running the state must also have rights according to the principle 'winner take all'[115].

The cost to Slovak taxpayers of corruption in the privatisation process has been spectacular. In the period between 1995 and 1998, the National Property Fund sold assets worth some 109.2 billion crowns and yet by November 1998 the NPF had only 50 million crowns in its current account, and was, in effect, insolvent – unable to honour liabilities through 1998 amounting to some 2.3 billion crowns[116]. This extraordinary state of affairs arose through a level of cronyism in the privatisation process that basically allowed for the massively subsidised selling off of state assets to political insiders, who might then asset-strip the viable enterprises, sometimes even reselling their degraded shares to the National Property Fund at inflated prices[117]. The incoming government under Mikuláš Dzurinda, inaugurated on 30 October 1998, subsequently made attempts to recoup some of the losses to the taxpayer through privatisation. A law passed in 1999 enabled a review of the privatisation contracts issued under the Mečiar regime with the possibility of revoking them and repossessing the privatised assets[118]. Although repossessions of equity have occurred in some of the most notorious cases, such as that of the gas storage firm Nafta Gbely[119], it is clearly impossible for the state to recoup even the majority of losses made in a period where the tunnelling and laundering of assets was essentially legalised. Having finally ousted Mečiar in September 1998, the incoming reformist coalition had little choice but to recommence the kind of austerity measures most Central European countries hoped they had seen the last of in the early 1990s. In this sense, Mečiar created an excellent political debt for his liberal reformist opponents, which his party may yet call in.

Both domestically and internationally, public perceptions of Slovakia's reform progress began to deteriorate through 1997 to 1998. According to the Wall Street Journal's Index of Economic Freedom, Slovakia went from being 'largely liberal' to being 'largely illiberal' between 1995 and 1997[120], the greatest deterioration of any country in the region – including Belarus, Russia and Ukraine. In May 1998 the numbers of those affirming that someone in their close family was considering emigration were significant – 30 per cent of those aged 18–24, and 20 per cent of those between 25 and 34 – figures which, given the additional preponderance of highly educated people considering emigration, stood as a potentially serious drain of youth and talent for a Slovakia in transition[121]. When asked if they would respond to an emigrating friend by saying 'You're right to leave because this place is going down hill' a staggering 43 per cent of 18–24-year-olds and 32 per cent of 25–34-year-olds said yes[122].

Controlling the state

In order to administer these more openly patronage-based arrangements, the continuity with the party-state patterns of the Communist era became ever more pronounced as the second Mečiar term wore on. After 1994 the MDS began to pressure officials of local and state administration (already thoroughly purged of supporters of the reformist parties back in 1992–3[123]) and workers in key industrial enterprises to join the party or risk their positions. At the level of basic education, school administrators were pressured to join the MDS, and party membership was clearly connected to appointments, a fact decried in a Bratislava high-school protest in 1997[124]. An amendment to the law on higher education in 1996 increased government control over the allocation of funding for and control over Slovak universities, and subsequently new universities were built in several towns with established universities critical of the government. Under the new regulations the Ministry of Education itself had to approve the appointment of all professors – a huge restriction on academic autonomy. By 1996 and 1997 the MDS was electing top officials of the state administration to party positions, beginning with the heads of regional and district state offices, who duly became the heads of regional party offices[125]. In March 1996 the government passed a Law on Territorial and Administrative Division that divided Slovakia into eight large regions and seventy-nine districts, establishing an entire new raft of expensive administrative offices before the government had begun to specify the powers it intended to devolve to them[126].

As we have seen, legislation towards an autocratic regime had seemed *ad hoc* until 1996, characterised more by splenetic bouts of state abuse rather than a fully-fledged plan to destroy democracy. By 1996, however, with the coalition consolidated, the efforts to centralise power[127] and to turn everything, including cultural institutions, the media, welfare provision and education, to the service of the regime, became systematic. Coalition legislation frequently contradicted the spirit of existing legal frameworks; however, it was in 1996 and 1997 that increasingly explicit attempts were made to legislate for blatantly authoritarian powers, the most striking example being an attempt in 1996 to amend the penal code to reintroduce the Communist coverall charge of 'crimes against the state'. The escalation of blatantly anti-democratic actions and legislation was clearly a miscalculation of the Slovak political climate; far from inuring the Slovak electorate to their incremental loss of freedom this anti-democratic legislation and the escalating conflict between the Mečiar government and other Slovak institutions – most notably the Constitutional Court and the Slovak President – reawoke Slovak society at large to the real dangers of a return to the bad old days.

Throughout the Mečiar period the Constitutional Court, made up of ten judges nominated by the President, stood as one of the most clear, and certainly the most publicly trusted, restraints on power. In 1997, the Court was considered the most credible political institution in the country. Cases could be brought to the Court by, amongst others, 30 deputies or more of the parliament, thus providing opposition deputies with a rare outlet for enforcing government accountability. Among other legislation the Court ruled against government attempts to gain presidential powers to adjudicate the validity of public petitions for referenda[128]; in relation to the National Property Fund legislation of 1994–5 the Court ruled that the government had surrendered its duty to administer state property to an institution not under its formal control – provoking the comment from Mečiar that the Constitutional Court was the one 'sick element on the Slovak political scene'. The President had also taken to the Court several laws from 1992 to 1995 that expanded the powers of public prosecutors, and that allowed the prosecutor general, the minister of justice and the Chair of the Supreme Court to reverse valid court decisions within six months. The Court, crucially, found in favour of the President, thus formally condemning what was anyway increasingly apparent – that this particular device was a favoured government tool for circumventing the law. Finally, the Court ruled against the government's treatment of MDS parliamentary deputy František Gaulieder, who was stripped of his parliamentary mandate after resigning from the Movement in December 1996. Gaulieder was expelled from parliament on the basis of a letter of resignation he claimed was a fraud, and two days later a bomb exploded at his residence[129] – one of the few outrageous actions in Slovakia that actually made its way into the international press. However, the Court ruled that the obligation to correct this event stood with the parliament itself, and, needless to say, the coalition-dominated parliament refused to reverse the decision[130].

As these cases illustrate, the second thorn in the side of the regime in addition to the Court, and the main counter to pure majority rule in the parliament, came in the person of former MDS party member Michal Kováč – the Slovak president. The Slovak constitution drafted in 1992 in fact created a hopelessly ambiguous division of powers between the presidency and premiership – to the point of making it unclear where ultimate executive authority actually lay. For example, although it was supposedly a parliamentary system with a powerful parliamentary executive, comprising the prime minister and his cabinet, the Slovak presidency also had the right to attend and even to chair government sessions. The president was also formally at liberty to demand reports from the government and its members[131]. At the time Mečiar had clearly believed that, as the parliament's choice, the new president would be a creature of the MDS, and this ambiguous division of powers would pose no problem. As it turned out, Michal Kováč, the final choice, surprised practically everybody by effectively renouncing his party loyalty, opting instead to fulfil the presidential role in the spirit intended by the constitution. Once he had established himself as a gate-keeper of the democratic process, the ensuing feud between him and Mečiar became bitter in the extreme.

Having quarrelled with Mečiar over his choice of ministers[132] and having been instrumental in excluding Meciar from power, Kováč effectively set himself up as the MDS's 'enemy of the people'. Kováč provoked all-out MDS fury after the September 1994 elections by encouraging a search for alternative coalitions to Mečiar's. When Kováč subsequently vetoed some of the legislation to emerge out of the notorious all-night legislative session of 3 November, he was answered swiftly with the slashing of half his office budget.

Although the presidency's powers relating to government were ambiguous and potentially strong – depending upon their interpretation by the incumbent – Kováč's powers *vis-à-vis* parliament were dangerously weak. One of the standard principles of a parliamentary system with a 'gate-keeping' president are that the president is understood to exist to defend the constitution and to guarantee against government abuse of power[133]. He or she should thus be elected for fixed terms and be protected from any possibility of arbitrary dismissal by parliament or government. It was thus a deep flaw in the Slovak constitution that the president could actually be dismissed by a three-fifths majority in parliament, if he or she 'undertakes activities directed against the sovereignty and territorial integrity of the Slovak Republic or a conduct aimed to destroy the democratic and constitutional regime in the Slovak Republic'. Just like the suggestions for the new penal code, these possible terms of impeachment were cast in exceptionally vague terms, open to dangerously elastic interpretations. Sure enough, on 5 May 1995, the governing coalition in the Slovak National Council passed a no-confidence vote against Kováč by 80 to 40, with 30 abstentions.

The MDS accused Kováč of having 'failed to respect the seriousness of the democratic decisions approved by parliament, and thus, the will of the majority of Slovak people'.

The evidence against Kováč had been compiled by the Separate Control Agency, the parliamentary committee responsible for oversight of the State Intelligence Services (SIS), now headed by Ivan Lexa. The report accused Kováč of using the state secret services in a conspiracy to undermine and overthrow the Mečiar government. A three-fifths majority was required to unseat a president, however, and Kováč duly refused to resign, despite the fact that Mečiar had asserted that his own re-election had brought Kováč's mandate to an end. That the President was almost impeached in a closed session of parliament, although he had not even received a report of the evidence against him – he had to read it in the press in order to defend himself in parliament some six days after the report was presented – shows how close Slovakia came in 1995 to absolute majority rule under Mečiar.

With the failure of the no-confidence vote, however, the MDS did not give up but simply changed tactics, removing presidential powers wherever possible with a simple majority in parliament or by other, less conventional, routes. In August 1995 Michal Kováč Jr, the President's son – wanted in Germany on charges of fraud – was abducted, tortured and deposited outside a Viennese police station. Just under a year later an independent commission headed by the Christian Democrat Ladislav Pittner issued a report that concluded that employees of the Slovak Information Service – including its director, Ivan Lexa – had organised the planning, execution and subsequent cover-up of the whole affair[134]. Lexa retaliated in parliament a few days later with his own *Report on Fulfilling the Duties of the Slovak Information Service*, wherein he accused the President, representatives of the opposition parties, journalists and church officials – essentially the entire democratic opposition to Mečiar – of inciting activities against the state and of maintaining contacts with foreign security services[135]. Various coalition members, including Mečiar himself, also came up with the fantastic suggestion that Michal Kováč Jr had actually engineered his own abduction in order to slander the government and security services.

The profound difficulty of gaining any legal redress for this political intrigue is well illustrated by the fact that in August 1996 the City Office of Investigation in Bratislava shelved defamation charges filed by the President against Mečiar for his assertion in a radio interview that the President had been fully aware of the planned abduction of his own son – the implication being that this was some elaborate presidential scheme for bringing the Mečiar regime into disrepute. The city officials commented that Mečiar's only offence had been that of making a 'factual error', which in no way constituted intentional defamation[136].

By the late 1990s Lexa and anyone else accused of involvement in the kidnapping had been granted a general amnesty by Vladimír Mečiar in his brief period with presidential powers, though that amnesty was in turn revoked by Dzurinda in December 1998, using those same presidential powers prior to the election of President Kováč's successor, Rudolf Schuster[137] – two amnesties which at the time of writing remain the subject of massive legal wrangling[138].

As it turned out, it was these issues of presidential succession that finally galvanised coherent opposition action and triggered public fears about an imminent loss of democratic rights in the September 1998 election. With Mečiar's return to power still possible at the time of writing, this broad and, in strictly ideological terms, rather incoherent anti-Mečiar coalition still survives in government two years on, its essentially pro-democratic and reformist energies still remarkably intact. On the plus side the Dzurinda government has secured the beginning of accession negotiations with the European Union (February 2000), and has passed not only essential macro-economic reform measures but also bankruptcy legislation. But in spite of the key austerity measures implemented since the Dzurinda government took power, it looks as though the next Slovak election will again fail to bring about any rationalisation of Slovak party politics, as yet again this government will have to fight across the basic divide of being for or against Vladimír Mečiar and a possibly seductive economic populism. Remarkably, ten years after the revolution, the Slovak party political scene remains hostage to the fortunes of the Movement for a Democratic Slovakia and its undaunted leadership, although these days it would be a brave party electorally that would enter into a Mečiar-led MDS coalition. If further proof were needed of the increasingly pernicious influence of the MDS on Slovak political life it came when Mečiar was seized by police at his home and taken to court – earlier subpoenas having been ignored – on the day before Good Friday 2000, and charged to give evidence on the abuse of state assets, the kidnapping of President Kováč's son, and fraud. The response of the MDS was repellent; it asserted that 'the Jews crucified Christ – now Dzurinda wants Mečiar'.

THE POST-COMMUNIST POLITICAL LEGACY –
TECHNOCRATS AND POPULISTS

In the Czech Republic, Klausite politics had produced a right-wing technocratic vision – a panoramic narrative of life and society that was complex enough to explain away or justify every anomaly, every administrative and political act. Mečiarism in the independent Slovakia, on the other hand, had put far less effort into intellectual and ideological justification, as it created a hollow caricature of the clientalist and state power practices of the 1980s. With its post-1992 constituency increasingly among rural and relatively uneducated voters, the MDS discovered that an emotive populism – given the ideological disarray of the opposition – was sufficient to stay at the top. While Klaus went for the squeaky-clean, radical-individualist hero role in the independent Czech Republic, Mečiar went increasingly all-out for folk-heroism – and its attendant unpredictability.

In many respects, however, the character of the post-independence Czech and Slovak regimes has been remarkably similar; by 1998 they had practically converged, the most obvious similarities being in the dominance of the political scene by demagogic populists and technocrats, with the latter resorting more and more to populist rhetoric. The main contrast lay in the sophistication of the technocratic solutions on offer and the degree of brute force employed.

Where Klaus's ideological dogmatism allowed a covert corruption of privatisation and reversion to patronage, Mečiar went quite publicly for the clan-economy, the placing of party men in crucial industrial, bureaucratic, educational and media positions, and the clientalistic distribution of state assets to loyal followers – signalling clearly that to be a 'party man' was once again the way to get ahead. Where Klaus accused press critics of crypto-Bolshevik sympathies, critical journalists in Slovakia found their cars being blown up and their phones tapped[139]. Where Klaus refused to legislate for state accountability, Mečiar legislated for unaccountable recentralised power. Where Klaus legislated to emasculate the powers of a critical president, President Kováč found his son kidnapped, tortured, allegedly by the Slovak security services, and deposited abroad. Both regimes carved up state influence between themselves and their coalition partners, both repoliticised their civil services – in Slovakia, right down to encouraging officers to join the party of power – and both routinely flouted the spirit of the law, even to the point of rejecting constitutional requirements and making blatant adjustments of electoral laws to suit their own ends. Both countries continued to operate as 'electocracies', in other words, as states in which the maintenance of truly minimal electoral endorsement was taken as an adequate definition of what it meant to be a democratic government – as the only binding constraint. By the late 1990s both Klaus and Mečiar had resorted to an aggressive and chauvinistic populism in an attempt to speak to the public disappointment for which they were, in no small part, responsible.

Having reduced Slovak politics to the formula that whatever he said, however incendiary, however contradictory, however outlandish, was for the higher good of the 'Slovak family', Mečiar, as during the break-up of Czechoslovakia, left himself far more vulnerable, politically, than Klaus. Having established himself as the proto-father of the nation as such, Mečiar was always more blatantly and brutally power-seeking, with fewer clear 'ends' on offer, to ultimately 'justify the means' employed. A continuing and worrying legacy of the Mečiar era, however, is the now deeply populist quality of Slovak political party competition, and the real problem faced by Slovakia's more democratic politicians who would dearly like to raise the level of policy debate. If the aspirations of the population were the measure, then the situation in Slovakia by the end of 2000 looked robust. Despite low growth and rising unemployment following the austerity measures of the Dzurinda government, public support for EU entry rose to three-quarters – a vote of faith in the government's efforts – and an attempt by Mečiar to call early elections through a referendum were also foiled in November 2000 by a 20-per-cent turn-out (50 per cent is required for validation). Such a constructive public will, however, needs constructive public servants, and although, as in the Czech Republic, there is much talk of how it will take 'the younger generation' to really improve things, many younger Slovak politicians appear to have learned the lessons of Mečiar's success in spades.

Slovakia's latest political innovation is called 'Smer' ('Direction'), a new party formed in 1999 and led by the PDL's former rising star Róbert Fico. Smer is in fact a one-man party, and Fico, suspected of seeking to be coalition kingmaker with the MDS, claims that the combination of his leadership – deputies hand-picked for their *lack* of political experience (thus guaranteeing their 'purity') and special 'committees of experts' – will transcend Slovakia's endless 'politicking' and solve all Slovakia's ills as it hears them from *vox populi*. Fico's appeal comes from his capacity to tap into popular discontent with the lack of accountability in Slovak politics – and it is not surprising that there are votes to be gained by presenting 'transition' purely as a technical problem deserving of undivided professional attention. When asked by this author what he 'actually believed in', however, Mr Fico replied that 'belief is not the point'[140] and clearly it is not. The younger generation of politicians have been shown that in practice, a populist or technocratic government – better still, one that can combine both strategies – may accrue far more power than any party playing by the harder rules of programmatic politics and ready accountability. Smer's proposed electoral slogan for 2002 is deceptively modest; it is 'No more promises'.

APPENDIX: 1990 AND 1992 ELECTION RESULTS

Election 8–9 June 1990
Percentage share of the vote

	Federal Assembly		Czech/ Slovak National Councils
	House of the People	House of the Nations	
Czech Republic			
Civic Forum (CF)	53.1	50.0	49.5
Communist Party of Czechoslovakia (CP)	13.5	13.8	13.3
Christian and Democratic Union (CDU)	8.7	8.7	8.4
MSD/SMS*	7.9	9.1	10.0
Others	16.8	18.4	18.8
Slovak Republic			
Public Against Violence (PAV)	32.5	37.3	29.3
Christian Democratic Movement (CDM)	19.0	16.7	19.2
Communist Party of Czechoslovakia (CP)	13.8	13.4	13.3
Slovak National Party (SNP)	11.0	11.4	13.9
Coexistence and HCDM**	8.6	8.5	8.7
Democratic Party (DP)	4.4	3.7	4.4
Slovak Green Party (SGP)	3.2	2.6	3.5
Others	7.5	6.4	7.7

Percentage share of seats

	Federal Assembly		Czech/ Slovak National Councils
	House of the People	House of the Nations	
Czech Republic			
Civic Forum (CF)	68	50	127
Communist Party of Czechoslovakia (CP)	15	12	32
Christian and Democratic Union (CDU)	9	6	19
MSD/SMS*	9	7	22
TOTAL	101	75	200

Election 8–9 June 1990 (*Continued*)
Percentage share of seats

	Federal Assembly		Czech/ Slovak National Councils
	House of the People	House of the Nations	
Slovak Republic			
Public Against Violence (PAV)	19	33	48
Christian Democratic Movement (CDM)	11	14	31
Communist Party of Czechoslovakia (CP)	8	12	22
Slovak National Party (SNP)	6	9	22
Coexistence and HCDM**	5	7	14
Democratic Party (DP)	–	–	7
Green Party (GP)	–	–	6
TOTAL	49	75	150

* Movement for Self-governing Democracy/Society for Moravia and Silesia.
** Hungarian Christian Democratic Movement.

Election results: 5–6 June 1992
Federal Assembly of the Czech and Slovak Federative Republic

	House of the People (150 seats)		House of the Nations (150 seats)	
	Votes (%)	Seats	Votes (%)	Seats
Czech Republic				
Civic Democratic Party and Christian Democratic Party	33.9	48	33.4	37
Left Bloc	14.3	19	14.5	15
Czechoslovak Social Democracy	7.7	10	6.8	6
Republican Party	6.5	8	6.4	6
Christian Democratic Union/Czechoslovak People's Party	6.0	7	6.1	6
Liberal Social Union	5.8	7	6.1	5
Others	25.8	0	26.7	0
TOTAL	100.0	99	100.0	75
Slovak Republic				
Movement for a Democratic Slovakia	33.5	24	33.9	33
Party of the Democratic Left	14.4	10	14.0	13
Slovak National Party	9.4	6	9.4	9

Election results: 5–6 June 1992 (*Continued*)
Federal Assembly of the Czech and Slovak Federative Republic

	House of the People (150 seats)		House of the Nations (150 seats)	
	Votes (%)	Seats	Votes (%)	Seats
Christian Democratic Movement	9.0	6	8.8	8
Hungarian Christian Democratic Movement and Coexistence	7.5	5	7.4	7
SDP in Slovakia	4.9	0	6.1	5
Others	21.3	0	20.4	0
TOTAL	100.0	51	100.0	75

Czech National Council

	Votes (%)	Seats
Civic Democratic Party and Christian Democratic Party	29.7	76
Left Bloc	14.1	35
Czechoslovak Social Democracy	6.5	16
Liberal Social Union	6.5	16
Christian Democratic Union/ Czechoslovak People's Party	6.3	15
Republican Party	6.0	14
Civic Democratic Alliance	6.0	14
MSD/SMS*	5.9	14
Others	19.0	0
TOTAL	100.0	200

Slovak National Council

	Votes (%)	Seats
Movement for a Democratic Slovakia	37.3	74
Slovak Democratic Left	14.7	29
Christian Democratic Movement	8.9	18
Slovak National Party	7.9	15
Hungarian Christian Democratic Movement and Coexistence	7.4	14
Others	23.8	0
TOTAL	100.0	150

* Movement for Self-governing Democracy/Society for Moravia and Silesia.

CZECH AND SLOVAK
POLITICAL PARTIES

1990–2

Czech political parties

AR/RPC	**Association for the Republic/Republican Party of Czechoslovakia**
ASD	**Association of Social Democrats** (formerly within the Civic Forum)
CDU	**Christian and Democratic Union**
Christ.DP	**Christian Democratic Party** (formerly part of the Christian and Democratic Union)
CDU/CPP	**Christian Democratic Union/Czechoslovak People's Party** (formerly part of the Christian and Democratic Union)
CDP	**Civic Democratic Party** (formerly within the Civic Forum)
CDA	**Civic Democratic Alliance** (formerly within the Civic Forum)
CF	**Civic Forum**
CM	**Civic Movement** (formerly within the Civic Forum)
CP	**Communist Party of Czechoslovakia**
CSD	**Czechoslovak Social Democracy** (formerly within the Civic Forum)
LB	**Left Bloc** (a coalition of the **Communist Party of Bohemia and Moravia,** following the split with the Slovak wing of the Party, and the minuscule (Czech) **Democratic Left**)
LSU	**Liberal Social Union** (a coalition of the **Agricultural Party,** the **Czechoslovak Socialist Party** and the **Green Party**)
MSD/SMS	**Movement for a Self-Governing Democracy/Society for Moravia and Silesia**

Slovak political parties

CDM	**Christian Democratic Movement**
CDU (PAV)	**Civic Democratic Union** (formerly the liberal wing of the Public Against Violence)
DP	**Democratic Party** (former Communist 'satellite' party – the Party of Slovak Renewal)
Egy.	**Együttélés (Coexistence)**
GP	**Green Party**
HCP	**Hungarian Civic Party** (formerly **Hungarian Independent Initiative**)
HCDM	**Hungarian Christian Democratic Movement**
MDS	**Movement for a Democratic Slovakia** (formerly part of the Public Against Violence)
PDL	**Party of the Democratic Left** (formerly the Communist Party of Slovakia)
PAV	**Public Against Violence**
SCDM	**Slovak Christian Democratic Movement** (formerly part of the Christian Democratic Movement)
SDPS	**Social Democratic Party of Slovakia**
SNP	**Slovak National Party**

1993–2000

Political parties in the Czech Republic

CDA	**Civic Democratic Alliance**
CDP	**Civic Democratic Party**
CDU/CPP	**Christian Democratic Union/Czechoslovak People's Party**
CP	**Communist Party of Bohemia and Moravia**
DU	**Democratic Union**
FU	**Freedom Union**
QC	**Quad (four-party) Coalition** (an electoral coalition comprising the CDU/CPP, FU, DU and CDA)
SDP	**Social Democratic Party**

Political parties in the Slovak Republic

CDM	**Christian Democratic Movement**
DP	**Democratic Party**
DU	**Democratic Union**

GPS	Green Party of Slovakia
MDS	Movement for a Democratic Slovakia
PCU	Party for Civic Understanding
PHC	**Party of the Hungarian Coalition** (formerly the Hungarian Christian Democratic Movement, Együtté-lés (Coexistence) and the Hungarian Civic Party)
SDC	**Slovak Democratic Coalition** (an electoral coalition uniting the five political parties, the CDM, the DU, the DP, the SDS and the GPS)
SNP	**Slovak National Party**
SDS	**Social Democratic Party of Slovakia**

NOTES

References included in the 'Secondary sources' section of the Bibliography below are cited here with author's name and date only.

CHAPTER 1

[1] The Hungarian territory of Ruthenia (Sub-Carpathian Ruthenia) eventually also accrued to Czechoslovakia as an autonomous region, Czechoslovakia seeming the least difficult choice. Ruthenia was administered by a Governor appointed by the Czechoslovak President and, though promised a separate civil administration for 1922, this was still not established when the Czechoslovak Republic fell in 1938. See Seton-Watson (1965), p. 324.

[2] Pryor (1973), p. 190.

[3] The Serb Orthodox Church acted as a bulwark against Magyar assimilation of Serbs culturally. Moreover, after 1878 an independent Serbia acted as a focus for Serbian identity, just as after 1859 the independent Kingdom of Romania encouraged an independent, indeed irredentist, Romanian identity. Macartney (1968), p. 730.

[4] Between 1910 and 1920 Bohemian Catholics began to leave the church in droves, perceiving the Catholic hierarchy to be an instrument of Habsburg oppression. Equally, anti-Magyar Slovak intellectuals who had sought refuge in the Czech education system tended to be from Protestant backgrounds precisely because their Protestantism had rendered them relatively immune to Magyarisation. Leff (1988), p. 19.

[5] Seton-Watson (1965), p. 13.

[6] In 1526 the Czech Diet elected Ferdinand I, a Habsburg, to the throne. The Czech nobility sought the strength of the established pan-European family as a way of reinvigorating the Czech kingdom. Ferdinand, however, proved so strong as to secure the succession of his descendants. Thereafter 'the Czech Diet ceased to elect kings and, instead, accepted them.' Bradley (1971), p. 68.

[7] Mason (1997), p. 13.

[8] Skilling (1994), p. 79.

[9] Connor (1994), p. 212.

[10] The First Republic embarked on the interwar period with some three million Germans and three-quarters of a million Magyars – in a population of 13,600,000. By 1930 Czechs constituted 49.9 per cent of the total population; Germans 21.9 per cent; Slovaks 15.9 per cent; Hungarians 4.7 per cent; Ukrainians, Ruthenians and Russians 3.7 per cent; Jews 1.3 per cent and Poles 0.6 per cent: Prucha (1995), p. 45.

[11] Bartlová (1995), p. 163.

[12] Skilling (1994), p. 71.

[13] Johnson (1985), p. 53.

[14] The Slovak National Council was viewed domestically as the representative forum of Slovak political feeling, having been reconstituted in May 1918 by the Slovak People's Party, the Social Democrats and the Slovak National Party.

[15] There existed a popular Czech notion that Slovak existed only as a backward form of Czech, which would soon dissolve as Slovak society passed through the modernisation already completed by Czech society, Johnson (1985), pp. 52–3.

[16] Beneš (1973), pp. 73–4.

[17] It should be remembered that these were chaotic postwar times. Bratislava was not occupied until 4 January 1919 and border security between Slovakia and Hungary was not achieved until August and the collapse of the five-month-old Hungarian Bolshevik regime under Béla

Kun, a situation not fully stabilised until the Treaty of Trianon of 4 June 1920. Seton-Watson (1965), pp. 322–4.

[18] The Cleveland Accord had already been swept aside. It was a joint declaration by émigré representatives of the Slovak League and the Czech National Association, calling for an independent federated Czechoslovak state. The Accord provided for Slovak autonomy to the extent of its own financial and political administrations and total cultural freedom. As Johnson points out, the significance of the document was that the American Slovaks could claim to represent the Slovak cause in northern Hungary, effectively silenced by the war. Johnson (1985), p. 47.

[19] Jelinek (1983), p. 5.

[20] T. G. Masaryk, *The Making of a State: Memories and Observations 1914–1918* (London: George Allen & Unwin, 1927), p. 208.

[21] Seton-Watson (1965), p. 334.

[22] Masaryk, op. cit., p. 209.

[23] Mamatey (1973), p. 9.

[24] Hlinka agitated for the adoption of the Agreement, making his way to Paris to lobby at the Peace Conference. He was arrested on his return and, untried, was only allowed to return to Slovakia after his election to the Prague Parliament in 1920: Kirschbaum (1983), p. 165.

[25] Leff (1988), p. 21.

[26] The works of Masaryk greatly influenced and shaped the anti-Habsburg feeling of many Slovak students in Prague during the 1890s. The newspaper *Hlas* (Voice) was a mouthpiece of the liberal democrats among the progressive student clubs advocating closer Czech Slovak cooperation on the basis of their common roots.

[27] The Council acted as temporary government before the first sitting of the Czechoslovak National Assembly. Bartlová (1995), p. 170.

[28] Before the first elections in 1920 the Czechoslovak National Council apportioned mandates among existing parties according to their results in the last election to the (Habsburg) Reichsrat, held under universal suffrage. This method could not be applied to Slovakia because of the distorting Hungarian franchise, which had left Slovakia with only three deputies.

The Czechoslovak National Council therefore, acting on Srobár's advice, had *nominated* forty-one leading Slovaks, to whom a further fourteen were soon added. This was later criticised, though at the time, according to Seton-Watson, 'it was universally accepted as a graceful compliment': Seton-Watson (1965), p. 317.

[29] Bartlová (1995), p. 171.

[30] Jelinek (1976), p. 5.

[31] Some 70.89 per cent of Slovaks were Roman Catholic and 6.46 Greek Catholic in 1921: Johnson (1985), p. 27.

[32] In the first years of the Republic Slovakia lacked sufficiently educated and politically reliable people to assure fair representation in the prestigious civil service – a legacy of Hungarian rule. By the time the reformed Slovak education system had produced large numbers of competent candidates in the Republic's second decade, however, they too found themselves unable to penetrate into the central administration. This persistent discrimination caused tension amongst Slovakia's educated classes, newly swelled with Catholics as these classes were. Some Czech politicians interpreted this frustration as rank ingratitude for the comprehensive new 'Czechoslovak' education system that had so elevated them, an appraisal which hardly helped matters. As late as 1938, a head count of all those employed in the ministries, together with the office of the president and executive council, totalled 10,825 positions, of which a staggering 123 were occupied by Slovaks; see Bartlová (1995), p. 173.

[33] *Budování státu* Volume II:1227: in Kirschbaum (1983), p. 161.

[34] Seton-Watson (1965), p. 917.

[35] Benes (1973), p. 83.

[36] Eduard Beneš's National Socialists, it should be noted, were not Nazis but non-Marxist radicals with a lower-middle and working-class constituency. This secular party was beleaguered by factional infighting and never gained a strong foothold in Slovakia; see Leff (1988), p. 57.

[37] Seton-Watson (1965), p. 330.

[38] The 1927 law gave Slovakia a Provincial President with wide powers and an elected Provincial Assembly. The latter was, however, a throwback to Hungarian practices in that it consisted of two-thirds

elected representatives and one-third selected directly by the civil service (ibid., p. 335). This latter third favoured central administration and keeping in line with central government policies, a factor exposing it to the HSPP's dissatisfaction, see Bartlová (1995), p. 174.

[39] In 1928 Hlinka's adviser, Dr Vojtech Tuka, repeated in the Hlinka Party's paper *Slovak* a long-established myth that there existed a potential legal vacuum as a result of a secret clause in the 1918 Martin Declaration stipulating the right of Slovaks, after ten years, to reconsider their decision to enter into a political union with the Czechs. He insisted that if autonomy was not granted by 31 October 1928, Slovakia might go its own way. Tuka was tried for treason as a Hungarian spy and sentenced to fifteen years' imprisonment (Seton-Watson (1965), p. 311). It was only after the war that Czechoslovak historians were able to produce unequivocal evidence proving Tuka's guilt, see Jelinek (1976), p. 10. Released from prison in 1938, Tuka would become Prime Minister of the clerico-fascist Slovak state from March 1939 to September 1944, and clearly and instrumentally pro-Nazi.

[40] In-fighting and Comintern dictates led the Communist Party at the time to engage in a leadership purge significant to postwar developments. The new elite centred on a Stalinist cadre around Klement Gottwald; 'young fanatics, whose greatest qualification was their willingness to accept Moscow's orders unconditionally'. At the end of the 1920s the Party presented the vision of a 'Soviet Slovakia' and while highlighting the differences between the Party and the Populists, Gottwald clearly played on L'udák ground. Mere autonomy, said the Communists, would only subject the Slovak worker to the Slovak bourgeoisie. Despite this Slovakia's branch of the Communist Party remained notoriously short of card-carrying members and functionaries during the Great Depression, see Jelinek (1983), pp. 17–25.

[41] Jelinek (1976), p. 10.

[42] See Johnson (1985), p. 51.

[43] Mamatey (1973), p. 157.

[44] When Hitler became German Chancellor in 1933 that other marginalised political group, the Communist Party, comprehended at last the true scale of the Nazi threat. Turning from its interminable attacks against the Social Democrats, the Party shifted its priorities to support the 'bourgeois state' and voted for the first time in favour of parts of the state budget. Following Masaryk's resignation in 1935, the Communists voted for Eduard Beneš (as did the L'udáks) rather than propose a candidate of their own. The slogan 'Soviet Slovakia' disappeared (Jelinek, ibid., p. 27), leaving the Hlinka party again alone in calling for Slovak autonomy, but this time with a new resonance.

[45] The Communist Party faced tremendous difficulties by this time: they had to demand pro-Slovak changes, for which they were accused of pro-L'udák behaviour. The minorities meanwhile rejected the Communists' brushing aside of self-determination and their apparent born-again Czechoslovakism. As Jelinek concludes, 'Communism was in retreat in the last years of the Republic': Jelinek (1976), p. 3.

[46] ibid., pp. 11–16.

[47] See Mamatey (1973), p. 164.

[48] In the confusion during September, Hodža's government had resigned and President Eduard Beneš appointed a cabinet of experts, led by General Jan Syrový, to replace it.

[49] Prochazka (1973), p. 260.

[50] The Czech historian Jan Rychlík has described this as a process of 'constructing Slovakia's independence paid for by the Czech taxpayer', a common Czech theme after 1989; see Rychlík (1995) (1995), p. 182.

[51] See Mamatey (1973), p. 167.

[52] See Leff on this issue (1988), p. 90.

[53] The Hungarians and Germans rejected the invitation to participate in the pre-1920 'Revolutionary National Assembly' which wrote the 1920 constitution; see Johnson (1985), p. 60. They boycotted the Parliament, hoping for reunion with Hungary and Austria respectively. When they eventually entered the legislature they were, of course, confronted by laws and principles established by Czechs and Slovaks.

[54] For an in-depth discussion, see Leff (1988), pp. 193–211.

[55] See Johnson (1985), p. 84.

[56] It is equally thought-provoking to ask whether the expulsion of ethnic Germans after the Second World War effectively removed all reason for the existence of Czechoslovakia.

[57] See Bartlová (1995), p. 169.

[58] Johnson (1985), p. 50.

[59] Ferdinand Peroutka, *Budování státu* Volume I, p. 213, in Kirschbaum (1983), p. 170.

[60] Churchill, *The Second World War: The Gathering Storm*, Volume 1 (Boston: Houghton Mifflin Company, 1948), p. 294.

[61] See Myant (1981), p. 41.

[62] Kirschbaum (1983), p. 287.

[63] Such interpretations have been greatly aided by Slovak L'udák and nationalist historians, who have proven consistent apologists for a Slovak state of highly dubious virtue – the virtue most openly claimed for it being that it 'safeguarded' the Slovak nation. There is, however, a correspondingly constant trend (contradictory to the prevailing stereotypes); liberal and some leftist Slovaks, like today's liberal Germans, have since tended to see harm in *every* 'national' idea – a hyper-conscientiousness, indeed, a phobia of nationalism that proved an important and problematic element in Slovak liberal policy after 1989.

[64] See Arendt (1994), p. 205.

[65] See Rychlík (1995), p. 186.

[66] In 1940 Czech and Slovak emigrants opposed to Beneš's 'Czechoslovakist' thinking had formed a 'Czecho-Slovak National Council' with the goal of securing a restoration of Czechoslovakia but on federative principles. In Beneš's favour, insofar as it secured him the British recognition decisive after the fall of France, was his ability to offer the Allies an entire network of secret service operations in Central Europe. From July 1940 Beneš's National Committee was duly recognised as the provisional Czechoslovak government in exile. Slovakia's hopes of being offered postwar choices were sunk when on 22 July 1941 it joined Germany in the war against the USSR. When Tuka declared war on the USA and Britain (in December 1941) it secured US, British and Soviet recognition of the Czechoslovaks in London; see Rychlík (1995), pp. 185–6.

[67] See Jelinek (1976), p. 125.

[68] See Rychlík (1995), p. 187.

[69] See Alexander Dubček's autobiography, *Hope Dies Last*, ed. and trans. J. Hochman (New York: Kodansha International, 1993), pp. 41–50.

[70] Golan (1971), p. 195.

[71] See Jelinek (1983), p. 75.

[72] See Leff on the full implications of the uprising (1988), p. 93.

[73] Sounding ever more distinctly like an émigré L'udák, Kirschbaum argues that 1944 brought down a 'tragedy' on the Slovak people and he calls the resistance 'accomplices in the imposition on the Slovaks of a state structure and system that was fundamentally inimical to their survival as a nation'; see Kirschbaum (1983), p. 291.

[74] The Czech lands, crucially, became more or less ethnically homogeneous. Across all of Czechoslovakia, the proportion of Czechs and Slovaks in the population rose from 64 per cent (1921) to 94 per cent, see Leff (1988), p. 93.

[75] ibid., p. 91.

[76] Rychlík (1995), pp. 189–90.

[77] Jelinek (1983), p. 83.

[78] ibid., p. 81.

[79] Mamatey and Luža (1973), p. 392.

[80] See Kirschbaum (1995), p. 227.

[81] Vnuk (1983), p. 325.

[82] See Rychlík (1995), p. 191.

[83] One of the Slovaks now preferred was Široký; hostile to the 'Uprising Generation', and burdened, for Slovak audiences, with a thick Hungarian accent: Jelinek, ibid., p. 92.

[84] Vnuk (1983), pp. 331–3.

[85] Article II. 1948 Constitution; see Pechota (1992), p. 8.

[86] See Leff (1988), p. 124.

[87] Viewed as the weak link in the Czechoslovak scene by Czech Communists, Slovakia fell prey to some paradoxical tactics. In 1947 the Communist Party assisted in fomenting anti-Communist activities in Slovakia – the logic being that these would hasten a final takeover (secured with the alleged L'udák conspiracy). '[E]xtra-parliamentary activity, anti-Czech, anti-Czechoslovakia, anti-Communist, and anti-Jewish demonstrations and riots were grist to the Communist mill', see Jelinek (1983), p. 99.

[88] All of these figures for levels of persecution are taken from Karel Kaplan's *Political Persecution in Czechoslovakia*

1948–1972, Research Project: Crisis in Soviet-Type Systems, Study Number 3, pp. 9–23.

[89] The show trials are often referred to as the 'Slánský process' after the trial's most senior victim and supposed ringleader, Rudolf Slánský (Secretary General of the Party). The particular persecution of Jews reflected the USSR's changing policy in the Middle East and the rising Soviet exploitation of anti-Semitism.

[90] From Suda (1981), p. 247.

[91] An experience which, to Dubček's horror, did not prevent Husák from launching a second wave of punishments when installed as First Secretary following the repression of Prague Spring in August 1968.

[92] See Leff (1988), pp. 167–9.

[93] Klement Gottwald had died suddenly in 1953, having contracted pneumonia at Stalin's funeral, and he was replaced as President by Antonín Zápotocký, who died in 1957. Novotný was a secretary of the Party, 1951–3 and First Secretary, 1953–68, combining this with the Presidency of the Republic after 19 November 1957.

[94] See Dubček, op. cit., p. 83.

[95] These included Gustáv Husák. Dubček found Husák a place at the Slovak Institute of History, where he applied himself to the history of the Slovak National Uprising, op. cit., pp. 86–93.

[96] A precursor to the more famous and feted 'Czechoslovak' writers' congress in June 1967.

[97] See Dubček, op. cit., p. 89.

[98] In June 1963 Novotný instructed the Slovak Party to restrain it – a clear sign that Slovak structures had broken out beyond central control, see Leff (1988), p. 111.

[99] In 1964 Dubček succeeded in wresting a limited expansion of National Council powers – another sign of the holding operation underway at the centre. The remnants of Slovak national institutions left after 1948 actually made Prague extremely prone to demands that they be operationalised when reformist moments arose, ibid., p. 112.

[100] In August 1964 the Slovak National Uprising was accorded some real recognition, with Kruschev and Novotný attending celebrations. There was even some acknowledgement of Slovak non-Communist, as well as Communist participation in the event, see Golan (1971), p. 195. Only months before his own downfall in October 1967 Novotný resorted to visiting Slovakia in an attempt to improve his image there. The visit was, however, disastrous. Most extraordinary was Novotný's suggestion that *Matica Slovenská* move its museum to Prague. Matica Slovenská, or 'Mother Slovakia', was Slovakia's main cultural organisation. Founded in 1861 it had since then safeguarded Slovak language/literature and was synonymous with national survival. As Dubček observed with glee, following this spectacle 'relations between Novotný and Slovaks of almost all stripes became irreparable', op. cit., p. 115.

[101] See Leff (1988), p. 119.

[102] ibid., p. 171.

[103] In 1960 a new constitution had been created for the sole purpose of signalling the supposed elevation of Czechoslovakia from the 'socialist stage' of development to that of its embarkation upon 'Communism' proper. The constitution of 11 July 1960 had claimed that a 'socialist democracy' had replaced the vaunted 'people's democracy' of 1948. This 1960 constitution neglected to address Slovak autonomy even more than had its predecessor, abolishing the already powerless Board of Commissioners.

[104] This stated 'that the very asymmetrical arrangement was unsuited by its very character to express the relations between two independent nations, because it expressed the standings of the two nations differently. The difference was mainly in the fact that the Czech national bodies were identical with the national central ones. . . . This prevented the Slovak nation, to all intents and purposes, from taking an equal share in the creation and realisation of a country-wide policy' Action Programme, reproduced in Robin Remington's *Winter in Prague: Documents on Czechoslovak Communism in Crisis* (Cambridge, Massachusetts: MIT Press, 1969), p. 107.

[105] Leff (1988), p. 122.

[106] Rychlik (1995), p. 196.

[107] ibid.

[108] Pechota (1992), p. 12.

[109] Hendrych (1993), p. 46.

[110] Leff (1988), p. 124.

[111] J. Lederer, *Reporter* 23 January 1969, quoted in Leff, ibid., p. 125.

[112] ibid., p. 127.

[113] ibid., p. 254.

[114] See Rychlík (1995), pp. 196–7.

[115] See Leff (1988), p. 247.

[116] Husák's post-invasion desertion to the forces of repression was a ready signal to many Czechs that Slovakia's prior engagement with reform had been motivated by nationalist expedience rather than democratic instinct, see Leff (1988), p. 174.

[117] Rychlík (1995), p. 195.

[118] The scale of Party efforts to suppress the notion of Slovak national identity can be seen from the fact that until 1968 Bratislava had no formal legitimacy as a Slovak political centre or capital; see Leff (1988), p. 107. This omission of institutional recognition reminded Slovaks of their predicament under Hungarian rule.

[119] From Dubček, op. cit., p. 277.

[120] Leff (1988), p. 163.

[121] In fact, in addition to the history of the movement's origins in Slovakia, Slovak public opinion in June 1968 clearly endorsed the full reform movement: in a June poll, 92.9 per cent of the respondents gave their support to the reform movement by agreeing that the Action Programme would positively influence the development of Czechoslovakia; in another poll a month later, 86 per cent of the respondents were in favour of broadening the measure for individual freedom, from Kirschbaum (1995), p. 242.

[122] Pithart (1995), p. 204.

[123] Leff (1988), p. 254.

[124] Following the recentralisation of the early 1970s, the concept of two national economies was treated as a 'rightist heresy propagated to disintegrate the state' (ibid., p. 248). Political 'achievements' were hardly to be attempted following the invasion, making Czech/Slovak economic parity one of the few available foci of Party propaganda. Economic achievements had to fulfil the legitimating role normally ascribed to the entire panoply of government – an unsustainable social contract, as it turned out.

[125] Jan Misovic, 'Názory na vzt'ahy národov a národnosti CSSR', *Informace*, March 1990, quoted in Wolchik (1991), p. 114.

[126] See Wehrlé (1994), p. 254.

[127] The Charter's spokesman, Jiří Hajek, commented that Slovaks were 'sufficiently enlightened' to be soft on each other, in Wehrle (1994), p. 254.

[128] *Die Welt*, 17 February 1977.

[129] Dubček, op. cit., p. 264.

[130] Kirschbaum (1995), p. 248.

[131] See Leff (1988), p. 266.

[132] '2,000 Words to Workers, Farmers, Scientists, Artists, and Everyone' was published in the respective journals of these workers in June 1968 – a call for 'action from below', in Golan (1971), p. 297.

[133] See Precan (1983) or Wehrle (1994).

[134] See Leff (1988), p. 264.

[135] Kirschbaum (1995), p. 248.

[136] Adam Michnik, *Letters From Prison: And Other Essays* (Berkeley: University of California Press, 1985), p. 50.

[137] As Miroslav Kusý has testified, Czech dissident visitors to their Slovak colleagues were typically arrested and sent back to Prague before reaching their destination. Václav Havel moreover has indicated that Charter 77 was exclusively Czech, at least at the very beginning, so as to ensure against police detection and intervention, in Wehrlé (1994), p. 253.

[138] ibid.

[139] Radio Free Europe, 'Are the Czech Lands or Slovakia Favored by the Federal Government?' Audience and Public Opinion Research Department, 1977, p. 9.

[140] Leff (1988), p. 262.

[141] Such 'favouritism' was eminently reversible, however, based unstably as it was on the Soviet expectation of a corrective Slovak influence at that time and compensation for the otherwise profound recentralisation of 1970. National representation in government seemed well established by the 1980s; between 1969 and 1983 Slovaks received about one-third of ministerial portfolios – a proportionate level hitherto never achieved, though Czechs continued to monopolise the head of security and control operations. While the advance was impressive it was also due to the persistence of individuals in office. It is thus difficult to separate the changes in 'principle' from the hard facts of 'oligarchic petrifaction' in the last twenty years of the state (ibid., p. 253). Such tactics were anyway only a minor part of the Soviets' wider plan through the 1970s –

the accelerated assimilation of Slovak and Czech identity. For a superb study on the uses of nationalism in Soviet-type states see Connor (1984), p. 447.

[142] Few authors have analysed Czechoslovakia in anything approaching its historical entirety (1918–92), the exceptions being F. Wehrlé and C. S. Leff, who have done much to explain the foundations behind evidently 'diverging constructions of history' (Wehrlé (1994), p. 241). Until recently, anyone reading Czech Slovak history faced an unusual burden of ideological 'decoding'. As several post-Second World War studies pointed out, Slovakia had tended to be subsumed within histories of the First Republic (1918–38) as if it represented no more than a province of the Czech-dominated whole. The perception that the story of Slovakia had been neglected spurred an alternative but often equally polemical literature, particularly from émigré Slovaks and their descendants. Within the country, the history of the state was thoroughly hijacked following the Communist takeover in 1948. It is thus important to appreciate how ill-served mediators in the national dispute would be, after 1989, by the overburdened ideological narratives within Czechoslovakia's history books.

[143] Vile (1982), p. 222.

[144] ibid.

CHAPTER 2

[1] See Schöpflin (1991), p. 9.

[2] Because to appeal to the more universalist and Enlightenment principle of the equal ability of all men in the governance of his own state did not look plausible in nineteenth-century Eastern Europe, where the majority of the population were the illiterate, entirely non-politicised peasantry.

[3] See Smith (1991) for a summary of Kohn's thesis and for an argument against it. Kohn's conception of 'Eastern' and 'Western' nationalism as two distinct types has been strongly criticised as an unsustainable generalisation. To begin with, Kohn ignored the many instances in modern history of distinctly illiberal nationalisms in Western Europe. At various times Irish, French, German and Italian nationalisms have all made violent and exclusive ethnic claims and have also used the most dim and distant myths, as chimerical as pure racial heritage in the fascist case. Given the enduring stereotypes, moreover, it is perhaps more significant that Kohn also completely ignored the strands of liberal Polish, Czech, Hungarian and Zionist nationalisms that existed through the nineteenth and twentieth centuries.

[4] See Bunce (1996), p. 10.

[5] Connor has emphasised that the leaders of nationalist movements anywhere may be merely opportunistic, motivated not by a nationalist vision at all but by some ulterior end. He cites personal gain and class-oriented philosophy, which they must cloak in a nationalist garb in order to mobilise the national sentiments of the masses – see 'The Seductive Lure of Economic Explanations', in Connor (1994), p. 161. Clearly, the conflict in Czechoslovakia may still be identified as nationalist in character if it proved possible to mobilise the electorate on that basis, whatever we may conclude about the 'real' motives of the elites (nationalism does not have to be a 'non-profit' business to be nationalism).

[6] Tom Nairn (1983), p. 198.

[7] ibid., p. 201.

[8] Walker Connor (1994) points out that causal connections between economic forces and nationalism should not be inferred simply because they tend to coexist, ibid., p. 160.

[9] ibid., p. 161.

[10] This can be found in a collection of Václav Klaus's speeches, *Renaissance: The Rebirth of Liberty at the Heart of Europe* (Washington: Cato Institute, 1997), p. 122.

[11] Quoted in Stein (1997), p. 264.

[12] *Lidové noviny* 26 October 1992, p. 1.

[13] It should be noted that the literature examining nationalism is vast and the range of theories huge – to select any definition, therefore, is to wish upon one's account a huge discussion about the reasonableness of the theoretical benchmark chosen. Following Anthony Smith, I was looking for a working definition 'stripped of essentialist notions . . . the only possible and fruitful one in the empirically indistinct field of nationalism', see Smith (1983), pp. 165–6.

[14] Breuilly (1993), p. 1.
[15] ibid., p. 2.
[16] ibid., p. 421.
[17] Of course, a crude application of Breuilly's definition could fail to capture important ambiguities peculiar to Czechoslovakia. The Czechs' tendency historically to regard 'Czech' and 'Czechoslovak' as synonymous is, indeed, analytically awkward, making it potentially difficult to distinguish nationalistic from federal-sounding rhetoric. Further complications might arise in that, after struggling for their own national status since their respective mid-nineteenth-century national revivals, both Czechs and Slovaks in the latter half of the twentieth century considered Breuilly's first trait, (a) that 'there exists a nation with an explicit character' – and some would argue (b) that 'the interests of this nation usually take priority over all other interests' – to be axiomatic. Breuilly insists that his criteria be applied strongly, however, and in that case we should accept as 'nationalist' only those statements which 'make the idea of a peculiar nation explicit; make this assertion the foundation of all political claims; and which are the central ideological statements deployed by a political movement or organisation' (Breuilly (1993), p. 3). Although this may seem somewhat extreme – there are many politicians in Europe, after all, who are self-evidently nationalistic, but who still fail to pin every assertion explicitly to their nationalist cause – these guidelines are still basically helpful. We should at least be wary of reading nationalism into acts that no-one is actually claiming for a nationalist cause.
[18] Disbarred under the Communist regime for criticising the government while defending religious dissidents in criminal trials, Čarnogurský was subsequently imprisoned for his own dissident activities, see Stein (1997), p. 15.
[19] See Shari Cohen's excellent *Politics Without a Past: The Absence of History in Post-Communist Nationalism* (1999).
[20] See Skilling and Wilson (1991), p. 25.
[21] This replaced the Communist regime until free general elections could be held.
[22] Zora Bútorová, 'A Deliberate 'Yes' to the Dissolution of the CSFR? The Image of the Parties and the Split of Czecho-Slovakia in the Eyes of the Slovak Population', in *Czech Sociological Review*, Volume 1, Spring 1, Prague, Academy of Sciences, 1993, p. 65.
[23] Quashing aspiring L'udáks within the Christian Democratic Movement was no easy matter for its leader, Ján Čarnogurský. His father, Pavol Čarnogurský, had been a member of parliament in the wartime Slovak state and he was one of the first in the post-1989 period to call for rehabilitating that state – see Cohen (1997).
[24] Similarly the SNP leader Jozef Prokeš had gone from party to party in 1990 attempting to join their candidate lists; he was turned down by the Public Against Violence before forming the SNP (ibid.).
[25] ibid.
[26] Throughout the period the Toronto-based World Congress of Slovaks remained vocally and militantly nationalistic.
[27] See Kusý (1995), p. 143.
[28] For an account of this see Cohen (1997).
[29] Kirschbaum (1995), p. 255.
[30] See Kusý (1995), p. 143.
[31] *Mladá Fronta dnes* 27 August 1990, pp. 1–2.
[32] It may be noted that scarcely 6,000 Jews remained in the entire federation following the Holocaust and Communist repressions.
[33] See Kusý (1995), ibid.
[34] In Bútorová, op. cit., p. 60.
[35] See Kusý (1995) – also confirmed by monthly polls carried out by the Association for Independent Social Analysis (AISA).
[36] For an account of the language dispute see Chapter 3.
[37] Breuilly (1993), p. 322.
[38] See Marian Timoracký, 'Verejná mienka o česko-slovenských vzťahoch', in Fedor Gál (ed), *Dnešni krize česko-slovenských vztahů* (Prague: Sociologické Nakladestelství SLON, 1992), p. 89.
[39] By 'populist' I mean parties which try to mobilise the entire electorate by convincing them that they, above all other parties, care most about the ordinary person. Populism is moralistic rather than programmatic, loosely organised and ill-disciplined; a movement rather than a party, with a loose, anti-intellectual and anti-'establishment' 'ideology'. See Wiles (1969).

[40] A mere 2,000 attended the parallel Initiative for a Common State demonstration, also in Bratislava, *Rudé právo* 25 September 1991.

[41] In June 1992, Slovak opinion was divided as follows: for a unitary state, 11 per cent; for a federation, 26 per cent; for a Lands-based republic, 6 per cent; for a confederation, 31 per cent; for independent states, 18 per cent (the highest since the revolution); and finally, those not knowing, 8 per cent. Back in December 1991 the figures had been 17 per cent for a unitary state, 31 per cent for a federation, 4 per cent for a Lands-based republic, 30 per cent for a confederation, 11 per cent for independence and 7 per cent undecided (public opinion poll from IVVM (Institute for Public Opinion Research)).

[42] The Slovak National Party actually consistently opposed the referendum option, knowing that it would guarantee defeat for the nationalists in any public consultation on the issue.

[43] Bútorová, op. cit., p. 61.

[44] In June 1992, Czech opinion was divided as follows: 29 per cent for a unitary state; 28 per cent for a federation; 21 per cent for a Lands-based republic; 5 per cent for a confederation; 13 per cent for independence, and 4 per cent undecided. Back in December 1991 the figures had been 36 per cent for a unitary state – the moderation of this view over a mere six months is surely striking; 27 per cent in favour of federation; 24 per cent in favour of a Lands-based republic; 4 per cent for confederation; 6 per cent for independence, and 3 per cent undecided (IVVM opinion poll).

[45] Kostelecky (1995), p. 87.

[46] IVVM polls suggested that up to December 1991 only a small minority fluctuating between 9 and 18 per cent in either republic supported the division of the state (IVVM 31 January 1992).

[47] As garnered from Czech and Slovak newspaper reports of the time.

[48] *Sociologické Aktuality* 5/1992

[49] *Zěmědělské noviny* 13 May 1992, p. 3.

[50] Though an important part of their rising political popularity through 1991 the CDP left the issue of the 'vetting' of former Communists to their electoral allies, the Christian Democratic Party.

[51] *Lidové noviny* 14 May 1992, p. 6.

[52] Interview 3 April 1992, quoted in Václav Klaus's *Rok málo či mnoho v dějinách země* (Prague: Repro-Media, 1993) (collected essays and speeches from 1992), p. 9.

[53] *Mladá Fronta dnes* 3 April 1992, p. 2.

[54] Article, *Zítra budou volby*, 4 June 1992, quoted in *Rok málo*, p. 23.

[55] *Lidové noviny* 29 May 1992, p. 8.

[56] Published 5 May 1992 and quoted in *Rok málo*, p. 17.

[57] *Mladá Fronta dnes* 4 June 1992.

[58] *Lidové noviny* 14 May 1992, p. 6. A remarkable comment given that the vast majority of MDS supporters preferred a common state, that the MDS was avowedly pro-common state in its electoral pronouncements and that Mečiar was offering the Slovak electorate a referendum on the state's future.

[59] *Telegraf* 2 June 1992.

[60] Marek Boguszak comments and polls in *Mladá Fronta dnes* 22 May 1992. Whereas only 13 per cent among those with basic education supported the Civic Democratic Party, among highly qualified specialists their support reached 45 per cent and among private owners and businessmen, some 35 per cent (ibid.). The results were from 1,363 respondents between 1 and 9 April 1992. Clearly the Civic Democratic Party managed to mobilise the support of a significant proportion of the technocratic elite, the frustrated class considered among the most potentially destabilising forces within stagnating Communist regimes.

[61] *Prostor* 12 May 1992, p. 2.

[62] ibid.

[63] The CM's Pavel Rychetský in *Hospodářské noviny* 29 April 1991, p. 1.

[64] Manifesto; *Co Chceme* (What We Want).

[65] *Sociologické aktuality* 5/1992.

[66] In *Co chceme*.

[67] *Respekt* 21 May 1992.

[68] Interview with Jana Šmídová in *Lidové noviny* 30 April 1992, p. 9.

[69] It is interesting to note that 53 per cent of Republican support came from the under-34s, *Lidové noviny* 29 May 1992.

[70] *Mladá Fronta dnes* 4 June 1992.

[71] The Electoral Commission recognised the group as constituting a political movement as opposed to a 'coalition', to

which a higher parliamentary threshold would have applied.

[72] See Kostelecky (1995), p. 81.

[73] Bútorová, op. cit., p. 8.

[74] This phenomenon was described by two of Slovakia's most well-known liberal sociologists as 'confusion and cognitive helplessness, evident in persistent misconceptions on issues related to the constitutional arrangement' – see Bútorová and Bútora (1995), p. 118. The same authors put it down to 'brainwashing' that Slovaks 'failed to appreciate that economic prosperity could best be achieved through the existing economic reform programme'. The Czech media likewise represented the Slovak electorate as fatally mesmerised by Meciar's populism. One campaign manager claimed that 'in a political campaign in Slovakia we would work with emotion . . . Slovakia needs personality, it needs its Janošik' (chief of Mark/BBDO marketing agency quoted in *Český deník* 28.5.1992). In fact a pre-election AISA poll showed that 64 per cent of Czechs surveyed would prefer to vote for personalities rather than parties, as against 54 per cent in Slovakia (*Mladá Fronta dnes* 13 May 1992, p. 14).

[75] *Rudé právo* 27 May 1992, p. 2.

[76] Where Klaus rejected the economic mafia as a hangover of communist practice the MDS's Milan Kňažko located them as at the heart of the privatisation process, which he depicted as 'the cheap selling off of national property to foreigners and the concentration of ownership in the hands of a narrow group' (ibid.).

[77] *Mladá Fronta dnes* 8 April 1992, p. 2.

[78] ibid.

[79] See chronology in *Czech Sociological Review*, p. 136.

[80] Sociologically, there were parallels in Civic Democratic Party and Movement for a Democratic Slovakia support. The Movement for a Democratic Slovakia support was strongest not only among those threatened by reform – the lowest qualified and high-school-educated population – but also among highly qualified specialists, where support reached beyond 50 per cent (data from AISA survey conducted by Marek Buguszak 1–9 April from a sample of 1,363: *Mladá Fronta* 22 May 1992). Again the 'technocratic elite' constituted an important body of support. Their support could rationally follow their expectation of professional benefits arising from a party that championed the Slovak economy without, so it could yet seem, rejecting links to the Czech Republic.

[81] Bútorová, op. cit., pp. 63–5.

[82] *Lidové noviny* 21 May 1992.

[83] Zora Bútorová, ibid.

[84] *Hospodářské noviny* 1 July 1992.

[85] ibid.

[86] A bi-national federation, where the 'other' nation is always the opposition, is of course particularly prone to such inferences.

CHAPTER 3

[1] Vile (1982), p. 222.

[2] See Leff (1997), p. 82.

[3] For a subtle and illuminating exploration, see Bunce (1999).

[4] See Offe (1995), p. 18.

[5] As it transpired, however, the media in both republics would tend only to report or to parrot the positions of the political parties, thus failing to assert any kind of independent argument or campaign for alternative state arrangements. The separateness of the media in the two republics, moreover, mirrored that of the political systems, reinforcing the tendency for insular and self-referential discussion.

[6] Radio Free Europe, *Report on Eastern Europe*, 6 April 1990, p. 7.

[7] Charter 77, the Czechoslovak Helsinki Assembly, the PEN (writers) Club, the Movement for Civic Freedom, the Committee for the Defence of the Unjustly Persecuted (VONS) and the independent Student Association, plus the creative unions, to name but a few, not to mention normal citizens.

[8] See Skilling and Wilson (1991), p. 148.

[9] *Svobodné slovo* 12 March 1990.

[10] See Kusín (1971), p. 99.

[11] See Peter Martin in *Report on Eastern Europe*, Radio Free Europe, 15 June 1990.

[12] The breakaway Democratic Initiative criticised the Forum's 'leftist bias' – an obvious slander against a movement whose only definite belief was in pluralism!

[13] Radio Free Europe, Report on Eastern Europe, 19 April 1991, pp. 9–10.

[14] The Finance Minister had successfully stolen the initiative from the earlier-formed and more intellectual right of the Civic Democratic Alliance (CDA).

[15] Other deputies chose between remaining independent or entering one of the various smaller groups which had left the Forum in January. On 2 April, Czechoslovak Social Democracy, which had failed to win representation in June 1990, announced that six deputies had joined, or, rather, created its ranks.

[16] See Wightman (1991), p. 67.

[17] *Mladá Fronta dnes* 7 January 1991.

[18] See Klaus von Beyme (1993), p. 423.

[19] Kipke and Vodička (1993), p. 48.

[20] See Chapter 5.

[21] *'Gen'* (television programme) interview with Václav Klaus (Juraje Jakubiska). Volume 1 of collected interviews edited by Martin Komárek (Prague: Hajek, AS, 1994), p. 13.

[22] M. Tuček and P. Manek, *Statistical and Survey Data* (Prague: Academy of Sciences of the Czech Republic, September 1993), p. 28.

[23] See Michal Kudernatsch's 'What type of capitalism is expected in the Czech Republic', in *Czech Sociological Review*, Volume 1, Spring 1 (Prague: Academy of Sciences of the Czech Republic, 1993), p. 115.

[24] From Václav Klaus's 'Proč jsem optimista', which first appeared in *Literární noviny* 26 November 1990.

[25] As the Polish dissident Adam Michnik observed, 'One can be astonished at the spectacle of these prudent people with clean hands accusing those who participated in the Prague Spring and in the democratic opposition of having maintained links with communism . . .' (from 'An Embarrassing Anniversary', *New York Review of Books*, 10 June 1993).

[26] Kundera wrote of 1968 that 'instead of the standard pattern of one group of people (a class, a nation) rising up against another, all the people (an entire generation) revolted against their own youth. Their goal was to recapture and tame the deed they had created, and they almost succeeded' (*The Book of Laughter and Forgetting* (London: Penguin Books, 1987), pp. 13-14).

[27] A foreign correspondent, Dienstbier was expelled from the Party in 1969 and fired after participating in anti-occupation broadcasts. From 1970 he worked predominantly as a stoker, was among the first signatories and spokesmen of Charter 77, and was imprisoned between 1979 and 1982.

[28] See Garton-Ash (1995), p. 36.

[29] *Mladá Fronta dnes* 30 January 1991.

[30] Having lost a third of its members, the Party seemed willing only to 'federalise' itself by establishing a Communist Party of Bohemia and Moravia to complement that of Slovakia (an action the Slovaks called for in 1968 to signal some autonomy of the Slovak Party).

[31] The government nevertheless announced that all party property would be confiscated as of 1 June 1990.

[32] The apparent death of a student from a police beating. This event has been much debated since with a theory emerging since that the body was actually that of a secret serviceman, playing dead, in aid of a conspiracy by Communist reformers to encourage demonstrations against the hardliners, thus allowing the reformers to seize power! In the event, the 'death' sparked the mass demonstrations of the November revolution.

[33] Exposing Communist infiltration in the new system was the clearest way for the Czech press, un-purged and still under the old titles of Youth Front and Red Truth etc., to rehabilitate themselves as editorially independent. Eager for conspiracy, new newspapers, notably *Respekt*, endeavoured to push de-bolshevisation to the fore. Having set out to 'vet' public life the press fastened onto personalities with greater rigour than onto policy.

[34] *Mladá Fronta dnes* 26 February 1991.

[35] Rudolf Kučera's 'Proč potřebujeme debolševizaci', in *Komentáře, Politické analýzy z let 1990-1992*, (Prague: ISE, 1992), p. 43.

[36] *Mladá Fronta dnes* 10 January 1991.

[37] *Občanský děnik* 5 February 1991.

[38] See Jonathan Stein and Susan Scarrow's excellent 'The Politics of Retrospective Justice in Germany and the Czech Republic' (1994), p. 25.

[39] *Mladá Fronta dnes* 5 October 1991.

[40] T. Marek, in *Mladá Fronta dnes* 4 September 1991, p. 2.

[41] It would be wrong to characterise those against the lustration law as the former dissidents *en bloc* (many of them, notably Václav Benda, were at the fore of the most impassioned called for legalised disqualification of past collaborators). The important distinction was between those strict liberal dissidents alarmed by the potentially abusive sweep of the law, and those, like Havel, who opted for an anti-Communist line, either out of conviction or from the perception that the government had yet to convince the public of its wholehearted rejection of past practices.

[42] Attended by the KAN, the Liberal Democratic Party, the Civic Democratic Alliance, the Club of the Democratic Right Wing, the Republic Union, and, notably, the right-oriented Prague Civic Forum Council.

[43] *Mladá Fronta dnes* 19 February 1991, p. 2.

[44] See Michnik, op. cit., p. 20.

[45] See Leff (1997), p. 85.

[46] See Jaroslav Veis in the *East European Reporter* 5 May 1992, p. 12.

[47] *Literární noviny* 26 November 1990.

[48] Quoted in Stein and Scarrow (1994), p. 25.

[49] Public anxiety had been fuelled by the attempted *coup d'état* in the Soviet Union in August 1991, following which the CDP had advertised for the publication of lists of collaborators and had acted as the sponsor of the new lustration bill (*Mladá Fronta dnes* 22 August 1991, p. 2).

[50] As early as November 1990 Klaus had argued that the 'forces which are against economic reform are identical with those which are against the formation of a political party' (*Lidové noviny* 2 November 1990).

[51] Having made much of its membership rules excluding ex-Communists the Civic Democratic Alliance proceeded to make a few exceptions for popular ministers, e.g. Vladimír Dlouhý.

[52] *Mladá Fronta dnes* 3 May 1991, pp. 1–2.

[53] See Stein and Scarrow (1994), p. 26.

[54] Author's interview with Václav Žák, former Member of Parliament for Civic Forum, 14 June 1995.

[55] *Rudé právo* 8 December 1990.

[56] Szomolanyí (1994), p. 63.

[57] Miháliková (1994), pp. 54–5.

[58] The repressive conditions of post-invasion 'normalisation' (1968–89), particularly Communist Party purges, had been more moderate in Slovakia. Artistic and intellectual circles were less violently harassed and consequently dissident groups were small and isolated both from the public and from one another, amounting only to 'islands of positive deviation' (ibid., p. 66).

[59] 'Revival' (*Obroda* in Slovak) was founded in February 1989 under the name 'O'. This political movement extolled democratic socialism and the principles of the Prague Spring and was legalised in November 1989.

[60] Radio Free Europe, *Report on Eastern Europe*, 10 October 1992.

[61] The Democratic Party, offspring of the Slovak Freedom Party, a former member of the 'National Front'. The DP stressed allegiance not only to democratic values but to a strong federal Czechoslovakia. It was led by Martin Kvetko, a returned exile and former leading member of the pre-Communist DP.

[62] At its founding convention at Nitra on 17 February 1990 the Christian Democratic Movement had formed around three theses; an 'Erhard-type' social market economy; two [European Community] stars and seats [Czech and Slovak]; and thirdly, if more implicitly, that the Christian Democratic Movement would gain the support of the 70 per cent of the Slovak population considering itself Catholic. The first two clearly addressed Slovak anxieties about national and economic conditions more explicitly than did the Public Against Violence, a point not lost on Vladimír Mečiar. Its third thesis, linking support with attitudes to the church, proved counterproductive. Slovak society had clearly begun to differentiate church and state since 1945.

[63] P. Zajac, 'Pät' Rokov Po', a series appearing in the newspaper *Domino*.

[64] See Szomolányi (1994), p. 71. The Communist Party meanwhile re-launched itself under the revitalising leadership of Peter Weiss. A member of the young Communist intelligentsia which had genuinely intimidated the Party before November '89, Weiss was determined to drag the Party into line with the

progressive Communist and social democratic parties of Western Europe. In contrast to the Czechs, the Slovak Communists also renamed themselves after the June 1990 elections. Under the new title the Party of the Democratic Left (PDL) required re-registration of its membership in the hope that this might further alienate the die-hards of the old regime. As will be remembered from the previous chapter, the Slovak National Party (SNP) also emerged just before the June election.

65 Šimečka (1991).

66 *Mladá Fronta dnes* 1 March 1991.

67 *Lidové demokracie* 4 March 1991.

68 *Rudé právo* 5 March 1991.

69 A ludicrous claim, given Gál's keen desire to avoid power beyond the Public Against Violence. The sinister aspect of Meciar's tactic is the spite he reserved for the Jewish Gál and the effect this had on mobilising deep-rooted Slovak anti-Semitism. In January 1993, 53 per cent of a representative sample claimed there was 'excessive influence of Jews on economic and social life': Zora Bútorová (ed), 'Current Problems of Slovakia after the Split of the CSFR', *Report on the Sociological Survey*, (Bratislava: Centre for Social Analysis, 1993), p. 9.

70 *Mladá Fronta dnes* 6 March 1991, pp. 1–2.

71 *Rudé právo* 7 March 1991.

72 *Mladá Fronta dnes* 8 March 1991, p. 4.

73 *Mladá Fronta dnes* 12 March 1991.

74 ibid.

75 *Pravda, Lidové noviny* 20 April 1991.

76 Jičíncský (1993), p. 75.

77 Szomolányi (1994), p. 72.

78 These 600,000 Hungarians constituted roughly 11 per cent of the Slovak population in 1989: see Leff (1997), p. 9.

79 Author's interview with Fedor Gál, former Chairman of the PAV, 4 April 1995.

80 *Svobodné slovo* 7 October 1990, p. 1.

81 *Lidové noviny* 29 October 1990.

82 In Kirschbaum (1995), p. 256.

83 *Svobodné slovo* 20 August 1990, pp. 1, 3.

84 *Svobodné slovo* 7 August 1990, pp. 1, 2.

85 *Svobodné slovo* 5 November 1990.

86 Though he envisaged Slovakia entering the European Union in the year 2000 as an independent state, Čarnogurský evidently feared damaging fragile rapprochement

with the West by a fractious separation. Čarnogurský's vagueness over exact constitutional conditions (despite being a lawyer) often elicited bewilderment from those involved in negotiations, he was, however, highly constrained by two Christian Democratic Movement factions, which threatened to come apart over economic policy and the national issue.

87 *Zemědělské noviny* 29 November 1990.

88 *Zemědělské noviny* 3 December 1990.

89 *Lidové noviny* 13 December 1990. Czech commentary in the same, major right-wing daily, however, ran as follows: in his editorial, J. Hanák argued that 'This is a battlefield campaign waged by the Slovak political representation against the "remainder" of the Czechoslovak Republic. Eighty-three per cent of the citizenry in this country wish to live in a common state. But the gentlemen from the Danube [Bratislava] are willing to tear this common state asunder in order to achieve their goals ... If the irrational and prestigious demands continue to be stoked over this burner, then one cannot consider a dramatic development impossible ... [and in an increasingly conspiratorial twist, he continued] The federal government could fall ... it is very probable that premier Mečiar will no longer be premier. Because the representatives of the powers that be, who have so far remained hidden behind him and for whom he has so unscrupulously elbowed out some room, will no longer have any need of him.' (*Lidové noviny* 10 December 1990).

90 IVVM opinion poll in *Mladá Fronta dnes* 25 January 1991, p. 2.

91 This impression was reinforced when the Slovak National Party took up Carnogursky's proposal suggesting the new constitution be seen as preparatory to the constitution of a sovereign state, able, of its own will, to link up with other states.

92 *Zemědělské noviny* 11 March 1991, pp. 1–2.

93 Zora Bútorová, 'A Deliberate "Yes" to the Dissolution of the CSFR?' in *Czech Sociological Review*, Volume 1, Spring 1 (Prague: Academy of Sciences of the Czech Republic, 1993), p. 66.

94 *Práce* 8 May 1991, p. 2.

95 *Práce* 13 June 1991, p. 3.

96 *Mladá Fronta dnes* 15 June 1991.

[97] M. Bohus, 14 August 1991, quoted in Kirschbaum (1995), p. 260.

[98] *Mladá Fronta dnes* 18 June 1991.

[99] *Zemědelské noviny* 2 July 1991, p. 1.

[100] Čarnogurský had outraged Czech opinion in September by asking Foreign Minister Dienstbier to change the preamble to the imminent Czechoslovak–German treaty to remove the statement of the legal continuity of the Czechoslovak state from 1918. While he deplored the politics of the clerico-fascist Slovak state, Carnogursky proposed its existence be acknowledged in deference to the nationals oppressed under Communism (*Pravda* 17.9.1991, pp. 1, 2). This appeal also condemned the CDM in the eyes of a Slovak electorate frustrated by the poor progress of talks and now widely suspicious of the Movement's potential, as the party of the clerical right wing, to re-introduce totalitarianism; see Zora Bútorová's 'A Deliberate "Yes"?', p. 68.

[101] Szomolányi (1994), p. 74.

[102] ibid., p. 75.

[103] Čarnogurský's was a religiously informed belief in the Slovak nation as repository of Slavic purity, a potential core for a new Christian Europe. In a spirit akin to that of the 19th-century pan-Slavists he rightly admitted: 'I shall give an argument which might not be well received in the Prague intellectual milieu: The Apocalypse of St John says that on the day of judgement nations will be admitted to heaven. Not therefore citizens, the Czech and Slovak Federal Republic, the European Community, or other man-made units' (*Lidové noviny* 3 June 1991, p. 16). Petr Pithart estimated correctly that Čarnogurský wanted to save his nation from the marasmus of consumerist, godless Western European teaching; 'the marasmus of the secularised modern society that Czechs appear to wish to be' (in *Zemědelské noviny* 14 August 1991).

[104] Though the two sides essentially acted *en bloc* through the autumn it was increasingly obvious that Čarnogurský was managing only through an unsustainable level of concession-giving. After Klepáč's supporters voted against the draft constitutional agreement in the Slovak National Council vote of the 13 February 1992 Čarnogurský presented them with an ultimatum; conform or leave. Thus on 7 March the two factions announced their separate candidacies for June 1992. Eleven of the Christian Democratic Movement's 31 deputies in the Slovak National Council defected to the Slovak Christian Democratic Movement, five from the 25 federal deputies.

[105] An independent since resigning from the Public Against Violence in July 1991, Dubček had been expected to follow up his frequent and controversial endorsement of Mečiar by joining the ranks of the Movement for a Democratic Slovakia. Had he joined the MDS he would have been used as a figurehead. Moreover, he opposed Mečiar's manipulation of the national question. After lustration it was clear that no Czech party of the centre/right would nominate him, thus ruling him out of a federal position.

[106] Jan Obrman's 'Dubček Joins the Social Democrats in Slovakia', *Radio Free Europe* 3 March 1992.

[107] This may have originated from the semantic difficulties arising from the existence of two Slovak words for sovereignty: *zvrchovanost'* and *suverenita*, which have the same meaning in a dictionary. Their meanings diverged during the constitutional debate, with the first referring to the sovereignty of the nation in metaphysical terms. The second meaning is sovereignty as understood in international legal terms; see Kirschbaum (1995), p. 263.

[108] *Lidové noviny* 14 September 1991.

[109] *Rudé právo* 25 September 1991.

[110] *Zemědelské noviny* 6 February 1992.

[111] Jan Obrman, Radio Free Europe 10 April 1992.

[112] *Národná obroda* 1 April 1992.

[113] ibid.

[114] *Lidové noviny* 31 March 1992.

[115] In a later interview with *Mladá Fronta dnes* Klaus cited three major steps toward the separation: The meetings of Lnáře in April 1990, when the Czech and Slovak Governments began to discuss future relations, fatally bypassing the federal authorities. Secondly, the Trenčianské Talks in August 1990, when an overpressured Federal Government carrying 'all the burdens of social and economic transformation' again lost the initiative. The third moment, Klaus argued,

was in the 'failure of the PAV'. 'Public Against Violence and later the Civic Democratic Union did not manage to produce personalities capable of addressing Slovak citizens, to move the Slovak scene in a certain direction. Thus PAV vacated a space for something quite different . . .' He made no judgement about the causes of PAV's subsequent electoral failure (*Mladá Fronta dnes* 3 July 1992, p. 7).

[116] See Chapter 2.

[117] Many of Mečiar's Slovak supporters could vote for him believing themselves to have protested against 'Pragocentrism' at the same time as expressing their desire to maintain a common state. See Vodička (1993), p. 92. Some 50 per cent of MDS supporters had apparently voted for the Public Against Violence in the previous election in June 1990 – a clearly pro-federal group; see Bohumil Jungmann's *Volby '92* (Prague: Institute for Public Opinion Research, 1993), p. 69.

[118] Quoted in Wolchik (1994), p. 171.

[119] IVVM opinion poll in *Lidové noviny* 29 July 1992, p. 3.

[120] Kirchheimer's thoughts on the development of catch-all parties are oddly resonant of the strategies adopted by the post-Communist successors: 'the mass integration party . . . is transforming itself into a catch-all people's party. Abandoning attempts at the intellectual and moral encadrement of the masses, it is turning more fully to the electoral scene, trying to exchange effectiveness in depth for a wider audience and more immediate electoral success'. See Kirchheimer (1990), p. 52.

[121] Further evidence of the underdeveloped state of the political scene in both republics is evident in the fact that the centre/right parties – the Civic Movement, the Civic Democratic Alliance, and Civic Democratic Party in the Czech Republic, and the Democratic Party and Civic Democratic Union in Slovakia – competed over more or less identical ideological space, thus effectively splitting the right-wing vote. All (excepting the victorious CDP), with some predictability, failed even to enter the Federal Assembly.

[122] See Olson (1994), p. 112.

[123] See Sewell (1992) and Swidler (1986).

[124] See Gamson (1992), pp. 7–8.

CHAPTER 4

[1] Constitutional Act 143/1968 stated that the two-chamber (bicameral) federal parliament, the supreme legislative body of the state, would become a three-chamber (tricameral) parliament when considering constitutional legislation, which would have to pass by a three-fifths majority in both the Chamber of the People and the now separated Chambers of the Nations. Since the House of the People had 150 deputies and the House of the Nations 75 deputies in each of the Czech and Slovak sections, some 30 deputies – or one-tenth of the total number of deputies – were enough to block a constitutional law. Significant bi-national consensus was thus essential to pass constitutional legislation; see Žák (1995), p. 254.

[2] Proportional representation was supposed to be an important consociational aspect of the state but of course it was merely a carry-over from the First Republic – not a consociational state.

[3] See Lijphart (1992), p. 217.

[4] It is hard to resist the thought that if this had been a discussion of Northern Ireland in 1974 Lijphart would hardly have dared to dive in and flatly infer the depth of ethnic consensus from institutional configurations – as he does here. It is deeply unfair to single out Lijphart, however; a lot of critical writing in the early 1990s assumed that East European states had wiped their slates clean in 1989.

[5] The copy of the 'collected laws' from 1968 including this veto amendment that I hunted down in Prague's Charles University library was uncut, i.e. it had not been read in almost thirty years.

[6] O'Leary and McGarry argue that 'the moment rival elites believe that the benefits of war exceed the costs of peace a consociational system is doomed' (McGarry and O'Leary (1993), p. 37).

[7] See McGarry and O'Leary (1993), p. 37. Note also Donald Horowitz's judgement that consociationalism might only function in moderately rather than deeply divided societies; see Horowitz (1985), pp. 571–2. The extremely low levels of mutual national animosity at the mass level in Czechoslovakia are thus again a striking fact.

8 See Arato (1993), p. 159.
9 See Stephen Holmes (1993) or Jose Maria Maravall (1994). 'Federalism', it has been noted, 'is concerned simultaneously with the diffusion of political power in the name of liberty and its concentration on behalf of unity or energetic government': Elazar (1987), p. 33.
10 Arato (1993), p. 155.
11 Bútora (1994), pp. 324–8.
12 ibid., p. 327.
13 *Lidová demokracie* 13 January 1990, pp. 1–3.
14 New Year's Speech, reported in *Rudé právo* 2 January 1990, pp. 1–3.
15 Havel was dismayed at the Assembly's rejection of his proposal and he attacked the Assembly publicly on 25 February; see Žák (1995), p. 251. This continuation of his tribune-like authority soured the relations between Havel and many parliamentary deputies.
16 *Svobodné slovo* 31 March 1990, pp. 1–3. The Slovak National Council's decision to ban broadcast coverage of the demonstration invited accusations of censorship: ibid., 3 April 1990. The following day the Czech and Slovak premiers broadcast strikingly contradictory statements: Czech premier Pithart noted that 'if the arguments and will of the Slovak nation are diverging from the joint road . . . we have no other option than to accept that will calmly'. Slovak premier Milan Čič meanwhile reassuringly stated that 'the Slovak National Council, Slovak government, Public Against Violence and the absolute majority of political parties and movements and citizens are unequivocally supportive of the principle of co-existence . . . in the common federation', rejecting the recent upheaval as rooted in 'outworn Czechoslovakism and, on the other side, in separatist extremes': *Svobodné slovo* 4 April 1990, pp. 1–3.
17 Kusý, a long-standing member of Charter 77, was now a PAV deputy and an adviser to President Havel.
18 *Lidové noviny*, 24 March 1990.
19 See Kirschbaum (1995), p. 255.
20 *Rudé právo* 12 April 1990.
21 An editorial appeared in *Lidové noviny* four days after Kusý's piece: 'In the Czech Republic, we feel that the strict Slovak requirement for a dividing hyphen in the name of the Republic is tactless and crude. Tactless because the last time the hyphen appeared was during the tragic post-Munich period, and it will be forever connected to those days. Crude because it foists upon us – why and by what right? – a nonexistent name for the Czech Republic: Cesko or cesko, the devil take it, it always turns out to be a humiliating 'tschechie' [i.e. Germanised] ... The last time that the dividing hyphen appeared, Slovakia lost its entire southern border and the town of Košice': *Lidové noviny* 28 April 1990.
22 *Lidové noviny* 12 April 1990.
23 Few significant changes were made before June 1990 following the removal of Party rule clauses (November 1989). Powers over agriculture, metallurgy and local government were formally devolved to the National Councils in July and, on the insistence of Slovak deputies, it was agreed to establish commissions with a view to further transfers by January 1991.
24 Council report, 2–3 July 1990, p. 36, quoted in Žák (1995), p. 252.
25 ibid., p.255. Prior to the meeting neither the participants nor the likely agenda were disclosed to the public.
26 A fact later acknowledged by Czech premier Pithart (1995), p. 209.
27 Viewpoint of the Democratic Right-wing Group at the ninth meeting of the Czech National Council, 28–29 November 1990.
28 See Elazar (1987), pp. 34–5.
29 From *Svobodné slovo* 10 August 1990, p. 1. At Lnáře in April 1990 the two republican governments had taken the remarkable decision that the simplest way to resolve all disputes over who subsidised whom was for each republic to live off the taxes collected on its own territory respectively. The federation would receive, from the republics, its necessary expenses (see Žák (1995), p. 251). Given the current tax and budgetary arrangements the two governments had effectively proposed removing the tax-gathering and coordinating powers of the federation. Václav Klaus, following his strengthened position after the June election, returned the agenda directly to this issue, aware that if legislated, the Lnáře agreement and the principles underpinning it would emasculate federal powers and authority over reform. To the Federal Assembly he

argued 'the national governments are working towards the dissolution of the federation, because without an economic centre and autonomy of revenues in all three budgets, it is impossible to imagine a unified economy' (ibid., p. 252). At Trenčianské Teplice the principle of independent budgets at the Czech, Slovak, and federal levels was agreed – see Chapter 7 for detail. This issue nevertheless became a parallel, but critical, element in what was to become a conflict set out like a musical canon: a piece in which the different parts take up the same themes successively.

[30] What this accusation ignored, moreover, was the chronic post-revolutionary tendency for ministries at *all* levels – in both republics and at the federal level – to compete quite single-mindedly over jurisdictions, not in a formal way, but by a process of creating *fait accompli* and through a sheer incapacity or refusal to coordinate; it was hard to tell which, but certainly coordination was hopeless. Thus, foreign embassies attempting to find partners for aid projects would discover three alternative policies for the Czech, Slovak and federal ministries respectively, with all ministries claiming to have unique jurisdiction over areas that formally were either at the republican or federal level. This process of empire building was hardly surprising but it added a further element of chaos to the ongoing debate about policy jurisdictions.

[31] The results of Trenčianské Teplice were in fact fully rejected at a meeting of ten minor Slovak parties convened by the separatist Slovak National Party and Slovak Independence Party (*Lidové demokracie* 15 August 1990).

[32] *Svobodné slovo* and *Zemědělské noviny* 14 August 1990.

[33] CTK 11 August 1990.

[34] *Svobodné slovo, Mladá Fronta dnes* 5 September 1990.

[35] Federal non-centralisation – or so-called 'symmetrical federalism' – it should be noted, has been conceptualised more conventionally 'as a matrix of governments, with powers so distributed that the rank order of the several governments is not fixed'. See Elazar (1987), p. 37.

[36] *Lidové noviny, Rude pravo* 2 November 1990.

[37] *Lidové noviny* 17 August 1990, p. 8.

[38] *Rudé právo* 29 October 1990.

[39] On the evening of 12 November Čalfa spoke on state television and laid down a more forthright statement of appropriate future federal powers. Amongst other things, he argued that the federation had to have, as a matter of minimal necessity, a unified international policy and it must ensure its internal security; it should have a single currency, a single monetary system and a unified system of taxes, finance, prices and customs policies, including the issue of united regulatory price measures; the federation had to be able to finance state administration, defence and other federal authorities and create financial reserves; it must have a unified concept of economic strategy and of external economic relations; it must have a unified power generation policy and be economically responsible for its network-creating infrastructures, including crude oil and gas pipelines. Finally, he declared 'we cannot imagine a Federal state without basic legislative competence for affairs which have an immediate impact on the rights liberties and position of its citizens' (*Svobodné slovo* 13 November 1990, pp. 1–4). Čalfa's arrogation of total responsibility for the welfare of 'the people' directly contradicted the basic federal principle that federations are founded upon dispersed majorities, and that the two planes of federal power, central and non-centralised (republican), are each possessed equally of such powers as have been delegated and guaranteed to them by 'the people'.

[40] Competences Law quoted in *Svobodné slovo* 21 December 1990, p. 20.

[41] The Slovak National Council approved the draft on the 19th.

[42] Klaus joined Dlouhý in condemning Slovak actions, concluding that 'These attempts spring above all from the activity of some Slovak Government representatives who demagogically confuse the failings of the surviving centralist system with the indispensable unifying role of Federal bodies' (*Svobodné slovo, Rudé právo* 8 December 1990).

[43] *Zemědělské noviny, Občanský deník* 28 November 1990.

[44] During the speech Havel drew deputies' attention to a recent opinion poll

showing that 70 per cent of respondents in Slovakia and 74 per cent in the Czech Republic considered the possible division of the state as an indulgence of politicians which would not reflect the interests of ordinary people.

[45] Mečiar responded by pointing out that 'in Bohemia there exist quite real and strong currents which think in the same way' (*Svobodné slovo, Lidové noviny* and *Občanský deník* 12 December 1990).

[46] *Svobodné slovo, Mladá Fronta dnes, Práce* 11 December 1990.

[47] See Žák (1995), p. 258.

[48] ibid.

[49] ČTK 2 January 1991.

[50] See Žák (1995), p. 258.

[51] One disputed clause was that on the Rights of Nationalities, which appeared inconsistent with the Slovak Language Law passed in October. The failure to approve more amendments protecting minorities provoked members of the Hungarian party, Coexistence (Együttélés), and the Christian Democratic Movement to walk out before the final vote (*Lidové noviny* 10 January 1991).

[52] The Federal Assembly subsequently created the constitutional court, and in July 1991 established the instrument of a referendum. The bill on referenda was passed at the second attempt, after the Slovak National Party and some Christian Democratic Movement deputies were persuaded to approve. The law stipulated that referenda could be declared in the solving of basic questions and forms of the state system, and when one of the republics proposed to secede from the federation. The referendum would be declared by the president at the proposal of the Federal Assembly if seconded by the National Councils. The results of the referendum were valid if voted for by more than 50 per cent of those entitled to vote in each of the republics (*Svobodné slovo, Mladá Fronta dnes* 19 July 1991). Of significance in 1992 was the stipulation that a referendum could not be declared in the five-month period before a general election.

[53] *Mladá Fronta dnes* 31 January 1991, pp. 1–2.

[54] *Mladá Fronta dnes* 5 February 1991.

[55] *Svobodné slovo* 6 March 1991, pp. 1–4.

[56] *Zemědělské noviny* 11 March 1991, pp. 1–2.

[57] *Mladá Fronta, Práce* 15 March 1991.

[58] *Mladá Fronta dnes* 26 March 1991, p. 2.

[59] *Mladá Fronta dnes* 14 March 1991, pp. 1–2.

[60] *Občanský deník, Mladá Fronta dnes* 24 April 1991.

[61] *Práce* 30 April 1991, p. 3.

[62] Quoted in *Mladá Fronta dnes* 3 April 1991, p. 7. Mečiar meanwhile had become embroiled in a dispute over cooperation with the Federal Ministry for Foreign Affairs, with whom he failed to consult before travelling to the already imploding Yugoslavia and the USSR.

[63] *Hospodářské noviny* 13 May 1991, p. 1.

[64] *Mlada Frontá dnes, Lidové noviny* 1 June 1991.

[65] 'The opinion currently expressed by J. Čarnogurský that Slovakia wants to be in the federation for the moment but that it will withdraw when the time is right is absolutely unacceptable to us. In Kroměříž I will put it clearly and bluntly – I will say that the Czech public is fed up with such opinions and that a clear barrier must be erected in this matter' (*Zemědělské noviny* 13 June 1991, p. 2). Regarding Kroměříž, Klaus also commented beforehand that the time when it was suitable for the talks to carry on in the extra-parliamentary arena was over as voters were under the impression the parliaments were being completely bypassed (*Mladá Fronta* 17 June 1991) – a comment designed to tap into the growing public frustration with the negotiated deadlocks.

[66] *Svobodné slovo, Mladá Fronta dnes* 18 June 1991.

[67] *Mladá Fronta dnes* 18 June 1991.

[68] *Zemědělské noviny* 2 June 1991, p. 1.

[69] *Hospodářské noviny* 5 September 1991, p. 2.

[70] *Svobodné slovo, Mladá Fronta dnes* and *Zemědělské noviny* 7 September 1991.

[71] *Mladá Fronta dnes* 10 September 1991, p. 2.

[72] *Mladá Fronta dnes,* In fact, Sweden, Switzerland and the Vatican had also recognized the Slovak state. 18 September 1991.

[73] *Rudé právo,* 25 September 1991. As of October 1991, an IVVM poll revealed the following, unhelpful results; in the Czech

Republic 38 per cent favoured a unitary state, 31 per cent a federation, 18 per cent a federal land system (i.e. Bundesrepublik), 4 per cent a confederation and 6 per cent two independent states. In the Slovak Republic 16 per cent favoured a unitary state, 34 per cent a federation, 6 per cent a federal land system, 25 per cent a confederation and 15 per cent two independent states (*Mladá Fronta dnes, Rudé právo* 1 November 1991).

[74] *Rudé právo* 1 November 1991, p. 3.

[75] *Lidové noviny, Hospodářské noviny* 4 November 1991.

[76] *Lidové noviny* 14 November 1991, pp. 1–12.

[77] *Mladá Fronta dnes, Hospodářské noviny* 15 November 1991.

[78] *Lidové noviny* 18 November 1991, pp. 1–8.

[79] *Mladá Fronta dnes, Lidové noviny, Český deník* 19 November 1991. According to an IVVM poll 73 per cent of Czechs and 59 per cent of Slovaks would vote in favour of a common state if a referendum took place in November (*Mladá Fronta dnes* 19 November 1991, p. 2).

[80] In May 1991, one month after Mečiar's ouster as Premier, only 33 per cent of Slovak respondents to a CSA poll agreed that the results of democratic elections should be binding during the whole electoral period, while 54 per cent disagreed. See Bútora (1994), p. 325.

[81] *Mladá Fronta dnes, Lidová demokracie, Lidové noviny* 20 November 1991. As it transpired, however, a potentially fractious meeting of the Financial Council was influenced favourably by the Slovak statement and a compromise was reached for the time being over the division of the proceeds of the turnover tax and profit tax. The Czech National Council, however, reneged on the budget agreements, apparently in protest against Slovak intransigence on the constitutional question. Their actions returning the budget to the limelight as both a symptom and vehicle of the by now full-blown constitutional crisis (see Chapter 5).

[82] John and Leschtina and *Mladá Fronta dnes* 10 December 1991, p. 6.

[83] *Lidové noviny* 22 January 1992.

[84] *Lidové noviny, Lidová demokracie* 23 January 1992.

[85] *Mladá Fronta dnes, Lidové noviny* 24 February 1992.

[86] *Hospodářské noviny* 12 March 1992, p. 1.

[87] Chapters 2 and 3.

[88] Eckstein (1979), pp. 14–15.

[89] See Batt (1993), Mathernová (1993) or Bunce (1999).

[90] Mathernová (1993), p. 64.

[91] ibid., p. 68.

[92] It should be noted that the *potential* for impasse in the Assembly offered the Czech media evidence for a virulent Slovak nationalism at work in the country's highest representative body. In *Literární noviny* no. 5 1990 the renowned dissident writer Ludvík Vaculík unleashed an article entitled 'Our Slovak Question', which effectively broke the taboo of public annoyance at Slovak actions, articulated with vigour by the press thereafter. In this Vaculík suggested that the Slovaks had no genuine history of their own and could only be supported with the assistance of other nations. He also claimed that Slovaks had been uncritical of the Slovak fascist state, renewing their adherence to 'good Czechoslovakia' only when it suited them, and, finally, that Slovak complaints about the Czechs were 'sociopsychological' (Radio Free Europe 7 September 1990). Perhaps most incendiary of all, Vaculik implied that the Slovaks had acted as a Quisling nation since 1968: 'Misled by their history, spoiled by Czech intervention on their behalf, the Slovaks do not know how an autonomous and proud nation should act' – a phrase Klaus would use to very precise effect at a later date (see Chapter 6).

[93] See Mathernová (1993).

[94] For example, as late as 3 November 1991, the Civic Movement (OH) representative and Chairwoman of the Czech National Council Dagmar Burešová was still explaining in talks that 'we are certainly willing to acknowledge that there must be confederative elements, but in principle to be a federation it must be a common state. Mr Premier [Marian Čalfa] [has confirmed that] a confederation is not a common state, it is a union of states' (*Slovenské Listy* 1994, p. 88).

[95] Mathernová (1993), p. 71.

[96] Elazar (1987), p. 29.

[97] *Hospodářské noviny, Mladá Fronta dnes, Český deník* 13 November 1991.
[98] In March 1991 the Slovak nationalist cultural organisation *Matica Slovenská* agreed to sue Havel's spokesman, Michael Žantovský, under the Penal Code paragraph 198 outlawing defamation of a race, nation or conviction, and paragraph 199 – the spreading of alarmist reports (*Zemědělské noviny* 21 March 1991, p. 1).
[99] See Batt (1993), p. 48.
[100] Mathernová (1993), p. 66.
[101] *Lidové noviny, Hospodářské noviny* 12 November 1991. This peculiar ire against Petr Pithart was in retaliation to his highly conciliatory television speech on 9 November. Pithart had acknowledged not only the flaws of Czechoslovakist ideology, declaring that the conception of the Czechoslovak federation in 1969 had been 'strange and not too democratic', but he had also identified widespread Czech paternalism. Czech Education Minister P. Vopenka lambasted Pithart for having 'taken over the Communist interpretation of Masaryk's republic and some inventions of primitive Slovak nationalists'. KAN chairman B. Dvořák advised Pithart to resign. Ján Čarnogurský of the Christian Democratic Movement and Peter Weiss of the Party of the Democratic Left on the other hand thanked Pithart for extending 'a friendly hand' and for his 'sober assessment' respectively (*Svobodné slovo, Lidové noviny* 11 November 1991).
[102] The consociational veto was of course originally conceived to 'exclude politically and constitutionally, the possibility of outvoting the Slovak nation as far as the state relations between the Czechs and Slovaks and the constitutional status of Slovakia are concerned' (p. 39, Action Programme 1968). The implication of objections to the veto as such (e.g. from the CDA) was a habituated Czech unitarianism; Czech and federal authority had evidently been synonymous for so long that sections of the Czech political elite considered effective Slovak intervention highly nationalistic.

CHAPTER 5

[1] Having occupied centre stage in the closeted economic debates of the late

1980s, Komárek was quickly outflanked after November 1989 by his professedly neo-liberal colleague Klaus. Komárek had recruited Klaus from the State Bank to Prognost in 1987.
[2] He moved on to lead *Matica Slovenská*.
[3] As the unit of output measurement at the macro-level in socialist accounting systems, NMP – the measure of net output – referred only to the production sphere and ignored the output of the service sphere. The state started to calculate GDP – the accounting unit used in the rest of the world, which includes the service sector – in 1991.
[4] See Martin Myant's excellent *Transforming Socialist Economies* (1993), p. 171.
[5] *The Times* 5 February 1990, p. 27.
[6] See Václav Klaus and Thomáš Ježek, 'Social Criticism, False Liberalism, and Recent Changes in Czechoslovakia' in *East European Politics and Societies*, Volume 5, Number 1 (Sage Publications, 1991) p. 39.
[7] The boldness of Klaus's statements and actions, such as his decision to contest the 1990 election in a north Moravian coal-mining district – in the Communist Party heartlands – was quickly establishing him as a confident and purposeful political figure. He won the seat. See Keane (1999), p. 440.
[8] *Rudé právo* 27 April 1990.
[9] As the weeks passed, however, demonopolisation – the micro-level restructuring of industrial enterprises – became an ever lower priority.
[10] *Rudé právo* 11 April 1990.
[11] See Myant (1995), p. 177.
[12] ibid., p. 78.
[13] Author's interview with Jan Klacek, Director of the Economics Institute of the Czech National Bank and former adviser to the Federal Minister of the Economy, Vladimír Dlouhý, 5 February 1995.
[14] Myant (1995), p. 179.
[15] ibid., p. 180.
[16] Author's interview with Jan Mládek, Former Federal Deputy Minister for the Economy and adviser to the Federal Minister of the Economy, Vladimír Dlouhý. 21 February 1995.
[17] Interview with Jan Klacek.
[18] It has been pointed out since that one reason the political left did not return to power in the early 1990s, as they did in the

ostensibly unlikely cases of Poland and Hungary, was that social democrats were in power at the beginning in Czechoslovakia – in 1990. The point is well taken since, as we shall see, Klaus would go on to 'borrow' much from the moderate liberal cabinet colleagues he affected to despise for their economic naivete. Between 1990 and 1992 Klaus would make his own several of the suggestions originating from his 'soft' political colleagues, which evidently contributed to maintaining the Czech social peace.

[19] Interview with Jan Mládek.

[20] Interview: ibid.

[21] *Financial Times* 8 November 1991.

[22] See Ian Jeffries, *Socialist Economies and the Transition to the Market: A Guide* (London, New York: Routledge, 1993), p. 379.

[23] *Zemědělské noviny* 11 March 1991, pp. 1–2.

[24] Next day, Kučerák, for his pains, received a vote of no confidence at the 13th meeting of the Slovak National Council. The Presidium also removed Huska and Kňažko, and the Minister for Labour and Social Affairs, Stanislav Novak, was replaced by the former Deputy Federal Minister, Helena Woleková. Ministers Kováč and Filkus resigned on 24 April 1991.

[25] Marcinčin (1994).

[26] The anti-reformists were also backed, academically, by NEZES – The Association of Independent Economists of Slovakia (actually constituted by old-structure economists and later joined by Huska) (*Hospodářské noviny* 19 March 1991). Their findings for Slovak economic sovereignty could, as reform progressed, be found echoed in the statements of the post-April 1991 Slovak opposition.

[27] Such as Federal Prime Minister Marián Čalfa (PAV).

[28] For examples see Karel Dyba and Jan Švejnar (1994), or Aleš Čapek (1992), or Aleš Čapek and Gerald Sazama (1993), or, most revealingly of all, O. Dědek (n.d.).

[29] This chapter is written with the proviso that any attempt to demonstrate the divisive powers of federal reform policy must look through the frequently opaque window of formal jurisdictions which were not only unclear in themselves, particularly

in the chaotic days of 1991, but were anyway frequently disregarded in practice (interview with Jan Klacek, 8 February 1995).

[30] Lukas (1992), p. 1.

[31] ibid., p. 8.

[32] Including, notoriously for the Slovaks, President Václav Havel.

[33] Lukas, ibid.

[34] Federal ministers, Vladimír Dlouhý in particular, counter-argued that a significant proportion of the armaments labour force was also employed in Southern Moravia (20 per cent) and Prague (17 per cent). To argue that unemployment in arms production was a problem of the regions, however, was clearly politically disingenuous in the light of the growing argument between the republics. Moreover, alternative employment in Slovakia did not exist, particularly in single-industry towns, whereas in tourist-rich Prague unemployment was persistently among the lowest in the country; indeed, Prague actually absorbed unemployment from neighbouring areas, indicating, if anything, a labour shortage.

[35] When financial crisis hit enterprises in early 1991 (bank credit became 'real' after January, carrying a 24-per-cent interest rate (see Myant (1995), p. 216), industry began to pass on bad debt, and primary and secondary insolvency spiralled. Though a consolidation bank was established, the federal Ministry of Finance publicly rejected selective help, deliberately leaving this issue to the nominally independent banks to resolve; even a scheme from Jan Vrba (Czech Minister for Industry) to encourage foreign partners was rejected as too interventionist (restructuring would subsequently become an electoral focus for the rival Civic Movement). Klaus supporters answered Western queries over the absence of export support with the claim that, of course there was an industry policy: it was implicit within the macro-economic strategy (through devaluation of the crown). Not until February 1992 was an agreement reached to establish an export credit agency, whose financial support remained negligible.

[36] See Aleš Bulíř, 'The Czech and Slovak Republics in 1992: The Process of Divergence' (Prague: *CERGE Working Paper*, Number 18, 1992), p. 5.

[37] See Myant (1995), p. 216.
[38] *Hospodářské noviny* 3 December 1991, p. 2.
[39] Myant (1995), p. 236.
[40] ibid., p. 239.
[41] Marcinčin (1994), p. 32
[42] Bulíř, op. cit., pp. 6–7.
[43] For this reason, it was avoided in Poland and Hungary, where more traditional methods, such as share flotations or liquidation and leasing, nevertheless produced unacceptable trends in ownership, so-called 'nomenklatura capitalism'.
[44] See Svejnar and Singer (1994), p. 44.
[45] Orenstein (1992), p. 21.
[46] See Bruszt and Stark (1996), p. 24.
[47] See Lukas (1992), p. 21.
[48] A mark of the Czechs' innately more conservative nature, according to Dĕdek: author's interview, 14 February 1995.
[49] See Horáková (1992), p. 39.
[50] Bulíř, op. cit., pp. 1–2.
[51] Horáková, ibid.
[52] Bulíř, op. cit., p. 15.
[53] See Przeworski (1993).
[54] See Dyba and Svejnar (1994), p. 6.
[55] Lukas (1992), p. 12.
[56] Orenstein (1992), p. 13.
[57] The author worked as a researcher on this project.
[58] Alan Cranston, *Study of Active Employment Policy in Czechoslovakia*, PHARE/Know How Fund sponsored report commissioned by the Czechoslovak Office of the Federal Government, 1992, p. 116.
[59] The Finance Ministry's control of the 1992 employment budget effectively overruled Petr Miller's attempts at consensus building in the Ministry of Labour and Social Affairs. In 1992, for the first time, the federal budget took on unemployment expenditure in order to give the pressured and bickering republics a better chance of balancing their budgets (expenditure on unemployment had previously fallen to the republics). The Federal Budget Act for 1992, however, reduced unemployment benefit by halving the eligibility period from 1 year to 6 months, contributing to a fall in the general (i.e. registered) rate from 6.6 per cent to 6.5 per cent in the first quarter and 5.5 per cent in the second quarter of 1992. This measure alone effectively indicated

that the federal state ignored and thus compounded the problem of long-term unemployment, building up disproportionately in Slovakia.
[60] Bulíř, op. cit., p. 9.
[61] A deal in which Volkswagen committed to maintain the existing level of employees at around 22,000.
[62] *Ekonomické Prohlédy*, ČR a SR (Paris: OECD, 1994), p. 27.
[63] Author's interview with Dr Kotulan of the Czech National Bank, 9 February 1995.
[64] *Ekonomické Prohlédy*, op. cit.
[65] Before 1989, the federal government had been the dominant tax collector, making sizeable transfers from the federal to the republican and local treasuries. By 1991 republican budgets had become dominant, accounting for nearly two-thirds of the total state budget. See Shen (1993), p. 105.
[66] *Ekonomické Prohlédy*, op. cit., p. 28.
[67] See Shen (1993), p. 103.
[68] See M. Havel's 'New Laws on Budgetary Rules in Czechoslovakia', *Czechoslovak Economic Digest*, Number 1 (Prague: Orbis, 1991), p. 4.
[69] See Shen (1993), p. 106.
[70] Author's interview with Jan Mládek, 21 February 1995.
[71] See former Deputy Federal Minister of Finance I. Kočárník's 'The Problems of Fiscal Management in the CSFR in a Time of Transition' (Prague: *CERGE Working Paper*, Number 13, 1992), p. 14.
[72] Kočárník, over-optimistically in the case of Slovakia, suggests that had revenue from privatisation been included in the budgets, they would have been close to balanced. ibid., p. 14.
[73] See Shen (1993), p. 107.
[74] *Mladá Fronta dnes* 22 November 1991, p. 2.
[75] *Hospodářské noviny* 3 December 1991.
[76] See Václav Klaus's 'Proč jsem optimista', *Literární noviny* 26 November 1990, which also appeared in the collected essays *O Tvář Zítřka* (Prague: Pražske Imaginace, 1991), p. 18.
[77] As part of the redivision of competences in December 1990 (Act 556/1990, amending Act 143/1968) the republican governments had inherited all other competences, notably the most politically fraught areas of agricultural

policy, social policy, industrial (structural) policy, energy policy, and the bulk of infrastructure. See I. Kočárník, op. cit., p. 15.

[78] See Bulíř, op. cit., p. 13.

[79] *Report on Eastern Europe*, Radio Free Europe, 6 April 1990.

[80] See Klaus's 'Proč jsem optimista', p. 16.

[81] See Václav Klaus's 'Jsem člověk konzervativní', *Lidové noviny* 2 November 1990; also in *O Tvář Zítřka*, p. 179.

[82] Orenstein (1992), p. 21.

[83] See Bulíř, op. cit., p. 1.

[84] From May 1992 Czech commercial banks, expecting a victory for Mečiar in the next month's election, were unwilling to buy new Slovak treasury bills and government bonds, and the holding of Slovak treasury bills in the portfolios of Czech banks declined steadily afterwards. ibid., p. 12.

[85] See Roland (1994), p. 29.

[86] e.g. through a wage agreement with the new Czech and Slovak Confederation of Trades Unions in January 1991, thus securing labour cooperation. Klaus dismissed the agreement as a gross error for which he held the 'Liberal club representatives in the Government' (i.e. future Civic Movement ministers) responsible (*Mladá Fronta dnes* 2 March 1991, p. 2). The federal government unilaterally abolished the agreement in July 1991.

[87] See Roland (1994), p. 28.

[88] See Klaus and Ježek, op. cit., p. 39.

[89] See Václav Klaus's 'The imperatives of long-term prognoses and the dominant characteristics of the economy at present' in *Czechoslovak Economic Digest* 7/1989, p. 42 (also appeared in Czech in the summer edition of *Politické Ekonomie*).

[90] See Klaus and Ježek, op. cit., p. 27.

CHAPTER 6

[1] An assumption of the leadership theory is that the maximum amount of autonomy that a state can have and still be called democratic is when elected politicians act on their own preferences even when their favoured options clearly and self-consciously diverge from society's preferences – *including those of their own political constituency.* (Adapted from

Nordlinger (1981), pp. 11–38.). It is only the possibility of rejecting these officials at a future date that keeps the state within even the most minimalist definition of democracy. Accepting this, I would argue that the post-Communist Czechoslovak state was highly autonomous insofar as the decision to separate the state was taken not only against the known majority will in regard to the continuation of a common state but even against the first preferences of a majority of voters for both Klaus's CDP and Mečiar's MDS.

[2] See Bunce (1996), p. 28.

[3] The cartoonist was the wonderful Vladimír Jiránek.

[4] *Rudé právo* 25 June 1991, p. 3.

[5] *Prostor* 8 June 1992, p. 1.

[6] *Pravda* 8 June 1992, pp. 1–2.

[7] Ivo Slávik, in *Mladá Fronta dnes* 9 June 1992.

[8] *Mladá Fronta dnes* 12 June 1992.

[9] *Mladá Fronta dnes* 9 June 1992, p. 1.

[10] *Lidové noviny* 18 June 1992, pp. 1–3.

[11] *Rudé právo* 11 June 1992, pp. 1–2.

[12] *Český deník* 15 June 1992.

[13] *Telegraf* 11 June 1992.

[14] *Mladá Fronta dnes* 11 June 1992, pp. 1–2.

[15] *Český deník* 15 June 1992

[16] *Lidové noviny, Mladá Fronta dnes* 12 June 1992, pp. 1–2.

[17] *Práce* 13 June 1992.

[18] *Svobodné slovo, Lidové noviny* 13 June 1992.

[19] *Mladá Fronta dnes* 15 June 1992.

[20] *Svobodné slovo, Lidové noviny* 13 June 1992.

[21] *Lidové noviny* 13 June 1992, p. 8.

[22] *Mladá Fronta dnes* 16 June 1992. Even as Havel sought consensus, however, his undiplomatic spokesman, Michael Žantovský, stated that in the event of agreement 'remaining impossible' Havel would agree with Klaus to proceed without protraction. He added for good measure that when one looked at how Czechoslovak bonds abroad had dropped by 10 per cent it represented 'an incentive for an accelerated course of action' (*Mladá Fronta dnes* 16 June 1992, p. 2). According to the Czechoslovak State Bank the price of bonds was in fact quite stable (*Hospodářské noviny* 16 June 1992, p. 1).

[23] *Telegraf* 17 June 1992.

[24] See Vodička (1993), p. 94.

[25] A decision was acknowledged at least the day before, when CDP Vice-Chairman Macek suggested that the talks be seen as procuring a 'velvet split' (*Telegraf, Mladá Fronta dnes* 17 June 1992). Following the first talks Klaus had declared 'I am not interested in chairing a self-liquidating Federal Government' (*Mladá Fronta dnes* 10 June 1992, pp. 1–2).

[26] *Práce* 19 June 1992, p. 1.

[27] *Mladá Fronta dnes* 22 June 1992, pp. 1–2.

[28] *Telegraf* 25 June 1992, p. 14.

[29] *Mladá Fronta dnes* 22 June 1992, p. 1.

[30] *Lidová demokracie, Mladá Fronta dnes* 22 June 1992.

[31] *Telegraf* 25 June 1992, p. 14.

[32] *Mladá Fronta dnes* 22 June 1992, pp. 1, 2. After a meeting of the Slovak Democratic Left council, Weiss announced that his party would not support Havel's candidacy (*Mladá Fronta dnes* 20 June 1992, p. 2), thus guaranteeing the blocking of his re-election in the Federal Assembly.

[33] *Lidové noviny* 22 June 1992, p. 8.

[34] *Mladá Fronta dnes* 24 June 1992, p. 1. In the Slovak National Council, the Christian Democratic Movement protested that the MDS had pushed for undemocratic majorities in major committees. In reply, two CDM members were demoted from the Security Committee to Education, and CDM Chairman Ján Čarnogurský was demoted from Foreign Affairs to the Environment. The Party of the Democratic Left's Pavol Kanis objected that the 'tooth for a tooth' principle was inappropriate to politics (*Pravda* 24 June 1992, pp. 1–2).

[35] *Telegraf* 24 June 1992, p. 1.

[36] The Movement for a Democratic Slovakia suggested to the Party of the Democratic Left and Slovak National Party on 27 June that a referendum on constitutional arrangements should be held in December, though all three objected to the current referendum law insofar as it enabled only one republic to withdraw from the federation and so risked Slovakia's successor status (*Mladá Fronta dnes* 19 June 1992, p. 1).

[37] *Telegraf* 30 June 1992, p. 2.

[38] *Hospodářské noviny* 30 June 1992, p. 2.

[39] *Mladá Fronta dnes* 1 July 1992, p. 6, and 14 July 1992, p. 2.

[40] *Rudé právo* 2 July 1992.

[41] *Mladá Fronta dnes* 2 July 1992.

[42] ibid., p. 2. On the same day a Bill on the Sovereignty and State Symbols of the Slovak Republic, proposed by the Slovak National Party, was withdrawn from the Slovak National Council presidium agenda. The draft provided for the right to veto federal laws. The Party of the Democratic Left objected that this would introduce an unacceptable legal dualism (ibid., p. 1).

[43] *Telegraf* 3 July 1992, p. 1.

[44] *Mladá Fronta dnes* 3 July 1992, p. 7.

[45] On 6 July 1992.

[46] *Mladá Fronta dnes* 9 July 1992.

[47] *Mladá Fronta dnes* 4 July 1992, pp. 1–2.

[48] *Telegraf* 7 July 1992.

[49] *Pravda* 8 July 1992.

[50] *Mladá Fronta dnes* 9 July 1992, pp. 1–2.

[51] *Telegraf* 10 July 1992.

[52] *Mladá Fronta dnes* 14 July 1992, p. 1.

[53] *Mladá Fronta dnes* 15 July 1992, pp. 1–2.

[54] Petr Pithart explained that a so-called 'catastrophic scenario' had indeed been prepared when a Slovak Declaration of Sovereignty first seemed possible – Slovak deputies had known of the report at the time and it had carried no plans of deportations. Stráský, one of the scenario's authors, retorted that the only 'horrifying' document he had seen concerned the economic risks of a Slovak secession (ibid.).

[55] *Pravda, Telegraf, Mladá Fronta dnes* 16 July 1992.

[56] *Hospodářské noviny* 14 July 1992, p. 1.

[57] *Mladá Fronta dnes* 15 July 1992, pp. 1–2.

[58] *Lidové noviny* 17 July 1992.

[59] *Lidové noviny* 18 July 1992, pp. 1–8.

[60] The Declaration: 'We, the democratically elected Slovak National Council, declare ceremoniously that one thousand years worth of efforts of the Slovak nation for sovereignty have been fulfilled. In this historical moment we declare the natural right of the Slovak nation for its self-determination as it is anchored in all international agreements and contracts on the rights of nations for their self-determination. Recognising the right of nations for their self-determination, we declare that we want freely to create the way and form of our national and state life while respecting the

rights of all, of each citizen, nations, national minorities and ethnic groups, and the democratic and humanistic legacies of Europe and the world. By this Declaration the Slovak National Council declares the sovereignty of the Slovak Republic as a basis of a sovereign state of the Slovak nation' (*Svobodné slovo* 18 July 1992, p. 1).
[61] *Mladá Fronta, Svobodne slovo* 18 July 1992.
[62] *Mladá Fronta dnes* 18 July 1992, p. 1.
[63] ibid.
[64] *Hospodářské noviny* 21 July 1992, p. 2.
[65] *Mladá Fronta dnes* 20 July 1992, p. 2.
[66] *Lidové noviny* 23 July 1992, p. 1.
[67] *Mladá Fronta dnes* 24 July 1992, p. 1.
[68] *Mladá Fronta dnes* 31 July 1992.
[69] *Mladá Fronta dnes* 4 August 1992, p. 1. The Social Democrats announced the candidacy of Jan Sokol (of the now extra-parliamentary liberal Civic Movement) for the fifth round of presidential elections. A widely respected contender, Sokol was doomed by Slovak opposition, however, and on 11 September withdrew his candidacy (*Český deník* 12 September 1992, p. 2).
[70] *Mladá Fronta dnes* 31 July 1992, p. 2.
[71] *Mladá Fronta dnes* 24 July 1992, p. 2.
[72] *Národná obroda* 3 August 1992.
[73] *Lidové noviny* 8 August 1992, p. 2.
[74] *Mladá Fronta dnes* 5 August 1992, p. 1.
[75] *Práce* 8 August 1992.
[76] *Mladá Fronta dnes* 11 August 1992, p. 1.
[77] *Národná obroda* 11 August 1992, p. 8.
[78] *Lidové noviny* 19 August 1992.
[79] *Mladá Fronta dnes* 20 August 1992, pp. 1–6.
[80] *Mladá Fronta dnes* 20 August 1992, p. 2.
[81] *Lidové noviny, Národná obroda* 21 August 1992.
[82] *Rudé právo* 22 August 1992, pp. 1–2.
[83] *Mladá Fronta dnes, Lidove noviny, Národná obroda* 25 August 1992.
[84] *Svobodné slovo, Nová obroda* 27 August 1992.
[85] *Mladá Fronta dnes* 4 September 1992.
[86] *Mladá Fronta dnes, Hospodářské noviny, Český deník, Nová obroda* 28 August 1992.
[87] The constitution failed to protect Hungarian rights – most obviously because it established Slovakia as the 'state of the Slovak people' as opposed to a state of the

citizens of Slovakia. The Christian Democratic Movement objected to various provisions it deemed undemocratic, un-Christian and at variance with the valid constitution. Among the latter were clauses stipulating the establishment of a Slovak customs zone and a Slovak central bank (*Český deník* 31 August 1992, p. 1). The final vote was once again by roll-call. Mečiar called it 'a constitution which stems from the ideas within our society, one which rejects fascism, anti-Semitism, and nationalism, being a guarantee of democracy, freedom and respect for law' (*Pravda, Mladá Fronta dnes* 1 September 1992).
[88] *Mladá Fronta dnes* 2 September 1992.
[89] *Mladá Fronta dnes* 30 September 1992, p. 2.
[90] *Mladá Fronta dnes* 4 September 1992, p. 2.
[91] *Mladá Fronta dnes* 5 September 1992, p. 1.
[92] *Lidové noviny* 8 September 1992, p. 16.
[93] *Mladá Fronta dnes, Prostor, Rudé právo* 9 September 1992.
[94] *Metropolitní Telegraf* 23 September 1992, p. 2.
[95] *Mladá Fronta dnes* 22 September 1992, pp. 1–2.
[96] *Lidová demokracie, Mladá Fronta dnes* 16 September 1992.
[97] *Mladá Fronta dnes, Zemědělské noviny* 24 September 1992.
[98] *Mladá Fronta dnes, Rudé právo* 10 September 1992.
[99] *Mladá Fronta dnes, Metropolitní Telegraf* 15 September 1992.
[100] *Mladá Fronta dnes, Hospodářské noviny* 17 September 1992. At this time Mečiar's attempts to use events abroad to distract attention from events at home became seriously counter-productive for Slovak international relations; ratification of the European Community Association Agreement had been made conditional on Slovakia's maintenance of good foreign relations. After visiting Bavaria, Mečiar declared himself for a new Slovak treaty with Germany, one which would tackle the unresolved problem of war reparations (*Metropolitní Telegraf, Práce, Lidová demokracie* 25 September 1992). To *Koridor* Mečiar suggested 'compensation to affected Slovak citizens for war damages, burnt-out villages, lost lives,

concentration camps and other things' (*Nová obroda* 29 September 1992, p. 12). German Foreign Ministry spokesman Hans Schumacher replied unequivocally: Germany did not wish to and would not negotiate new treaties with either republic – the very reasoning behind ratification of the current treaty. Slovak violation of the federal treaty would release Germany from all its contractual obligations to Slovakia (*Mladá Fronta dnes, Národná obroda* 28 September 1992).

[101] *Mladá Fronta dnes, Národná obroda* 17 September 1992.

[102] *Metropolitní Telegraf* 21 September 1992, pp. 1–3.

[103] *Hospodářské noviny* 1 October 1992, p. 2.

[104] *Mladá Fronta dnes* 1 October 1992, p. 1.

[105] *Pravdá* 25 September 1992, p. 1.

[106] *Metropolitní Telegraf, Mlada Fronta dnes* 29 September 1992.

[107] *Mladá Fronta dnes* 30 September 1992, pp. 1–2.

[108] *Pravda* 30 September 1992, p. 2.

[109] *Hospodářské noviny* 30 September 1992, p. 2.

[110] *Mladá Fronta dnes, Metropolitní Telegraf* 30 September 1992.

[111] *Mladá Fronta dnes, Hospodářské noviny, Metropolitní Telegraf* 2 October 1992.

[112] The following day the Assembly also failed to propose a candidate for the sixth round in the presidential elections. The seventh would take place on 26 November.

[113] *Svobodné slovo* 3 October 1992, p. 1.

[114] *Mlada Fronta dnes, Pravda* 5 October 1992.

[115] *Mladá Fronta dnes, Pravda* 6 October 1992.

[116] *Metropolitní Telegraf, Mladá Fronta dnes* 6 October 1992.

[117] *Mladá Fronta dnes, Český deník* 7 October 1992.

[118] *Mladá Fronta dnes* 7 October 1992, p. 1.

[119] *Mladá Fronta dnes* 9 October 1992, p. 8.

[120] *Mladá Fronta dnes, Národna obrodá* 7 October 1992.

[121] *Hospodářské noviny, Mladá Fronta dnes* 7 October 1992.

[122] *Hospodářské noviny* 9 October 1992, pp. 1–2.

[123] *Rudé právo* 8 October 1992, p. 1.

[124] *Mladá Fronta dnes* 9 October 1992, p. 1.

[125] *Mladá Fronta dnes, Metropolitní Telegraf* 12 October 1992.

[126] *Hospodářské noviny* 13 October 1992, p. 2. This last pledge came to haunt the government when conflict over the Gabčikovo Nagymáros dam erupted. The project had been agreed in 1977 but was now condemned by Hungary as a border change. The dispute forced the federal government to intervene and cooperate with international arbitration (*Mladá Fronta dnes, Český deník and Národná obroda* 20 October 1992; *Telegraf* 21 October 1992, p. 6), leaving Mečiar free to threaten 'force' even though he excluded military aggression. Germany and the EC threatened Slovakia with diplomatic non-recognition (*Mladá Fronta dnes* and *Rudé právo* 24 October 1992), and the dispute did much to bolster the Czechs' reputation as the honourable party in the divorce.

[127] *Pravda, Mladá Fronta dnes* 14 October 1992.

[128] *Hospodářské noviny* 15 October 1992, p. 1.

[129] Having rejected the Slovak proposal for dual citizenship the CDP also prevailed at Javorina with the decision that each republic would regulate the issue separately.

[130] *Hospodářské noviny, Mladá Fronta dnes, Pravda* 27 October 1992. Earlier, several thousand people had attended the celebration of the renewal of the Czech state, organised by the CDP at Prague's Vyšehrad (*Lidové noviny* 26 October 1992, p. 1).

[131] *Hospodářské noviny* 29 October 1992, pp. 1–2.

[132] *Mladá Fronta dnes* 30 October 1992, p. 2. Having agreed that it was important for politicians to avoid creating an atmosphere of confrontation (*Mladá Fronta dnes* 31.10.1992:1,2), Klaus and Havel personified the deal on TV's 'This Week's Outcome', complimenting each other and expressing their joint interests in the new Czech Republic; Havel acknowledged his defeat over the issue of direct election for the new presidency (*Rudé právo* 2 November 1992, pp. 1–2).

[133] *Mladá Fronta dnes* 30 October 1992, p. 2.

[134] *Mladá Fronta dnes, Svobodné slovo* 27 November 1992, p. 1.
[135] *Mladá Fronta dnes, Český deník* 4 November 1992. The leader of the Party of the Democratic Left, Peter Weiss, offered a coalition if 'MDS changes the policy statement and admits its errors' (*Mladá Fronta dnes, Český deník* 4 November 1992). Mečiar only accused the Party of endangering the 'calm domestic atmosphere'.
[136] The Bratislava Division of the Federal Police had recently stopped criminal investigation of St.B. (Communist secret police) files stolen from Trenčin, an issue that had loomed over Mečiar before the election (*Lidové noviny* 6 November 1992, p. 1).
[137] *Národná obroda, Metropolitní Telegraf* 5 November 1992.
[138] *Mladá Fronta dnes* 9 November 1992, p. 1.
[139] *Svobodné slovo, Mladá Fronta dnes* 6 November 1992.
[140] *Mladá Fronta dnes, Lidové noviny* 10 November 1992.
[141] *Mladá Fronta dnes* 14 and 16 November 1992, p. 1.
[142] *Mlada Fronta dnes* 14 November 1992, p. 2.
[143] *Lidové noviny* 17 November 1992.
[144] *Hospodářské noviny, Mladá Fronta dnes* 18 November 1992.
[145] *Mladá Fronta dnes* 18 November 1992, pp. 1–2.
[146] In the House of the Nations the Bill was supported by the Civic Democratic Party, Movement for a Democratic Slovakia, Slovak National Party and Christian Democratic Union/Czechoslovak People's Party. Conversely, deputies of the Christian Democratic Movement, Slovak Democratic Left, Coexistence, Left Bloc, Czechoslovak Social Democracy, Slovak Social Democracy and the Republicans either voted against or abstained. In the House of the People, the Civic Democratic Party, Movement for a Democratic Slovakia, Christian Democratic Union/Czechoslovak People's Party, Left Social Union and parts of Czechoslovak Social Democracy and the Slovak National Party supported the Bill.
[147] *Mladá Fronta dnes* 19 November 1992, pp. 1–2.

[148] *Hospodářské noviny* 19 November 1992, pp. 1–2.
[149] *Mladá Fronta dnes, Hospodářské noviny* and *Lidové noviny* 20 November 1992.
[150] *Lidová demokracie* 20 November 1992, p. 1.
[151] *Mladá Fronta dnes* 23 November 1992, p. 2.
[152] In continuing talks between the presidia of the Czech and Slovak governments in Bratislava (Klaus was absent due to a tennis injury), Mečiar and Kočarnik continued to disagree over the division of the real-estate property of federal institutions. They agreed, however, that no common military doctrines would exist, so ending any vestiges of military union.
[153] *Svobodné slovo* 25 November 1992, p. 1.
[154] The Law confirmed in Article 4 that 'legislative power in [both republics] will be transferred to a legislative body, consisting of deputies elected in the 1992 elections in [both republics] to the Federal Assembly of the ČSFR, and those elected to the [National Councils]. The detailed conditions of this legislative body will be set in harmony with Article 7' (*Mladá Fronta dnes, Národná obroda* and *Rudé právo* 26 November 1992).
[155] During the four rounds of coupon privatisation so far, Slovak holders of investment coupons and Slovak investment privatisation funds had gained stocks of Czech enterprises amounting to Kčs 18,800 million, whereas Czechs had sought out only some Kčs 4,500 million of Slovak property (*Mladá Fronta dnes* 27 November 1992, p. 1).
[156] *Mladá Fronta dnes* 28 November 1992, p. 1.
[157] *Mladá Fronta dnes, Rudé právo* and *Lidové noviny* 1 December 1992.
[158] *Svobodné slovo* 28 November 1992, p. 1.
[159] *Mladá Fronta dnes* 30 November 1992, pp. 1–2.
[160] *Svobodné slovo, Český deník* 3 December 1992.
[161] *Mladá Fronta dnes, Zemědělské noviny* 1 December 1992, p. 2.
[162] *Hospodářské noviny* 4 December 1992, p. 2. *Mladá Fronta dnes* 5 December 1992, p. 1. Mečiar's proposal to form a second

chamber with federal deputies was rejected by the MDS Council, the Movement's advisory body, and later by the MDS presidium, meeting on 12 December. Mečiar, unperturbed, said the establishment of a second chamber would anyway have been too complicated (*Mladá Fronta dnes* 14 December 1992, p. 2). As for the presidency, Mečiar announced a likely election in January 1993, the anticipated candidate being Michal Kováč (MDS) (*Český deník* 5 December 1992, p. 2).

[163] *Mladá Fronta dnes, Slobodné slovo* 16 December 1992, p. 1.

[164] *Mladá Fronta dnes* 17 December 1992, pp. 1–2.

[165] *Český deník* 18 December 1992, p. 1.

[166] *Mladá Fronta dnes, Český deník* 18 December 1992, p. 1.

[167] *Mladá Fronta dnes* 18 December 1992, p. 2.

[168] *Metropolitní Telegraf* 2 December 1992, p. 3. Slovakia's reputation fell under further scrutiny when an operative bugging device was found in the US consulate in Bratislava (*Telegraf, Mladá Fronta dnes* 7 December 1992). Mečiar claimed that the discovery was orchestrated by Prague to discredit the Slovak state and that 'a bug is to be discovered at the offices of the Christian Democratic Movement and the government is to be accused of bugging political parties or their leaders. Other provocations are under preparation. Of course we shall reject and withstand them' (*Mladá Fronta dnes* 12 December 1992, pp. 1–2). Few doubted that Mečiar's forces were responsible.

[169] *Mladá Fronta dnes* 19 December 1992, p. 2.

[170] *Mladá Fronta dnes* pp. 1–2. *Rudé právo* 23 December 1992, p. 2.

[171] *Mladá Fronta dnes, Rudé právo, Český deník* 23 December 1992, p. 1.

[172] *Rudé právo* 22 December 1992, p. 2.

[173] *Hospodářské noviny* 23 December 1992, p. 2.

[174] *Lidové noviny* 31 December 1992, p. 2.

[175] See Draper (1993), p. 26.

[176] See Zbořil (1995), p. 207.

[177] *Zemědělské noviny* 22 October 1992, p. 3.

[178] By November, 50 per cent of Czechs, as compared to some 40 per cent of Slovaks, considered the dissolution of the federation as 'necessary'; 43 per cent of Czechs and 49 per cent of Slovaks saw separation as 'unnecessary' (IVVM poll 2/22, quoted in *Mladá Fronta dnes* (pp. 1, 2), *Svobodné slovo* 27 November 1992, p. 1). Given the choice of voting in a referendum simply for or against the division of the federation, 42 per cent of Czechs would have voted for division as against 32 per cent of Slovaks; 36 per cent of Slovaks chose the option 'don't know' (IVVM 2/22: 4–9 November 1992).

[179] Precision on this point is thwarted by the lack of systematic opinion-taking during the last six months. While IVVM took monthly samples they changed the phrasing of the questions in such a way as to make comparison over time dubious; ideal preferences and pragmatic endorsements became blurred.

[180] See Wolchik (1994), p. 180.

[181] Institute for Public Opinion Research (IVVM) 2/24, 8 February 1993.

[182] Reflections of these problems can be seen in public opinion polls. In Slovakia, 50 per cent of Slovaks, when asked in March 1993 'Would you have voted for the dissolution of the CSFR?', maintained that they would have answered 'no' (only 29 per cent 'yes'): see Zora Bútorová's 'Current Problems of Slovakia after the Split of the CSFR', *Report on the Sociological Survey* (Bratislava: Centre for Social Analysis, 1993), p. 3. Had elections been held in March, the Movement for a Democratic Slovakia would have secured only 18.6 per cent of the vote, almost half its June figure (ibid., p. 25). Only 13 per cent of Slovaks said they trusted the Slovak government completely, and 66 per cent judged that their politicians had not been ready to face complete independence (ibid., pp. 30–31). When asked to name their 'most trusted politician', Mečiar's support had dwindled steadily from just under 80 per cent in February 1991 to just over 20 per cent in March 1993 (ibid., p. 37).

[183] See Connor (1994), p. 140.

[184] The depth of this conflicting view only increased over time; while 61 per cent of Slovaks in March 1993 attributed the split to the uncompromising attitude of Czechs, 84 per cent identified the cause of separation as the 'aggravated economic and

social situation of the Slovak population' (Butorova, op. cit., p. 25).

[185] See Breuilly (1993), p. 85.

[186] The broad claim of historical institutionalists is that institutions structure political battles and, in so doing, influence their outcomes. For a discussion of the institutionalist argument see Steinmo and Thelen (1992), p. 3. In our case the failure of political institutions was critical in giving autonomy to political leaders. It seems to me that it would be stretching a point to claim this as an institutionalist argument; the *absence* of constraint cannot positively structure a political outcome, but can only open up political opportunity.

[187] See Žák (1995), p. 263.

[188] *Mladá Fronta dnes* 19 November 1992, pp. 1–2.

[189] *Mladá Fronta dnes* 25 September 1992, p. 24.

[190] See Václav Havel's *Summer Meditations* (trans. Paul Wilson) (London and Boston: Faber and Faber, 1992), p. 34.

[191] As Nordlinger has argued, 'nonmanipulable cultural, social and economic conditions may go a long way in accounting for the emergence of an intense conflict but, once it has become severe, its successful or unsuccessful regulation will be largely dependent upon the purposeful behaviour of political elites'. See Nordlinger (1972), p. 4.

[192] See Bunce (1996), p. 3.

[193] See First (1983), p. 210.

[194] Our case is an apt illustration for Lustick's discussion of why traditional distinctions between 'secession' and 'decolonisation' are problematic. Noting that 'separation of an outlying territory from an established state is usually considered 'secession' if the link between the state and the outlying territory is or was presumed permanent and 'decolonization' if the link is or was considered temporary', Lustick points out that this leaves little terminology to describe departures from states that have always suffered from ambiguous permanence and identity. See Lustick (1993), p. 23.

[195] See First (1983), p. 208.

[196] ibid., p. 213.

[197] The phrase has been used by Ken Jowitt, who has written persuasively of the dangers of the Western European neglect of this region. See Jowitt (1992), p. 305.

CHAPTER 7

[1] See Klaus's *Renaissance: The Rebirth of Liberty at the Heart of Europe* (Washington: Cato Institute, (1997), p. 106.

[2] Two of the most divisive issues were the status of the Catholic Church and the restitution of Church property, and the CDP's unwillingness to implement regional administrative reform.

[3] See Leff (1997), p. 197.

[4] In the 1 June elections, the Civic Democratic Party won 29.62 per cent of the vote and 68 seats, the Christian Democratic Union/Czechoslovak People's Party won 8.08 per cent of the vote, the Civic Democratic Alliance 6.36 per cent, the Social Democrats under Zeman came a close second with 26.44 per cent and 61 seats (behind Klaus's 68 seats), and the Communist Party won 10.33 per cent of the vote and the Republicans 8.01 per cent (ČTK 3 June 1996). The Christian Democratic Party had merged with the Civic Democratic Party in March 1996.

[5] Although promised in the 1992 Czech constitution, elections for the Senate were delayed until 1996, creating the potential for a constitutional crisis – the Senate being required for the emergency dissolution of parliament. Coalition party leaders, after a year of debate, agreed to fill the Senate seats in Autumn 1994, with local and Senate elections combined. The draft electoral law submitted by the CDP in February 1994, however, advocated a simple majority system for eighty-one single-seat districts and the CDP's coalition partners objected on the basis that polls indicated the CDP would gain some 90 per cent of Senate seats. The failure to fulfil the 1992 constitution served CDP interests. Until the creation of the Senate the Chamber of Deputies carried the responsibilities of both chambers, and as the dominant force in the lower Chamber Klaus had little to gain from an upper chamber in any form. Eventually, in September 1995, the Chamber of Deputies approved the creation of the 81-member Senate, agreeing

eventually on its election under the CDP's original system. The grudging and politicised creation of the Senate left it scarred and unpopular, as repeatedly low turnouts for Senate elections would later attest – in 2000 turnout was 34 per cent in the first round and a mere 15 per cent in the second, with young voters participating the least. The Senate was to be elected under a majority system, in contrast to the proportional representation for the lower Chamber of Deputies, and in the Senate elections would be held every two years for one-third of the seats. Senators, who had to be over the age of 40 (21 for the Chamber of Deputies), would hold office for six years.

[6] Wagner's condition was that Klaus must finally submit his plans for the privatisation of bank and state infrastructures to the parliament, something he had previously refused to do on the basis that such decisions were 'administrative' in nature.

[7] The sixth of sixteen cabinet members to resign since taking office in July 1996.

[8] Czech political parties received money from the state budget according to the percentage of votes secured in elections. The regulations for party financing had long been feeble, however – no sanctions were stipulated for parties failing to list large donations, and anyway parliament consistently failed to call parties to account. Through 1996 and 1997 the Civic Democratic Alliance, with poor electoral results, had been dogged by major party funding scandals. According to CDA's own accounting documents this small party – which headed the privatisation and industry ministries – received more than 52 million crowns in 1996, the most of any Czech party. *The Prague Post*, 11 February 1998.

[9] *The Prague Post* 26 November 1997.

[10] *The Prague Post* 10 December 1997.

[11] For the full text of this devastating speech to the Czech Senate see Vaclav Havel, 'The State of the Republic', *New York Review of Books*, 5 March 1998, trans. Paul Wilson.

[12] *The Prague Post* 10 December 1997.

[13] With CDP support down to below 20 per cent the risks of breaking away to establish a new right-wing party were clear; a breakaway party would have to convince the electorate that it bore the true mantle of the neo-liberal right and that it was untainted by corruption. If it failed to outpace Klaus a new faction stood in great danger of becoming, at best, just another minor party. Klaus ran again as chair of CDP at the party conference in mid-December 1997 – a move that at the time looked like sacrificing the party for his own power – but he retained tremendous grass-roots popularity and was re-elected. The Freedom Union duly set out in January 1998 to articulate a more moderate, less dogmatic version of pro-market politics, with a particular emphasis on democratising the state and anti-corruption.

[14] See *Transition*, June 1998.

[15] According to polls published in January, 24 per cent of respondents said they would vote for a new right-wing party, and 55 per cent welcomed the establishment of a new party, whilst 58 per cent sympathised with oppositionists to Klaus (*Lidové noviny* 9 January 1998).

[16] STEM Opinion Poll, May 1998.

[17] Klaus had been in Sarajevo at the time of Pilip and Ruml's resignations.

[18] *The Prague Post* 24 June 1998.

[19] Having run a prominent campaign, the Republicans made the mistake of producing policy declarations instead of being merely a party of protest. Their performance was such that their traditionally poor, young and disaffected electorate apparently shifted to the Social Democrats. The Republicans' antics in the 1996–8 parliament had not helped. In this period the Republicans were accused of blackmailing their own party members, manipulating candidate lists in order to secure mandates for friends and family members, making racist statements on parliamentary ground and hiding a fugitive in the party's parliamentary headquarters (*The Prague Post* 24 June 1998).

[20] The Czech Parliament sacked the entire Television Council governing state television in March 1999, so that of its eight serving members four were given to the Social Democrats and three to the CDP – though the Council is officially 'non-partisan'. See *The Prague Post* 6 January 2001. Further apparently politically motivated appointments to Czech television caused a TV strike, a

shutdown of the station and a public storm through Christmas 2000, bringing an estimated 100,000 demonstrators on to Prague's streets to protest at political party interference in supposedly independent institutions – the greatest number since November 1989.

[21] *The Prague Post* 15 July 1998.

[22] A group of prominent intellectuals, several of them former signatories of Charter 77, were so incensed by the spirit of the opposition agreement that in July 1999 they formed a group calling itself 'Impulse 99'. The idea behind Impulse was that it should be a civic initiative: a spontaneously developing movement intended to protest against the agreement and more specifically to reinvigorate the idea of civic life and participation in politics. Although the organisers and their petition caused a mild media stir – midsummer being an otherwise quiet period in Czech public life – the venture quickly went quiet, its public debates and public rallies notwithstanding.

[23] Havel's regular statement from Lany, 9 July 1998.

[24] Andrew Stroehlein in the *New Presence*.

[25] *Pravo* 16 November 1998.

[26] In contrast to the Irish constitution, for example, which specifies both PR and the system used (STV with a minimum of three-member constituencies) (Article 15/2/6), precisely to prevent gerrymandering efforts from incumbents.

[27] See Václav Klaus's *Česká cesta* (Prague: Profile, 1994), p. 74.

[28] Reed (1999b). See also Reed (1999a), p. 7.

[29] Civil service reform consequently proved one of the most controversial points in EU/Czech relations (EU Enlargement Report 11/98).

[30] These IPFs eventually controlled 73.3 per cent of voucher points in the first wave of voucher privatisation (1992–3), and 63.5 per cent from the second wave (1993–4) – 69 per cent in total. Consequently, as Reed points out, the success of voucher privatisation was thus hugely dependent upon the sophistication of IPF investment practices. (See Q. Reed's excellent Oxford University Ph.D. (1996), p. 158.)

[31] Over 60 per cent of assets privatised by 'standard privatisation methods' (i.e. non-

voucher) – or 32.6 per cent of total assets – were 'State Residual Holding', under the auspices of the National Property Fund, as of December 1995. As Reed points out, this locked the state into a dual role as administrator and privateer of state assets – a tension which, in the absence of regulation, created obvious problems (Reed, ibid., p. 170).

[32] The lack of due diligence or anti-fraud legislation meant that majority shareholders could legally transfer company assets to personally owned dummy companies, or could generate liens on company assets, and then simply pocket the loans (Reed, ibid., p. 191).

[33] See *The Economist*, 21–30 September 1996.

[34] CEEPN conference, December 1993.

[35] Quoted in *Respekt* 23–29 June 1997.

[36] Throughout 1993 the Czech parliament had debated the *need* to adopt a law on conflict of interests, but kept postponing the law itself – doing nothing for the credibility of Czech deputies as disinterested public servants.

[37] See Reed (1999a), p. 9.

[38] Government representatives admitted explicitly that 'short sharp sleaze' was the price to pay for a successful mass privatisation of the economy. As Thomáš Ježek, the CDA former Minister of Privatisation, noted, 'this special, transitional period . . . justifies things that would be unthinkable in mature capitalist economies' (Ježek interview with Reed, ibid., p. 14).

[39] Chaired by prominent CDP member R. Salzmann, then chairman of Komerční-Bank – one of the Big 4 Czech banks.

[40] See Reed (1996), p. 169.

[41] Only days before the finance scandal fully hit the CDP the party had moved to neuter the only recently created Czech Securities and Exchange Commission. Led by the CDP the Lower Chamber transferred the proposed right of the parliament to nominate its five commissioners to the Cabinet; the Commission was also stripped of its power to issue its own regulations and the right to be funded from a surcharge on securities transitions. Instead, the SEC – established to depoliticise and clean up the financial markets – would be funded by the state and would only be allowed to

enforce regulations issued by the Ministry of Finance.
[42] Institute for Public Opinion Research (IVVM) poll.
[43] In Reed (1999a), p. 2.
[44] *Lidové noviny* 7 March 1994.
[45] Interview with Czech Radio, quoted by Jeremy Druker in *The Prague Post* 7 December 1997.
[46] From Milan Šimečka's *The Restoration of Order: The Normalisation of Czechoslovakia 1969–1976*, (London: Verso, 1984), pp. 121–2.
[47] The text of Klaus's speech to the Heritage Institute is given in his *Renaissance* (op. cit.), pp. 7–13.
[48] Review of Klaus's *Renaissance* (op. cit.).
[49] *The Prague Post* 10 December 1997.
[50] See Michale Shafir in *Radio Free Europe* online report 1 June 2000.
[51] The Civic Democratic Union dissolved itself as an electoral entity in November 1992 after it was accused of having misused funds back in 1990 and 1991. The leadership was unable to resolve the question of the PAV's debts and was fearful that Meciar would use the opportunity to finally humiliate the entire liberal movement. The end of the PAV/CDU meant the collapse of the Slovak civic network that had evolved with it. A few months later some refugees from the Civic Democratic Union formed a party of Conservative Democrats. When it split the liberal vote with other liberal formations in the 1994 elections, however, many of its members finally moved into the Democratic Party – the small liberal conservative party that had fought with Klaus's CDP back in the June 1992 election – a long-overdue rationalisation of the small liberal streak in Slovak politics. Over the next few years, moreover, Slovakia would see the evolution of an active 'Third Sector' or civic/non-governmental organisation sector – spurred on, not least, by many of the liberal refugees from the PAV. This increasingly vibrant Third Sector would play a critical role in preserving and asserting a debate about the possible dimensions of Slovak democracy. By the late 1990s their arguments were part and parcel of a societal reaction against Mečiarism.
[52] ČTK 15 April 1993.
[53] The MDS's pro-Western Foreign

Minister after Kňažko, until expelled from the party for his dissent in February 1994.
[54] See Leff (1997), p. 245.
[55] In 1996 a school textbook, *A History of Slovakia and the Slovaks*, was published – sponsored by the European Union – that distorted wartime history to the point that the EU demanded its money back. The government also sponsored *Matica Slovenská* to publish a book called *The Suppressed Truth About Slovakia* that defended the wartime Slovak state.
[56] After 1994, the governing coalition organised majorities in ten out of the Council's eleven permanent legislative committees. When the liberal economist Ivan Mikloš was eventually allowed, as the first and only opposition member, onto the supervisory board of the National Property Fund in October 1997, he emerged with a catalogue of scandals and eventually resigned in disgust in September one year later.
[57] See Mesežnikov (1998), p. 17.
[58] Unusually, the minister responsible for foreign affairs, career diplomat Pavol Hamžík, actually resigned after only nine months in office following the referendum crisis.
[59] See Mesežnikov (1999), published in the comprehensive *The 1998 Parliamentary Elections and Democratic Rebirth in Slovakia* edited by Martin Bútora, Sharon Fisher, Zora Bútorová and Mesežnikov (Bratislava: Institute for Public Affairs, 1999), p. 53.
[60] ibid., p. 54.
[61] Krivý (1999), p. 67.
[62] The coverage of the government-owned newspaper *Slovenská Republika* was overwhelmingly hostile to the opposition – depicting opposition parties as conspiring agents of the 'anti-Slovak foreign lobby' and Civic Campaign OK '98 as agents of the financier and philanthropist George Soros – a classic Communist-style anti-Semitic conspiracy theory.
[63] Radio Free Europe online, 29 September 1998.
[64] See Školkay (1999), p. 115.
[65] *Praca* 25 June 1998.
[66] Školkay (1999), p. 119.
[67] Mesežnikov (1999), p. 31.
[68] *Slovenská Republika*, 29 April 1998.
[69] RFE/RL 23 September 1998.

[70] Školkay (1999), p. 127.
[71] Školkay (1999), p. 126.
[72] Lebovič (1999), p. 39.
[73] Mesežnikov (1999), p. 58.
[74] RFE/RL 23 September 1998.
[75] These two parties had been previously supported by the MDS in order to help split the existing Catholic and Green vote.
[76] Školkay (1999), p. 130.
[77] Quoted in the *Slovak Spectator* 14–20 September 1998.
[78] See Školkay (1999), p. 124.
[79] See Krivý (1999), p. 45.
[80] See Školkay (1999), p. 127.
[81] See Krivý (1999), p. 45.
[82] See Školkay (1999), p. 130.
[83] ibid., p. 131.
[84] ibid., p. 129.
[85] See Krivý (1999), p. 63.
[86] See Mesežnikov (1999), p. 53.
[87] ibid., p. 16.
[88] State funding officially allocated to minority groups for the publication of minority language newspapers was also rescinded. The Mečiar government allegedly gave the R-press publishing company, with owners close to MDS, $270,000 to publish bimonthly minority-language supplements in the pro-government *Slovenská Republika*. Of this money less than $120,000 was reportedly used for this purpose: see US Department of State, 'Slovak Republic Country Report on Human Rights Practices for 1998' (1999).
[89] See Sharon Fisher, *Transition* 29 November 1996.
[90] ibid.
[91] *Sme*, 16 August 1996.
[92] *Národná obroda*, 22 October 1996.
[93] See Fisher, op. cit.
[94] See Milan Žitný, *Transition* July 1998.
[95] See Sharon Fisher in *Radio Free Europe*, Volume 2, Number 49, 10 December 1993.
[96] See Alexander Duleba, *Transition*, 20 September 1996.
[97] ibid.
[98] See Juraj Marušiak et al., 'The Foreign Policy and National Security of the Slovak Republic', in G. Mesežnikov et al. (ed), *Slovakia 1998–1999: A Global Report on the State of Society* (Bratislava: Institute of Public Affairs, 1999), p. 185.
[99] Surveys by the Slovak Institute for Public Affairs, April/October 1997–1998;

see Zora Bútorová's 'Development of Public Opinion: From Discontent to the Support of Political Change', in M. Bútora et al. (ed), *The 1998 Parliamentary Elections and Democratic Rebirth in Slovakia* (Bratislava: Institute of Public Affairs, 1999), p. 201.
[100] See Zora Bútorová, 'Public Opinion', in G. Mesežnikov et al. (ed), *Slovakia 1998–1999: A Global Report* (1998), p. 138.
[101] See Malová (1997).
[102] ibid.
[103] See Mesežnikov (1997), p. 46.
[104] In 1995, the SNP objected to the MDS's ratification of the Slovak–Hungarian basic treaty. In February 1997 the AWS rejected MDS attempts to privatise key financial institutions (see Mesežnikov (1997), p. 45).
[105] See Mikloš (1998), p. 124.
[106] Slovakia's growth rates in the 1990s in fact became one of the puzzles of the region for Western economists. With Slovak government rhetoric, in contrast to the Czech, an ambiguous mix of pro-market and strong social protection, Slovakia's decent macro-economic trends provided an apparently freak phenomenon in a region where it was assumed that fiscal austerity was the only path to renewed and sustainable economic growth.
[107] See Mikloš (1997), pp. 61–3.
[108] At the start of 1997 out of 4,000 declarations only two bankruptcies were carried out (one of which had been filed in 1992) – the result not only of a bad bankruptcy law but also an entirely overloaded commercial court system. According to January 1996 figures from the Statistical Office some 69 per cent of enterprises were affected by insolvency (see Mikloš (1998), p. 111).
[109] See Jurzyca et al.(1999), p. 220.
[110] Other non-legislated tendencies included the systematic discrimination against foreign investors (the OECD described foreign buyers as being 'bullied' (*OECD Economic Surveys*: Slovak Republic, 1995–1996, Bratislava; quoted in Mikloš (1998), p. 110). Out of 367 privatisation decisions in 1995, only 5 favoured foreign investors; in 1996 the proportion declined to 2 out of 400 (quoted in Mikloš (1997), p. 65).
[111] The scale of infrastructural investment under Mečiar was clearly beyond the

capacity of domestic lenders, prompting the government to increase public debt beyond levels that could be easily refinanced. According to the National Bank of Slovakia, the net debt of the public sector was about 76 billion crowns in 1994, but this increased to approximately 145 billion crowns by the end of 1998 (Jurzyca *et al.* (1999), p. 213). Government priorities were such that the immediate impact of the excessive growth in public debt was felt in welfare spending – spending on education, both at school and university level, and on health effectively stagnated, and the government's refusal to honour its obligations to health and other insurance funds pushed them close to collapse (ibid., p. 212).

[112] ibid., p. 204.

[113] *Slovak Spectator* 18 January 1999. Prime Minister Dzurinda speculated that 'it could be a sign to the government from certain groups not to proceed in investigating crimes and mismanagement of state property during the most recent period [of the Mečiar government]' (ibid.).

[114] *Pravda*, 28 September 1996.

[115] *SME* 1 February 1997.

[116] See Jurzyca *et al.* (1999), p. 221.

[117] To offer just one example; as Jurzyca *et al.* (1999) report, on 9 July 1998, the NPF approved the sale of 73.9 per cent of shares in an aluminium smelter Zavod SNP (ZSNP) Žiar nad Hronom to an unknown firm, ZHK, effectively for 65 million crowns, despite the fact that ZSNP was worth some 20 billion crowns in assets. The NPF also issued a guarantee for the ZSNP's liabilities so that failure by the ZSNP to honour these would result in the Property Fund repossessing the privatised assets and the ZSNP's liabilities together. As Ivan Mikloš commented, the 'buyer acquired the assets at better terms than if they had been given away for free'.

[118] See Jurzyca *et al.*(1999), p. 226.

[119] In 1995 Nafta Gbely, a.s., was Slovakia's fourth most profitable company and its shares the most lucrative on the Slovak capital market. On 1 August 1996, the National Property Fund decided on the direct sale of a 45.9-per-cent stake in Nafta Gbely to an unknown company, Druha Obchodna, a.s., for 500 million crowns – $17 million (Nafta Gbely's profit before taxes in 1995 reached 1.075 billion

Slovak crowns – $35.8 million!). The first payment was 150 million crowns to be paid within 30 days. The balance, however, could be paid over the following 10 years, and payments could be invested into the company rather than paid to the National Property Fund – investments into the company were thus effectively deducted from the purchase price. Since Nafta Gbely generated more than 1 billion crowns annually the new owners could simply repay their debt to the National Property Fund out of company dividends. The first registered residence of Druha Obchodna turned out to be an abandoned family house. The media later reported that shares in NG were being sold to the Russian company Gazprom. (See Mikloš (1997), p. 69.)

[120] Cited in Mikloš (1997), p. 81.

[121] See Bútorová, op. cit. (1998), p. 196.

[122] Poll taken in May 1998, ibid.

[123] Already as part of the separation process there had been some administrative reorganisation, with five ministries being abolished and the management structure of those remaining being revised. Most importantly, in terms of Mečiar's influence through the state, these structural changes were accompanied by a major purging of personnel connected with the opposition parties and their replacement by officials loyal to the MDS (see Adele Kalniczky in Radio Free Europe, Volume 2, No. 6, 5 February 1993).

[124] See Butorá and Demeš (1999), p. 158.

[125] See Mesežnikov (1997), p. 46.

[126] See Nižnanský (1998), p. 48.

[127] The proportion of total tax receipts going to the central state budget increased from 79.5 per cent in 1994 to 90.4 per cent in 1997 (ibid.)

[128] Law on Referenda 269/1995.

[129] See US State Department *Slovak Republic Country Report on Human Rights Practices for 1998.*

[130] ibid., pp. 33–4.

[131] See Article 102/1992.

[132] Most notably Kováč twice refused to appoint Ivan Lexa as privatisation minister on the grounds that Lexa was unqualified and unfit to hold the post – an anxiety over character that Lexa would vindicate in his role as Mečiar's over-active head of the security services from 1996 onwards.

[133] See Žifčák (1995), p. 62.

¹³⁴ *SME* 16 May 1996.

¹³⁵ See Mesežnikov (1998), p. 12.

¹³⁶ ibid., p. 16.

¹³⁷ Finally elected – over Mečiar – in May 1999 through direct election. Rudolf Schuster, chair of the Party of Civic Understanding and former mayor of Košice, was inaugurated as Slovak president in June 1999. Slovakia had been without a president from March 1998 to June 1999.

¹³⁸ The Kováč case more than any other during the Mečiar period revealed the return to the use of targeted terror by the state security services. Clearly, however, the Slovak police force in 1995 retained men of integrity. The two Slovak police investigators homing in on the security services found themselves dismissed from the police service. Following their withdrawal from the case a Major Jozef Číž attempted to table it for lack of evidence. In October 1995 Major Peter Vačok, one of the police investigators recalled from the case, made public accusations against two SIS officers, and

one, Oskar Fegyveres, confessed to involvement in the kidnapping. Fegyveres fled into hiding abroad. In April 1996, however, his close friend and another former SIS agent, Róbert Remiáš, was killed in a car explosion, allegedly while under SIS surveillance (see Ivantyšyn and Toth (1998), p. 173).

¹³⁹ *SME* editor Peter Tóth, who had investigated the Kováč Jr kidnapping, had his car burned in September 1997, after finding a dead cat nailed to his door in May. Two journalists from Radio Twist and Nový Čas, Karol Lovas and Slavomir Klikusovsky, were the victims of anonymous flyers sent around Bratislava accusing them of being paedophiles and pornographers. Arpad Soltesz was assaulted in a Košice restaurant after writing about the relationship between the East Slovak Iron Works (VSŽ) and the Meciar government (US State Department Slovak Country Report, ibid.).

¹⁴⁰ Conversation at London University's School of East European and Slavonic Studies, 27 November 1999.

BIBLIOGRAPHY

OPINION POLL DATA

AISA (Association for Independent Social Analysis, Prague). (1992) 'Czechs and Slovaks Compared: A Survey of Economic and Political Behaviour', *Studies in Public Policy*, 198, Centre for the Study of Public Policy, University of Strathclyde.

Boguszak, M., Rak, V., and Gabal, I. (1990) *Vyzkum 'Československo'* (May), Prague: Association for Independent Social Analysis.

Bútorová, Zora. (March 1993) 'Current Problems of Slovakia after the Split of the CSFR' – *Report on the Sociological Survey*, Bratislava: Centre for Social Analysis.

Bútorová, Zora. (1993) 'A Deliberate "Yes" to the Dissolution of the CSFR? The Image of the Parties and the Split of Czecho-Slovakia in the Eyes of the Slovak Population' (58–73) in *Czech Sociological Review* Volume 1, Spring 1, Prague: Academy of Sciences of the Czech Republic.

Bútorová, Zora. (1998) 'Public Opinion', in Bútora, Martin, and Skladony, Thomas (eds), *Slovakia 1996–7: A Global Report on the State of Society*, Bratislava: Institute of Public Affairs.

Bútorová, Zora. (1999) 'Development of Public Opinion: From Discontent to the Support of Political Change', in Bútora, Martin, Fisher, Sharon, Bútorová, Zora, and Mesežnikov, Grigorij (eds), *The 1998 Parliamentary Elections and Democratic Rebirth in Slovakia*, Bratislava: Institute of Public Affairs.

Bútorová, Zora, Gyárfášová, Oľga, and Velsič, Marian. (1999) 'Public Opinion', in Mesežnikov, Grigorij, Ivantyšyn, Michal, and Nicholson, Tom (eds), *Slovakia 1998–1999: A Global Report on the State of Society*, Bratislava: Institute of Public Affairs.

Institute for Public Opinion Research (IVVM). Selected data covering electoral preferences and views on nationality between 1990 and 1994, Prague.

Jungmann, Bohumil (ed). (1993) *Volby '92*, Prague: Institute for Public Opinion Research (IVVM).

Kudernatsch, Michal. (1993) 'What type of capitalism is expected in the Czech Republic?' *Czech Sociological Review* Volume 1, Spring 1, Prague: Academy of Sciences of the Czech Republic.

Misovič, Jan. (March 1990) 'Názory na vzťahy národov a národnosti ČSSR', *Informace*.

Piekalkiewicz, Jaroslaw. (1972) *Public Opinion Polling in Czechoslovakia, 1968–1969: Results and Analysis of Surveys Conducted During the Dubček Era*, New York: Praeger Publishers.

Radio Free Europe. (March 1977) 'Are the Czech Lands or Slovakia Favored by the Federal Government?' Audience and Public Opinion Research Department.

Timoracký, Marian. (1992) 'Verejná mienka o česko-slovenských vzťahoch' in Gál, Fedor (ed), *Dnešní krize česko-slovenských vztahů*, Prague: Sociologické Nakladatelstvi (SLON).

Tuček, M., Manek, P. (September 1993) *Statistical and Survey Data*, Prague: Academy of Sciences of the Czech Republic.

ECONOMIC REPORTS

Aspekty a dôsledky rozdelenia ekonomiky ČSFR na oddelene ekonomiky SR a ČR, (1991), Bratislava: Vydavateľstvo slovenskej akademie vied.

Bulíř, Aleš. (November 1992) 'The Czech and Slovak Republics in 1992: The Process of Divergence', *CERGE Working Paper* Number 18, Prague.

Čapek, Aleš, *et al.* (1991) *Varianty vývoje česko-slovenských vztahů, jejich ekonomické implikace*, Prague: Ekonomický ustav, Československé akademie věd.

Cranston, Alan. (January 1992) *Study of Active Employment Policy in Czechoslovakia*, PHARE/Know How Fund sponsored report commissioned by the Czechoslovak Office of the Federal Government.

Czechoslovakia in the International Economy. (October 1992) Volume 2, Number 2, Prague: Institute for Foreign Economic Relations.

Ekonomické Prohlédy. (1994) ČR a SR, Paris: OECD.

Havel, M. (1991) 'New Laws on Budgetary Rules in Czechoslovakia', *Czechoslovak Economic Digest*, Number 1, Prague: Orbis.

Kočárník, I. (August 1992) 'The Problems of Fiscal Management in the CSFR in a Time of Transition', *CERGE Working Paper* Number 13, Prague.

Prusa, L. (1993) 'Životní minimum – základní prvek zachranne sociální sitě', *Narodní hospodářstvi* (33–38), Number 4, Prague.

FEDERAL LEGAL DOCUMENTS/REPORTS

Constitutional Law on the Dissolution of the Czech and Slovak Federal Republic of November 25, 1992, in Pechota (ed), *Transnational Juris* Vol. 2.

Constitution of the Czechoslovak Socialist Republic (1960), Prague: Orbis.

Hendrych, D. (1972) 'Central organs of state administration in the Czechoslovak Socialist Republic', *Bulletin of Czechoslovak Law* 1–2, 5–17.

Slovenské Listy: 'poločas rozpadu' (1994) [a stenographic record of the constitutional talks between President Havel and 'highest institutional functionaries' on 3 November 1991].

Ústavní zákon (constitutional law) c. 143/1968 (constitutional amendment).

Ústavní zákon (constitutional law) c. 125/1970 (constitutional amendment).

NEWSPAPER ARTICLES

'Gen' (television programme). (1994) Interview with Václav Klaus: interviewed by Juraje Jakubiska. Collected interviews Volume 1, ed Komárek, Martin. Prague: Hájek AS.

Hubl, M. (1968) 'Community of Czechs and Slovaks' in *Práce*, 28 January in Czechoslovak Press Survey Number 2005 (24:27).

Klaus, Václav. (1989) 'The imperatives of long-term prognoses and the dominant characteristics of the economy at present', in *Czechoslovakia Economic Digest* 7/1989 (also appeared in Czech in the summer edition of *Politické Ekonomie* in the same year).

Klaus, Václav. (1991) 'Proč jsem optimista', first appeared in *Literární noviny*, 26 November 1990a, latterly in *O Tvář Zítřka* (*The Face of Tomorrow*: collected articles, essays and speeches) (15–16), Prague: Prazske Imaginace.

Klaus, Václav. (1991) 'Finance a životní prostředí', first appeared in *Věda a technika mládeži* 16/1990b, latterly in *O Tvář Zítřka* (see above) (135–138), Prague: Prazske Imaginace.

Klaus, Václav. (1991) 'Jsem člověk konzervativní', first appeared in *Lidové noviny* 2 November 1990c, latterly in *O Tvář Zítřka* (see above) (176–181), Prague: Prazske Imaginace.

Klaus, Václav. (1991) 'The Transition From a Centrally Planned Economy: the Czechoslovak Approach' (February 1990) in *Cesta k tržní ekonomice*, selected articles and speeches in both Czech and English, Prague: Top Agency.

Klaus, Václav. (1993) *Rok málo či mnoho v dějinách země* (collected essays and speeches from 1992), Prague: Repro-Media.

Klaus, Václav. (1994) 'Strašný i krásny srpen 1968' (first published 15 August 1993) appearing in *Česká cesta*, Prague: Profile S.R.O.

Klaus, Václav, and Ježek, Thomáš. (1991) 'Social Criticism, False Liberalism, and Recent Changes in Czechoslovakia' in *East European Politics and Societies*, Volume 5, Number 1, Berkeley, CA: Sage Publications.

Mezinárodní Forum. (1992) *Důsledky Rozdělení Československa*, Prague: ústav socialné politických věd Univerzita Karlova.

Zajac, P. (1994) 'Pät' Rokov Po', a series appearing in the newspaper *Domino* (on disk).

Znoj, M. (1994) 'Anatomie Klausova Conservatismu', in *Listy* (69–79), Number 2, volume XXIV.

MEMOIRS AND TESTAMENTS

Churchill, Winston S. (1948) *The Second World War: The Gathering Storm*, Volume 1, Boston: Houghton Mifflin Company.

Ciganka, Frantiska. (1992) *Kronika demokratického parlamentu 1989–1992*, Prague.

Djílas, Milovan. (1962) *Conversations With Stalin*, New York: Harvest Books, Harcourt, Brace and World Inc.

Dubček, Alexander. (1993) *Hope Dies Last: The Autobiography of Alexander Dubček*, ed. and trans. J. Hochman, New York: Kodansha International.

Havel, Václav. (1992) *Summer Meditations*, trans. Paul Wilson, London and Boston: Faber and Faber.

Havel, Václav. (9 December 1997) 'The State of the Republic', speech to the Czech Senate reproduced in *The New York Review of Books*, 5 March 1998, trans. Paul Wilson.

Klaus, Václav. (1997) *Renaissance: The Rebirth of Liberty at the Heart of Europe*, Washington DC: Cato Institute.

Klaus, Václav. (1999) *Země, kde se již dva roky nevládne*, Centrum pro Ekonimku a Politiku, Prague: Rabbit and Rabbit.

Kučera, Rudolf. (1992) 'Proč potřebujeme debolševizaci', in *Komentáře, Politické analýzy z let 1990–1992*, Prague: ISE.

Kundera, Milan. (1987) *The Book of Laughter and Forgetting*, London: Penguin Books.

Masaryk, T. G. (1927) *The Making of a State: Memories and Observations 1914–1918*, London: George Allen & Unwin Ltd.

Michnik, Adam. (1985) *Letters From Prison: And Other Essays*, Berkeley, Los Angeles, London: University of California Press.

Michnik, Adam. (1993) 'An Embarrassing Anniversary' *New York Review of Books*, 10 June.

Remington, Robin (ed.) (1969) *Winter in Prague: Documents on Czechoslovak Communism in Crisis*, Cambridge, Massachusetts, and London: MIT Press.

Šimečka, Milan. (1984) *The Restoration of Order: The Normalisation of Czechoslovakia 1969–1976*, London: Verso.

CZECH NEWSPAPERS AND PERIODICALS CONSULTED FOR THE YEARS 1990–2

ČTK (Czech Press Agency)

Ekonom, Prague, economic weekly

Hospodářské noviny, economic and political daily

Lidová demokracie, People's Party daily

Lidové noviny, independent daily supportive of Havel

Mladá Fronta dnes, independent daily (formerly the Union of Youth daily)

Občanský deník, Civic Forum daily

Práce, labour/union movement daily

Respekt, weekly independent, eventually supportive of Czech separatism

Rudé právo, left-wing daily, formerly the Czechoslovak Communist Party paper

Svědictiví, paper of Czech emigration, published in Paris by Pavel Tigrid

Svobodné slovo, Socialist Party daily

Telegraf, right-wing/conservative daily supporting Vaclav Klaus

Zemědělské noviny, daily traditionally connected to farming community

SLOVAK NEWSPAPERS AND PERIODICALS CONSULTED FOR THE YEARS 1990–2

Kultúrny Život, weekly cultural paper, formerly Slovak Writers Union paper

Národná Obroda, weekly independent

Novy Slovák, nationalist paper with uncritical attitude to the wartime Slovak state

Pravda, left-wing daily, formerly the Slovak daily of the Czechoslovak Communist Party

Práca, labour/union movement daily

Slovenský denník, Christian Democrat daily

Slovenské národné noviny, moderate nationalist weekly of *Matica Slovenská*

Slovensky národ, nationalist paper (pro-wartime state/Tiso and prone to 'World Jewish conspiracy' theorising)

Smena, daily of the Union of Youth

Verejnost, Public Against Violence daily (Veřejnosti proti násiliu)

Zmena, Slovak nationalist daily with highest circulation of the nationalist press (openly anti-Semitic and tending toward the extreme right – writing includes frequent labelling of 'enemies' as 'Jew', 'Freemason', 'cosmopolitan', 'communist', etc., and pro-Tiso/wartime Slovak state)

ENGLISH-LANGUAGE PERIODICALS

Radio Free Europe Research Reports and Report on Eastern Europe:

11 March 1970 'Which Way Federation in Czechoslovakia', Jiří Hajek and Ladislav Nižnanský.

10 January 1979 'Czechoslovakia After a Decade of Federation', Ladislav Nižnanský and William F. Robinson.

7 September 1990 'Relations Between Czechs and Slovaks', Peter Martin.

7 December 1990 'Difficult Power-Sharing Talks', Jan Obrman and Jiří Péhe.

22 March 1991 'Growing Slovak Demands Seen as Threat to Federation', Jiří Péhe.

7 June 1991 'The State Treaty Between the Czech and Slovak Republics', Jiří Péhe.

30 August 1991 'Controversy Over the Referendum On the Future of Czechoslovakia', Jiří Péhe.

20 September 1991 'Further Discussion on the Future of the Federation', Jan Obrman.

11 October 1991 'Bid for Slovak Sovereignty Causes Political Upheaval', Jiří Péhe.

28 November 1991 'Czech and Slovak Leaders Deadlocked Over Country's Future', Jiří Péhe.

20 March 1992 'Slovakia, Calculating the Cost of Independence', Peter Martin.

11 February 1994 (Volume 3, Number 6) 'Czech Government Coalition: Striving for Stability', Jiří Péhe.

Transition (19 April 1993) 'In the Czech Republic, all Eyes are on TV Nova', Normandy Madden.

Transition (28 June 1996) 'Elections Result in Surprise Stalemate', Jiří Péhe.

Transition (7 February 1997) 'Maverick Czech Reformers Get Bogged Down', Jiří Péhe.

SECONDARY SOURCES

Arato, Andrew. (n.d.) 'Revolution, Civil Society and Democracy: Paradoxes in the Recent Transition in Eastern Europe', *Working Papers on Transitions from State*

Socialism #90.5, Cornell Project on Comparative Institutional Analysis, Ithaca, New York: Cornell University.

Arato, Andrew. (1993) 'Constitution and Continuity in the East European Transitions' (155–171) in Grudzinska Gross, I. (ed) (1994).

Arendt, Hannah. (1994) *Eichmann in Jerusalem: A Report on the Banality of Evil*, London: Penguin Books.

Banac, Ivo (ed). (1992) *Eastern Europe in Revolution*, Ithaca and London: Cornell University Press.

Barbiari, R. (1992) 'Czechoslovakia's Move Towards a New Constitution: the Challenge of Establishing a Democratic Multinational State', *The New York Law School Journal of International and Comparative Law*, 13:1.

Bartlová, Alena. (1995) 'Political Power-Sharing in the Interwar Period' (159–1800) in Musil, Jiří (ed) (1995).

Batt, Judy. (1993) 'Czechoslovakia', in Stephen Whitefield (ed) *The New Institutional Architecture of Eastern Europe* (proof copy for review) Basingstoke: Macmillan.

Beneš, V. (1973) 'Czechoslovak Democracy and Its Problems, 1918–1920' (39–99) in Mamatey, Victor S., and Luža, Radomir (ed) (1973).

Bennett, C. (1995) *Yugoslavia's Bloody Collapse*, New York University Press.

Beyme, K. von. (1993) 'Regime Transition and Recruitment of Elites in Eastern Europe' *Governance*, Volume 6, Number 3 (409–426), Cambridge, Massachusetts, and Oxford: Blackwell Publishers.

Binns, C. (1989) 'Federalism, nationalism and socialism in Yugoslavia' (115–147) in Forsyth, M. (ed), *Federalism and Nationalism*, New York: St Martins Press.

Blanchard, O. J., Froot, K., and Sachs, J. (1993) 'Introduction' in *The Transition in Eastern Europe*, Volume 2, University of Chicago Press.

Bosák, Edita. (1983) 'Czech-Slovak Relations and the Student Organisation Detvan, 1882–1914' (6–42) in Kirschbaum,

Stanislav (ed), *Slovak Politics*, Cleveland, Ohio: Slovak Institute.

Brada, J. (1991) 'The Economic Transition From Plan to Market' (171–177), *Journal of Economic Perspectives*, Volume 5, Number 4, Fall.

Bradley, J. (1981) *Politics in Czechoslovakia*, Washington DC: University Press of America.

Bradley, J. F. N. (1971) *Czechoslovakia, A Short History*, Edinburgh University Press.

Breuilly, J. (1993) *Nationalism and the State*, Second Edition, Manchester University Press.

Brubaker, Rogers. (1996) 'Nationalizing States in the Old "New Europe" – and the New', *Ethnic and Racial Studies*, Volume 19, Number 2, April.

Bruszt, Laszlo, and Stark, David. (1996) 'Restructuring Networks: Network Properties of Assets and Liabilities in the Postsocialist Transformations', paper presented at the conference on *Democracy, Markets and Civil Societies in Post-1989 East Central Europe*, Harvard University, Center for European Studies, 17–19 May 1996.

Bunce, Valerie. (1996) *From State Socialism to State Disintegration: A Comparison of the Soviet Union, Yugoslavia and Czechoslovakia*, paper presented at the conference on *Democracy, Markets and Civil Societies in Post-1989 East Central Europe*, Harvard University, 17–19 May 1996.

Bunce, Valerie. (1999) *Subversive Institutions*, Cambridge University Press.

Bunce, Valerie, and Csanadi, M. (1993) 'Uncertainty in the Transition: Post Communism in Hungary', in *East European Politics and Societies*, 7 (2): 240–75.

Bútora, Martin. (1994) 'Constitutionalism in Values and Stories', in Grudzinska Gross, I. (ed) (1994).

Bútora, Martin, and Demeš, Pavol. (1999) 'Civil Society Organisations in the 1998 Elections', in Mesežnikov, Grigorij, Ivantyšyn, Michal, and Nicholson, Tom (eds), *Slovakia 1998–1999: A Global Report on the State of Society*, Bratislava: Institute of Public Affairs.

Bútorová, Zora, and Bútora, Martin. (1995) 'Political Parties, Value Orientations and Slovakia's Road to Independence', in Wightman, Gordon (ed) (1995).

Čapek, Aleš. (1992) 'The Past and Future of Czecho-Slovak Economic Relations', *Program on Central and Eastern Europe Working Series #22*, Harvard University.

Čapek, Aleš, and Sazama, Gerald. (1993) 'Czech and Slovak Economic Relations', *Europe-Asia Studies* (211–235), Volume 45, Number 21.

Castle-Kanerová, Mita. (1992) 'Social Policy in Czechoslovakia', in Deacon, Bob (ed), *The New Eastern Europe*, London: Sage Publications.

Císař, J., and Benda, S. (1992) *Rozvod po Československu*, Prague: Orbis.

Cohen, Shari. (May 1997) *Politics Without a Past: The Absence of History in Post-Communist Nationalism*, Ph.D. dissertation, University of California, Berkeley.

Connor, Walker. (1984) *The National Question in Marxist-Leninist Theory and Strategy*, Princeton University Press.

Connor, Walker. (1994) 'Illusions of Homogeneity' and 'The Seductive Lure of Economic Explanations ("Eco- or Ethno-Nationalism?")' in *Ethnonationalism: The Quest for Understanding*, Princeton University Press.

Dědek, O. (n.d., unpublished) *Ekonomická Historie Zániku Československá: Příklad kulturního rozchodu národů* (Economic History of the Separation of Czechoslovakia: an example of culturally different nations); published in English as *The Break-up of Czechoslovakia: an In-Depth Economic Analysis*, Aldershot: Averbury, 1996.

Deutsch, Karl. (1966) *Nationalism and Social Communication: An Inquiry into the Foundations of Nationalism*, Second Edition, Cambridge, Mass.: MIT Press.

Draper, Theodore. (1993) 'The End of Czechoslovakia', *New York Review of Books* XL:3, 28 January (20–26).

Dunleavy, Patrick, and O'Leary, Brendan. (1987) *Theories of the State: The Politics of Liberal Democracy*, London: Macmillan.

Dyba, Karel, and Svejnar, Jan. (1994) 'Stabilisation and Transition in Czechoslovakia' in Blanchard, O., Froot, K., and Sachs, J. (ed), *The Transition in Eastern Europe*, Volume 1, University of Chicago Press.

Eckstein, Harry. (1979) 'On the Science of the States', in Grauberd, S. R. (ed), *The State*, New York: W. W. Norton.

Elazar, D. J. (1987) *Exploring Federalism*, University of Alabama Press.

Elster, J. (1995) 'Consenting Adults or the Sorcerer's Apprentice'. *East European Constitutional Review*, Volume 4, Number 1, Winter, Chicago: University of Chicago Law School.

Evans, Geoffrey, and Whitfield, Stephen. (1993) 'Identifying the Bases of Party Competition in Eastern Europe', *British Journal of Political Science*, 23 (521–548), Cambridge University Press.

First, Ruth. (1983) 'Colonialism and the Formation of African States', in Held, David, *et al.* (ed), *States and Societies*, New York and London: New York University Press.

Gagnon, A. (1989) 'Canadian federalism: a working balance', in Forsyth, M. (ed), *Federalism and Nationalism*, New York: St. Martins Press.

Galanda, Milan, and Valko, Ernest. (1998) 'The Legislative Process and Constitutional Jurisprudence', in Mesežnikov, Grigorij, Ivantyšyn, Michal, and Nicholson, Tom (eds), *Slovakia 1998–1999: A Global Report on the State of Society*, Bratislava: Institute of Public Affairs.

Gamson, W. A. (1992) *Talking Politics*, Cambridge University Press.

BIBLIOGRAPHY

Garton-Ash, Timothy. (1995) 'Prague: Intellectuals and Politicians', *New York Review of Books*, 15 January.

Geddes, Barbara. (1995) 'A Comparative Perspective on the Leninist Legacy in Eastern Europe', *Comparative Political Studies*, Volume 28, Number 2, Beverly Hills, CA: Sage Publications.

Gellner, Ernest. (1964) *Thought and Change*, London: Weidenfeld and Nicolson.

Golan, Galia. (1971) *The Czechoslovak Reform Movement: Communism in Crisis 1962–1968*, Oxford: Cambridge University Press.

Goldman, P., *et al.* (1992) 'Introduction: Soviet federalism – its origins, evolution and demise', in Lapidus, G. W., Zaslavsky, V. and Goldman, P. (eds), *From Union to Commonwealth: Nationalism and Separatism in the Soviet Republics*, Cambridge University Press.

Grudzinska Gross, I. (ed). (1994) *Constitutionalism and Politics – (IV) Bratislava Symposium 1993*, Slovak Committee of the European Cultural Foundation.

Hendrych, D. (1993) 'Czechoslovakian Public Administration', in Hesse, J. (ed), *Administrative Transformation in Central and Eastern Europe*, Oxford: Basil Blackwell.

Hirzsowicz, Maria. (1980) *The Bureaucratic Leviathan: A Study in the Sociology of Communism*, Oxford: Martin Robertson.

Hobsbawm, E. J. (1990) *Nations and Nationalism Since 1780: Programme, Myth, Reality*, Cambridge University Press.

Holmes, Stephen. (1988) 'Gag rules or the politics of omission' in Elster, Jon, and Slagstad, Rune (eds), *Constitutionalism and Democracy*, Cambridge University Press.

Holmes, Stephen. (1993) 'Back to the drawing-board: An argument for constitutional postponement in Eastern Europe', *in East European Constitutional Review*, University of Chicago Law School.

Horáková, I. (July 1992) *Personal Consumption in Czechoslovakia and its Changes After the Economic Reform*, Central European University Thesis, Prague.

Horowitz, D. (1985) *Ethnic Groups in Conflict*, Berkeley and Los Angeles: University of California Press.

Huntington, Samuel P. (1991) *The Third Wave: Democratization in the Late Twentieth Century*, Norman and London: University of Oklahoma Press.

Ivantyšyn, Michal, and Tóth, Peter. (1998) 'Crime, Criminality, and Domestic Security', in Mesežnikov, Grigorij, Ivantyšyn, Michal, and Nicholson, Tom (eds), *Slovakia 1998–1999: A Global Report on the State of Society*, Bratislava: Institute of Public Affairs.

Jelinek, Yeshayahu. (1976) *The Parish Republic: Hlinka's Slovak People's Party 1939–1945*, Boulder, Colorado: East European Monographs, Columbia University Press.

Jelinek, Yeshayahu. (1983) *The Lust for Power: Nationalism, Slovakia, and the Communists 1918–1848*, East European Monographs, Boulder, Colorado: Columbia University Press.

Jičíncský, Zdeněk. (1993) 'Ke ztroskotání československého federalismu', in Kipke, Rudiger, and Vodička, Karel. (eds) (1993).

Johnson, P. (1985) *Slovakia 1918–1938*, East European Monographs, Boulder, Colorado: Columbia University Press.

Jowitt, Ken. (1992) *New World Disorder: The Leninist Extinction*, Berkeley, Los Angeles and London: University of California Press.

Judt, Tony R. (1992) 'Metamorphosis: The Democratic Revolution in Czechoslovakia', in Banac, Ivo (ed) (1992).

Jurzyca, Eugen, *et al.* (1999) 'The Economy of the Slovak Republic', in Mesežnikov, Grigorij, Ivantyšyn, Michal, and Nicholson, Tom (eds), *Slovakia 1998–1999: A Global Report on the State of Society*, Bratislava: Institute of Public Affairs.

Kaplan, Karel. (1983) *Political Persecution in Czechoslovakia 1948–1972*, Research Project: Crises in Soviet-Type Systems (directed by Mlynař, Z.), Study Number 3, Cologne: Index Publisher.

Keane, John. (1999) *Václav Havel: A Political Tragedy in Six Acts*, London: Bloomsbury.

King, P. (1982) *Federalism and Federation*, Baltimore: Johns Hopkins University Press.

Kipke, Rudiger, and Vodička, Karel. (eds) (1993) *Rozloučení s Československem – příčiny a důsledky česko-slovenského rozchodu*, Prague: Patriae.

Kirchheimer, Otto. (1990) 'The Catch-all Party' (orig. 1966) in Mair, Peter (ed) (1990).

Kirschbaum, Stanislav. (1983) 'The Slovak People's Party: The Politics of Opposition, 1918–1938' and 'The Revolt of 1944', in Kirschbaum, Stanislav (ed), *Slovak Politics*, Cleveland, Ohio: Slovak Institute.

Kirschbaum, Stanislav. (1995) *A History of Slovakia: The Struggle for Survival*, New York: St Martin's Press, Macmillan.

Kitschelt, Herbert. (1992) 'The Formation of Party Systems', *East European Politics and Society* (7–50), Volume 20, Number 1, Berkeley, CA: Sage Publications.

Kohn, Hans. (1955) *Nationalism: Its Meaning and History*, Princeton, New Jersey: D. Van Nostrand Company Inc.

Kohn, Hans. (1994) *The Idea of Nationalism*, New York: Macmillan.

Kostelecky, Thomas. (1995) 'Changing Party Allegiances in a Changing Party System: the 1990 and 1992 Parliamentary Elections in the Czech Republic' in Wightman, Gordon (ed) (1995).

Kostunica, V. (1988) 'The Constitution and the Federal States', in Rusinow, D. (ed), *Yugoslavia: A Fractured Federalism*, Washington DC: The Wilson Center Press.

Krejčí, O. (1990) *Czechoslovakia at the Crossroads of European History*, London and New York: I. B. Tauris & Co.

Krejčí, O. (1995) *History of Elections in Bohemia and Moravia*, East European Monographs, Boulder, Colorado: Columbia University Press.

Krivý, Vladimír. (1999) 'Election Results 1998–1999', in Mesežnikov, Grigorij, Ivantyšyn, Michal, and Nicholson, Tom (eds), *Slovakia 1998–1999: A Global Report on the State of Society*, Bratislava: Institute of Public Affairs.

Kusín, V. (1971) *The Intellectual Origins of the Prague Spring*, Cambridge University Press.

Kusý, Miroslav. (1995) 'Slovak Exceptionalism' in Musil, Jiří (ed) (1995).

Lebovič, Peter. (1999) 'Political Aspects of the Election Law Amendments', in Bútora, Martin, Fisher, Sharon, Bútorová, Zora, and Mesežnikov, Grigorij (eds), *The 1998 Parliamentary Elections and Democratic Rebirth in Slovakia*, Bratislava: Institute of Public Affairs.

Leff, Carol S. (1988) *National Conflict in Czechoslovakia: The Making and Remaking of a State, 1918–1987*, Princeton University Press.

Leff, Carol S. (1997) *The Czech and Slovak Republics: Nation Versus State*, Boulder, Colorado, and London: Westview Press.

Lijphart, Arend. (1992) 'Democratization and Constitutional Choices in Czechoslovakia, Hungary and Poland 1989–1991', *Journal of Theoretical Politics* 4(2): 207–223, London: Sage Publications.

Lipset, Seymour Martin, and Rokkan, Stein. (1990) 'Cleavage Structures, Party Systems and Voter Alignments' (orig. 1967), in Mair, Peter (ed) (1990).

Lomax, Bill. (1995) 'Impediments to Democratisation in Post-Communist East-Central Europe', in Wightman, Gordon (ed) (1995).

Lukas, Zdeněk. (1992) 'Standing of Both Republics and Effects of Separation', *Current Analysis*, Number 3, Vienna: WIIW.

Lustick, Ian. (1993) *Unsettled States, Disputed Lands: Britain and Ireland, France and Algeria, Israel and the West Bank-Gaza*, Ithaca, New York: Cornell University Press.

Macartney, C. A. (1968) *The Habsburg Empire 1790–1918*, London: Weidenfeld and Nicolson

Mair, Peter (ed). (1990) *The West European Party System*, Oxford University Press.

Malová, Darina. (1994) 'The Relationship Between the State, Political parties and Civil Society in Postcommunist Czecho-Slovakia' (111–59), in Szomolányi, Soňa, and Mesežnikov, Grigorij (eds) (1994).

Malová, Darina. (1997) 'The Development of Interest Representation in Slovakia after 1989: From "Transmission Belts" to Party-State-Corporatism'?, in Gould, John A., and Szomolányi, Soňa (eds), *Slovakia: Problems of Democratic Consolidation*, Bratislava: Slovak Political Science Association and Friedrich Ebert Stiftung.

Mamatey, Victor S. (1973) 'The Establishment of the Republic' and 'The Development of Czechoslovak Democracy, 1920–1938', in Mamatey, Victor S., and Luža, Radomir (eds) (1973).

Mamatey, Victor S., and Luža, Radomir (eds) (1973) *A History of the Czechoslovak Republic 1918–1948*, Princeton University Press.

Maravall, Jose Maria. (1994) 'The Myth of the Authoritarian Advantage', *Journal of Democracy*, October, Volume 5, Number 4, Baltimore: Johns Hopkins University Press.

Marcinčin, Anton. (1994) *The Political Framework of Slovak Privatisation*, Draft mimeo 10 November 1994, Prague.

Mason, John W. (1997) *The Dissolution of the Austro-Hungarian Empire, 1867–1918*, London: George Allen & Unwin.

Mathernová, K. (1993) 'Czecho? Slovakia in Constitutional Disappointments' in Dick Howard, A. E. (ed), *Constitution Making in Eastern Europe*, Washington DC: Woodrow Wilson Center Press.

McGarry, John, and O'Leary, Brendan (eds). (1993) *The Politics of Ethnic Conflict Regulation*, London and New York: Routledge.

Mesežnikov, Grigorij. (1994) 'The Programs of Political Parties in Slovakia: in Practice and Declaration', in Szomolányi, Soňa, and Mesežnikov, Grigorij (eds) (1994).

Mesežnikov, Grigorij. (1997) 'The Open-Ended Formation of Slovakia's Political Party System', in Gould, John A., and Szomolányi, Soňa (eds), *Slovakia: Problems of Democratic Consolidation*, Bratislava: Slovak Political Science Association and Friedrich Ebert Stiftung.

Mesežnikov, Grigorij. (1998) 'Domestic Politics', in Bútora, Martin, and Skladony, Thomas (eds), *Slovakia 1996–7: A Global Report on the State of Society*, Bratislava: Institute of Public Affairs.

Mesežnikov, Grigorij. (1999) 'The 1998 Elections and the Development of the Party System in Slovakia', in Bútora, Martin, Fisher, Sharon, Bútorová, Zora, and Mesežnikov, Grigorij (eds), *The 1998 Parliamentary Elections and Democratic Rebirth in Slovakia*, Bratislava: Institute of Public Affairs.

Mihál{i}ková, Silvia. (1994) 'The End of Illusions: Democracy in Post-Communist Slovakia', in Szomolányi, Soňa, and Mesežnikov, Grigorij (eds) (1994).

Mikloš, Ivan. (1997) 'Economic Transition and the Emergence of Clientalist Structures in Slovakia', in Gould, John A., and Szomolányi, Soňa (eds), *Slovakia: Problems of Democratic Consolidation*, Bratislava: Slovak Political Science Association and Friedrich Ebert Stiftung.

Mikloš, Ivan. (1998) 'Privatisation', in Bútora, Martin, and Skladony, Thomas (eds), *Slovakia 1996–7: A Global Report on the State of Society*, Bratislava: Institute of Public Affairs.

Miller, Robert F. (1992) 'The dilemmas of civil society in Yugoslavia: The burdens of nationalism', in Miller, Robert F. (ed), *The Developments of Civil Society in Communist Systems*, Sydney: Allen and Unwin Ltd.

Mishler, W., and Rose, R. (1994) 'Representation and Effective Leadership in Post-Communist Political Systems', *Studies in Public Policy*, 232, University of Strathclyde.

Murrell, P. (1992) 'Conservative Political Philosophy and the Strategy of Economic

Transition', *East European Politics and Societies*, Volume 6, Number 1, Berkeley, CA: Sage Publications.

Musil, Jiří. (1995) 'Czech and Slovak Society', in Musil, Jiří (ed) (1995).

Musil, Jiří (ed). (1995) *The End of Czechoslovakia*, Budapest: Central European University Press.

Myant, Martin. (1981) *Socialism and Democracy in Czechoslovakia, 1945–1948*, Cambridge University Press.

Myant, Martin. (1993) *Transforming Socialist Economies: The Case of Poland and Czechoslovakia*, London: Edward Elgar.

Nairn, Tom. (1983) 'Nationalism and the Uneven Geography of Development', in Held, David, *et al.* (ed), *States and Societies*, New York and London: New York University Press.

Nižnanský, Victor. (1998) 'Public Administration', in Mesežnikov, Grigorij, Ivantyšyn, Michal, and Nicholson, Tom (eds), *Slovakia 1998–1999: A Global Report on the State of Society*, Bratislava: Institute of Public Affairs.

Noel, S. J. R. (1993) 'Canadian responses to ethnic conflict: consociationalism, federalism and control', in McGarry, John, and O'Leary, Brendan (eds) (1993).

Nordlinger, E. (1972) *Conflict Regulation in Divided Societies*, Occasional Papers in International Affairs Number 29, Cambridge: Center For International Affairs, Harvard.

Nordlinger, E. (1981) *The Autonomy of the Democratic State*, Harvard University Press.

O'Donnell, G. (1993) 'On the State, Democratisation and Some Conceptual Problems: A Latin American View with Glances at Some Post-Communist Countries', *World Development* 21, 8 (1355–69).

Offe, Claus. (1995) 'The Future of Democracy' in Hausner, Jerzy, *et al.* (ed), *Evolution of Interest Representation and Development of the Labour Market in Post-Socialist Countries*, Cracow Academy of Sciences.

Olson, David M. (1994) 'The Sundered State: Federalism and Parliament in Czechoslovakia', in Remington, Thomas F. (ed), *Parliaments in Transition: The New Legislative Politics in the Former USSR and Eastern Europe*, Boulder, San Francisco, Oxford: Westview Press.

Orenstein, Mitchell. (1992) 'The Political Success of Neo-Liberalism in the Czech Republic', *CERGE Working Paper Series* Number 68, Prague.

Orenstein, Mitchell. (1998) 'Vaclav Klaus: Revolutionary and Parliamentarian', *East European Constitutional Review*, Winter, Volume 7, Number 1.

Pěchota, V. (1992) 'Czechoslovak Constitutionalism', *Czechoslovak and Central European Journal*, Volume 10, Number 2, Winter.

Pithart, Petr. (1995) 'Towards a Shared Freedom, 1968–1989', in Musil, Jiří (ed) (1995).

Potůček, Martin. (1999) *Not Only the Market: The Role of the Market, Government and Civic Sector in the Development of Postcommunist Societies*, Budapest: CEU Press.

Prečan, V. (ed). (1983) *Human Rights in Czechoslovakia: A Documentation*, Paris.

Pridham, Geoffrey. (1995) 'Political Parties and Their Strategies in the Transition from Authoritarian Rule: the Comparative Perspective', in Wightman, Gordon (ed) (1995).

Prochazka, Theodor. (1973) 'The Second Republic, 1938–1939', in Mamatey, Victor S., and Luža, Radomir (ed) (1973).

Průcha, Václav. (1995) 'Economic Developments and Relations, 1918–89', in Musil, Jiří (ed) (1995).

Pryor, Zora P. (1973) 'Czechoslovak Economic Development in the Interwar Period', in Mamatey, Victor S., and Luža, Radomir (ed) (1973).

Przeworski, Adam. (1991) *Democracy and the Market: Political and economic reforms in Eastern Europe and Latin America*, Cambridge University Press.

Przeworski, Adam. (1993) 'Economic reforms, public opinion, and political institutions: Poland in the Eastern European perspective', in Pereira, Luiz Carlos Bresser, Maravall, Jose Maria, and Przeworski, Adam (eds), *Economic Reforms in New Democracies: A Social Democratic Approach*, Cambridge University Press.

Reed, Quentin. (1996) 'Political corruption, privatisation and control in the Czech Republic: a case study of problems in multiple transition', Ph.D, Oxford University.

Reed, Quentin. (1999a) 'Political corruption in a post-communist society', mimeo (or in Czech, in Frič, Pavol (ed), *Korupce na český způsob*, Praha, G & G).

Reed, Quentin. (1999b) 'Corruption in Czech Privatisation', mimeo.

Remington, T. (1990) 'Regime Transition in Communist States', in *Soviet Economy 6* (160–190).

Reschová, Jana (1992) 'Nova politika s novymi l'ud'mi', *Sociologický casopis*, XXVIII, (2), Prague.

Reschová, Jana, and Syllová, Jindřiška. (1996) 'The Legislature of the Czech Republic', in Olson, David M., and Norton, Philip (eds), *The New Parliaments of Central and Eastern Europe*, London and Portland, Oregon: Frank Cass Publishers.

Roland, Gerard. (1994) 'The Role of Political Constraints in Transition Strategies', *Economics of Transition*, Volume 2 (1) (27–41).

Rosenberger, Chandler. (1994) *Nations of influence: the role of German nationalism in Czechoslovakia's 'Velvet Revolution'*, Fall, seminar paper, Workshop on Eastern European Politics, Harvard University.

Rychlík, Jan. (1995) 'From Autonomy to Federation, 1938–1968', in Musil, Jiří. (ed) (1995).

Sartori, Giovanni. (1990) 'A Typology of Party Systems' (orig. 1976) and 'Structuring the Party System' (orig. 1968) in Mair, Peter (ed) (1990).

Schöpflin, George. (1991) 'National Identity in the Soviet Union and East Central Europe', *Ethnic and Racial Studies*, Volume 14, Number 1.

Schöpflin, George. (1993) 'The Road from Post-Communism', in Whitefield, Stephen (ed), *The New Institutional Architecture of Eastern Europe*, London: Macmillan.

Schöpflin, George. (1993) 'The Rise and Fall of Yugoslavia', in McGarry, John, and O'Leary, Brendan (eds) (1993).

Schumpeter, J. (1944) *Capitalism, Socialism and Democracy*, London: Allen and Unwin.

Seton-Watson, Robert W. (1965) *A History of the Czechs and Slovaks*, Connecticut: Archon Books.

Sewell, W. Jr. (1992) 'A Theory of Structure: Duality, Agency and Transformation', *American Journal of Sociology* 98 (1) 1–29.

Shen, R. (1993) *Economic Reform in Poland and Czechoslovakia: Lessons in Systematic Transformation*, London and Westport: Praeger.

Šimečka, M. (1991) 'Good Democrats All', in Whipple, T. (ed) (1991).

Sivaková, Danica. (1992) 'Slovenská národná rada', *Sociologický časopis* XXVII (2) Prague.

Skilling, H. Gordon. (1976) *Czechoslovakia's Interrupted Revolution*, Princeton University Press.

Skilling, H. Gordon. (1994) *T. G. Masaryk*, London: Macmillan.

Skilling, H. Gordon, and Wilson, Paul (eds). (1991) *Civic Freedom in Central Europe: Voices from Czechoslovakia*, Basingstoke and London: Macmillan.

Školkay, Andrej. (1997) 'Journalists, Political Elites and the Post-Communist Public: The Case of Slovakia', in O'Neil, Patrick H. (ed), *Post-Communism and the Media in Eastern Europe*, London: Frank Cass.

Školkay, Andrej. (1999) 'The Media and Political Communication in the Election Campaign', in *The 1998 Parliamentary Elections and Democratic Rebirth in*

Slovakia, Bútora, Martin, Fisher, Sharon, Bútorová, Zora and Mesežnikov, Grigorij (eds), Institute for Public Affairs, Bratislava.

Smith, Anthony D. (1979) *Nationalism in the Twentieth Century*, New York University Press.

Smith, Anthony D. (1983) *Theories of Nationalism*, Second Edition, New York: Holmes and Meier Publishers.

Smith, Anthony. (1988) 'The Myth of the "Modern Nation"*T*', *Ethnic and Racial Studies*, Volume 11, Number 1, January.

Smith, Anthony. (1991) *National Identity*, London: Penguin Books.

Stark, David. (1996) 'Recombinant Property in East European Capitalism', *American Journal of Sociology*, Volume 101, Number 4 (993–1027), January.

Stein, Eric. (1997) *Czecho/Slovakia: Ethnic Conflict, Constitutional Fissure, Negotiated Break-up*, University of Michigan Press.

Stein, Jonathan, and Scarrow, Susan. (1994) 'The Politics of Retrospective Justice in Germany and the Czech Republic' *Program on Central and Eastern Europe Working Paper #35 Series*, Harvard University.

Steinmo, Sven, and Thelen, Kathleen. (1992) 'Historical institutionalism in comparative politics', in Steinmo, Sven, Thelen, Kathleen, and Lonstreth, Frank (eds), *Structuring Politics: Historical Institutionalism in Comparative Analysis*, Cambridge University Press.

Stepanek, P. (1993) *Jan Stráský – prezident na půl úvazku*, Prague: Nakladatelství irma.

Suda, Zdeněk. (1981) *Zealots and Rebels: A History of the Ruling Communist Party of Czechoslovakia*, Stanford, California: Hoover Press.

Suda, Zdeněk. (1995) 'Slovakia in Czech National Consciousness', in Musil, Jiří (ed) (1995).

Suny, R. (1992) 'State, civil society, and ethnic cultural consolidation in the USSR – roots of the national question', in Lapidus, G. W., Zaslavsky, V., and

Goldman, P. (eds), *From Union to Commonwealth: Nationalism and Separatism in the Soviet Republics*, Cambridge University Press.

Švejnar, J., and Singer, M. (1994) 'Using Vouchers to Privatise an Economy: The Czech and Slovak Case', *Economics of Transition*, Volume 2 (1) (43–69).

Swidler, A. (1986) 'Culture in Action: Symbols and Strategies', *American Sociological Review* 51: 271–86.

Syllova, Jindriska. (1992) 'Ceska narodni rada v roce 1990', *Sociologicky casopis*, XXCIII (2) Prague.

Szomolányi, Soňa. (1994) 'Old Elites in the New Slovak State and Their Current Transformations', in Szomolányi, Soňa, and Mesežnikov, Grigorij (ed) (1994).

Szomolányi, Soňa, and Mesežnikov, Grigorij (eds). (1994) *The Slovak Path of Transition – to Democracy?*, Bratislava: Slovak Political Science Association and Interlingua.

Sztompka, Piotr. (n.d.) 'Dilemmas of the Great Transition: A Tentative Catalogue', *Harvard Program on Central and Eastern Europe Working Paper Series #19*, Cambridge, Massachusetts: Harvard University.

Taborsky, Edward. (1981) *President Edvard Beneš: Between East and West 1938–1948*, Stanford, California: Hoover Press.

Tismaneanu, V. (1994) 'Discomforts of Victory: Threats to Fledgling Democracies in Postcommunist Societies', in Grudzinska Gross, I. (ed) (1994).

Urban, J. (1991) 'The Politics and Power of Humiliation', in Whipple, T. (ed) (1991).

US Department of State. (1999) 'Slovak Republic Country Report on Human Rights Practices for 1998', Bureau of Democracy, Human Rights, and Labor, 26 February.

Vile, Maurice. (1982) 'Federation and Confederation: The Experience of the United States and the British Commonwealth', in Rea, Desmond (ed.), *Political Co-operation in Divided Societies: A series of papers relevant to the conflict in*

Northern Ireland, Dublin: Gill and Macmillan.

Vnuk, Frantisek. (1983) 'Slovak-Czech Relations in Post-War Czechoslovakia, 1945–1948', in Kirschbaum, Stanislav (ed) (1983).

Vodička, Karel. (1993) 'Koaliční Ujednání: Rozdělíme stát! Volby '92 a jejich důsledky pro československou státnost', in Kipke, Rudiger, and Vodička, Karel (eds) (1993).

Wehrlé, Frédéric. (1994) *Le Divorce Tchéco-slovaque*, Paris: L'Harmattan.

Weschler, Lawrence. (1992) 'The Trials of Jan Kavan', *New York Review of Books*, 19 October.

Whipple, T. (ed). (1991) *After the Velvet Revolution*, Focus on Issues Number 14, New York: Freedom House.

Wightman, Gordon. (1991) 'Czechoslovakia', in Szajkowski, B. (ed), *New Political Parties of Eastern Europe and the Soviet Union*, Harlow: Longman Current Affairs.

Wightman, Gordon. (1993) 'Notes on Recent Elections: The Czechoslovak Parliamentary Elections of 1992', *Electoral Studies* 12: 1 (83–6).

Wightman, Gordon. (1995) 'The Development of the Party System and the Break-up of Czechoslovakia', in Wightman, Gordon (ed) (1995).

Wightman, Gordon (ed). (1995) *Party Formation in East-Central Europe: Post-Communist Politics in Czechoslovakia,*

Hungary, Poland and Bulgaria, Aldershot: Edward Elgar.

Wiles, Peter. (1969) 'A Syndrome, Not a Doctrine', in Ionescu, Ghita, and Gellner, Ernest (eds), *Populism, Its Meaning and National Characteristics*, London: Macmillan Company.

Wlachovsky, Miroslav, *et al.* (1998) 'The Foreign Policy of the Slovak Republic', in Mesežnikov, Grigorij, Ivantyšyn, Michal, and Nicholson, Tom (eds), *Slovakia 1998–1999: A Global Report on the State of Society*, Bratislava: Institute of Public Affairs.

Wolchik, Sharon. (1991) *Czechoslovakia in Transition: Politics, Economics and Society*, London and New York: Pinter Publishing.

Wolchik, S. (1994) 'The Politics of Ethnicity in Post-Communist Czechoslovakia', *East European Politics and Societies*, Volume 8, Number 1, Winter, Berkeley, CA: Sage Publications.

Wolchik, Sharon. (1995) 'The Politics of Transition and the Break-Up of Czechoslovakia', in Musil, Jiri (ed) (1995).

Žák, Václav. (1995) 'The Velvet Divorce – Institutional Foundations', in Musil, Jiří (ed) (1995).

Zbořil, Zdeněk. (1995) 'Impediments to the Development of Democratic Politics: a Czech Perspective', in Wightman, G. (ed) (1995).

Zifčak, Spencer. (1995) 'The Battle Over Presidential Power in Slovakia', *East European Constitutional Review*, Volume 4, No. 3, Summer.

INDEX

A

Action Programme (1968) 27–8, 283n104
administration, state 7–9, 280n32, 11,
   281n38, 284n141, 119, 295n30, 194; in
   the independent Czech Republic 230–3,
   309n29, 240, 270; in independent
   Slovakia 256, 258, 265–70, 312n123,
   312n127
Agrarians 9–12, 18–19
Andráš, Anton 107
anti-Semitism 12, 17, 282n87, 24–5, 54,
   286n32, 291n69, 156, 193, 303n87,
   310n62, 252, 257, 269; in independent
   Slovakia 310n62, 252, 257, 269
arms industry 152–9, 299n34, 171
army (Czechoslovak) 127–8, 142, 178,
   194–5, 305n152
Association of Workers of Slovakia 244,
   249, 254, 261
authoritarianism x, 17–18, 209, 212–20;
   accusations of 64–5, 97, 110, 190, 194,
   200, in the independent Czech Republic
   237–42; in independent Slovakia 220,
   245–9, 255–7, 260, 265–72

B

Belgium 74–5
Benda, Václav 90, 290n41, 92, 183, 190
Beneš, Edvard 281n44, 281n48, 282n66
Bratislava 15–16, 284n118
Breuilly, John 47–9
Britain 19, 74
Budmerice 100, 103–4, 129
Bunce, Valerie 76, 288n3
Burešová, Dagmar 128–9, 131, 135, 297n94

C

Čalfa, Marián 95, 123, 295n39, 133, 297n94
Canada 74–5, 144, 223
Čarnogurský, Ján, as CDM party leader
   286n18, n23; 95–8, 100–5, 291n86,
   292n100, n103, n104, on the national
   question 51–5, 70–1; during 1990–1992
   constitutional talks 123, 126, 128–31,
   134, 141, 298n101; on economic policy
   155, 157, 163; during partition process
   302n34, 187, 202, 209–10; in independent
   Slovakia 252, 254

Charter 77 36, 284n132, 284n137, 56,
   289n27
Christian Democratic Movement, on the
   national question 50–3, 62–3, 70–1;
   developments between 1990–1992 81–2,
   290n62, 95–107, 291n86; during 1990–
   1992 constitutional talks 120, 123, 126,
   296n51, 129–32, 134, 140, 142; on the
   economy 150, 155, 157, 159; during the
   partition 186–9, 193, 303n87, 201; in
   independent Slovakia 242–3, 246–8,
   254–5, 268; see also Slovak Christian
   Democratic Movement
Christian Democratic Party 60–3, 91–2,
   183–4, 190
Christian Democratic
   Union/Czechoslovak People's Party 60,
   62–3, 68, 81, 89–90, 133, 184, 193; in the
   independent Czech Republic 227–9, 240
Čič, Milan 95, 119, 294n16
Civic Democratic Party, on the national
   question 58–67, 71; party development
   through 1990–1992 83–94, 108–14;
   during 1990–1992 constitutional talks
   126, 133–4, 137–9, 143, 146; on economy
   173–5; during partition process 176–219,
   304n129, 304n130; in the independent
   Czech Republic 220–42, 308n13,
   309n41; CDP, CDA, Christian DP,
   Christian DU coalition 220–37
Civic Democratic Alliance, on the national
   question 58–62, 64, 66–8, 71; party
   development through 1990–1992 91, 93,
   290n51, 105, 108; during 1990–1992
   constitutional talks 133, 138, 143, 146;
   on the economy 153; during the
   partition process 184, 202–3, 205; in the
   independent Czech Republic 309n38,
   228, 308n8, 240
Civic Democratic Union see Public
   Against Violence
Civic Forum, on the national question 49–
   50, 67; developments through 1990–1992
   75–6, 288n12; disintegration of 79–84,
   88–92, 103; during 1990–1992
   constitutional talks 117–23, 126, 137,
   143, 148; on the economy 152,
   167

civil society, Czechoslovakia 1990–1992 78–9, 82, 89, 92, 112–14, 133, 149–50, 208–12; in the independent Czech Republic 228, 241–2, 309n20, n22; in independent Slovakia (also known as the 'Third Sector') 310n51, 246, 249–50, 252, 258, 266

clerico-fascism 5–19, 50–2, 131–2, 210

Cleveland Accord 6, 280n18

Coexistence (Együttélés) 62–3, 81, 296n51; during partition 186–8, 193, 200–1

Communism, February 1948 22, 24; 'Normalisation' 33–8; legacies of vii, 50, 83–94, 109, 112; constitutional legacies 115–16, 138–9; economic legacies 154, 156, 173–5; affecting partition 205, 208, 212, 214, 231; in the independent republics 233, 237–42, 255–72

Communist Party 10, 281n40, n44; during Second World War 18–19; post-war 20–6; Prague Spring 26–7, 87; 'Normalisation' 29–34, 38, 290n58; post-1989 60–3, 65, 68, 75, 80–2, 289n30, n31, 89–90, 95, 112, 132, 173–5, 201; Communist Party of Bohemia and Moravia in the independent Czech Republic 222, 225, 227, 229, 231, 239, 241; see also Party of the Democratic Left (Slovakia)

confederation 38, 287n41, 66, 69, 70–1, 106, 297n94, 140, 177–8, 180, 184, 197–8, 207

Connor, Walker 285n141, 209, 285n5

consociationalism 115–17, 293n1, n2, n6, n7, 125, 145–6, 298n102

constitutional court, Czechoslovak 120, 296n52, 141–2, 184; Czech 231; Slovak 199

constitutionalism 23, 33–4, 117–18, 182–3, 186–7, 199–201, 205, 213–15, see also rule of law; in the independent Czech Republic 307n5, 229–37, 270; in independent Slovakia 245, 254, 266, 270

constitutions, Czechoslovak; (1920) 279n15, 5 (1968) 27–30, 101, 121, 167, 186 (1970 amendments) 30, 293n1, 115–16, 121, 188; Czech constitution (1992–) 194, 202–5; Slovak constitution (1992–) 193, 195, 199, 303n87, 246, 265–70

constitutional legislation (1990–1992) 102, 119, 294n23, 124–6, 133–4, 145–6, 188–207, 305n146, 305n154

constitutional talks 58, 66–7, 96, 100–11; renegotiating the state 1990–1992 115–46, 97n94, 165–6; for the dissolution of the state 177–207

corruption 201, in the independent Czech Republic 308n8, 223–5, 308n13, 309n32, 309n36, 309n38, 231–8, 240–1, 270; in independent Slovakia 220, 243, 310n56, 251, 253, 256, 261–5, 312n117, 312n119, 270–1

Czech National Council 28; during 1990–1992 constitutional talks 120, 124–7, 129–30, 133, 135–6, 141; on the economy 162, 166; during the partition 182, 184, 188–9, 191–3, 197, 201–3, 206; in the independent Czech Republic 221–2, 228, 308n20, 231, 309n36, 309n41

Czechoslovak-German Treaty 292n100, 131–2, 303n100

Czechoslovak government in exile (Second World War) 282n66, 20–1

Czechoslovakia (–1989), foundation of 4–7, constitutional models for First Republic 5–7, demise of First Republic 12–16; nationalities policy in 20, 23; national minorities in 279n1, 4, 10–12, 14–16, 281n45; expulsion of minorities 19, 23, 282n56, see also Hungarian minority and Roma; religious differences in First Republic 2, 7–9, 14, 20, 22, 24, 36–7; social democracy in 7, 9–12; post-war restoration of 18–24, Communism in 19–39; federalisation of 21–4, 283n103, n104, 27–30

Czechoslovak Social Democracy 60–3, 68, 289n15, 89, 133, 187, 196–7, 201–2; in the independent Czech Republic 221–2, 222–6, 228; in government (1998–) 228–31, 240

Czech national stereotypes of Slovaks 14–16, 23–5, 29–32, 34–8, 46–9, 84, 94, 97, 101, 104, 109–110, 297n92, 138, 131–2, 156–7, 196, 205

Czech Republic, before 1918 2–3; Reich's Protectorate 14–16; independent Czech Republic 142, 220–42, 270–1

Czech Senate, 1996 elections 307n5, 222, 223; 1998 elections 229–30; 2000 elections 239–40

D

de-colonisation 217–19, 307n194

Democratic Party 71, 81, 96, 290n61, 102, 134; in independent Slovakia 242, 310n51, 246–8

Democratic Union 240, 243, 246–8

demonstrations 49, 287n40, 73, 78, 97, 101, 106–7, 112–14, 119, 133, 304n130, 202, 208, 211–12

Dienstbier, Jiří 58, 68, 83, 88, 289n27, 292n100, 131, 153

Direction (Smer) 271–2

dissent/dissidents 35–8, 50, 65, 75, 288n7, 80, 82–4, 86–99, 290n41, 290n58, 110–11, 117–19, 150, 210, 212

dissolution of the state 39, 61, 73–4, 78, 112, 141, 176–219, 221

Dlouhý, Vladimír 58, 290n51, 102, 124, 295n42; on the economy 148, 150, 152, 158, 299n34

Dubček, Alexander, as leader of Prague Spring 24, 26–8, 31–3, 36, 49; 1990–1992 71, 75, 93–5, 98, 105–7, 292n105, 182; death of 193, 200

Dzurinda, Mikuláš 252, 254, 264, 312n113, 269, 271

E

economy in Czechoslovakia 1990–1992, party policies 54–5, 58, 63, 65–70, 288n76, 80, 85, 3–4, 99, 101, 105, 109–11, 113; in constitutional talks 118, 294n29, 122–4, 128, 297n81, 138, 140, 142–3; reform ideas 147–55, 299n26, 159–61, 167–75; Scenario for Economic Reform 151–4, 157; bankruptcy law 171, 193; banking 299n35, 300n84; budgets 163–7, 300n59, n65, n72, 171, 182, 184, 204; fiscal and monetary policy 149–52, 162, 169, 189, 198–9; foreign investment 158, 160–1, 163, 185; market regulation 149; living standards in 161–2, 301n86; national stereotypes in decision-making 151, 153, 156–60, 167–73; performance, Czech 153, 157, 160–3, 166–7, 169–70, 208–9, Slovak 153–4, 157, 160–3, 166–7, 169, 170, 186, 189, 198, 208–9; privatisation 149–51, 155–6, 159–61, 169–70, 201, 300n43, 305n155; unemployment 157–8, 299n34, 161–4, 300n59, n61, 166, 169–70, 184; during partition talks 178, 180–1, 184–5, 189, 191–2, 196, 198–9; division of property during partition 194–5, 197–9, 305n152, 204, 260

economy in the independent Czech Republic (1992–), banking 222, 308n6, 230, 233–7; bankruptcy 230; budget 222, 234; economic reform strategy 220, 222, 225, 228, 330, 231–42; investment privatisation funds (IPFs) 233–7, 309n30, 309n31; market regulation 224, 231, 233–7, 309n36, 309n41; performance 220, 222, 225, 229, 231, 238; privatisation 220, 308n6, 231, 233–7; unemployment 220, 230, 234

economy in independent Slovakia (1992–) banking 242, 263, bankruptcy 242, 263, 311n108, 269; fiscal policy 262–5; foreign investment 242, 263, 311n110, 271; International Monetary Fund and 244; 'party-state corporatism' 261–5; performance of 242, 244, 261–5, 311n106, 271; privatisation 244–5, 310n56, 251, 153, 261–6, 312n117, 312n119; public spending in 311n111; unemployment in 242, 263

education, in independent Slovakia 242, 245, 253, 255, 311n111, 265

elections, inter-war 7, 10–12; post-war 22; post-revolution (1990) 57, 60, 80–1, 96, 150 (1992) 57, 60–72, 77, 79–82, 89, 91, 93–4, 97, 105–11, 293n121, 133; in the independent Czech Republic (1996) 221, (1998) 224–5, 227–30, 234; in independent Slovakia (1994) 243–5, 247, (1998) 249–55, 267, 254–5; see also Czech Senate

electoral laws, in the independent Czech Republic (1992–) 307n5, 229–31, 309n26, 270; in the independent Slovakia 247–8; 1998 amendment to 1992 law 252, 270

émigrés 52

ethnic conflict regulation 40–2, 75–7, 112, 115–18, 293n6, 293n7, 136–9, 143, 165, 216, 397n191, 257

Europe and the European Union 45, 68–9, 72, 80, 86–8, 101–2, 291n86, 129, 140, 303n100, 200, 206, 218–19; and the independent Czech Republic 231, 239–40; and independent Slovakia 242, 310n55, 252–3, 259–61, 269, 271

F

Federal Assembly, structure of 293n1; 29, 75, 90–110, 111; during 1990–1992 constitutional talks 124–5, 127, 132–5, 141–2, 144; during partition process 178–207, 212–15

federal deputies, proposed transfer of 182, 200, 202, 205

Federal Government of National Understanding (1989–90) 39, 286n21, 53, 80–2, 148

federalism 40, 115–16, 294n9, 295n35, 295n39

federations, Czechoslovak federation (1968–1989) 8–24, 27–30, 31–8, Soviet-type vii, 217; democratic federations 75–7, 121–2, 133–6, 168
federal models (and others) for Czechoslovakia (1990–2) 65–72, 78–9, 82, 100–5, 108–10, 113–14, 118–46, 295n39, 173–5, 176–207
flag, Czechoslovak 202, 205–6
Fico, Róbert 253, 271–2
Filkus, Rudolf 96, 154, 299n24, 183, 189, 194–5
foreign policy, of independent Slovakia 310n58, 256, 258–61
Freedom Union 308n13, 224–5, 227–9, 239, 240–1

G

Gabčíkovo Nagymáros 304n126, 250
Gál, Fedor 95–7, 291n69, 100, 127–8, 130, 56, 193
Germany (post-war) 19, 142, 303n100, 219
Gottwald, Klement 281n40, 22, 24, 26, 283n93
Green Party 68, 81, 95

H

Habsburg Empire 279n6, 2–3
Havel, Václav vii, 34, 284n137, 39, 53, 56, 59, 64, 69, 88, 290n41, 95–7, 100–3, 105; during 1990–1992 constitutional talks 118–20, 294n15, 123–8, 295n44, 130, 132–6, 141–3, 289n98, 145, 299n32; during partition talks 178, 180–3, 185–8, 304n132, 202, 204, 208, 214–16; in the independent Czech Republic 222–4, 229, 241, 260, 270
historical record 282n63, 282n73, 34–8, 285n142, 50–2, 86–7, 89, 154, 310n55
Hlasists 7–8, 280n26, 15
Hlinka, Andrej 6, 12–13, 252
Hlinka Slovak People's Party (L'udaks) 6, 8–14, 16–19, 22, 25
Hodža, Milan 9, 12–13
Holocaust 17
Hungarian Alliance (Coexistence + HCDM) 242 (+ Hungarian Civic Party) 248
Hungarian Christian Democratic Movement 62–3, 81; during partition 186–8, 193
Hungarian minority 49, 99–100, 296n51, 185, 193, 303n87, 219; in independent Slovakia 243, 251–2, 154, 157–8
Hungary 2–4, 280n17, 281n39, 285n3, 298n18, 300n43, 304n126; and

independent Slovakia 253, 258; Slovak-Hungarian state treaty 259, 311n104, 260–1
Husák, Gustáv 25, 283n91, 283n95, 284n116, 32
Huska, Augustin 154, 299n24
'hyphen war' 53, 118–20, 294n21, 142

I

Independence (Czech and Slovak day of) 206–7
International Monetary Fund (IMF) 206, 244
invasion of Czechoslovakia 28, 218

J

Ježek, Thomáš 58, 150, 152, 161–2, 172, 309n38

K

Kalvoda, Jan 67–8, 138, 203
Klaus, Václav, as party leader 1990–1992 39, 46, 58, 61, 64–8, 288n76, 72–3, 78, 83, 85–94, 100, 104, 108–11, 292n15; role in 1990–1992 constitutional talks 123–4, 295n42, 296n65, 130–1, 134, 137–8, 144–6; on the economy 148–51, 298n7, 161, 165–75; during the partition 176–215, 302n25, 304n132; in independent Czech Republic 220–42; resignation of 223; evolution of Klausite politics 237–42, 270–2; compared with Mečiarism in 2000 270–1
Klepáč, Ján 55, 105, 292n104
Kňažko, Milan 288n76, 96, 135, 299n21, 191; in independent Slovakia 242–3
Kohn, Hans 43, 285n3
Komárek, Valtr 148–9, 298n21, 152
Kováč, Michal 154, 299n21, 179, 199, 205, 306n162; as Slovak president 243, 245–6, 266–70, 312n132; Kovac Jr. 268–70
Kroměříž 100, 104–5, 130–1, 296n65
Kučerák, Jozef 97–8, 130, 148, 154–5, 299n24, 157
Kundera, Milan 87, 289n26
Kusý, Miroslav 36, 119, 294n17, 294n21, 284n137

L

Language laws (Slovakia 1990–2) 54, 286n35, 99–100, 123, 296n51; in independent Slovakia 257
Lány 100, 103–4, 128–30
Left Bloc 62–3, 68, 180, 187, 190, 193, 201, 205; in the independent Czech Republic 221

Lenin, Leninism 173–5, 217
Lexa, Ivan 312n132, 268–70
Liberal Social Union 60–2, 68, 201; in the
    independent Czech Republic 221
Lijphart, Arend 115–16, 293n4
Lnáře 292n115, 119, 122, 294n29, 165
lustration (vetting) 287n50, 65, 67, 80, 88–
    94, 289n38, 290n41, 290n49, 290n50,
    108, 110–11, 148
Lux, Josef 224–8

M
Macek, Miroslav 179, 302n25, 183, 195
Markuš, Jozef 100, 148, 154
Martin Declaration (1918) 5
Masaryk, T. G. 4, 6, 281n44, 14–16
Matica Slovenská 283n100, 54, 100, 106,
    298n98, 298n2, 186, 310n55
Mečiar, Vladimír 39, on the national
    question 55–8, 61, 67, 69–70, 72–3; role
    in 1990–1992 party political
    developments 78, 90–2, 95–111, 291n89,
    292n105; during 1990–1992
    constitutional talks 121–5, 127–9, 131,
    134, 137, 141, 145–6; on the economy
    154–7, 163, 169, 172–3; during the
    partition 176–215, 305n152, 306n168;
    after Slovak independence 220, 242–72;
    evolution of Mečiarism, nationalism of
    255–61, economic policy of 261–5,
    state-building ideology of 256–61, 265–
    70
media 54, 288n5, 78–9, 89, 289n33, 96–7,
    291n89, 104, 106–7, 119–20, 163; during
    partition 178, 183, 186–7, 190, 193, 205;
    in the independent Czech Republic 221,
    223–4, 229, 308n20, 236; Czech T. V.
    strike (2000) 308n20; in independent
    Slovakia 245, 249–55, 258, 263, 265, 268,
    270, 313n139
Michnik, Adam 37, 289n25, 92
Mikloš, Ivan 152, 159, 161; in independent
    Slovakia 310n56, 263, 312n117
Mikloško, František 37, 128, 135, 186
Miller, Petr 152–3, 300n59
Mílovy 105, 135
Moravčík, Jozef 183, 185, 189, in
    independent Slovakia 243, 310n53;
    Moravčík government (1994) 243–5, 249
Movement for a Democratic Slovakia, on
    the national question 55–8, 61–2, 66,
    69–70; party developments through
    1990–1992 96–111; during 1990–1992
    constitutional talks 127–9, 131, 134–5,
    137, 139, 145–6; on the economy 154–5,
    172–3; during partition 177–215,

306n162; in the independent Slovak
    Republic 220, 242–72; splits at the top
    of 242–6; government coalition with
    AWS and SNP 245–9, 255–71, 311n88,
    311n104
Movement for Self Governing
    Democracy/Society for Moravia and
    Silesia 62–3, 81, 84, 205
Munich diktat 13, 132

N
nationalism, defined 285n13, 47–9, 268n17,
    72–4; in Eastern Europe 39, 43–9,
    285n2, 285n3; in the Czech Republic
    (1990–2) in the party political scene 58–
    61; during the 1992 election 64–8; as
    such 20, 27, 34, 64–8, 71, 84, 86, 108,
    174, 213, 217–19; in the independent
    Czech Republic (1992–) 239–42; in the
    Slovak Republic (1990–2) in the party
    political scene 49–58; during the 1992
    election 68–72; as such 12–19, 24–5, 34,
    46–9, 68–72, 96–107, 174, 178, 196, 205,
    209–10, 219; in the independent
    Slovakia, 244, 310n55, 25–7, 254–61, 271
nationalism as an explanation for the
    break-up; the 'inevitability argument'
    41, 44, 72–4, 113, 207; the 'inequality
    argument' (relative deprivation) 41, 44–
    5, 285n5, 285, 8, 48, 68, 72–3, 143–6,
    169, 214; 'phantom nationalism' 69, 72–
    4, 108, 128, 196, 205, 207
National Socialists (Czechoslovak) 10,
    280n36
Nazism 12–14, 16–19 (see also 'clerico-
    fascism')
neo-liberalism 80, 83, 86–7, 149–54, 157,
    165, 167–75, 210–12, 220, 231–42
net material product (defined) 298n3
Normalisation 29, 31–8
North Atlantic Treaty Organisation
    (NATO) 218–19; regarding independent
    Czech Republic 223, 240; regarding
    independent Slovakia 246–7, 259–60

O
Obroda (Revival) 49, 95, 290n59
Opposition Agreement 220–31, 309n22
OSCE (formerly the Conference on
    Security and Cooperation in Europe)
    218–19

P
Party of Civic Understanding 252–5
Party of the Democratic Left 62–3, 70–1,
    290n64, 106–7; during constitutional

talks 129; on the economy 154; during the partition 178, 180, 302n32, 186, 193, 200–1, 305n135, 209–10; in independent Slovakia 242–3, 248, 252–4, 262
Party of the Hungarian Coalition 248, 251–5
party system, Czech developments (1990–2) 75–9, 80–94, 126; Slovak developments 68–9, 94–108, 127–9, 154–7, 159; in Czechoslovakia as a whole 63, 108–14, 293n120, 292n121, 115–18, 125, 138–9, 143–6, 152, 173–6, 192, 208–9, 212, 216; in the independent Czech Republic 220, 308n8, 224–31, 308n13, 239–42, 270–1; in independent Slovakia 242–9, 311n75, 258, 261–2, 270–2
Pensioners' Party 225–7
Pithart, Petr 32, 94, 97, 100, 103, 294n16, 122–3, 294n26, 128, 131, 145, 298n101, 166, 183, 302n54
Pittsburgh Agreement 5–7, 280n24
Poland 37, 285n3, 86, 148, 298n18, 300n43; and independent Slovakia 253
population 279n10, 282n74, 291n78
populism, defined 286n39; 56–7, 69–70, 96, 98–9, 110–11, 124, 271–2; in the independent Czech Republic 226, 237–42; in independent Slovakia 255–70
Prague Agreements (1945–6) 21–2
Prague Spring 26–30, 87–8, 92, 290n59, 101–21, 149
president, powers of Czechoslovak president 125, 133–5, 142–3, 145, 179; elections for (1992) 185–7, 302n32, 189, 303n69, 195, 304n112, 304n132, 204; Czech president (1992–) 186, 202, 215–16; Slovak president (1992–) 178–9; 306n162; 246–7, 266, 269, 313n137
Prokeš, Jozef 286n24, 178
Public Against Violence, on the national question 49–50, 55–7, 69; political developments through 1990–1992 75–6, 79–81, 94–103, 107–8, 292n105, 292n115; during 1990–1992 constitutional talks 117–18, 120–2, 124, 126–8, 132, 134; on the economy 154–7, 169; PAV-Civic Democratic Union, on the national question 71; political developments 1990–1992 98–9, 100, 107–8; during 1990–1992 constitutional talks 143; in independent Slovakia 242–3, 310n51
public opinion, on different state models, Czech opinion 287n44, 296n73, 297n79, 176, 200, 306n178, 306n179, 208; Slovak

opinion 287n41, 55, 287n46, 58, 70, 288n74, 296n73, 297n79, 297n80, 176, 200, 306n178, n179, 208; combined 291n89, 293n119, 113, 169, 189, 193, 200, 212; priorities in and beliefs about transition, Czech opinion 84–5, 295n44, 169, Slovak opinion 48, 54, 70, 73, 85, 99, 169, 306n184; regarding Czech political parties/leaders 66, 287n60, 288n80, 80, 91, 308n15; regarding Slovak political parties/leaders 50, 52, 286n35, 288n80, 71–2, 95, 97–8, 292n100, 105, 193n117, 306n182; on current political/socio-economic situation 284n121, 288n74, 80, 86, 109, 117, 295n44, 297n80, 207, 208, 306n182; on Czech-Slovak relations 35, 37, 52, 84, 184, 306n184; on Jews in public life 291n69 (Slovakia); in the independent Czech Republic 224–5, 230–1, 236–7, 241; in independent Slovakia 243, 247, 261, 264–5, 270

R
Reagan, Ronald 149
referenda, on the future of the state 61, 67, 72, 78, 105, 107–8, 125, 296n52; Havel fights for 132–4, 141–2, 145; as a possibility during the partition process 177, 179, 181, 183, 302n36, 189–91, 194, 199, 202–3, 306n178, 211, 215; in independent Slovakia, on presidency 246–7, 310n58; on state industries 251; powers to call referenda 266; early elections 2000 271
religion 279n4, 7–8, 280n31, 9, 84, 95, 107; in independent Czech Republic 307n1; in independent Slovakia 244, 251, 257–8
Republican Party 59, 62–3, 68, 287n69, 187, 205; in the independent Czech Republic 221, 225, 227–8, 308n19
revolution (November 1989) 38, 64–5, 68, 82, 89, 289n32, 211, 241–2
Roma minority 53, 59, 187, 223, 240, 252–3, 257, 258
rule of law 65, 67, 83, 88–99, 107–8, 110–11, 117–18; in the independent Czech Republic 220, 224, 231–7; in independent Slovakia 220, 266–72
Ruml, Jan 90, 93; in the independent Czech Republic 223, 225, 228, 308n17, 241
Russia 206, 257, 259–61, 264, 312n119, see also Soviet Union
Rychetský, Pavel 122, 131, 153

S

Schuster, Rudolf 243, 269, 313n137
Second World War 14–18; resistance
during 18–20, 303n100; *see also* Slovak
state
security, international/geopolitical 68,
306n162, 218–19
security services 90–1, 95, 97, 107–8, 191–
2, 305n136, 306n162, 201, 237; in
independent Slovakia 245, 256, 261,
268–71, 313n138
self-determination, right to 29, 126
Senate (Czech) 200, 305n154, 305n162,
214–15, 307n5
separatism 29, 296n52, 302n42, 43–61, 72–
4, 101, 106, 120–3, 128–9, 140, 146, 166–
7, 177, 179, 186, 191–2, 197, 209–10, 216,
307n194
Šimečka, Milan 95, 237–8
show trials ('Slansky process') 293n89,
24–6
Sládek, Miroslav 59, 187; in the
independent Czech Republic 227
Slota, Ján 258
Slovak Christian Democratic Movement,
formation of/on national question
292n104; 55, 69; political development of
105–6; during 1990–1992 constitutional
talks 105–6, 135, 139
Slovak Democratic Coalition 246–7
Slovak National Party, on the national
question 51–8, 286n35, 62–4, 71–2;
political development through 1990–
1992 97, 100, 102–3, 107; during 1990–
1992 constitutional talks 295n31, 127,
129, 131, 135, 140; on the economy
155–6; during partition 178, 180,
302n42, 186–8, 200–2
Slovak national uprising (1944) 18–19,
282n73, 24–5, 283n100
Slovak National Council, First Republic 5,
279n14, 7, 280n27, 18–22, 283n99, 28,
50, 69–70, 95–6, 100, 102, 104–5,
292n104, 107, 118, 120, 124–7, 295n41,
129–33, 135–6, 141, 166; during partition
talks 179–82, 302n24, 186–9, 191–2, 193,
197, 200–2, 206
Slovak Republic, before 1918 2–3;
constitutional proposals 1918–1968 9,
14, 16, 281n38, 18–24; wartime Slovak
state 14, 16–19, autonomy removed
21–4; 37, 51–4, 97, 292n100, 127, 132,
297n92, 251–2, 258, 310n55
Slovak national stereotypes of Czechs 14–
16, 20, 22–4, 32–3, 34–8, 46–9, 70, 138,
141

Slovenská Republika 310n62, 253,
311n88
Social Democratic Party (Slovakia) 71,
105–6, 182, 193, 201; in independent
Slovakia 247–8, 252–5
Slovak Republic, (1992–) as relating to
Czechs 256, 260, 270–2
Socialist Party 68, 80
sovereignty 27; in the party political
debate 53, 54, 56, 60, 69, 102–7, 291n91,
292n107, 119; as discussed during
1990–1992 constitutional talks 122,
126–7, 131, 138, 140–1; during partition
177, 179, 182, 184–207, 302n42, 302n53,
214; Slovak Declaration of Sovereignty
187–8, 302n60
Soviet Union (USSR) vii; between
1918–1989 18, 20–1, 25–6, 35; post-1989
290n49, 101, 296n62, 54, 217 (see also
'Russia')
Stalinism 23–7
Stráský, Jan 179, 182, 184, 302n54, 193–4,
199, 200–1, 204–6
Sudetenland 4, 12–14, 19, 23

T

technocracy 85–7, 144, 167–75, 210–19; in
independent Czech Republic 237–42; in
independent Slovakia 253, 270–2
Tiso, Jozef 12–14, 17–19, 53
'Thank you, now leave!' 241–2
Thatcherite conservatism 86–7, 149
theories of the break-up 38–42; the
inevitability argument 41, 44, 72–4, 113,
207; the inequality argument 41, 44–5,
285n5, 285n8, 48, 68, 72–3, 143–6, 169,
214; the institutionalist
argument/separate party systems 41,
75–7, 108–14; party competition
argument/party autonomy 41, 77–9,
108–14; institutionalist argument/path
dependency 41, 115–16, 121, 136–46,
307n186; democratisation argument 42,
108, 121, 136–41, 143–75; realist
argument/leadership 42, 109, 113–14,
300n1, 176–7, 207–15, 307n186
Tošovský, Josef, interim government of
224, 233
trades unions 300n86, 182; in independent
Slovakia 252–62
transition (from Communism) ix, 30–3,
38, 40, 42, 64–7, 76–80, 84, 94, 110–14,
117–18, 143–7, 167–76, 300n1, 211; in
the independent Czech Republic 220–1,
225–6, 228; in independent Slovakia 220,
245, 255

treaty, between Czechs and Slovaks
(1990–2) 69, 102–5, 126–30, 132, 134–5,
138, 140–2, 177, 201
Trenčianské Teplice 100, 292n115, 120–5,
294n29, 295n31, 137, 144
Tuka, Vojtech 11, 281n39

U
Uhde, Milan 46, 184, 193, 206, 222
United Nations 179

V
Valeš, Václav 149, 152
Vaculík, Ludvík 36, 101, 297n92, 142
veto, constitutional right of 22, 29, 30, 67;
during 1990–1992 constitutional talks

67, 293n1, 115–17, 125, 136–8, 145–6,
28n102; during partition 178, 213
Vikárka (restaurant talks) 102, 126–7

W
Warsaw Pact 28, 24, 218
Weiss Peter 290n64, 298n101, 302n32,
305n135; during partition 209–10

Y
Yugoslavia vii–viii, 46, 101, 296n62, 184,
194, 204, 217, 259

Z
Žák, Václav 84, 121, 215
Žantovský, Michael 97, 298n98, 301n22
Zeman, Miloš 196; in the independent
Czech Republic 222, 224, 228–31, 240–1